Small Group
Communication
A Reader

p. 306

Robert S. Cathcart
Queens College of the City University of New York

Larry A. Samovar
California State University, San Diego

Third Edition

Small Group Communication

A Reader

wcb

Wm. C. Brown Company Publishers
Dubuque, Iowa

Copyright © 1970, 1974, 1979 by Wm. C. Brown Company Publishers

Library of Congress Catalog Card Number: 77—94283

ISBN 0—697—04156—5

Printed in the United States of America

Contents

Preface

We present our third edition with a feeling of confidence borne in part by the favorable responses of many students and teachers to the first and second editions, and largely because the systematic study of small group communication has become an established and important area of learning and training. We sincerely hope that we have been able to contribute in our small way to the importance of small group communication study and that we can continue to do so through this new edition. As was the case with the two earlier editions, this revision is meant for the student of group process and group communication, no matter whether that person be a student of speech communication, business and industrial management, nursing, human relations or teacher education.

We again offer a carefully arranged selection of readings drawn from a wide variety of disciplines and publications designed to give students an awareness of the latest theoretical and practical advances in the field, as well as an understanding of how this discipline has developed over the last several decades. We have tried to give the student and teacher an overview of the field and, at the same time, present the most recent processes and techniques available for small group training. It is our hope that this collection will provide greater insights into the principles and processes of group communication and a heightened awareness of the techniques and methods available for the improvement of such communication. We believe that this carefully selected and organized collection of readings from many fields can be more effective than can the usual textbook.

Our philosophy and approach remain the same. The collection of essays presented is both selective and comprehensive. Selective in that we have carefully chosen the forty-six readings presented from over five hundred previewed selections. Comprehensive in that we have endeavored to cover all facets of small group communication from theoretical constructs about "groupness," to specific analysis of language and thought, to practical exercises that can be performed to improve group communication. This collection makes available in one place representative articles from psychology, sociology, anthropology, philosophy, business and industrial management and speech communication; all arranged to give readers easy access to the basic principles of small group communication. The editors have avoided pressing the case for any one particular approach to small group processes opting to give readers a sampling of the diverse philosophies and concepts that constitute this fascinating area of study. We have brought together writings from the human potential movement, from behaviorists who study laboratory groups, from practitioners in the business world, and from those who have developed principles and methods of effective communication; all selected to give students and teachers knowledge of the research and practices which are continually reshaping our thinking and teaching about small group communication.

This third edition brings another extensive revising and updating. Over fifty percent of the selections in this revision are new, reflecting our desire to keep abreast of the rapidly developing trends in the field. The number of selections have been increased from forty-three to forty-six. Six of them are original essays that have not appeared elsewhere. Many of them reflect a new and growing interest in communication *per se*. The first section of the book has been revised and reorganized to place a greater emphasis on the relationship of the individual to the group. The second section has been completely revised to include new chapters on Task Groups, Growth Groups and small group experiential activities. The section on Theory and Practice has been updated by the inclusion of several original essays written especially for this section. In each instance we have retained those essays which have been judged highly successful in actual classroom situations while supplementing them with selections which, we believe, enable this anthology to stand on its own as a complete text for the small group communication class.

The third edition retains the same format found in the second edition. All readings are grouped in four sections according to their focus on certain aspects of group communication. Section I, *Small Groups: Definitions, Individuals and Groups contains* eleven readings grouped in two chapters. The first introduces students to the various ways of defining a small group while the second reveals influence patterns as individuals relate to groups and are influenced by groups. Section II, *Group Operations: Task Groups, Growth Groups, Experiencing and Evaluating* has a total of fifteen essays selected to inform the reader of what transpires as groups perform various acts and functions. Section III, *Small Group Communication: Theory and Practice* offers two chapters each containing six selections that examine the nature of the communication process in small groups and provide means and methods of overcoming obstacles to communication. Section IV,

Group Leadership: Concepts and Performance is divided into two chapters, with a total of nine readings devoted to contemporary concepts of leadership, its dimensions and its practice. Each major section of the book is introduced by an essay by the editors that explains the background, current theories, and practices relevant to the areas covered. This introduction contains, also, a brief overview of each selection in the section. A bibliography is included at the end of each chapter to guide students to other works which expand on the ideas developed in the chapter.

The editors are extremely pleased to present five original essays written expressly for this revised edition as well as the original essay by Charles Kelly that has appeared in the first two editions. We are deeply indebted to Norman Page, Edith Folb, Edward Rynte, Stephen King and Bruce Eckman for their excellent contributions to this reader. It gives us great pleasure to introduce these outstanding contributions to the field of small group communication.

The editors acknowledge the assistance of Dolores Cathcart and Cora Cochran in helping to assemble this revised edition.

Finally, we acknowledge the contributions of our students and colleagues who helped indirectly to shape this revision; and to the many writers and publishers who have made this book possible we express our appreciation. We now offer a thoroughly revised and updated version which hopefully will provide both old and new users of this book a better understanding of where we have been and where we are now in the field of small group communication.

ROBERT S. CATHCART
LARRY A. SAMOVAR

SMALL GROUPS: DEFINITIONS, INDIVIDUALS AND GROUPS

"Modern life is group life," wrote Eduard C. Lindeman in 1924. He was confirming the twentieth-century view of man as the social interactant shaped by the conditions of group life. Traditionally, man had been viewed as an individual or an isolated unit of society and only incidentally a member of the groups within society: the family, the guild, the community, the class.

It was this traditional view of man and society that produced the classic descriptions for the various forms of social or political organizations: Plato's republic, Machiavelli's city-state, Hobbe's Leviathan, Rousseau's social contract, and Locke's social compact. All of these formulations were based upon assumptions about the inherent nature of man and the inflexible structure of society. It was assumed that there were only two major variables, man and society. Groups, e.g., the family, were fixed and played little part in theorizing prior to the nineteenth century. This traditional view has gradually given way in the twentieth century to the view of *groups as society*. Modern sociologists and psychologists, focusing on man's behavior rather than his inherent nature, have found that the primary or informal groups are the warp and woof of man's daily life. They are the shapers of man's values and attitudes. Small groups are now recognized as the very mechanisms of socialization. Societies and cultures are seen as a maze of interlocking and overlapping groups in which the individual plays various roles.

The study of man and his group life has developed at an ever-increasing pace since early in this century when John Dewey recognized that the child could not be truly educated apart from the groups which formed his immediate world, and psychologist, Floyd Allport, found that experiments with individual behavior were always influenced by the groups of which the subjects were a part. The rapid growth of a psychology of groups has developed mainly along two tracks: the political-practical and

1

the theoretical-experimental. The political-practical stream has focused on means and methods of improving group processes, operating on the assumption that this would, in turn, improve society. It has led to a concern for the processes by which democratic decisions are made, how democratic leadership can be improved, how individual participation can be enhanced, and overriding all these concerns, the need for improving communication within groups. The practitioners of group process have produced an ever-growing array of techniques for understanding and improving groups. They are responsible for the now widely known practices of role-playing, feedback, brainstorming, buzz sessions, T-groups, encounter groups, and sensitivity training.

It is the political-practical approach which produced the group-discussion movement in the college, the community, and the business world. Hundreds of courses and workshops in group communication and group process are held annually, all designed to increase the individual's ability to function more effectively in groups and, in turn, to make groups more effective contributors to our democratic society. Rare is the teacher or business executive today who does not use group methods or task committees to enhance learning and decision making. Even anti-establishment organizations like Women's Lib and Gay Lib are applying group methods and techniques in what is known as "consciousness-raising" sessions to enhance and expand their movements.

The principle behind this approach to group study is summed up by Dorwin Cartwright and Alvin Zander in *Group Dynamics.*

> A democratic society derives its strength from the effective functioning of the multitude of groups which it contains. Its most valuable resources are the groups of people found in its homes, communities, schools, churches, business concerns, union halls, and various branches of government. Now, more than ever before, it is recognized that these units must perform their functions well if the larger system is to work.[1]

More recently, group techniques have been applied to the improvement of the individual and his *intra*-personal communication. A group, usually unrelated to any specific task, is used as a laboratory for helping the individual explore his self-image and to sensitize him to his own feeling and that of others. In this way, the study of group processes has come full circle and is used not only to help the group function more effectively as a contributor to our sociopolitical system, but the group becomes a source for and means of enhancing the life of the individual. The whole panoply of human potential group programs from Esalen to EST, from TM to Therapy, reflects this approach of improving individuals through group activities and improving groups through individual growth.

---

1. Dorwin Cartwright and Alvin Zander, *Group Dynamics: Research and Theory,* 2d ed. (New York: Harper and Row, 1962) ix.

The theoretical-experimental track to group study is inextricably tied to the growth of the social sciences. Its roots lie in the movement which has produced the sciences of human behavior: psychology, sociology, and anthropology. It is a part of the tradition which holds that man's behavior and social relationships can be subjected to scientific investigation equally as well as can natural and biological phenomena. The social psychologists of this century brought "man" into the laboratory and developed the techniques of scientific research and statistical measurement which led eventually to the experimental study of groups. The contributors to the theoretical-experimental side of group study are seeking a theory of human behavior based upon scientific experimentation. For the most part, they are behavioral scientists who are more concerned with theoretical research than with finding practical answers for the improvement of group functioning.

The scientific study of groups received its greatest impetus in the late 1930s when Kurt Lewin established the Research Center for Group Dynamics, where theoretical problems of group interaction were studied, and when Muzafer Sherif developed ingenious experimental techniques for the investigation of social norms. Thus, an identifiable field of scientific study was established which has come to be known as *group dynamics*. "Group dynamics is [that] field of inquiry dedicated to advancing knowledge about the nature of groups, the laws of their development, and their interrelations with individuals, other groups, and larger institutions."[2]

Not all of the investigations of the group dynamicists have been conducted in the artificial atmosphere of the laboratory. W. F. Whyte and Robert Bales, in particular, adapted scientific techniques of observation and measurement to the field and took their studies into the streets, the classrooms, the board meetings, etc. There they tested theories of interaction and group process. Whether in the laboratory or in the field, the researcher in group dynamics is concerned with advancing our knowledge about group life.

We are far from formulating a complete theory of human interaction or group dynamics. However, the student of group communication has, today, a wide array of theoretical and practical information from which to choose. Experimental research proceeds apace, and practitioners are continually evolving new techniques for the improvement of group communication and interaction. It is our purpose here to bring to you some of the more significant theories, principles, and practices which have contributed to our knowledge about groups and the part the individual plays in them.

Section I of this book is devoted to writings about the nature and form of small groups, models, and the variables affecting the performance of the individual within a group. The first chapter of Section I focuses on definitions and presents some of the current thought on what constitutes a

---

2. *Ibid.*, p. 29.

small group. The second chapter explores the relationships of individuals to each other and to the group.

The first selection in Chapter 1 by Ivan Steiner examines the impulses which lead men to collective action. He illustrates how collective action satisfies human needs and at the same time creates dilemmas about which patterns of collective behavior are the most satisfactory. He states that "collective behavior may be examined at any of three levels: the group, the organization, or the society," and goes on to discuss the importance of defining the group in preparation for the study of collective behavior.

The second selection in this chapter asks the question, "What do we mean by 'a group,' anyway?" and answers that an absolute definition of "group" can probably never be achieved. Yet Bernard Davies, the author of *The Use of Groups in Social Work,* recognizes that those who work with groups need to understand how and why individuals come to sense their own involvement with others, and he proceeds to provide a working definition of small groups based upon where and how and under what circumstances individuals might meet and operate with other individuals.

In the third selection, John DeLamater, a sociologist, explains why it is necessary to define "small groups." He establishes a formal definition and explains the four variables that make up his definition of a small group.

Patrick Penland and Sara Fine in their essay on "Group Dynamics" take the position that "a group is a system within a system within a system" and they explain how every group is responsible to some larger system which becomes the reality base for that group. They look carefully at the structure and goals of both structured and unstructured groups and conclude that every group is a product of the social context out of which it is created.

Taking a rather unique approach to understanding what is a group, Jerry Wofford, Edwin Gerloff and Robert Cummins ask the reader to assume the role of a case observer for a market-research group which examines the communication processes within the market-research group. The authors lead the case observer (reader) through an examination of the variables: group identity, social structure, goals, cohesiveness, and norms, which define the nature of the group.

The final piece in Chapter 1 reflects the current interest in communication models. Martin Andersen's model of a group discussion offers a method of establishing the boundaries of a small group as well as a tool for examining the components of the communication process. As Andersen suggests, a model focuses "on integral socio-psychological constructs and their interrelationships, and provides an operational guide for practice and prediction in discussion."

For many people the word "group" seems to imply a collection of people that in some way transcends and supersedes the individuals within that group. This myth of "the" group holds that individuals become something less than individuals once they affiliate with others. While we would grant that each group does indeed impose a "personality" or group identity on its members, we would nevertheless take the position in Chapter 2 that those members of a group function within the group as separate individuals. Individuals have unique personal histories and varied group experiences, ranging from large, complex groups, such as one's culture, to subtle groups such as neighborhoods and political parties which they bring to each small group they join. Chapter 2, therefore, presents readings that focus on the role of the individual before and during the group encounter—what he brings and how he behaves because of his uniqueness.

The first selection in Chapter Two, "The Individual and the Group," presents the findings of a medical doctor who derived a game theory of human behavior from his experiences with psychotherapy groups. Eric Berne, in this excerpt from his book, *Games People Play,* points out that all individuals have biological and psychological needs which can be fulfilled only through suitable group contact. He claims all individuals have "life plans" and "provisional group imagos" which, if they could be fulfilled, would provide the individual with the maximum possible satisfaction. Berne sees most of us struggling to fit our group imagos to real groups. He advances the interesting notion that one's successful adjustment to group reality is determined by the "script" or life plan which each individual carries with him on the subconscious level.

The piece by Gerald Philips and Eugene Erickson considers what happens when the individual enters a group. They assume that each individual possesses desires and motives which determine his approach to a group and his initial interactions within the group. On the other hand, they maintain that any group holds to norms and riutals which control or influence the activities of new members. The essay provides insights into the strategies that individuals use to achieve their personal goals and the countervailing pressures to make them conforming members of the group.

Joseph Luft, by employing the "Johari Window," offers a rather unique approach to the study of individual behavior. He maintains that to understand our own behavior we must examine it "in relation to others." The small group is an ideal arena for that examination. By using words and diagrams, Luft discusses the four areas of human awareness and then relates these to both intra- and inter-group processes.

We have already suggested that each individual within a group functions as a unique and specific entity. One is both in and apart from the group at the same time. Often the individual's psychological distance from the group is determined by his purpose and the purpose of the group. Norm Page, in his essay "Bargaining: Communication and Process," discusses a communication experience where the individual is in conflict with the group, yet needs the group to accomplish his goals. Page looks at the bargaining group, with its special problems, and advances some observations concerning how the individual uses aspects of forcing, compromise, problem-solving, and on occasion, smoothing and withdrawal to reach his desired ends. He also points out various strategies and tactics that individuals often employ within the group.

As you have seen, the role of the individual within the group, what he brings to the group, and how he behaves in the group, have been the general themes in all of the essays in this chapter. These same ideas are further developed by Richard Porter in a selection that focuses on culture as a factor in how the individual communicates while acting as a member of a group. Porter's analysis is predicated on the assumption that our past experiences, which are largely determined by our culture, will influence how we communicate. By examining some of the major ingredients of culture, such as cultural values, social perception, language, and non-verbal elements, Porter helps us understand our own communication behavior within the small group as well as the behavior of others.

The materials in Section I have been selected to aid the student of group communication in his understanding of what makes a group a group, and to help him increase his own effectiveness in groups by adding to his awareness of his role as an individual within the group.

Definitions

Collective Action

Ivan D. Steiner

Living things survive collectively. The tiny clostridium is wedded to bacterial partners which remove the oxygen from its atmosphere, leaving only the nitrogen it needs. Countless generations of protozoa have been sheltered inside the stomachs of termites where they perform functions their hosts cannot manage for themselves. There are tree roots that ally themselves with fungi, and algae and fungi that combine to accomplish the joint colonization of bare rock. Ants exchange hospitality for the milk of the aphid, and the plover flies into the open mouth of the crocodile to eat the blood-sucking leeches from its gums.

Mutual assistance by members of different species is only one aspect of the process by which living things achieve collective survival. Cooperation by members of the *same* species is equally common. Although the social insects provide the most obvious examples of this phenomenon, nature is replete with cases in which one individual contributes to the creation of the environment needed by another of the same species. Goldfish in large numbers are better able to resist poisons in their habitat than is the solitary goldfish. A herd of deer can more readily cope with deep snow than can the individual animal, and a flock of birds can survive where a single member of the species cannot. When attacked by wolves, musk oxen assemble themselves into a star-shaped formation with their antlers poised to fend off their assailant; in this fashion, each animal avoids an attack from the rear, against which musk oxen are almost totally helpless.

Man is no exception to the rule. Biologically, he is the least specialized of Earth's creatures, and poorly equipped to survive alone. By comparison with many other species, his body is weak; it is unprotected by hair, scales, or shells; and it lacks claws, tusks, or stingers. Upright posture leaves man's pelvic organs exposed to injury, and his two-legged gait is slower than that of many four-footed animals. He cannot climb, dig, or conceal himself as well as can many of his competitors, and he is equipped with less sensitive organs of sight, hearing, and smell. Nature has left him no alternative; he can combine his efforts with those of his fellows, or he can perish. But man has survived. Indeed, he has achieved "dominion over the fish of the sea, and the fowl of the air, and over every living thing that moveth upon the Earth [Genesis I, 28]."

Social scientists have attributed man's success to a variety of factors that include an opposable thumb, superior cortex, linguistic abilities, and the capacity to develop and transmit cultural solutions to recurring problems. Equally important is the ingenuity with which humans pool their resources to produce outcomes that no single individual can accomplish alone. For, although collective action is found at all levels of biological development, when practiced by man, it assumes a distinctive character. Among lesser creatures, cooperation reflects the push of instinctive tendencies, augmented and tempered by meager learning and limited insight. Musk oxen achieve collective survival because each does what comes naturally, and the same is generally true of infrahuman primates. But nature has failed to equip man with an elaborate repertoire of collective responses. Instead it has endowed him with the intellectual capacity to discover for himself how his interpersonal efforts should be organized, and with communicative abilities that permit him to tell his associates what he believes should be done.

It is obvious that man's approach to collective action can be far more flexible than that of any other creature. Humans can more readily modify their behaviors to meet the changing demands of their environments, and can discard one interpersonal arrangement in favor of another that seems more appropriate. Unlike musk oxen that assume the same star-shaped formation regardless of whether their assailant is a wolf or an armed hunter, humans can adjust their reactions to fit the problem at hand. Man's comparative freedom from instinctual determination and his vastly greater ability to evaluate and plan, permit him to employ collective action in a highly selective, flexible and adaptive manner. His triumph over other creatures has, in large measure, been a consequence of his superior ability to devise new and more effective ways of combining his own efforts with those of his associates.

Man's freedom to decide for himself how he will relate to his fellow men is not an unmixed blessing. Among the many possible patterns of collective action that may be employed to meet a given need, some are likely to be much more productive than others, and a few may be utterly disfunctional. Freedom to choose entails the obligation to choose wisely—at least as wisely as nature has chosen in behalf of its less thoughtful creatures, and as prudently as other human beings. For, having achieved supremacy over other animals, man vies with his kind for prestige, space, and material goods; and the success of his undertakings depends largely upon the quality of the alliances he forms with his associates, and upon the comparative merits of his own and other people's social units. Some groups, organizations, and societies function better than others, and the rewards received by participating members are likely to vary accordingly. Freedom to construct one's own social units implies the right to fail as well as the right to succeed.

Because the satisfaction of human needs is so often contingent upon the kind of collective arrangements people devise, man has shown a continuing concern for the adequacy of his social structures. Some of his oldest written documents offer advice to those who wish to enjoy harmonious family or group relationships, or who seek to establish a just and productive society. However, until very recently, such prescriptions have been based on casual observation rather than upon scientific inquiry. Knowledge about social systems has, on the whole, remained less abundant than knowledge about biological or physical systems. During the 20,000 years since our progenitors emerged from their caves, human curiosity has penetrated the problems of the land and the seas, and even the stars and planets that rise above them. But man himself, and the groups in which he thrives, have yielded their secrets less readily. Although recent decades have brought striking developments in the social sciences, no discipline has succeeded in charting group processes with the precision of a botanist who analyzes the structure of a fallen leaf, or the accuracy of a chemist who evaluates the processes of a hydrocarbon molecule. Moreover, our meager knowledge of human behavior is distressingly uneven. We know more about the individual man, the solitary mortal in the laboratory, than we know about man in his social habitat—the group. The psychology of semi-isolated *Homo sapiens* has been more rigorously explored than has the psychology of men in interaction with one another.

To be sure, everyday experience offers valuable lessons concerning the nature and consequences of collective behavior. Insights that are based on informal observation though, are often rather imprecise and even contradictory. Consider, for example, the following pairs of adages.

Two heads are better than one, but
   Too many cooks spoil the broth.
The more the merrier, but
   Three is a crowd.

If you would have a thing well done, do it yourself, but,
    Jack of all trades, master of none.
In unity there is strength, but
    A chain is no stronger than its weakest link.

Propositions such as these express the wisdom of the ages that has accumulated as people have noticed interesting regularities in human behavior. Undoubtedly, each is correct part of the time, but the circumstances under which any one of them is valid are not specified. Adages permit an observer to "explain" events that have already occurred, but they provide little real understanding of the phenomena with which they deal, and they have very limited predictive value. Understanding, prediction, and control are goals that can be fully realized only when the insights of everyday life are supplemented by the conclusions generated by carefully controlled research....

Task Groups

Collective action can involve as few as two persons or as many as a million. In some respects, everyone on earth is probably dependent upon everyone else, though such interdependencies often go unrecognized and are generally too indirect and weak to be of great practical importance. Within a single society, people rely upon one another for the satisfaction of many needs, including military security, protection from disease, and economic stability. However, awareness of such mutual relationships is likely to be intense only when wars, epidemics, or depressions are imminent. On other occasions, the behaviors of members may be so effectively guided by norms and role systems that people scarcely realize they are participating in a nationwide network of cooperative activity. In the case of a specific organization, such as a church, business enterprise, army, or political party, people are likely to be quite aware of their commonality of fate and to recognize the necessity of finding a collective solution to their problems. In smaller units—families, work groups, or committees—mutual interrelationships are even more apparent, and people generally employ direct, face-to-face, communication to harmonize and coordinate their individual efforts. Social aggregations of this kind are the building blocks out of which organizations and societies are constructed. The quality of the collective actions that transpire in such "primitive" social units tends to color the character of the larger units.

It is evident that man's collective behaviors may be examined at any of three levels: the group, the organization, or the society. Conceptual distinctions among these three kinds of social units are often blurred and artificial, but it is helpful to view groups as collections of mutually responsive individuals, to conceive organizations as sets of mutually responsive groups, and to regard societies as clusters of mutually responsive organizations. As attention is shifted upward in the conceptual structure, more and more human beings are implicated, but the immediacy and strength of the influence any one person is likely to exert on another decreases. Although members of a single group can ordinarily communicate directly and frequently with one another, people who are members of the same organization but of different groups generally cannot. Indeed, contacts among members of different groups tend to be routed "through channels," or to be mediated by third parties who function as communication specialists, liaison agents, or leaders. Members of different organizations ordinarily affect one another in an indirect manner either through the somewhat formal and stylized encounters of their elected or appointed representatives, or through the impact of their own organization's activities and products on those of the organization in which the other person functions. Face-to-face interchange among rank-and-file members of different societies tends to be even more rare. Although we may be exaggerating the differences among the three social levels, the units we call groups are the only ones in which all members may easily, rapidly, and effectively exercise deliberate and selective influences on all others.

To say that a group consists of a set of mutually responsive individuals is to provide only a minimal definition of the phenomenon with which this book is concerned. How intense, direct, and persistent must the responsiveness of the members be in order for a collection of individuals to qualify as a group? When the members go their separate ways after a period of interpersonal activity, does the group cease to exist? Is it a new group when members resume their collective actions? By what criteria can one specify who belongs in the group and who does not? Do groups possess attributes that entitle them to be regarded as entities in the sense that separate individuals are deemed to be? Or is it true, as some writers have contended, that groups have no reality apart from that of their individual members, the word "group" being only a convenient label for a class of people who are most accurately viewed as separate and distinct behavioral agents? These and other questions are best deferred until the collective behaviors of group members have been examined in considerable detail. For the present, it is only necessary to establish the fact that we are dealing with small sets of people who influence one another through direct, generally face-to-face, contacts.

What Is a "Group"?

Bernard Davies

Problems of Defining 'A Group'

For many social workers taking on group work roles for the first time, one somewhat academic question frequently seems to overshadow all others: What do we mean by 'a group,' anyway? Here, it often seems, is a major theoretical obstacle which has to be cleared away before any practical progress can be made.

It is doubtful, however, if the question 'What is a group?' can ever be finally answered. Despite long and abstruse discussions, argument seems invariably to persist. Take the matter of the *size* of a group, for example. It may be readily agreed that most social workers are concerned with small groups. But, do *two* people constitute such a group? Or must there be at least *three?* And when does a small group cease to be small and become large, or even a crowd? When its numbers have risen to ten? To twenty? Or higher?

And what about the *physical properties* of a group? Must all individuals be in the same place at the same time for the group to be said to be in existence? Or does the group continue to exist even when its members are geographically dispersed, even if only by a few yards or miles?

Then there are questions about *time:* How long have individuals to be in contact with each other before it can be said that they constitute a group? Must they meet at least fortnightly for a minimum of two hours? What if they meet for just ten minutes each week or on six occasions only in the year? Can they then be said to be a group?

Finally, there are questions of *perspective:* who says that a gathering of individuals is, or is not, a group? Does the group really exist if only outsiders call the gathering a group, without the individuals to whom they are referring, feeling or knowing of their collective identity? Or must this subjective sense of belonging exist too?

None of these, of course, is a totally irrelevant question. They raise or imply issues which, for very practical purposes, do need to be considered and if possible clarified. Anyone trying to work with groups in a disciplined way needs to understand how and why an individual comes to sense his

From *The Use of Groups in Social Work Practice* by Bernard Davies. (Routledge & Kegan Paul, London), 1975.

own involvement with other individuals, and how and why he is willing to commit himself to them.

Unfortunately, however, many discussions on 'What is a group?' seem not to have this practical purpose. Instead, they seem to be carried on as if, by verbal exchange, the participants will be able to discover some carefully concealed definition of 'group' which is divinely inspired, and therefore final, perfect and worthy of blind emulation in their practice. It is a form of Utopian thinking which in the long run is unlikely to be helpful to the practitioner.

Such an ultimate definition of 'group' can probably never be achieved because, *in reality,* groups do not exist as discrete, concrete entities. They are not, perhaps, figments of our imagination. But they are formulations of the human mind. That is, the word 'group' is no more than a way of summarising and expressing a very wide and complicated range of human experiences and phenomena. True, in recent years, some elements of this summary have gained quite widespread acceptance, and the probability of their occurring has been tested by experiment. Nonetheless, the term 'group' provides no more than an approximate and subjective representation of the 'realities' of human experience, and this representation is in many respects quite arbitrary.

Moreover, as has already been made clear, 'set-piece' situations are not the only ones in which a group work perspective might be helpful. A great variety of (to an onlooker) ill-defined, only partially formed, and very fluid situations might also call for the application of group work insights because, in them, the *interaction* between individuals is crucial. Family 'interviews,' encounters with three or more clients in the waiting-room or the street, at school or at their place of work, 'social clubs,' tenants groups and other neighbourhood groups, 'recreational activity groups' —all these and many others potentially constitute such situations. In them, it may be vital that a worker understand and utilise the exchanges between people, rather than just develop and exploit his own direct relationship with each of them individually. This therefore makes it even more difficult to produce a single and final definition of 'group.'

A Working Definition of 'Group'

In the statements that follow, therefore, a selection has been made of those elements of collective human behaviour and experience which seem to me to fit the needs and purposes of those who are most likely to read this book. It is thus a 'definition' of 'group' which is by no means definitive. Rather, it bears in mind where, how and under what circumstances, this plurality of individuals might meet and operate. And so, when in this book reference is made to a group, it is intended to imply:

A gathering of three or more individual human beings; who may, but who may not, expect to go on meeting permanently; in which direct person-to-person exchanges (verbal or non-verbal) between *each* individual are at least possible; and in which there exists, *or is possible,* between and among these individuals some common interests and/or purposes, some sense of identity and some mutual acceptance of interdependence.

The base-line of this definition—'three or more individual human beings'—is intended to highlight (firstly) that, even though we are discussing group situations, it is still uniquely *individual* personalities which are involved (and secondly it is meant to emphasise), that being involved with a third person (and also of course a fourth, fifth, sixth and so on) modifies, not only this individuality, but also the *exchanges* between just two individuals. Thus, in the diagram

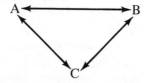

the intervention of C not only affects A as a person and B as a person; it also alters the interaction between A and B. A and B are thus likely to respond to each other, as well as to other elements in their situation (including, of course, other individuals such as D, E and so on), to some degree differently from the way they would have responded if C were not present. It is this possibility of modifying the relationship between individuals because of the intervention of other individuals which is crucial to our conception of a group.

This definition, though quite categorically laying down a minimum size for a group, is much less specific about an upper limit, and indeed deliberately avoids stating this in numerical terms. It does assume the *possibility* of direct person-to-person exchanges among *all* the individuals. And this, even though it may never become a reality, inevitably sets a 'natural' limit on the size of the group. The *actual* maximum number among whom such direct communication and contact could be achieved may vary somewhat according to circumstances. In some cases it may be as few as three, in others rather more. It is, however, an unmistakable way of distinguishing this type of small group from, say, a crowd or mob.

This insistence on the possibility, at least, of direct, person-to-person interaction among all participants has another practical consequence. It means that on some occasions, anyway, and for some periods of time, all participants must be gathered in physical proximity. Again, it is not necessary to be specific; indeed, it is not possible to be specific, since once again the circumstances of the group will vary. Nonetheless, this criterion of at least potential face-to-face exchange does in a general way deal with the spatial and time elements of group life, as well as with group size.

The problems of time, space and size are also dealt with indirectly in the suggestion that common purposes and/or interests, and a sense of identity and interdependence, should (actually or potentially) exist among individuals involved in the collective situation. This is even more of an evaluative criterion than those suggested so far, even more dependent on the subjective interpretations of a supposedly objective onlooker. And again, in practice, such identity and interdependence may never establish themselves—they may remain forever potential. Nonetheless, even given a change in one or more of the variables in this situation—the physical environment, what the individuals are doing and so on—the fact that it *could* exist, has important implications. Again it suggests that time may be needed, and that for some of this time individuals need to be a physical proximity.

Nonetheless, though there are indications of what may be involved, the definition is deliberately vague about maximum size, where the gathering meets and especially how much time is needed. By being imprecise in this way, allowance is thus once again made for these situations of collective human exchange which are spontaneous and transient, but which, in social work terms anyway, may be at least potentially productive. Take, for example, those passing and accidental combinations of individuals which are formed or emerge to deal with a crisis (like a sudden bereavement in a neighbourhood). They may never subsequently reform in exactly the same way. However, while they last, they produce a very strong feeling among participants of being involved with each other, and might be particularly beneficial to some individuals if they are deliberately supported and encouraged.

Or, take those informal, often social and recreational events like a youngsters' street 'kick-about' or a small gathering of mere acquaintances in a pub. Here again, the combination of individuals is likely, in its original form, to be impermanent and ostensibly superficial in its impact. But again, the individuals might already feel some investment with each other, or might begin to do so given some new opportunity or reason. The interactions which exist could thus be extremely helpful to them, even though no formal 'group' has ever been recognised or defined.

For social workers, these unplanned group situations could offer new, perhaps once-for-all, perhaps more long-term, openings for providing appropriate help. No definition of group should, in itself, discourage them from applying any group work insights and skills they possess to such situations. The need for a constantly active, interactionist perspective must again be stressed.

The insistence in the definition on an actual or potential sense of identity and interdependence has another useful consequence. It by-passes those incessant theoretical and largely sterile discussions about all those situations in which a number of individuals—passengers in a railway compartment, patients in a doctor's waiting-room and so on—happen to be in the same place at the same time, without having any direct need for or concern with *each other*. The question that seems permanently to fascinate is: Do they or do they not constitute a group?

It is of course true that an accident—the sudden illness of one of the passengers, the doctor's non-arrival for surgery—may create some, even temporary, feeling of identity among these separate individuals. By our definition, they might then be a group which, hypothetically anyway, could 'use' or 'be used' by a social worker. And the steps by which they move from a state of separation from each other, to greater mutual involvement might theoretically be exploitable. . . .

For most practical purposes, however, the question 'Are such gatherings *really* groups?' seems largely irrelevant to most social workers. What, above all, the social worker needs to know is: Are such gatherings usable: can they, in their present form, help him to fulfill his purposes, or at least, are they, in any realistic sense, capable of development so that they can be so helpful? Unless the answers to these questions are clearly positive, the whole debate must remain almost entirely academic.

Indeed, the main purpose of discussing what is meant by the term 'group' has throughout been very practical—hence, in part, the vagueness and flexibility of the definition offered. Social workers should feel confident about moving within a very wide variety of situations of human interaction as they arise. And they should feel able to use them in ways best suited to their clients' needs. They should be able to form groups deliberately for a period of time to be determined by them and/or by the clients involved. They should be able to intervene in groups which already exist (assuming of course that they do this in ethical ways which are acceptable to the group members). They should be able to recognise and utilise short-term and spontaneous interactional situations which lack any formal definition. And ideally they should be able to combine any or all these approaches as and when appropriate, both with each other, and also with a casework approach. If they are really to adjust their ideas of time, space, size and content according to the nature of the interactions and the people involved, then an absolute, handed-down definition of groups will be of very little use to them.

A Definition of "Group"

John DeLamater*

The "small group" is one of the most enduring and most frequently studied areas of inquiry in social psychology. Studies of individual behavior in and of groups have occupied social scientists since Floyd Allport's research on social facilitation in the 1920s. Bibliographies of material in this area (e.g., Raven, 1961) typically include more than 1,500 entries, in part demonstrating the amount of interest which this topic has generated. In addition, the small group has been studied in a tremendous variety of settings, ranging from the laboratory to the delinquent gang and the large industrial organization.

Yet in spite, or in part because, of the tremendous amount of empirical knowledge which exists about groups, there has yet to appear a major conceptual synthesis dealing comprehensively with the small group. A recent paper on small group theory points out that there are at least six important conceptualizations, and that there are marked differences in their orientation and content (DeLamater et al., 1965). Some of these differences are no doubt due to differences in the training of the theorist(s) and in the research methods typically employed. More importantly, it would appear that these differences in conceptualization are perhaps primarily a function of differences in the definition of the "small group" itself.

Definitions are of primary importance because they provide the scientist with an implicit orientation toward the world. By stating explicitly what is to be included within the concepts with which he is working, and at least implicitly excluding all other phenomena, the investigator has determined those events with which he is concerned. Thus, if one defines a "group" as individuals who share affective ties, he would be excluding by implication much of the work on "secondary groups," whose ties are formally determined and often are not characterized by affective ties among members. He might go on to construct a comprehensive theory of groups with or without recognizing that his theory is primarily applicable to informal or primary ones. Often, one suspects that the failure to recognize limitations on the generality of a given theory grows precisely out of the fact that the author's focus was highly restricted by his definitions, and yet the author himself was unaware of such restrictions. In effect, important characteristics and processes in the phenomena of interest may be ignored systematically due to the nature of one's definitions.

In addition, the definition and surrounding theory frequently determine the research strategy. Measures designed to operationalize con-

This excerpt from "A Definition of 'Group'" by John DeLamater is reprinted from *Small Group Behavior* Vol. 5, No. 1 (February 1974) pp. 33-41 by permission of the Publisher, Sage Publications, Inc.

cepts are often developed using the criterion of face validity, at least initially. Secondarily, the experimental setting whch one chooses is heavily influenced by one's concepts and theory. Thus, for example, studies in the group dynamics tradition which deal with cohesiveness frequently rely on paper and pencil measures in a laboratory setting of the three aspects of cohesiveness specified by the conceptualization (compare DeLamater, 1964): attraction to the task, attraction to other members, and the prestige of the group (e.g., Pepitone and Reichling, 1960; Schachter et al., 1960). Thus, the empirical results which one obtains, in this case about cohesiveness and groups, are heavily dependent on the underlying conceptualization. This introduces biases and omissions of unknown types and importance in empirical data concerning the phenomena of interest.

These problems become especially important when one attempts to synthesize information in a particular problem area, since one will encounter concepts of varying degrees of precision and arbitrariness, and biases in conceptual orientations and supporting data. Such inconsistencies cannot long be tolerated if one is to make real progress in delineating the major variables, events, and processes in the area. While differences in definitions and conceptions are tolerable and perhaps inevitable in the early stages of investigation of an area, we cannot in truth claim to understand meaningfully that area until these divergencies have been synthesized, and major definitions brought into as close agreement as possible with the empirical world (and therefore with each other). Only from a base of precisely defined, empirically valid, and comprehensive definitions of basic concepts can we proceed to organize and integrate knowledge in an area of inquiry.

It is the purpose of this paper to attempt to provide a precise, empirically useful, and relatively comprehensive definition of the concept of "group," and thereby hopefully to contribute to the integration of knowledge about groups. Small groups are the empirical focus *par excellence* for social psychology and related areas of sociological inquiry, since many important phenomena—perception, interaction, socialization, roles, deviant behavior, and social control—occur and can be readily studied empirically in this context. Yet there is a striking lack of consensus about the definition of "group," which has produced important divergencies in the conceptual treatments of and empirical data about groups. These differences in definition and resulting knowledge are especially frustrating in view of the importance of the phenomena. . . .

Formal Definitions of Group

In the realm of formal definitions, it is instructive to note first that a major textbook dealing with small groups makes no attempt to formally define the concept (Cartwright and Zander, 1968). However, an indication of the characteristics of groups which these authors consider important for purposes of analysis is given by those to which they give primary treatment: pressures to uniformity, power and influence, leadership and performance of group functions, motivational processes, and structural properties of groups. These five allow for a fairly comprehensive treatment of the available literature, but they are not presented as defining properties of the concept. More importantly, they lack the unidimensionality which is important in a theoretically and operationally adequate definition.

Bales (1953) defines a "small group" as

> any number of persons engaged in interaction with one another in a single face-to-face meeting or a series of such meetings, in which each member receives some impression or perception of each other member distinct enough so that he can . . . give some reaction to each of the others as an individual person, even though it be only to recall that the other was present.

This is obviously a research-oriented definition. Its principal fault seems to lie in its generality. It is quite probable that a group of strangers waiting at a bus stop who converse for a few minutes could recall the presence of each of the others. A definition such as this seems too inclusive, classifying temporary aggregations together with stable groups.

According to Cattell (1951) "a group is a collection of organisms in which the existence of all (in their given relationships) is necessary to the satisfaction of certain individual needs in each." Again, this is overly general, so much so that it would appear to include animal social groups. While animal groups may show some similarities to human ones, classifying them within the same definition is only justified if it can be demonstrated empirically that they are the same on all dimensions considered important.

For Homans (1950),

> a group is defined by the interaction of its members. If we say that individuals A, B, C, D and E form a group, this will mean that . . . A interacts more with B, C, D, and E than he does with M, N, O . . . who we choose to consider outsiders or members of other groups.

In essence, each member must interact more frequently with other members than he does with anyone else. There are many difficulties with such a strictly quantitative definition, the foremost being the application of it in any real situation. Frequency counts would have to be made of each "member's" interactions with every other individual, perhaps over a considerable period of time—an expensive, if not impossible, task. Second, this definition implies that each person has only one major group membership; it is not readily apparent how such a definition allows for the phenomenon of multiple group membership, so characteristic of complex societies and an important factor in individual behavior. Further, the lack of specification of the content of interaction makes it difficult to draw any implications about the psychological aspects of group membership. This, however, is consistent with Homans' sociological orientation toward groups.

Krech and Crutchfield (1948) define "group" as

> two or more people who bear an explicit psychological relationship to each other. This means that for each member of the group the other group members must exist in some more or less immediate psychological way so that their behavior and their characteristics influence him.

This definition emphasizes mutual perception and influence. A major problem is the failure to specify interaction as a necessary property; this implies that nonexistent persons could form part of a group, a difficult problem to deal with in empirical studies.

According to Merton (1957),

> The sociological concept of a group refers to a number of people who interact with one another in established patterns. . . . One *objective* criterion of the group . . . [is] frequency of interaction. A second criterion . . . is that the interacting persons *define themselves* as members, i.e., that they have patterned expectations of forms of interaction which are morally binding on them and on other "members." . . . The correlative and third criterion is that the persons in interaction be *defined by others* as "belonging to the group."

There are several problems with this definition. First, while the term "patterned" is emphasized in relation to both interaction and expectations, its meaning is not clear; a criterion is needed which states at what point expectations or interaction becomes "patterned." With respect to the third criterion, definition by others, a critical empirical issue is the specification of those "others." Does each member of the group have to define each other as a member, or does one only need to be considered a member by a majority of the others? If the former, research studies would continuously face the problem of how to treat persons who are not unanimously defined as "members," perhaps a common phenomenon empirically. Further, no relation between self-definition and definition by others is specified. If, as Merton implies by his use of the word "correlative," these should be in agreement, there is still the question of how much agreement. Thus, the major problems with this definition revolve around its lack of specificity.

Finally, Newcomb (1963) states that

> the distinctive thing about a group is that its members share norms about something. The range covered by the shared norms may be great or small, but at the very least they include whatever it is that is distinctive about the common interests of the group members. . . . They also include, necessarily, norms concerning the roles of the

group members—roles which are interlocking, being defined in reciprocal terms.

Thus, the critical properties of a group are that its members share norms about their common interests and that its members have roles—i.e., structured and interdependent relationships which are agreed upon.

In analyzing these formal definitions, there are three characteristics which recur as defining properties.

First, several authors include or focus on *interaction* as a defining property. Bales (1953) and Homans (1950) include interaction explicitly; for the latter, frequency of interaction is the sole defining property. Newcomb's (1963) definition presupposes interaction, through its emphasis on shared norms and interlocking roles. Merton (1957) stresses interaction, albeit of a more limited but undefined type—i.e., "interaction in accord with established patterns."

The second common characteristic is *perception*. Bales' definition requires that members perceive one another as individuals, and that of Krech and Crutchfield (1948) seems to refer in part to perception in requiring that members exist for each other in an "immediate psychological way." The authors differ over whether these perceptions must be shared by the members or may be individualized. Merton and Newcomb both state that it is shared perceptions which are necessary, either shared perceptons ("definitions") of membership (Merton) or shared norms (Newcomb).

The third characteristic is *interdependence*. For Cattell (1951), it is interdependence in the satisfaction of needs. Cartwright and Zander (1968) view interdependence as a prerequisite for group performance and the basis of group structure. Newcomb stresses interdependence due to the interlocking roles of group members.

Analysis of Variables

Another approach to explicating the common properties of groups, as viewed by the scientist, is to analyze those variables employed by small group researchers. Specifically, one can look at the conceptual statement of these variables, assuming that the choice of variables reflects at least in part the scientists' conceptions of major group properties.

Such an analysis was carried out as part of a larger study of conceptual orientations toward the small group (DeLamater et al., 1965). An attempt was made to develop a classification system which would encompass the content of some 160 independent and dependent variables which have been used in small group research. After trying several such systems, the following five-category scheme was elaborated, and it was judged most adequate for that sample of variables.

Affect: This class included all variables which were defined or conceptualized as internal affective states, both positive and negative.

Cognition: This class contained all variables defined or conceptualized in terms of cognitive states or processes, including beliefs, attitudes, and perceptual variables.

Behavior: All variables which referred to the overt behavior of individuals or groups were classified in this category, including interaction and group achievements through member efforts.

Position: This class included variables which dealt with a given individual's relationships to other persons in the group—e.g., variables dealing with one's role, sociometric status, and leadership position.

Structure: This class included all variables referring to the location or distribution of parts within a unit—e.g., the distribution of roles. This category is the group-level equivalent of the position class; the positions of members taken collectively comprise the structure of the group. Thus, variables in this class occurred only at the group level in the original analysis.

Therefore, the relevant substantive content categories are affective, behavioral, cognitive, and position/structural variables. The latter three are highly similar to the common properties discussed in connection with formal definitions: interaction (behavior), perception (cognition), and interdependence (position-structure). The failure to include affective ties or reactions explicitly in any of the formal definitions considered above is worthy of note. This is perhaps partly due to the predominance of laboratory studies of the small group. Affective reactions are perhaps not significant influences in a twenty- to thirty-minute interaction with strangers when one is *playing the role of a subject*. In the laboratory setting, task and structural variables often account for so much of the variance that researchers and theorists overlook the importance of affective reactions. At the same time, persons playing the role of a subject may not have strong emotional reactions toward other subjects.

Although theorists do not include affective factors in formal definitions of group, several of them do introduce affect in more extended discussions as an important determinant of behavior in groups. For example, those who follow the group dynamics tradition consider affect in their focus on cohesiveness, defined as a positive attraction to the group arising from attraction (i.e., liking) toward other members, the group task, or the group's prestige (Festinger, 1960). Similarly, Bales (1965) recognizes socioemotional or affective factors as one of the three basic aspects of group structure and function. As a final example, Homans (1950) distinguishes the "external system" of the group, the demands of and behavior oriented toward the task and the environment, from its "internal system," the interpersonal relations within the group. The failure to include affective ties in formal definitions is even more interesting in light of the attention it has received in these conceptual analyses.

A Tentative Definition

Thus, an analysis of formal definitions and a systematic study of the variables employed in small group research point to four important defining properties of a group. *A comprehensive definition of "group" can be formulated in terms of the following properties: interaction between individuals, perceptions of other members and the development of shared perceptions, the development of affective ties, and the development of interdependence or roles* (i.e., group structure).

Interaction, as employed here, refers to face-to-face contact between persons in which each individual's behavior is affected by the behavior of others. Thus, imagined associations, considered by some as "reference group" phenomena, are not included.

Perception refers not only to the fact that we perceive those with whom we interact in an immediate sense, but also to the perceptions which each member develops concerning group norms, perceptions which are typically shared (compare Newcomb, 1961). It also refers to perceptions of the personalities of each of the other members, which may or may not be shared.

By *affective ties* are meant the positive and negative feelings which each member develops vis-à-vis other members as he interacts with them. These emotional reactions are partly influenced by how the others perform their roles, whether their behavior meets group norms. But an often stronger determinant is how the individual perceives the personalities of others, what he views them to be like as individuals. To the extent that affective reactions are due to such personal factors, they are less likely to be shared, to be common to other group members.

Interdependence can be viewed as basically interdependence with respect to the completion of some task(s) or goal achievement. This interdependence is the basis of the group, since members are attempting to achieve something which would be harder or impossible to achieve as individuals. The goal may be the exchange of affect, of cognitive orientations, and attitudes toward the world, the production of a product, or any of the multitude of outcomes toward which groups strive. If the group is to be stable over time, there must be continual goal-directed activity, and it is the nature of the goal which gives coherence and direction to perception and behavior, while one is part of the group. As the basis of organization, it is the group's goal(s) which determine the role structure to a large extent. The role system—the positions and activity of group members—is designed (consciously or not) to fulfill in a stable and reliable fashion the functions necessary to goal achievement. The role system may be formal, with rights and duties written down for each position to which all adhere, or it may be informal, with a (perhaps unspoken) consensus about who does what. It is in this informal sense that we sometimes speak of roles in friendship groups—e.g., the "joker." Thus, because the role structure exemplifies and is determined by the interdependence of members, that structure provides a good logical and empirical criterion of that interdependence.

These variables need not be conceptualized as possessing only two states, as either present or absent. Such an "all or none" approach creates the need for arbitrary logical and empirical cutoff points, on one side of which a set of persons does not have the characteristics and is not a group, while on the other side it does and is. The determination of these qualitatively differentiating points can be extremely hard, and, when accomplished, the criterion chosen may not be truly meaningful. An approach in terms of dimensions, viewing each variable as a dimension capable of assuming a range of specific values, avoids these problems and perhaps accords better with reality. Also, the integration of large segments of the research literature on small groups would be facilitated by such a dimensional approach. It is for this reason that affective ties, perception, and roles are stated above in terms of development, a development which may produce varying degrees of affect among members, different amounts of consensus concerning roles, and different degrees of sharing of perceptions.

References

Bales, R. F. (1965) "Task roles and social roles in problem-solving groups," pp. 321-333 in I. Steiner and M. Fishbein (eds.) Current Studies in Social Psychology. New York: Holt, Rinehart & Winston.

———. (1953) "A theoretical framework for interaction process analysis," pp. 29-38 in D. Cartwright and A. Zander (eds.) Group Dynamics: Research and Theory. Evanston, Ill.: Row, Peterson.

Cartwright, D. and Zander, A. (eds.) (1968) Group Dynamics: Research and Theory. New York: Harper & Row.

Cattell, R. B. (1951) "New concepts for measuring leadership, in terms of group syntality." Human Relations 4: 161-184.

DeLamater, J. (1964) "Operational measures of cohesiveness and their validity." (unpublished)

———. McClintock, C. G., and Becker, G. (1965) "Conceptual orientations of contemporary small group theory." Psych. Bull. (December): 402-412.

Festinger, L. (1960) "Informal social communication," pp. 286-299 in D. Cartwright and A. Zander (eds.) Group Dynamics: Research and Theory. Evanston, Ill.: Row, Peterson.

Heinicke, C., and Bales, R. F. (1953) "Developmental trends in the structure of small groups." Sociometry 16: 7-38.

Homans, G. C. (1950) The Human Group. New York: Harcourt, Brace.

Krech, D. and Crutchfield, R. S. (1948) Theory and Problems of Social Psychology. New York: McGraw-Hill.

Merton, R. K. (1957) Social Theory and Social Structure. New York: Free Press.

Newcomb, T. M. (1963) "Social psychological theory: integrating individual and social approaches," pp. 7-20 in E. P. Hollander and R. G. Hunt (eds.) Current Perspectives in Social Psychology. New York: Oxford Univ. Press.

————. (1961) The Acquaintance Process. New York: Holt, Rinehart & Winston.

Pepitone, A. and Reichling, G. (1960) "Group cohesiveness and the expression of hostility," pp. 141-151 in D. Cartwright and A. Zander (eds.) Group Dynamics: Research and Theory. Evanston, Ill.: Row, Peterson.

Raven, B. (1961) A Bibliography of Small Group Research. Los Angeles: Univ. of California Press.

Schachter, S.; Ellerston, N.; McBride, D.; and Gregory, D. (1960) "An experimental study of cohesiveness and productivity," pp. 152-162 in D. Cartwright and A. Zander (eds.) Group Dynamics: Research and Theory. Evanston, Ill.: Row, Peterson.

Whyte, W. F. (1955) Street Corner Society. Chicago: Univ. of Chicago Press.

Group Dynamics

Patrick R. Penland and Sara Fine

A group is a system within a system within a system. The group has boundaries, and outside those boundaries is the larger social entity of which it is a part. A committee is responsible to the agency out of which it was created. A learning group may depend for sustenance and support and approval on an educational or informational institution. A training group may be beholden to a library or a service agency for its existence. A therapy group may be created under the auspices of a mental health clinic or hospital.

Each sponsoring agency is in turn accountable to a larger system—a board of directors, a citizens' committee, the state, a funding agency, the electorate. Even the most independent group is responsible to generalized societal boundaries. Sometimes the "parent" is very stern, very present, and has very strong censure and approval power over the behavior and processes of the group; sometimes the authorizing agency is completely uninvolved, at least on an overt level. In any event, the group is affected by its existence, for each group has limitations imposed on it from without.

The larger system can affect the operation of the group in many ways, sometimes directly, sometimes subtly. For example, the system may put direct pressure on the leader to direct the group's activities and decisions into certain directions. On the other hand, the leader may simply sense that the system is exerting some control over his leadership in ways he cannot quite identify, but which seem to be bound up with his status in the larger system. The group members themselves may be under explicit operational and goal instructions. Even when they are directed to resolve a problem or reach a decision independently, they know that they are ultimately accountable to the goals, beliefs and rules of the system within which the group is operating, and even to the larger social climate outside the system. A jury, for example, must face the judge, the prisoner, their own families, and friends with their "independent" decision.

Sometimes a group may appear to be responsible only to itself for its own process; yet even so, there is generally some higher authority that can affect the death of the group should it disobey some social ground rule. A university may offer a course in "Group Dynamics" and the course may be run as an open, unstructured, virtually leaderless experience in group and interpersonal dynamics with no structure, no explicit goals, no specific

Reprinted from Patrick Penland and Sara Fine, *Group Dynamics and Individual Development*, Marcel Dekker, Inc., N.Y., 1974, pp. 45-53, by courtesy of Marcel Dekker, Inc.

rules, no directive leader. Yet, on some level, the members and the leader both feel the pressure to attend and to "succeed." Perhaps the attainment of a degree depends on the course. Perhaps to the nonleading leader-teacher, a continuation of the course offering is at stake. No word is spoken about this undercurrent of reality, but all participants react to their awareness of it. Should the group decide to defy the system's rules, they are still reacting in some way to the system's pressure.

The impact of the system is a very subtle component of the group's dynamics, complicated further by the fact that the larger system is usually invisible to the group. It generally cannot be directly confronted, nor does it present itself for modification or change. Sometimes it sends a representative to participate in the group, and then the group has a different experience from one in which no system agent is visible. The dynamics become more inhibited and group behavior more constrained. In one way or another, the group will deal with that representative. It may try to entice him into group rather than system loyalty. The group may begin to negotiate with him, or overtly ignore him while yet taking him into account with every word and act. Participants may try to please him and win his approval, or go into combat with him in a simulated rebellion against the system he represents.

The existence of the larger system is a reality base, and its effect is felt in every group. But generally the system is present only as a spirit, or in some sense, as a conscience. System "invisibility" may cause another kind of dynamic to come into play—the group myth about the system. This myth grows up in response to the group's own fantasy about the power and omniscience of the superstructure, about how much control it could exert on the group or on its members.

But in reality, the supersystem seldom possesses the degree of actual censuring and approving power with which the group perceives it. In fact, the "system" may be a myth, with only as much power as the group is willing to endow it. In some real sense, it is the group that confers on the system all kinds of demands, prohibitions, and power, rather than the other way around. The group endows the system with demands rather than face its own reluctance to direct itself. The group imposes mystical limits on its own freedom rather than accept accountability for its own success or failure. The phrased excuse "The library board wouldn't approve this new idea" may be easier for a group to accept than the realization "If we try this, there will be a terrific battle in the group."

While all groups are affected by the larger system, all groups do not attempt to change their relationship to it. Task and agenda groups tend to see that relationship as a given imperative within which the group will operate. Thus, group myths tend to be quickly formulated and unquestioningly maintained. When, however, the agenda itself concerns a confrontation with the supersystem, as when a grievance committee forms to negotiate with the parent institution, the myths come under some intellectual scrutiny and the group mobilizes its own counterpower to challenge the superauthority. It is the counterpower that all groups have, whether or not they use it, whether or not they are aware of it.

Unstructured groups, on the other hand, may deny the existence of any force outside themselves. Members often see themselves as a self-sustaining entity, responsible only to the group, and hardly affected by the world outside the meeting room. Yet, individual participant behavior reflects the expectations of the social climate outside, and group behavior reflects the rules and boundaries set upon it. In some way, every group is a product not only of the individual members that make it up, but of the social context out of which it was created.

Group Happenings

If a group is composed of living, breathing members, then something is always happening. A group is a dynamic organism, always awake, never really still; group dynamics and interpersonal dynamics and intrapersonal dynamics are operating all the time. A glance, a shift of chairs, a moment of embarrassment may be small moments, small movements—hardly noticed—yet in a constant and cumulative manner they affect the members in mysterious ways. A member sitting silently still, his eyes glued to his shoes, is not only himself a complex, operating, thinking, feeling, and responding being, but he can also arouse complex responses in members around him and affect the total process of the group. Sometimes, in fact, the silent member is the most powerful individual in the group by virtue of the intensity of the responses he arouses in other members.

Whether a group that is sitting in moody silence or engaging in comfortable chatter it is active in its process and in its effects on the members within that process. There is no such thing as "nonparticipation" or "nonresponsiveness." Nor is there any group that does not behave on an affective, reactive level as well as on a cognitive and verbal level. A group is always in a dynamic state, but groups differ widely on the level of consciousness on which they operate.

Do we ignore what is happening or do we talk about it? If a group has bogged down into inaction and indecision or into confrontation and conflict, there are both overt and unconscious forces at work. The members will perceive the dynamics both as part of the group's process and in terms of their own reactions to them. The way they respond to those dynamics will to a great degree be determined by the structural limits within which the group is functioning.

There seems to be a direct correlation between traditional structure and the absence of any discussion about the underlying group dynamics, the "hidden agenda," or the focal encounters between members. In a highly structured group, acceptable social behavior will be the norm. If conflict arises, it will be dealt with only on a rational and intellectual level. More likely, it will be politely ignored, because ignoring intense feelings and avoiding personal verbal exchanges are part of the social ethic of our culture. It is not even considered acceptable social form to discuss the subtleties of any human process. One does not ordinarily discuss the undercurrent dynamics and social need fulfillment of a cocktail party when at a cocktail party!

But even in a structure-oriented group, there is sometimes a break-through. A member will point out what is happening in the group or he will begin to talk about himself, his personal feelings, and his reactions. At that moment a remarkable phenomenon occurs—structure will be abandoned, if only for a moment. Chairs will shift out of place. Other members will somehow move toward the speaker. Formal titles may be replaced by first names. Time schedules will be abandoned and agendas will be neglected. But it is likely that before long, a task-oriented member will recall the meeting to order. Other members, frightened by the sudden human involvement, will gratefully resume their former distant postures, somehow vaguely uneasy, somehow feeling unsettled by the experience.

There are many small moments and small movements within every group, but there is also an overall movement and flow—highs, lows, and level places, overall patterns of general shifts in mood and need. Movement and activity will take hold of the group, giving way to inertia and apathy. Movement will begin again, and then inertia will once more immobilize the process. Authority will be challenged by the group as though by unanimous consent; then direction will be demanded, and challenged again. The group will become anxious, then comfortable. Anxiety and comfort will play their alternate parts in the drama.

Perhaps the most remarkable aspect of this flow pattern is that it happens at all. Whereas individual members, with their individual needs and stresses, press for their individuality and for their place in the group, one might expect that this multiplicity of needs, demands, and styles of expression would result in chaos, in constant and unconcerted individual movements. But there is also the *group* phenomenon. It is as though, at some invisible signal, a group will fall silent, or make a decision, or talk of trivialities, or call itself to order.

The control of this flow pattern is one function of group structure. When operational procedures play an important role in the group process, it is possible to control highs by calling a meeting to order, to moderate lows by moving to the next item on the agenda, to respond to attacks or demand for leadership by taking a vote, to deal with anxiety by changing the subject, to flee from apathy by adjourning the meeting.

An open process group, however, lives with the flow, agonizes with it, and is exhilarated by it. Basically it *deals* with it, tries to understand its effects, in order to learn from the experiencing of it. Member A, for example, may be so unnerved by the silence that his anxiety forces him to break it. Member B responds to demands for leadership by assuming it, only to be ignored for his effort. Member C is so exasperated by the inertia that she leaves the group. And so it goes! Group actions and the members' reactions become the focus for group work and the raw material for personal and group development. Does Member A always confront his anxiety by talking? Does Member B always assume leadership when there is a vacancy? Does Member C always walk away from a situation when she is frustrated?

In an open process group, it is not unusual to hear a long silence broken with words like, "I wonder what's going on in this group right now," or "The silence is making me very uncomfortable." The words are followed by group relief that at last the process is moving again. But in the process, members are left with some insight about how they react to anxiety or to apathy or to anger or to not being able to take over. Learning has taken place, learning about oneself.

In an unstructured group, where there is no sharply defined leadership role and no superimposed set of goals and regulations, members experience a kind of freedom to explore, along with a concommitant anxiety about that freedom and the responsibility it imposes on them. When group agreement is reached, it will likely be the product of both the loose structure and the anxiety it produces. The group's way of functioning will become legitimate fodder for discussion. Feelings will be dealt with as feelings: conflicts will be viewed not as intellectual debating exercises, but as behavioral and emotional issues among the parties to that conflict.

Because an unstructured group gropes to handle its own direction and its own responsibility, it is more likely to become aware of the way in which unresolved issues among members, and group issues about authority and anxiety, can either hamper the movement of the group or bring it into dynamic confrontation and growth. The unstructured group has a greater potential for this kind of awareness than does a tightly structured one. It has more potential to free itself from prescribed social behavior that prohibits involvement with "strangers" and explicating than which is implicit in a social encounter.

Group Goals

Every group meets to "do" something. All groups have goals, goals that were part of the initial "contract" when the group formed itself, and goals that evolve and are modified by the experience and the process of the group itself. Sometimes these goals are concrete and explicit. They may be concerned with decision making or establishing policies, fulfilling a designated task or learning a skill—goals concerned with some outer-directed accomplishment. Other groups move towards goals that are more inner-directed, more vague, harder to define and defend. Even when such goals can be articulated, they tend to be self-oriented or person-oriented and subject to a diversity of interpretation. It becomes much more difficult to relate specific group processes and activities to the accomplishment of those goals.

But whether goals are well-defined and explicitly understood by the group or whether they remain abstract and generalized, goals are in one sense a group purpose, a commonality that is a primary factor in the emergence of a group spirit. A goal may be as vague as "getting well" (in a therapy group or Alcoholics Anonymous, or a group of patients with a common illness). It may seek "to learn more about oneself" (in a sensitivity group), or to explore ways of enhancing interpersonal relations (in a T-group or staff development group). Goals may aim to affect change or increase production in a system (staff meetings, agenda meetings) and conduct their business toward that end. Groups may meet to defend themselves against some threat, real or imagined (protest groups), or to nurture an ideal (religious discussion groups), or to promote a cause (political action groups, citizens groups). Groups come together in all styles and modes for activity, enlightenment, and gratification. . . .

Group Unity

Groups move toward a spirit of unity. The natural movement of the group, the movement forward that goes beyond the clashes of conflict and the peaks and levels and lows of activity, is toward a state in which the group has an ego and a momentum of its own. Sometimes a group never reaches this state. At other times, it seems as though the moment of harmony and fellowship that has been reached will last forever. When a group has a momentary experience of unity and purpose, it is inevitable that another crisis will disrupt its euphoria.

Nevertheless, the group keeps straining toward that comfortable, productive state. Group unity is an unspoken expression of group movement toward goals that are generally acceptable to all the members. It is the unvoiced recognition that all the members are involved with the group process; it is a group feeling that here is a place where contribution and creativity are valued. Basically it is a state in which the group can accept its own dynamics without being threatened by them.

When a group experiences this spirit of unity, it is secure enough to accept new members and entertain strangers without the fear that the stranger will unbalance the strength of the group. It is secure enough to withstand the absence of a strong member without feeling helpless and resentful. It can accept the subgroups in its midst without fearing that the group will dissolve as a result of their existence. It will have come to recognize that group discontent and member conflicts will not destroy the group. Members will have freedom to move and breathe and behave within the group limits. Each member will be valued for his individuality, and this will not be a threat to the group.

All groups—structured and unstructured—task and training—press toward this end. The need for a feeling of unity is so powerful that groups will often "fake it." When a difficult decision has been reached or a difficult task accomplished, a task group or an agenda group will applaud itself on how effectively it works together and how limitless its potential is for further action. But such an expression, made after action where members have been enticed into compliance or challengers legislated into submission, where members have been hurt and are quietly nursing wounds, is a smug assertion of power, not an expression of real group unity.

In an open process group, the pressure for a group spirit of unity is even greater, for has the group not expressly met for the purpose of growth and maturity? An expression of warmth in the group by a member is often met with silent resentment by other members, who feel anything but warmth and who hesitate to admit their coldness lest they be labeled as unfeeling or unresponsive, but who continue to feel that they are being manipulated by a false expression of unity.

Moments of group unity are rare and precious, and often they go by without attention being called to them. It is in those moments, when the conflicting and blocking group dynamics have reached some crisis and then some real resolution, that for a brief time the group is aware, generally on a level that goes beyond verbalization, that a real potential for group productivity has been released. And it is during those moments that members will risk the most, will contribute the most, and that the group will accomplish the most. It is these precious moments that reassure members when it is yet possible for people to work together toward some common goal.

Group Behavior and the Communication Process

Jerry C. Wofford, Edwin A. Gerloff and Robert C. Cummins

Much of our communication occurs in small groups. From the family of our birth to our funeral entourage, groups have a significant impact on our development and behavior. Communication is the basic tool for the operation of these groups. Whether it be the family members influencing one another in the daily conduct of life affairs, the work team on the engineering project, the board of directors, the chamber of commerce, the church school, or the social group, communication is the vital thread that holds the group together and provides the conduit for influence and action.

We are members of many more groups today than at any other time. These groups tend to be less permanent, stable, and enduring in nature. Consequently, communication skill becomes increasingly more important; one must be able to interact quickly and to relate effectively on a limited time basis. The successful manager today must become adept at establishing close, open relationships. One who remains guarded and defensive in the group context will be unable to succeed in a wide range of situations in the work environment. The typical manager spends much time in small groups. To perform effectively, the manager must be able to communicate effectively in the group for decision making, planning, and task execution. An understanding of certain group processes is an important determinant of the manager's ability to communicate effectively.

In the present chapter, we shall examine more closely the basic processes of group functioning and how they relate to the communication process. You are again asked to assume the role of the case observer for the market-research group and examine the group-process variables. The variables which concern us include group identity, social structure, goals, cohesiveness, and norms. These variables define the nature of the group and establish the group bahavioral patterns.

Each of the group-process variables influences the flow, form, content, purpose, and quality of the communication process. Each is in turn influenced by the communication process (see Figure 1). You might begin your case observation with a look at the process of establishing group identity.

From *Organizational Communication: A Keystone To Managerial Effectiveness* by Wofford, et al. Copyright © 1977 by McGraw-Hill, Inc. Used with permission of McGraw-Hill Book Company.

Establishing the Group Identity Through the Communication Process

The communication which establishes the identity will vary widely from one group to another. Groups which have vague purposes and structure spend a great deal of time and communication in developing their identity. If the association with the group is only to be of a temporary nature, less attention will be given to group identity. Groups which are established for a five- to ten-year duration give much more attention to identity. In addition, if the members are strongly ego-involved in the group, greater attention will be given to the discussion of identity.

The identity of our market-research group was defined in terms of *location* and *time,* which were already set when the group was first formed. Members learned that they were to appear at a particular address on a certain date. However, from the moment they first entered the building,

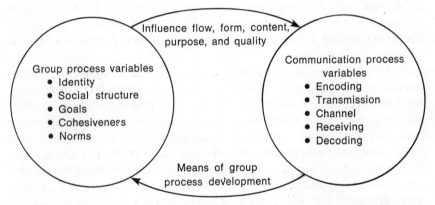

Figure 1. Interaction of group-process variables and communication-process variables

the locational aspects of their future group activities rapidly refined and expanded. A more explicit, fuller, and richer perception of the group's identity is formed over time.

For this market-research group, the *membership* is externally assigned and is easily identified. Since it is small, each member knows the other members. Large groups with fluctuating memberships such as university student bodies have a far less defined membership identity than is the case for the market-research group. The defined, stable membership of the group facilitates communication in that senders and receivers can build their understanding and their awareness of the language and semantics typically used by one another. Encoding, transmission, and other elements of the communication process will be enhanced through continuous practice and use. An enlightened manager can make good use of such effects in linking his or her group to other units of the organization.

The group has defined *territorial space.* Certain offices, conference rooms, coffee lounges, and buildings "belong" to the group. The members refer to them as "our" or "ours." This territorial space may be expanded or contracted informally. Once established, the group tends to resist variations in the use of the space. Seating patterns become fixed. Particular locations become associated with specific activities. In groups such as an inner-city gang, the territorial space may be defended to the death against invasion. While not to this extreme, we all hold a degree of proprietary protectiveness for "our" territorial work space. Group communication may be directed toward defining or protecting the group's territorial space.

The *values* of the members also begin to be revealed early. As the members describe their backgrounds, they reflect their values. In our market-research group, the introductory discussion focused upon work and educational background. These were the valued aspects of their history as it applied to this group. In time, the values of the members will be reflected in many different ways and will become a point of identity for the group. These values become a basis for exercising control within the group.

With continued interaction, *expectations* about a number of factors become apparent. These expectations include those regarding various roles, interaction patterns, and member behavioral patterns. In our market-research group, the members developed the expectations that would assure Sam's leadership role. They also developed the expectation of a close interaction and participation in decisions. Job-performance expectations were discussed and agreed upon in open communication. By their behavior at coffee breaks and lunches, they developed clear expectations about who would interact with whom. These communication channels become the tasks for group activities.

The group establishes its identity when its members define the situations and characteristics which set them apart as an entity. The awareness of group identity may be either conscious or subconscious. The identity may be either external- or internal-systems-oriented. The primary external-system-oriented elements of identity include location, routine patterns, and membership. Values and expectations are elements of identity that relate closely to the internal system.

The Relationship of Social Structure to the Communication Process

The second phase of development of the group process involves the social structure. The establishment of social structure and group identity are not totally independent processes. The structure of the group is one of the bases for group identity. Social structure includes *status systems, role relationships, subgroups, interaction relationships,* and *social-influence pat-*

terns. The effectiveness of both the managerial and communication processes will be influenced by the social structure within which they occur. Accordingly, the manager and the communicator should be acquainted with the important variables which determine social structure.

The Relationship of the Status System Within the Group to Communication

Achieved and Ascribed Status.   Status is the social position a person holds as compared with that of other members of his or her group. Status identifies the evaluation of a position of an individual in the group. Status may be sought through striving and competitive mastery of the roles linked to status, or it may be ascribed to a person on the basis of characteristics such as sex, age, race, and kinship. The first type of status is referred to as *achieved status;* the second is *ascribed status.* Achieved status is attained through performing valued roles, activities, and efforts. On the other hand, the personal qualities of the individual are the basis for ascribed status and cannot be readily altered. In the film *The King and I,* the King of Siam is asked by his son how he will know when he possesses the omniscience associated with inheritance of the kingship. The King explains, "When you become King you will know." The King is suggesting that the ascribed status must precede the attainments associated with the status. This is not always the order of events.

In our market-research group, we can see evidence of both ascribed and achieved status. Sam comes to the group with the assigned, formal authority and position of group manager. This position within the external organizational system gives him a certain level of status. He has the authority to direct the work of others in the group, yet he elects to maintain a flexible group structure and to allow participation. As the group structure develops into an internal system, Keith and Betty appear to be striving to achieve a higher status rank than that aspired to by Dutch and Bryant. The status ascribed to them by virtue of their age and experience facilitate their ability to attain the desired status rank.

Deference.   When group members act as if a group member holds status, these acts are referred to as *deference* behaviors. The group immediately shows deference for Sam. They accept his right to determine the group's method of organizing action. Deferential behavior takes the form of responding to the influence of the person with high status rank in satisfying that person's needs and aiding the achievement of his or her goals. The use of ingratiation as a deference behavior to gain conformity from a higher-status person was discussed in Chapter 10 [Wofford et al text].

In an organization, the amount of status is usually tied closely to the organizational position, power hierarchy, and chain of command. Status symbols are acquired to communicate the existence of the status and to

facilitate its recognition by others within the organization. D
havior generally includes providing the most well-decorated
rooms, most courteous treatment, gifts, attentiveness, praise, and imitation.
Consequently, people with high status generally will carry with them
symbols which help others recognize their status position.

Distributive Justice. Distributive justice refers to the perception of
a person's status rank as proportional to the deferential behavior and the
rewards associated with that rank. If people feel that their status rank is
commensurate with their rewards and recognition, then distributive justice
is maintained. If, however, this perception of their rank by virtue of
achievement or ascribed status is below the level of the rewards and benefits afforded to them, then they feel a lack of distributive justice. Lack of
distributive justice is usually attributed to favoritism and produces dis-
harmony within the organization. Distributive justice is a significant consideration for the manager in determination of the relationship of wages and
performance. Workers who perceive the status of their work to be low
relative to the level of their pay will attempt to offset this imbalance by
increasing their performance (Adams and Rosenbaum, 1962). If the
manager arranges the work so that quantity cannot be increased, the quality
of the work will be increased (Adams and Jacobsen, 1963).

The Impact of Status on Communication. Status has a significant
impact upon the communication process in groups. Communication variables such as "how often," "who," "to whom," and "what" are influenced
by status. High-status people generally communicate more frequently than
do low-status people. They also have greater influence and more power
than low-status people. Communication patterns tend to emerge along
status lines. Persons of equal status tend to communicate with one another
rather than with persons of different status. Consequently, status differen-
tials facilitate communication at the same or similar status rank, but inhibit
communication between people of differing ranks.

When people are introduced without the benefit of identifying status
cues, there is a tendency to avoid communication. The ambiguity of the
status positions results in discomfort in communication and is a threat to
the status-related communication. To continue communication in the face
of ambiguous status risks the loss of status position. The person may communicate in a manner that denotes lower status when his or her status is
actually higher. Communication among persons of different status levels
tends to be directed with more upward than downward reference. Persons
of a given status position tend to direct their communication to higher-status
persons rather than to persons of a lower-status level. Consequently,
communication is greater among and toward high-status persons in a group.

The content of communication also varies among status levels. In
group discussions, high-status people tend to give information and opinions,

whereas low-status people assume a more passive role involving such responses as agreement, disagreement, and requests for information. Higher-status people also tend to sustain their positions by avoiding criticism of their role and tasks. Low-status people tend to be more critical of their own role.

The implications of these effects of status upon communication for the manager are quite apparent. Since managers hold a position which in our society provides high status, they may find difficulty in communicating with workers with whom they have the greatest need for communication. They may communicate unnecessarily with peers simply because they are more comfortable in doing so. Managers should also be aware of the barrier which their status provides for getting information and opinions from lower-status people. Managers can often improve their communication with subordinates by reducing the perceived status differential between themselves and subordinates.

If we examine the market-research group in terms of status and communication, we find that the higher status of Sam in the group is a basis for his being the most frequent communicator and the most influential group member. He will be the most frequently listened to, agreed with, supported, and reinforced member of the group. In the brief communication samples recorded in the example, the tendency for the communication tends to remain within status levels, particularly during coffee and lunch breaks and other informal situations.

Role Relationships Within the Group and Communicaton

Roles define the kinds of interaction that are prescribed for certain types of interpersonal relationships. Managers may play a number of roles concurrently. They are supervisors to their employees, subordinates to higher-level managers, colleagues to their professional club members, fathers to their children, and husbands to their wives. Each role requires a different set of behaviors and attitudes. The content and style of communication is strongly influenced by the individual's role. The nature of the communication to one's wife, daughter, and supervisor are clearly very different in nature. Sam, of the market-research group, served as supervisor to his team and subordinate to his boss, a colleague to managers of other departments, and a market analyst to key customers. His communication experiences in each situation were likely to be quite different.

The relative significance of the roles for an individual and the amount of time that is spent performing each vary widely. The role of a monk in a monastery is essentially a full-time role. By contrast, the role of a customer for the person at the drive-in bank window is very brief and of little significance in a person's life. A role may be clearly established, as that of the bride at her wedding, or it may be as flexible as that of a professor in defining how and what will be done in class, research, or university activities.

Distinctions should be made between the perceived role, expected role, and enacted role. The *perceived role* is the set of behaviors that the occupant of the position believes he or she should perform. The *expected role* is the set of behaviors that others believe he or she should perform. *Enacted role* is the actual set of performed behaviors. Obviously, these types of roles may be at considerable variance. The greater the variance between the three types of roles, the greater the stress upon the individual and the persons associated with the individual. This stress is called *role strain*. A difference between the perceived role and the enacted role reflects a barrier: either internal to the person performing the role, such as incompetency, or external to the person, such as lack of resources or support from others. Differences between the expected role and the enacted role produce interpersonal conflict which results in change or eviction of the occupant from the position.

Role conflict occurs when a person is required to enact two incompatible roles simultaneously. Recently, in New York City, a news reporter rushed to the scene of an automobile accident to find his own son was the victim. An insurance salesperson is encouraged to sell to friends, but in doing so establishes a conflict of roles which may place the salesperson in a highly stressed situation. In the disastrous Texas City fire, when oil refineries exploded and resulted in fires which endangered the entire city, police officers were faced with the question of whether they would enact the police officer role and help protect the community or give first attention to the needs of their families in the parent role. Only one person resolved the conflict in favor of the police officer role. This man did so in the knowledge that his family was visiting in another city and enactment of the parent role was not needed. Role conflicts, like forms of role strain, stem from a wide range of perceptual, environmental, and behavioral elements. They are resolved either by altering the perceived role, the expected role, or the enacted role or by eliminating the behavioral constraints.

Role relationships, whether externally or internally determined, significantly influence communication. Each role will require a certain level of communication. Other communication which is not required emerges because of the circumstances in which the role occurs. The manager's role requires a large amount of communication and encourages even more. Certain routine, isolated jobs provide roles which require and permit little communication. The content of the communication is equally influenced by the role. Each role within a group has an information requirement and encourages the discusson of a definable range of topics.

Subgroups as Channels for Communication

Another aspect of social structure which influences the communication process is that of subgroup formation. Just as organizations are occasionally factionalized into groups, so groups are sometimes factionalized into subgroups. We usually think of subgroups as those factions or cliques which emerge spontaneously in the group. These are internal-system elements. However, subgroups can be external and required as well. A particular task may require that a subgroup be formed. For instance, two members of a research team may be sent to another laboratory to carry out a study that requires special equipment. A subgroup of design engineers may be assigned the task of selling the results of the work of the entire design team to a potential user.

Subgroups influence the channels of communication flow. The frequency of interaction among members of a subgroup is greater than that for nonmembers. Should special jargon be developed, barriers to communication from outside the subgroup may exist. For formal task-oriented subgroups, this communication is work-content-related. For cliques or factions most of the communication content will be oriented to the common needs, interests, or goals.

Interaction Relationships Within the Group

Interaction relationships are the emergent, recurring interactions among group members. These relationships are significant aspects of the group process and are intimately tied to the communication process. Interaction relationships become established rather quickly. These relationships are influenced by the status and role structure in the work situation. For example, Keith and Betty have similar functions to perform. Sam has a related activity with the two of them, and so the social-interaction relationship tends to be directed among these three. Bryant and Dutch have closely coordinated functions and responsibilities. Consequently, they communicate frequently. The geographical location of the work stations for Bryant and Dutch facilitate their close interaction relationships. Sam communicates frequently with Bryant and Dutch because of his responsibility for coordination.

Social-Influence Patterns and Communication

The social-influence patterns relate closely to the other aspects of social structure. As the accepted, informal group leader as well as the formal leader, Sam has the greatest amount of social influence. Keith and Betty have greater influence over the activities of Bryant and Dutch than vice versa. Keith and Betty are collecting the information. Therefore, the rate of information collection and transmittal by Keith and Betty will determine to a large extent the work load and work output of Bryant and Dutch. The reverse is not the case. This arrangement, by which the higher-status persons are the influence initiators, is favorable for the communication process. An adverse communication situation results when low-status persons become the influence initiators.

We have seen that each of the elements of social structure relates closely to the communication process. Communication serves to influence the development of the social structure and it is significantly influenced by the social structure.

The Goals of the Group and the Communication Process

Group goals are the internal-oriented, emergent goals. We refer to the goals imposed upon the group from without (such as by higher management) as superordinate goals. While superordinate goals influence the group's own goals, the group goals hold the dynamic force for mobilizing group activity. Thus, the group goals are our primary concern here.

The Needs of Group Members

In terms of motivational structure, groups operate very similarly to individuals. In fact, the motivational forces at work within a group are a particular combination of the motivational forces at work within the individual members constituting the group. Like individuals, groups have needs and attentive goals. The needs of the group are more than the simple summation of the needs of the individuals within the group. The very existence of the group brings additional needs and alters existing ones. Communication helps to estaiblish and alter the needs. It also helps the group obtain the goals which will satisfy the needs. The group goals are not a simple composite of the goals for the individual members. Within the same group, one person will emphasize satisfaction of interpersonal needs while another person will be motivated primarily by the need for achievement or self-esteem. Other persons will be striving for security in group membership. Out of this complex array of needs, group goals emerge. . . .

Group Norms and Communication

A group norm is any standard of value or belief which is held by the members of a group. Norms are vital and viable forces influencing the behavior of members of the group. Groups have norms in most of the areas of their functioning. These areas include codes of dress, conduct, speech, choice of words, performance level, quality of performance, etc. Norms are similar to goals in that they are often not expressed verbally. They may not be a part of conscious awareness for group members. However, they are always communicated among the members of the group in one form or another. They may be communicated by way of example, grimace, smile, verbal criticism, or praise. The norms tend to be within the internal organizational system.

Not all group members are willing to conform to every norm. Those who choose not to follow group practice for a behavior are considered *deviants*. A group member who persists in disparate behavior will become ostracized or separated from other group members and is referred to as an *isolate*. . . .

Summary

A number of group-process variables have been discussed which are significant in their impact upon organizational communication. These include group identity, social structure, group goals, cohesiveness, and norms. The general nature of such variables has been described and we have attempted to show the interrelationship of the various process variables and the communication process itself. The various process variables influence the internal-external context in which the communication process occurs. Thus, such variables affect the content, purpose, and quality of communication. Communication is frequently the means of establishing group-process variables. For example, in establishing its identity, the group discusses such things as its membership, location, and expectations. Group goals may also be developed through the discussion process.

The process of communication and the group-behavior process are closely intertwined in the dynamics of group functioning. Clear examples of this are seen in the effects of status and cohesiveness upon the freshness and openness of communication and in the effects of norms upon the sanctions communicated to the groups. Since the managerial role involves a good deal of functioning in groups, the manager should be aware of the group-process variables in their relationship to the communication process. The kinds of interactions between communication and group processes which influence managerial effectiveness were examined in this chapter.

A Model of Group Discussion

Martin P. Andersen

Historical antecedent and current practice attest to the widespread use and practical value of group discussion as a tool for decision-making and learning, a training method, and a technique for therapy and research. The situation is well stated in these words:

> Executives hold conferences at all levels in an organization; scientists work in teams; educators serve on committees; church workers hold conferences; parents serve on action groups; teachers educate by the use of participation methods; psychologists and psychiatrists practice group therapy; and teen-agers hold meetings.[1]

Currently there are evidences that, while widely used, the discussion process is not always understood and is frequently misused or abused. One author has noted that there is a "dilemma as to just what principles and concepts make up the rhetoric of discussion and how they should be presented."[2] An earlier article pointed out that at times certain characteristics of discussion are idealized (emphasized) to the exclusion of others.[3] This disparity in focus is seen in the different approaches of persons who employ discussion in research. At one extreme, discussion appears to be viewed as a form of stimulus-response activity, a unidimensional variable mediating relatively simple, predetermined goals and outcomes. At the other extreme, discussion is seen as a complex form of goal-seeking behavior, a multidimensional variable mediating the life space[4] of the group and the need-value-skill systems of its members.

Differences in the understanding of discussion are also revealed by its practice. A few persons deliberately hide authoritarian decision-making and advocacy under the cloak of discussion.[5] Others seem to believe that an

Reprinted from *Southern Speech Journal*, XXX, No. 4 (Summer, 1965), pp. 279-293. Reprinted with the permission of the author. This is a slightly abridged version of the original article.

1. Norman R. F. Maier, *Problem-Solving Discussions and Conferences* (New York: McGraw-Hill Book Company, Inc., 1963), v.

2. Harold P. Zelko, *The Quarterly Journal of Speech*, L (April, 1964), 202.

3. Dean C. Barnlund, "Our Concept of Discussion: Static or Dynamic," *The Speech Teacher*, III (January, 1954), 8.

4. See Kurt Lewin, *Field Theory in Social Science* (New York: Harper & Row, Publishers, 1951), xi.

5. See the description of "pseudo-discussion" in William S. Howell and Donald K. Smith, *Discussion* (New York: The Macmillan Company, 1956), 7-9.

"unstructured situation" and a "permissive atmosphere" are the essential components of a successful discussion. Apparently there is a need to attempt to answer the question, "What constitutes the principles and concepts of discussion?" We need periodically to formulate an integrated statement of the rhetoric of discussion.[6]

The purpose of this paper is to present a broad conceptual model of discussion, including its essential components, their interrelationships, and the cognitive-perceptual processes involved. The model is descriptive. It ties together a variety of observed characteristics of discussion and portrays the ways in which people act as participants. The model is normative. It indicates the ways in which people should behave, and the characteristics of the output when productivity in discussion is maximized. The model is tentative. Refinements and modifications can and should be made. Finally, the model is incomplete and necessarily oversimplified. For example, one element of discussion is oral communication, a process which in itself has been the object of a large number of model representations.[7] The values of the model are that it seeks to establish boundary lines for the discipline of discussion, focus on integral socio-psychological constructs and their interrelationships, and provides an operational guide for practice and prediction in discussion.[8]

In this paper discussion is viewed as a system of communicative and adaptive behavior growing out of imbalances in the need-value systems of the participants, both individually and collectively, and dynamically interrelated to specified properties of the "field sub-region"[9] in which the discussion occurs. A model of such behavior is concerned with the components of the system itself (structure), the sociological, psychological, and physical forces which determine the type, intensity, and direction of the interaction within the system (movement) and the outcomes as they relate to the sub-region in which the interaction takes place (productivity). In other words, the model should describe input into a system, interactive processes within the system, and output. The components and processes must be considered as functionally and dynamically interrelated at all times, even though we may consider them separately in our analysis.

---

6. See Daniel Fogarty, *Roots for a New Rhetoric* (New York: Bureau of Publications, Teachers College, Columbia University, 1959), 132–140, for a preliminary exploration of the rhetoric of discussion.

7. F. Craig Johnson and George R. Klare, "General Models of Communication Research: A Survey of the Developments of a Decade," *Journal of Communication*, XI (March, 1961), 13–33.

8. See Irwin D. J. Bross, *Design for Decision* (New York: The Macmillan Company, 1953), 161–182, for a statement of types, criteria, and values of models.

9. An illustration will make the meaning of this expression clear. The decisions made by a group research team in a local branch (sub-region) of a national organization constructing a missile component (region) are affected by the current needs and plans of the National Aeronautics and Space Administration (field).

Bases for the Model Construction

Numerous sources have contributed to the construction of the model. Empirical data covering a large number and variety of group discussions have been examined. A survey of approximately sixty currently-used discussion and communication textbooks revealed considerable unanimity as to the essential elements of group discussion.[10] An analysis of books on small group process directed attention to socio-psychological conceptualizations relative to human communicative and adaptive behavior. Pertinent research studies in discussion and related disciplines provided two types of helpful findings: (1) reconfirmation of conclusions based on the sources listed above, and (2) a set of tested hypotheses which verified certain of the theoretical assumptions incorporated in the model. Finally, critical evaluation by graduate students and colleagues resulted in several revisions of the model.

We now turn to a detailed description of our discussion model, which is diagrammed in Figure 1.

Essential Components of Group Discussion

The solids in Column 1 represent the six essential components of the discussion process: *purpose, thought pattern, content, the group, leadership,* and *communication.* Each is considered as one-sixth of the total. The descriptive terms near each solid designate the prediscussion characteristics of that component as it forms a part of the input. These characteristics are manifested through the group members, both individually and collectively.

1. One essential component is purpose. Discussion is not an end in itself; it is a means to some group goal which individuals cannot achieve alone. Discussion usually has one of three purposes: to solve a problem, to aid in learning, and to secure commitment to later action. Depending on circumstances before a discussion, its purpose may be *predetermined* or *emergent.*

2. Every discussion starts with a varying quantity and quality of meaningful content: reliable *facts* and *considered opinion* which are related to the discussion purpose. This content is brought to the discussion by the group members. At one extreme the essential information is available or accessible; at the other it is partially lacking or unavailable. In every instance

---

10. The reader may be interested in checking on the following sampling: Harold A. Brack and Kenneth G. Hance, *Public Speaking and Discussion for Religious Leaders* (Englewood Cliffs, N.J.: Prentice-Hall, Inc., 1961), 153–254; Laura Crowell, *Discussion: Method of Democracy* (Chicago: Scott, Foresman and Company, 1963), 7; Jon Eisenson, J. Jeffrey Auer, and John V. Irwin, *The Psychology of Communication* (New York: Appleton-Century-Crofts, 1963), 253–268; Giles Wilkeson Gray and Waldo W. Braden, *Public Speaking: Principles and Practice,* 2nd ed. (New York: Harper & Row, Publishers, 1963), 416; and Halbert E. Gulley, *Discussion, Conference, and Group Process* (New York: Henry Holt and Company, 1960), 4–5.

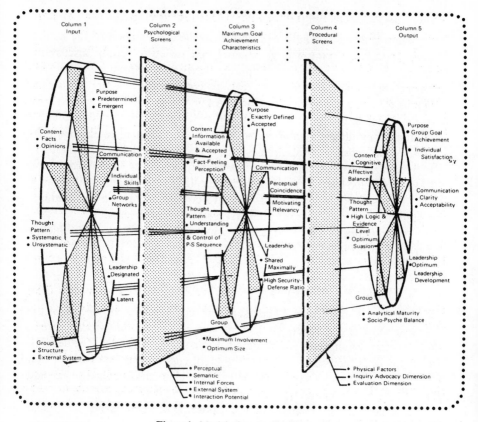

Figure 1. Model of group discussion.

the facts and opinions which each individual brings with him are set in the perceptual field of that individual.[11]

3. The third component of discussion is the thought pattern. Facts and opinions alone are not enough; they must be dealt with in a way which will contribute to the purpose. Almost without exception authorities say that discussion is a process of reflective thinking. Its success depends on the way a topic is developed systematically, moving from the location and definition of the problem through a consideration of possible solutions to the selection of the one preferred. Obviously, the quality of group thinking is a function of the members' skills in inquiry. Some persons are objective, thorough, logical, and have the ability to suspend judgment; others are at the opposite pole.

11. The implications of this statement and a definition oi "perceptual field" are found in Arthur W. Combs and Donald Snygg, *Individual Behavior: A Perceptual Approach to Behavior*, rev. ed. (New York: Harper & Row, Publishers, 1959), 16–36.

Therefore, the thought pattern input in discussion, as it applies both to individuals and the group, may be described as *systematic* or *unsystematic*.

4. A fourth component of any discussion is the group in which it occurs. This may be a small face-to-face, informal group or a large, more formal, co-acting group. The pre-discussion characteristics of any group are *structure* and its *external system*. Some discussion groups meet only once. In this case there is little prior structure, or differentiations among the members and their relationships, which together determine the flow of information, the flow of work,[12] and power relationships. When a group has stability (has continued over time) some hierarchical structure may have developed.[13] In every case a discussion group also functions within the matrix of some external system, by which we mean the configuration of interlocking individual and group frames of reference impinging on the movement within the group. Thus, decisions made by a local chapter of the Congress of Parents and Teachers are affected by the state and national policies of that body as well as by the school system with which the local PTA is associated and the community in which the school is located.

5. The leadership pattern is a fifth component of discussion. This element is conceived of as being of two possible conditions before discussion: *designated* or *latent*. There are two situations in which we have designated leadership: (1) where there is a single leader (moderator, chairman, president, etc.) who is named in advance, and (2) where leadership is shared among several who know their responsibilities in advance. In contrast leadership may be latent. Then the potential lies within the group members who —once discussion has started—exercise initiative in carrying out whatever leadership functions are needed.

6. The sixth component in discussion is communication, which is manifested in input in *individual skills* and *group networks*. Each group member brings with him varying skills in the use of verbal and nonverbal symbols, the media of communication. Also, each member has a potential for listening. When a group has met over a period of time it may have developed some dominant pattern of communication which is a function of both the dimensions of the group structure and the potency of the external system. This network of communication gives intensity and direction to the interaction. When a discussion group meets for the first time the potential communication networks are latent; then there can only be a predisposition to interact in a certain way.

---

12. See Dorwin Cartwright and Alvin Zander, *Group Dynamics: Research and Theory*, 2nd ed. (Evanston: Row, Peterson and Company, 1960), 648–649.

13. A meaningful statement of the dimensions of the group structure is found in John K. Hemphill and Charles N. Westie, "The Measurement of Group Dimensions," *Journal of Psychology*, XIX (April, 1950), 325–342.

Socio-Psychological Screens in Discussion

In the diagram of our model, the horizontal lines connecting Columns 1 and 2 represent different group members, who function unilaterally until the start of the discussion. When the discussion begins a number of socio-psychological processes becomes immediately operative in interpersonal and intrapersonal interaction. These processes function in both speakers and listeners as screens which filter all contributions. Every individual has a uniquely different filtering mechanism so that how a contribution is structured by a speaker or perceived by a listener is always a function of the filtering mechanism operating within that person. Five of these screens are of special significance: the *perceptual, semantic, internal forces, external system,* and *interaction potential.* While considered separately here, they are in reality closely interrelated; each affects and is affected by the others.

The first screen is that created by each member's *perceptual* field, which is defined as "the entire universe, including himself, as it is experienced by the individual at the instant of action."[14] All behavior of an individual is completely determined by his perceptual field which, in fact, is the only reality he can accept. He sees another's perceptual field as containing much error and illusion.[15] It becomes important in discussion, therefore, to establish a "common ground" of content and deal with that content objectively and impersonally.

A second screen, stemming from the first, is a *semantic* one. This screen filters the word meanings; it determines whether the signification of a symbol-stimulus is denotative or connotative. Even when this differentiation is perceived, it is still essential that sender and receiver understand the frame of reference in which a word is used. For example, an "extremist" might be understood to be "a person who holds extreme, or advanced views," but there might be a misunderstanding in discussion because two different frames of reference were used, one being "to the left" and the other "to the right." One writer says that content "must be susceptible to similar structurizations by both communicator and interpreter."[16]

The third screen is designated as that of *internal forces,* of both the individual and the group. Each individual in discussion seeks some combination to overt or covert personal or group goals. This goal-seeking behavior stems from and is shaped by the perceived instabilities in the members' beliefs, attitudes, statuses, values, desires, and needs as these are related to the discus-

---

14. Combs and Snygg, *Individual Behavior,* p. 20.

15. Ibid., 21.

16. Franklin Fearing, "Toward a Psychological Theory of Human Communication," *Journal of Personality,* XXII (Sept., 1953), 73. This article provides an excellent theoretical statement of the conceptual framework within which communication occurs.

sion topic. Forces within the group also filter the discussion content. These forces might be any of the group's dimensions: norms, cohesiveness, extent of cooperation or competition, hedonic tone, permeability, and stability, to mention only a few.[17] Research has shown beyond any doubt that these and other group dimensions have significant impact on the behavior of the group members.

The nature of the third screen just described is partially determined by a fourth, the *external system,* which includes the total physical, technical, and social environment in which the discussion occurs: its "field." Sometimes the external system has the characteristics of a primary group, as when discussion occurs in a family, a peer group, or a play group. In other situations the external system takes on the character of secondary groups, such as the nation, political party, church, union, industry, or social movement. Frequently, the external system combines the characteristics of both, as when the frames of reference of a discussant include his family, the union of which he is a member, the company for which he works, and the political party in which he is registered. The filtering effect on discussion content of each of these types of external systems will vary in directness, intensity, frequency, duration, and formality.

A final screen in discussion is the group's *interaction potential.* This is defined by one author as "the tendency of a given pair of members of a group to interact."[18] This concept has been expanded to apply to all possible combinations of group members and to include the "freedom" as well as the "tendency" to interact. It is generally accepted that productivity in discussion is a function of the extent to which this potential is maximized, how well the group's resources are used. One of the theoretical assumptions underlying the use of such techniques as brainstorming. T-Group training, role-playing, buzz groups, and the audience interaction panel is that optimum participation improves the quantity and quality of the outcomes and the members' satisfactions. Research also supports the conclusion that full involvement improves productivity.[19] It becomes apparent, then, that when interaction is kept at a low level because of status barriers, personal differences, semantic problems,

---

17. See Edgar F. Borgatta, Leonard S. Cottrell, and Henry J. Meyer, "On the Dimensions of Group Behavior," *Sociometry,* XIX (Dec., 1956), 223–240; Raymond B. Cattell, "New Concepts for Measuring Leadership, In Terms of Group Syntality," *Human Relations,* IV (1951), 161–184; Hemphill and Westie, *Group Dimensions;* George C. Homans, *The Human Group* (New York: Harcourt, Brace and Company, 1950); and George A. Theodorson, "Elements in the Progressive Development of Small Groups," *Social Forces,* XXXI (May, 1953), 311–320. These articles present different approaches to the analysis of group dimensions.
18. Bernard M. Bass, *Leadership, Psychology and Organizational Behavior* (New York: Harper & Row, Publishers, 1960), 342.
19. See Ralph K. White and Ronald Lippitt, *Autocracy and Democracy: An Experimental Inquiry* (New York: Harper & Row, Publishers, 1960), 282–285.

group size, or variance in discussion skills, productivity will be directly affected.

These screens act as a unified filter on all six components of discussion. They are always present and are partial determinants of the discussion outcomes. They are operative at the start and during the discussion and hence we place them immediately after input in our model.

Conditions Essential for Maximum Goal Achievement

As indicated earlier, the separate horizontal lines between Columns 1 and 2 suggest that prior to discussion each individual functions unilaterally. Once the process starts, it may be assumed that there is some concern for goal achievement. This is indicated by the convergence of lines between Columns 2 and 3.

One value of a model is its use in prediction. To know the conditions under which the discussion process functions at its best, the characteristics of each component which are essential for maximum goal achievement must be considered.

1. The two essential characteristics for the first component are that the purpose must be *exactly defined* and *accepted*. Problem location and definition is the first step in the reflective thinking process and is equally important when understanding or commitment are the goals. In a summary of the characteristics of productive groups, one author states: "The most productive groups . . . are found to be those which can best carry out the steps in the problem-solving process."[20] A second condition under which purpose contributes maximally to goal achievement is when the defined goal is accepted by the group members. While it is impossible to suppress completely the hidden agendas of some group members, the publicly stated goal must take precedence. Membership in any discussion group is predicated on the assumption that goal achievement is desired.

2. The second component in discussion is content. Maximum productivity should occur under two conditions: (1) when needed *facts and opinions are optimally available and accepted,* and (2) when their *fact-feeling* (cognitive-affective) *qualities are perceived.* Discussion cannot take place in a vacuum, in a situation in which facts and opinions are not available.[21] When this extreme situation exists, the discussion should be postponed or not held. Then, too, these facts and opinions, when properly tested, must be accepted.

---

20. A. Paul Hare, *Handbook of Small Group Research* (New York: The Free Press of Glencoe, 1962), 375.

21. See Maier, *Problem-Solving Discussions,* 138–139, 211–238, for a statement of methods of decision-making when all desired facts are not available.

A second essential characteristic of content is that its cognitive-affective (fact-feeling) qualities be perceived by the group members. A person who cannot differentiate between the objective meaning of a contribution and the subjective feelings of the contributor is apt to focus on personalities rather than issues.

3. The characteristics of the thought pattern which are essential for maximum productivity are that the members *understand the problem-solving sequence* and *exercise control* over its progress. Persons who do not understand the reflective thought process are apt to perceive discussion as advocacy, indoctrination, compromise, or as an unsystematic approach toward goals. However, understanding what constitutes solid thinking is not enough. The members must be free to make procedural decisions in discussion; they must be aware of the progress being made; and they must be courageous in their insistence that the best thinking procedures be followed.

4. As far as the group itself is concerned, productivity is dependent on *maximum involvement* of the members and *optimum size*. People become members of a discussion group because they have a contribution to make or an interest in the topic. To the extent that group members are not maximally involved the end product suffers. A second essential is that the group be of optimum size for the achievement of its task and social needs. The group must be large enough to accomplish its goal and small enough to insure member satisfaction through participation. This is related to Thelen's "principle of individual challenge in the least-sized group," which he describes in these words:

> The central assumption of this principle is that the quality of performance depends on how one is motivated to perform, and that it is possible to compose groups in such a way that motivation is high. Such groups are the *"smallest groups in which it is possible to have represented at a functional level all the social and achievement skills required for the particular required activity."*[22]

In large discussion groups, as the panel-forum, special techniques may be employed to increase participation.

5. The leadership component characteristics which are essential for highest productivity are that leadership tasks be *shared maximally* and that there be a *high security-defense ratio*. In practice the division of leadership functions in discussion varies greatly. There is considerable support, however, for the belief that "the experience of group discussion will be more satisfying psychologically when the leader shares this responsibility with qualified

---

22. Herbert A. Thelen, *Dynamics of Groups at Work* (Chicago: The University of Chicago Press, 1954), 187.

members, or when they exercise initiative in undertaking these tasks themselves."[23] The second essential of the leadership component concerns the leader-member relationships. To participate effectively in discussion the members must feel secure in the feeling that their contributions will be understood and accepted. At the same time there must be a minimum of feelings of defensiveness, of always having to "fight" for or against ideas presented.

6. Finally, for maximum achievement communication in discussion must be characterized by maximum *perceptual coincidence* and *motivating relevancy*. The first characteristic refers to the need for establishing "common ground" in the discussion. What is said must be similarly structured (perceived) by both speaker and listeners. Group members must be able to differentiate between the affective and cognitive aspects of discussion content. The second characteristic means that what is said must be relevant to the goal of the group and the need-value systems of the participants. It also means that member contributions must be presented with the forcefulness sufficient to insure their thorough examination.

Procedural Screens in Discussion

In the diagram Columns 3 and 4 are connected by three parallel lines to suggest that the interaction of the members, through which the dynamic interrelationships among the six components are manifested, is primarily goal and group centered. This interaction is also filtered through a second set of screens shown in Column 4. These three screens are placed together because they seem to lend themselves to more direct control by the group members than the screens in Column 2.

The first screen encompasses all the *physical factors* of the situation in which the discussion occurs. For example, the acoustics of the meeting room, its size and shape, the availability and comfort of tables and chairs, the heating and lighting, the timing, outside noises and disturbances, and the availability of presentation aids such as projection equipment and blackboards are factors which affect both the quantity and quality of the discussion. Consideration must be given to these factors in preplanning.

A second procedural screen may be designated as the *inquiry-advocacy dimension*. As already stated, discussion is characterized by reflective thinking, in which the best or correct answer to some problem is sought. In contrast, intentional thinking, which characterizes debate, is that in which support for some predetermined answer is sought. In any given situation, an appropriate balance between inquiry and considered support of ideas must be maintained.

---

23. Eisenson, Auer, and Irwin, *The Psychology of Communication*, 262.

A third procedural screen in discussion is its *evaluation dimension*. This refers to the extent and nature of the "assessment of progress" made during and after a discussion. The implication is that there should be a balance in discussion between content and process. Too infrequently are discussion group members concerned with such questions as "How well are we doing?" and "How can we improve?" Too frequently there is little concern about standards for effectiveness.

Output Characteristics for Maximum Productivity

Obviously, the outcome of any discussion ought to represent the highest possible achievement. Column 5 presents the essential characteristics of each component under conditions of maximum output productivity. Columns 4 and 5 are connected by a wide (three strand) horizontal line suggesting that under conditions of highest achievement the group interaction is unitary. The size of the solids in Column 5 are smaller than in Columns 1 or 3 to suggest that the output in discussion is less inclusive, more refined, more focused than the input.

1. The purpose of every discussion is twofold: (1) to insure *group goal achievement* and, (2) to provide some *member satisfaction*. The first is of primary importance but the second cannot be overlooked.

2. Under conditions of maximum productivity the component of content should be characterized by a *cognitive-affective-balance*. Denotative meanings must be understood. Connotative meanings must be understood and accepted.

3. The output characteristics of the thought pattern are that the decisions and understandings reached should be based on the *highest level of logic and evidence* and *optimum suasion*. This again suggests a balance: sound reasoning, well-supported facts and opinions, a proper inquiry-advocacy relationship, and sufficient motivating relevancy to insure that decisions made will be supported.

4. Two qualities should characterize the group under conditions of maximum productivity. The first is *analytical maturity*. That is, the group must have reached a point where it can and does assess its own progress critically. At the point of maximum productivity the group must also have achieved a *socio-psyche balance*. It should be able to satisfy ego-needs while working effectively toward goals.

5. When a discussion group is functioning at its peak, there should be optimum *opportunity for leadership development*. Leadership tasks should be shared when possible; members should have opportunities to practice different leadership roles.

6. Finally, at its best the communication component should be characterized by *clarity* and *acceptability*. What is said must be mutually understood by the members; what is said must also contribute to behavioral or attitudinal change.

Summary

This paper presents a theoretical-operational model of group discussion. The paper describes the basic and essential components of discussion at three sequential points: (1) at the time of input, (2) during discussion under conditions of maximum goal achievement, and (3) at the time of output under conditions of maximum productivity. Brief descriptions are also given of two sets of screens, one composed of socio-psychological and the other of procedural factors, which filter the discussion interaction. The model proposes that group discussion is a form of communicative-adaptive, goal-seeking behavior having structure, movement, and productivity, which acts as a multidimensional variable mediating the field subregion in which the discussion occurs and the need-value systems of the group members. Specific relationships among the elements of input, process filters, and output are hypothesized. The model is not definitive. It attempts to describe a set of relationships which are sufficiently general to account for and enable predictions to be made about the phenomena of discussion.

SUGGESTED READINGS

Chapter 1

Applbaum, Ronald L., *et. al. The Process of Group Communication.* Chicago: Science Research Associates, 1974.

Borman, Ernest G. *Discussion and Group Methods.* New York: Harper and Row Publishers, 1969.

Borgatta, Edgar F. *Social Interaction Process.* Chicago: Rand, McNally and Co., 1955.

Burgoon, Michael, Heston, Judee K. and McCroskey, James. *Small Group Communication: A Functional Approach.* New York: Holt, Rinehart and Winston, Inc., 1974.

Cooper, C. L. (ed.) *Theories of Group Process.* New York: John Wiley & Sons, 1975.

Fisher, B. Aubrey. *Small Group Decision Making.* New York: McGraw-Hill Book Company, 1974.

Goldberg, Alvin A. and Larson, Carl E. *Group Communication: Discussion Processes and Applications.* Englewood Cliffs, N.J.: Prentice-Hall, 1975.

Johnson, F. Craig and Klare, George R. "General Models of Communication Research: A Survey of the Developments of a Decade." *Journal of Communication,* XI (March, 1961): 13-33.

Larson, Carl E. "Speech Communication Research on Small Groups," *Speech Teacher* 20 (March 1971), 89-102.

MacKenzie, Kenneth D. *Theory of Group Structure.* New York: Gorden and Breach Science Publishers, 1976.

Mills, T. *The Sociology of Small Groups.* Englewood Cliffs, N.J.: Prentice-Hall, 1967.

Porter, David and Andersen, Martin P. *Discussion in Small Groups: A Guide to Effective Practice.* 3rd edition. Belmont, CA: Wadsworth Publishing, 1976.

Rosenfeld, Lawrence B. *Human Interaction in the Small Group Setting.* Columbus, Ohio: Charles E. Merrill, 1973.

Shaw, M. *Group Dynamics.* New York: McGraw-Hill Book Co., 1971.

Shepherd, Clovis. *Small Groups: Some Sociological Perspectives.* San Francisco: Chandler, 1964.

Thibaut, John W. and Kelley, Harold. *The Social Psychology of Groups.* New York: John Wiley & Sons, Inc., 1959.

The Individual and the Group

The Games Individuals Play in Groups

Eric Berne

Each individual enters a group with the following necessary equipment: (1) biologic needs, (2) psychological needs, (3) drives, (4) patterns of striving, (5) past experience, and (6) adjustive capacities. It is just this equipment which makes it possible for leaders to exploit their members for good or evil, and which hampers the independent flowering of individual personalities. But that is another matter which does not belong in a technical book on group dynamics, any more than a discussion of human morality belongs in a textbook of medicine. After he sees what forces people are up against when they join groups, the reader will be better able to form his own philosophy.

Biologic Needs

The well-known sensory deprivation experiments indicate that a continual flow of changing sensory stimuli is necessary for the mental health of the individual. The study of infants in foundling hospitals, as well as everyday considerations, demonstrates that the preferred form of stimulation is being touched by another human being. In infants, the withholding of caresses and normal human contact, which Rene Spitz calls "emotional deprivation," results directly or indirectly in physical as well as mental deterioration. Among transactional analysts, these findings are summarized in the inexact but handy slogan: "If the infant is not stroked, his spinal cord shrivels up."

From *The Structure and Dynamics Of Organizations and Groups,* by Eric Berne. (Grove Press, Inc., New York), 1966. Copyright © 1963 by Eric Berne. Reprinted by permission.

As the individual grows up, he learns to accept symbolic forms of stroking instead of the actual touch, until the mere act of recognition serves the purpose. That is why the elements of greeting rituals are called "strokes." What is said is less important than the fact that people are recognizing each other's presence and in that way offering the social contact which is necessary for the preservation of health. Thus, both infants and grown-ups show a need for, or at least an appreciation of, social contact even in its most primitive forms. This can be easily tested by anyone who has the courage to refuse to respond when his friends say "Hello." The desire for "stroking" may also be related to the fact that outside stimulation is necessary to keep certain parts of the brain active in order to maintain a normal waking state. This need to be "recharged," as it were, by stimulation, and especially by social contact, may be regarded as one of the biologic origins of group formation. The fear of loneliness (or of lack of social stimulation) is one reason why people are willing to resign part of their individual proclivities in favor of the group cohesion.

Psychological Needs

Beyond that, human beings find it difficult to face an interval of time which is not allotted to a specific program: an empty period without some sort of structure, especially a long one. This "structure hunger" accounts for the inability of most people simply to sit still and do nothing for any length of time. Structure hunger is well known to parents. The wail of children during summer vacation and of teen-agers on Sunday afternoon—"Mommy, there's nothing to do!"—recurrently taxes their leadership and ingenuity.

Only a relatively small proportion of people are able to structure their time independently. As a class, the most highly paid people in our society are the ones who can offer an entertaining time structure for those whose inner resources are not equal to the task. Television now makes this advantage available in every home. In a group, it is principally the leader who performs the necessary task of structuring time. Capable leaders know that few things are more demoralizing than idleness, and soldiers have said that risking their lives in active combat is preferable to sitting out a "bore war." Psychotherapists see the same thing in a milder degree when their group patients beg them for instructions as to how to proceed and resent it if a program is not forthcoming. One product of structure hunger is "leadership hunger," which quickly emerges if the leader refuses to offer a program or if he is absent from a meeting and there is no adequate substitute. No doubt there are other factors involved here, but the fact remains that a long unexpected silence at any group meeting or on the radio arouses increasing anxiety in most people.

Because a group offers a program for structuring an interval of time, the members are willing to pay a price for their membership. They are willing to resign still more of their individual proclivities in favor of ensuring the survival of the group and its structure. They also appreciate the fact that the leader is the principal time-structurer, and that is one factor in awakening their devotion.

The reason given by Mrs. Black for playing her games throws some light on why people seek time-structuring. Unless the Adult is kept busy, or the Child's activities are channeled, there is a danger that the Child may run wild, so to speak, in a way the individual is not prepared to handle. The need to avoid this kind of chaos is one of the strongest influences which sends people into groups and disposes them to make the sacrifices and the adjustments necessary to remain in good standing.

The need for social contact and the hunger for time-structure might be called the preventive motives for group formation. One purpose of forming, joining and adjusting to groups is to prevent biologic, psychological and also moral deterioration. Few people are able to "recharge their own batteries," lift themselves up by their own psychological bootstraps, and keep their own morals trimmed without outside assistance.

Drives

On the positive side, the presence of other human beings offers many opportunities for gratification, and everyone intuitively or deliberately acquires a high proficiency in getting as many satisfactions as possible from the people in the groups to which he belongs. These are obtained by means of the options for participation listed in the previous chapter. The surrounding people contribute least to the satisfactions reaped from fantasy and most to those enjoyed in intimacy. Intimacy is threatening for various reasons, partly because it requires independent structuring and personal responsibility; also, as already noted, it is not well suited to public situations. Hence, most people in groups settle for whatever satisfactions they can get from games, and the more timid ones may not go beyond pastimes.

Nevertheless, hidden or open, simple or complicated, a striving for intimacy underlies the most intense and important operations in the group process. This striving, which gives rise to active individual proclivities, may be called the individual anancasm, the inner necessity that drives each man throughout his life to his own special destiny. Four factors lend variety to its expression: (1) the resignations and compromises that are necessary to ensure the survival of the group. This is the individual's contribution to the group cohesion. (2) The disguises resulting from fear of the longed-for intimacy. (3) Individual differences in the meaning of intimacy: to most it means a loving sexual union, to some a one-sided penetration into the being of another through torture; it may involve self-glorification or self-abasement.

There are differences in the kind of stroking received or given. Most want a partner of the opposite sex, some want one of the same sex, in love or in torment. All of these elements are influenced by the individual's past experiences in dealing with or being dealt with by other human beings. From the very day of birth, each person is subjected to a different kind of handling: rough and harsh or soft and gentle or any combination or variation of these may signify to him the nature of intimacy. (4) Differences in the method of operation, the patterns of behavior learned and used in transacting emotional business with other people.

Patterns of Striving

Each person has an unconscious life plan, formulated in his earliest years, which he takes every opportunity to further as much as he dares in a given situation. This plan calls for other people to respond in a desired way and is generally divided, on a long-term basis, into distinct sections and subsections, very much like the script of a play. In fact, it may be said that the theatre is an outgrowth of such unconscious life plans or scripts. The original set of experiences which forms the pattern for the plan is called the protocol. The Oedipus complex of Sigmund Freud is an example. In transactional analysis the Oedipus complex is not regarded as a mere set of attitudes, but as an ongoing drama, divided, as are Sophocles's *Oedipus Rex, Electra, Antigone,* and other dramas, into natural scenes and acts calling for other people to play definite roles.

Partly because of the advantages of being an infant, even under bad conditions, every human being is left with some nostalgia for his infancy and often for his childhood as well; therefore, in later years he strives to bring about as close as possible a reproduction of the original protocol situation, either to live it through again if it was enjoyable, or to try to re-experience it in a more benevolent form if it was unpleasant. In fact, many people are so nostalgic and confused that they try to relive the original experience as it was even if it was very unpleasant—hence the peculiar behavior of some individuals who are willing to subject themselves to all sorts of pain and humiliation, repeating the same situation again and again. In any case, this nostalgia is the basis for the individual anancasm. This is something like what Freud calls the "repetition compulsion," except that a single re-enactment may take a whole lifetime, so that there may be no actual repetition but only one grand re-experiencing of the whole protocol.

Since the script calls for the manipulation of other people, it is first necessary to choose an appropriate cast. This is what takes place in the course of pastimes. Stereotyped as they are, they nevertheless give some opportunity for individual variations which are revealing of the underlying personalities of the participants. Such indications help each player to select the people he would like to know better, with the object of involving suitable ones in his favorite games. From among those who are willing and able to play his games, he then selects candidates who show promise of playing the roles called for in his script; this is an important factor in the choice of a spouse (the chief supporting role). Of course, if things are to progress, this process of selection must be mutual and complementary.

Because of its complexity, it is fortunate that it is not necessary to consider the script as a whole in order to understand what is going on in most group situations. It is usually enough to be aware of the favorite games of the people concerned.

The Provisional Group Imago

There are various forces which determine group membership, and the individual is not necessarily attracted mainly by the activity of a group. If it is the kind of group in which he will meet other members face to face, his more personal desires become important. As soon as his membership is impending, he begins to form a provisional group imago, an image of what the group is going to be like for him and what he may hope to get out of it. In most cases, this provisional group imago will not long remain unchanged under the impact of reality; but, as already noted, the internal group process is based on the desire of each member to make the actual, real group correspond as closely as possible to his provisional group imago. For example, a man may join a country club because that will offer him an opportunity to engage in his favorite pastimes. If the club is not equipped for one of them, he may try to introduce it. Membership in any group that includes unmarried people is nearly always influenced by the hope of finding a mate, and this may give rise to a very lively and colorful provisional group imago.

Psychotherapists often have to deal with provisional group imagoes when they suggest that a patient join a therapy group. The patient questions the therapist either to adjust an imago he has already formed from reading or gossip or to start forming one so that he will know what to expect. If the picture offered by the therapist does not meet his desires, the patient will not be favorably inclined and may join only to please the doctor rather than with the hope that "the group" will be of value to him.

While the script and the games that go along with it and set it in action come from older levels of the individual's history, his provisional group imago is based on more recent experiences: partly first-hand, from groups he has been a member of, and partly second-hand, from descriptions of groups similar to the one he desires or expects to join. One branch of the advertising and procurement professions is particularly concerned with favorably influencing provisional group imagoes.

It should be clear now that each member first enters the group equipped with: (1) a biologic need for stimulation; (2) a psychological need for time-structuring; (3) a social need for intimacy; (4) a nostalgic need for patterning transactions; and (5) a provisional set of expectations based on past experience. His task is then to adjust these needs and expectations to the reality that confronts him.

Adjustment

Each new member of a group can be judged according to his. ability to adjust. This involves two different capacities: adaptability and flexibility.

Adaptability is a matter of adult technics. It depends on the carefulness and the accuracy with which he appraises the situation. Some individuals make prudent estimates of the kinds of people they are dealing with before they make their moves. They are tactful, diplomatic, shrewd, or patient in their operations, without swerving from their purposes. The adaptable person continually adjusts his group imago in accordance with his experiences and observations in the group, with the practical goal of eventually getting the greatest satisfaction for the needs of his script. If his script calls for him to be president, he picks his way carefully and with forethought through the hazards of political groups.

On the other hand, the arbitrary person proceeds blindly on the basis of his provisional group imago. This is typical of a certain type of impulsive woman, who will launch a sexually seductive game immediately on entering a group, hardly glancing around the room to see what company she has to reckon with. Occasionally her crude, unadapted maneuvers may be successful, and she will get the responses her script calls for: advances from the men and jealousy from the women. However, if the other members are not so easily manipulated, she may be ignored or rebuffed by both sexes. Then she is faced with the alternatives of either adjusting or withdrawing; otherwise, she may be extruded by the other members.

The second variable, flexibility, depends on the individual's ability and willingness to modify or sacrifice elements of his script. He may decide that he cannot obtain a certain type of satisfaction from a group and may settle for other satisfactions which are more readily available. Or he may settle for a lesser degree of satisfaction than he originally hoped for. The rigid person is unable or unwilling to do either of these things.

Adaptability, then, concerns chiefly the Adult, whose task it is to arrange satisfactions for the Child. The adaptable person may keep his script intact by modifying his group imago in a realistic way. Flexibility becomes the concern of the Child, who must modify his script to accord with the possibilities presented by the group imago. From this it can be seen that adaptability and flexibility often overlap, but they may also be independent of each other, as consideration of four extreme cases will demonstrate.

The adaptable, flexible individual will carry out his operations smoothly and with patience and will settle for what is expedient. ("Politics is the science of the possible.") He is the rather uninspiring "socially adjusted" person that some school systems take as their ideal, the "common-ground finder" who sacrifices principle to convenience in a "socially acceptable" way. In certain professions, such capacities may be desirable or profitable and may be deliberately cultivated.

The adaptable, inflexible member will carry on patiently and diplomatically but will not yield on any of the goals he is striving for. In this class are many successful business men who do things their own way. The arbitrary, flexible person will shift from one goal to another, showing little skill or patience, and will settle for what he can get without changing his tactics. The arbitrary, inflexible person is the dictator: ready to accomplish his aims without regard to the needs of others and inflexible in his demands. The others play it his way, and he gets and gives what he wants to.

The above descriptions are transactional and refer to the individual's behavior in a group situation, but they resemble character types described from other points of view.

It should be noted that it is the group process and not the group activity that leads to adjustment. For example, a certain type of bookkeeper may never adjust himself to the office group; he may concentrate on his work and do it well while remaining an isolate year in and year out except for participating in greeting rituals.

The Group Imago

The complete process of adjustment of the group imago involves four different stages. The provisional group imago of a candidate for membership, the first stage, is a blend of Child fantasy and Adult expectations based on previous experience. This is modified into an adapted group imago, the second stage, by rather superficial Adult appraisals of the other people, usually made by observing them during rituals and activities. At this point, the member is ready to participate in pastimes, but if he is careful and not arbitrary, he will not yet start any games of his own, although he may become passively involved in the games of others. Before he begins his own games, his adapted imago must be changed into an operative one, which is the third stage. This transformation works on the following principle: the imago of a member does not become operative until he thinks he knows his own place in the leader's group imago, and this operative group imago remains shaky unless it has repeated existential reinforcement. To become operative, an imago must have a high degree of the differentiation mentioned in Chapter 5.

Grim examples may be found in the memoirs of officers of secret police forces. Many of these officers felt uncertain of their positions in the hierarchy until they thought they knew how they rated with their superiors, whom they were continually trying to impress in the course of their work. Once they felt that their positions were established, they were then able to differentiate themselves and their colleagues more clearly in their own group imagoes, whereupon they felt free to unleash the full force of their individual proclivities. They grew more and more confident in their atrocious actions and in their relationships with other party members as the approval of their leaders was reinforced.

A more commonplace example of operative adjustment is the case of the inhibited boy in kindergarten. He may find it difficult to associate with the other children until he feels sure that he knows how he stands with the teacher. Of course, this principle is intuitively known to all capable teachers, and they act accordingly. If they are successful, they will then note that "this boy has improved his adjustment and has now made some friends," i.e., he has differentiated some of the other children in a meaningful way. Similarly, in a psychotherapy group, an adaptable member will not begin to play his games until he thinks he knows how he stands with the leader. If he is arbitrary and not adaptable (e.g., the impulsive type of woman mentioned in the previous section), he may act prematurely and pay the penalty.

The operative principle may sound complicated, but it is really very simple. After a new child is born into a family, the other children treat him cautiously until they think they know how they stand in relation to the baby in the group imagoes of their parents, which they find out by testing. If a father is replaced by a stepfather, the wise child walks softly with the other children until he finds out how he and they stand with the new parent.

The operative principle is what makes it advisable to draw an authority diagram in considering an ailing group. The imago of each person on such a diagram operates according to how he thinks he stands with his superiors, and what he thinks they expect from him; this determines how he will behave in his role in the organizational structure. The primal leader, or the leader who is on his own, has to raise his imago by its own bootstraps, as it were. But even here the operative principle may come into play. An independent leader, such as a group therapist in private practice, may feel responsible to his own Parent, and his group imago becomes operative on that basis. Thus it may be said that the true leader of some psychotherapy groups is the therapist's father. The leadership slot in such an imago is occupied by a phantom, and the therapist operates as the executive of his father's canon. (Incidentally, a phantom is also left whenever a well-differentiated member leaves a group, and it persists until the mourning process is completed, if it ever is. Since only autistic transactions are possible with phantoms, they give rise to many interesting and complex events.)

The fourth phase of the group imago is secondary adjustment. At this stage the member begins to give up his own games in favor of playing it the group's way, conforming to its culture. If this occurs in a small group or subgroup, it may prepare the way for game-free intimacy. However, activity may be carried on effectively regardless of the state of an individual's group imago.

The four stages of adjustment of the group imago and their suitability for structuring time are: (1) the provisional imago for rituals; (2) the adapted imago for pastimes; (3) the operative imago for games; and (4) the secondarily adjusted imago for intimacy.

Knowledge of this progression makes it possible to define with some exactness four popular terms which are usually used carelessly and even interchangeably: participation, involvement, engagement and belonging.

An individual who gives any transactional stimuli or transactional responses, in words or otherwise, is to that extent participating. Thus, participation is the opposite of withdrawal. It may occur at any stage of adjustment. A member may participate in activities, rituals, pastimes or games, depending on how far his provisional group imago has been adjusted.

A person who plays a passive role in the game of another member, without taking the initiative, is involved. Involvement may occur with an adapted group imago which is not yet operative.

A member who takes the initiative in starting one of his own games, or who actively tries to influence the course of someone else's game to his own advantage, is engaged. This occurs only after his group imago becomes operative. As already noted, this may happen prematurely and inappropriately in arbitrary individuals.

Belonging is more complicated. A member belongs when he has met three conditions: eligibility, adjustment and acceptance. Eligibility means that he can meet the requirements for membership. Adjustment means that he is willing to resign his own games in favor of playing it the group's way. Such a resignation results from secondary adjustment of an operative group imago. Those who are "born to belong" are taught very early certain rituals, pastimes, and games which are acceptable to their class; their secondary adjustment takes place during their early training. Acceptance means that the other members recognize that he has given up some of his individual proclivities in favor of the group cohesion, and that he will abide by the group canon. If he fails to do so, acceptance may be withdrawn. The sign of belonging is assurance, and the sign of acceptance is that the members give the responses required by the canon. If they break the social contract and show rudeness, the member loses his assurance. All this is well illustrated in the process of naturalization. The foreigner must first be eligible to cross the external boundary by immigration. Then he is required to study the canon of his adopted country. The better he adjusts his group imago, the more he is accepted and the more he belongs.

The Script

The script is the most important item and, at the same time, the most difficult to investigate of all the items of equipment which the individual brings with him when he enters a group. For example, in choosing a new president from among the vice-presidents of a corporation, a psychologist can test the capacities of the various candidates for the job, but the script will determine what use each individual will make of his capacities, and the script cannot be reliably brought to light by any form of testing. Its unmasking requires a long period of psychiatric investigation by a skilled script analyst. Fortunately, however, the intuition of the member's associates or superiors, especially those who have known him a long time and have seen him react to a variety of pressures, is sometimes fairly reliable in this respect. There are outstanding vice-presidents whose scripts call for them to excel the deceased president in effectiveness, and there are equally capable vice-presidents who may give no indication to an untrained observer that their scripts call for them to destroy what the deceased president has built up and also destroy themselves in the process.

The adjustment of a script is similar to the adjustment of a group imago, but the preparatory stages occur before the individual enters the group.

The original drama, the protocol, is usually completed in the early years of childhood, often by the age of 5, occasionally earlier. This drama may be played out again in more elaborate form, in accordance with the growing child's changing abilities, needs and social situation, in the next few years. Such a later version is called a palimpsest. A protocol or palimpsest is of such a crude nature that it is quite unsuitable as a program for grown-up relationships. It becomes largely forgotten (unconscious) and is replaced by a more civilized version, the script proper: a plan of which the individual is not actively aware (preconscious), but which can be brought into consciousness by appropriate procedures. The script proper is closely related to the provisional group imago and can be found along with it among the fantasies of a candidate about to enter a group. Once he becomes a member, the script goes through the same processes of adjustment as the provisional group imago, depending on the individual's flexibility. In a clear-cut case there is an adapted script, called the adaptation, then an operative script and finally a secondary adjustment. The similarity to the development of theatrical and movie scripts is evident, and sometimes it is remarkable.

Since some scripts may take years or even a whole lifetime to play out, they are not easily studied in experimental situations or in groups of short duration. They are most efficiently unmasked by a careful review of the life history or in long term psychotherapy groups, which are much better than individual therapy for this purpose. But in some measure, the script influences a large percentage of the individual's transactions in any group meeting in which he participates actively.

One of the easiest scripts to observe in action is that of the man whose individual anancasm tragically drives him to failure. He can be followed through his expulsion from college to his discharge from one job after another, and the acute observer can soon spot the decisive moment in each of these performances which set the stage for the final outcome and can see the same drama being played over and over again with a different cast.

The adjustment of a script can be illustrated by a more constructive example. A therapist whose protocol had to do with "curing lots of people" (siblings) had a palimpsest by the age of 5 where he would invite his neighborhood contemporaries en masse to his house to play doctor. The protocol was based on a beloved family physician and much illness in the family. The palimpsest was necessary because Davy's siblings, being of various ages up to adolescence, were not readily available for his performances, so that he had to fill his cast with extras off the street. The script proper was active for a while during his grade-school years when he would invite various clubs to "meet at my house," hoping in this way to become a leader. The adaptation occurred years later when he was able to become a group therapist, which was a socially acceptable way of trying to "cure a lot of people, who meet at my house." During the period of the adaptation, his efforts were tentative and not very successful. During the phase of his operative script when he took more initiative in structuring his therapy groups, he was more efficient but became heavily involved ("identified") with his patients. Finally, his script underwent a secondary adjustment, in which his therapeutic efforts were better controlled, involved fewer games, and were still more successful. He still had "lots of sick people meeting at my house" but was flexible enough to give up the magical satisfactions of "curing" them, acting in accordance with Ambroise Pare's dictum "I treated them, but God cured them." This "meeting at my house" was the first act of a long script which led to a satisfactory professional career when it was properly adjusted.

Summary

We have now studied the individual's course from infancy until the time he belongs to a group; the kinds of transactions he may participate in and the manner in which he sets up and becomes engaged in chains of trans-actions. This is sufficient information to understand the operations of any individual in any group in terms of social dynamics and complements the study of the structure and the dynamics of groups as a whole.

The most important hypotheses on which this discussion of the adjustment of the individual to the group is based are as follows:

1. Social contact and time-structuring are necessary for psychological survival and probably for biologic survival as well.
2. Therefore, the problem of the healthy individual is primarily to find a suitable group for structuring his time. Secondarily, he strives to attain the maximum possible satisfactions from the facilities available.
3. The secondary considerations lead to the emergence of a provisional group imago before entering the group.
4. The individual then adjusts his operations in the group according to his adaptability and flexibility.
5. His participation is programmed by a mental picture of the group, its social customs, certain idiosyncratic patterns of manipulation and specific predetermined long-term goals, or, more concisely, his group imago, the group culture, his games and his script.
6. He will not take the initiative in the group process until he thinks he knows his place in the leader's group imago, although he may be premature in his inferences.
7. The group imago and the script go through well-defined phases of adjustment.

The Johari Window: A Graphic Model of Awareness in Interpersonal Relations

Joseph Luft

Like the happy centipede, many people get along fine working with others without thinking about which foot to put forward. But when there are difficulties, when the usual methods do not work, when we want to learn more—there is no alternative but to examine our own behavior in relation to others. One trouble is that it is so hard to find ways of thinking about such matters, particularly for people who have no extensive backgrounds in the social sciences.

When Luft and Ingham (1955) first presented the Johari Window to illustrate relationships in terms of awareness, they were surprised to find so many people, academicians and nonprofessionals alike, using and tinkering with the model. It seems to lend itself as a heuristic device to speculating about human relations. It is simple to visualize the four quadrants of the model:

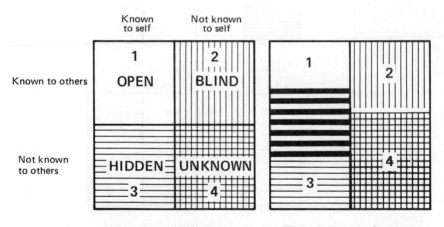

Figure 1. The Johari Window.   **Figure 2.** Degrees of openness.

Quadrant 1, the area of free activity, or open area, refers to behavior and motivation known to self and known to others.

Quadrant 2, the blind area, is where others can see things in ourselves of which we are unaware.*

Quadrant 3, the avoided or hidden area, represents things we know but do not reveal to others (e.g., a hidden agenda or matters about which we have sensitive feelings).

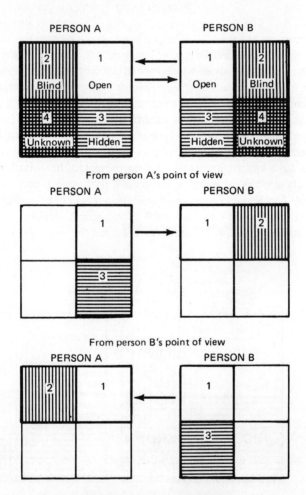

Figure 3. Interpersonal Relations.

*"Undoubtedly you know much of what goes on in your mind and can report it. Undoubtedly you have private evidence that bears on the current activity of your mind. Thus, in important respects, your knowledge of yourself is more complete and reliable than the knowledge others may have. Yet it is clear that this knowledge must be inferential and theoretical—at least in part. A second person may be better able than you to evaluate your present mental state and predict your behavior. In principle self-knowledge may depend on the same kinds of inference that knowledge of another depends on" (Hebb, 1969, p. 55).

Quadrant 4, the area of unknown activity, points to the area where neither the individual nor others are aware of certain behaviors or motives. Yet we can assume their existence because eventually some of these things become known, and we then realize that these unknown behaviors and motives were influencing relationships all along.

In a new group, Q1 is very small; there is not much free and spontaneous interaction. As the group grows and matures, Q1 expands in size, and this usually means we are freer to be more like ourselves and to perceive others as they really are. Quadrant 3 shrinks in area as Q1 grows larger. We find it less necessary to hide or deny things we know or feel. In an atmosphere of growing mutual trust, there is less need for hiding pertinent thoughts or feelings. It takes longer for Q2 to reduce in size because usually there are "good" reasons of a psychological nature to blind ourselves to certain things we feel or do. Quadrant 4 changes somewhat during a learning laboratory, but we can assume that such changes occur even more slowly than shifts in Q2. At any rate, Q4 is undoubtedly far larger and more influential in an individual's relationships than the hypothetical sketch illustrates.

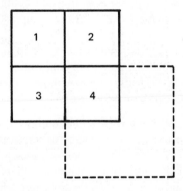

Figure 4. The relative size of Q4.

The Johari Window may be applied to *intergroup* relations. Quadrant 1 then means behavior and motivation known to the group and also known to other groups. Quadrant 2 signifies an area of behavior to which a group is blind, but other groups are aware of the behavior, e.g., cultism or prejudice. Quadrant 3, the hidden area, refers to things a group knows about itself, but which are kept from other groups. Quadrant 4, the unknown area, means a group is unaware of some aspects of its own behavior, and other groups are also unaware of this behavior. Later, as the group learns new things about itself, there is a shift from Q4 to one of the other quadrants.

Principles of Change

1. A change in any one quadrant will affect all other quadrants.
2. It takes energy to hide, deny, or be blind to behavior which is involved in interaction.
3. Threat tends to decrease awareness; mutual trust tends to increase awareness.
4. Forced awareness (exposure) is undesirable and usually ineffective.
5. Interpersonal learning means a change has taken place so that Q1 is larger and one or more of the other quadrants has grown smaller.
6. Working with others is facilitated by a large enough area of free activity. An increased Q1 means more of the resources and skills in the membership can be applied to a task.
7. The smaller the first quadrant, the poorer the communication.
8. There is universal curiosity about the unknown area, but this is held in check by custom, social training, and diverse fears.
9. Sensitivity means appreciating the covert aspects of behavior, in quadrants 2, 3, and 4, and respecting the desire of others to keep them so.
10. Learning about group processes as they are being experienced helps to increase awareness (enlarge Q1) for the group as a whole as well as for individual members.
11. The value system of a group and its membership may be noted in the way *unknowns* in the life of the group are confronted.
12. A centipede may be perfectly happy without awareness, but after all, he restricts himself to crawling under rocks.

Having familiarized himself with this outline, a group member might learn to use it to help himself to a clearer understanding of the significant events in a group. Furthermore, the outline is sufficiently broad and loose so that it may have heuristic value in stimulating the identification and elaboration of problems in new ways. Several illustrations of different kinds of intergroup and intragroup behavior are given below.

The Objectives of a Group Dynamics Laboratory

Using the model, we may illustrate one of the general objectives of the laboratory, namely, to increase the area of free activity (Q1) so that more of the relationships in the group are free and open.* It follows, therefore, that

---

*"The fact that others know reality is something which we never doubt; communication puts the 'world in their reach' within our reach, too. A crucial prototype of this process occurs in person-to-person interaction. Here, in the direct communication between two people who attend to each other fully and speak the same language, the shared vivid present of the 'We' establishes shared reality" (Holzner, 1968, p. 8).

the work of the laboratory is to increase the area of Q1 while reducing the area of quadrants 2, 3, and 4. The largest reduction in area would be in Q3, then in Q2, and the smallest reduction would be in Q4.

An enlarged area of free activity among the group members implies less threat or fear and greater probability that the skills and resources of group members can be brought to bear on the work of the group. The enlarged area suggests greater openness to information, opinions, and new ideas about each member as well as about specific group processes. Since the hidden or avoided area, Q3, is reduced, less energy is tied up in defending this area. Since more of one's needs are unbound, there is greater likelihood of satisfaction with the work and more involvement with what the group is doing.

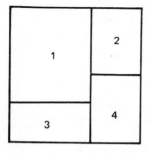

Figure 5. Laboratory objectives.

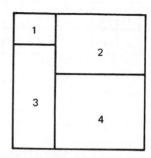

Figure 6. Beginning interaction in a new group.

The Initial Phase of Group Interaction

Applying the model to a typical meeting of most groups, we can recognize that interaction is relatively superficial, that anxiety or threat is fairly large, that interchange is stilted and unspontaneous. We also may note that ideas or suggestions are not followed through and are usually left undeveloped, that individuals seem to hear and see relatively little of what is really going on.

The Model May Depict Intergroup Processes as Well as Intragroup Processes

The group may be treated as an entity or unit. Cattell (1956), for instance, uses the term "syntality" to mean the quality of a group analogous to the personality of an individual. Lewin conceives of the group as an organized field of forces, a structured whole. In this model, a group may relate to other groups in a manner similar to the relationship between individuals. The first quadrant (Fig. 8) represents behavior and motivation of a group which is known to group members and also known to others.

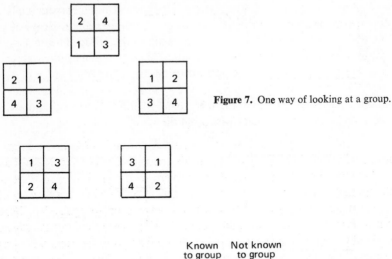

Figure 7. One way of looking at a group.

Figure 8. A group as a whole.

A college seminar, for instance, may share certain knowledge and behavior about itself with other classes on campus, such as requirements for the course, subject matter of the seminar, or the amount of work it sets out to do. However, many things occur in a seminar that are known to its members, but not known to outside groups (quadrant 3).

An illustration of an area of avoided behavior might be the students' feeling that their seminar is very special or quite superior to other classes. Or they might feel the course is a waste of time, but for some reason they do not share this attitude with outsiders. Or sometimes a special event occurs, and this is kept from outsiders.

Quadrant 2, the blind area, is characteristic of certain cults that are unaware of some aspects of their own behavior, though outsiders are able to discern the cultish qualities. Or the prejudices of a certain group may be perfectly apparent to outsiders but not to the group members themselves.

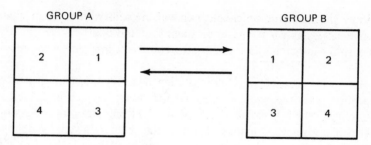

Figure 9. Interaction between two groups.

Quadrant 4 applies to attitudes and behavior that exist in the group but for some reason remain unknown to the group and to outsiders. An illustration of this might be an unresolved problem with regard to over-all goals of the group. If the group is covertly split and some members want to go off in different directions—and if this fact has never been recognized or brought out in the open—then we could see the development of difficulties which remain unknown to the group members and unknown to the members of other groups. For example, in a large scientific enterprise, the physicists and engineers were having great difficulty with the machinists. Only after a long period of investigation did it become apparent that the question of status and privilege was producing bitter feelings between groups, yet the members of the various groups were unaware of the ramifications of this problem.

Representations of Interaction

Another way of representing a relationship is shown in Fig. 10, where all the information bearing on the relationship is contained in the matrix. Each person in the relationship has blind spots in areas open to the other person, and both are blind or lack awareness with respect to certain aspects of their relationship, as represented by quadrant 4. A critical factor in the rela-

	Known to supervisor	Not known to supervisor
Known to employee	1 Open area	2 Employee aware Supervisor is blind
Not known to employee	Supervisor aware Employee is blind 3	Both unaware 4

Figure 10. A model of person-to-person interaction: employee—supervisor.

tionship is the manner in which the unknowns are dealt with; recurring interaction patterns establish the style or quality of the interpersonal tie. Every relationship can be characterized by the constraint inherent in the relationship.

The persons represented are interdependent in Q1, and each is both independent and dependent in Q2 and Q3. Independence is defined here as awareness which is exclusive; the dependent one lacks awareness of an interpersonally relevant matter of which the other *is* aware. Withholding information or feelings which are interpersonally relevant is therefore a way of controlling or manipulating the other. Both persons are dependent where both are unaware, in Q4.

The representation lends itself to consideration of a variety of questions. Regarding Fig. 10, for instance, what kinds of information or feelings are apt to be found in Q2? In Q3? In Q4? What happens when information flows from Q2 to Q1 or from Q3 to Q1 or from Q4 to Q1? Or, regarding Fig. 11,

	Known to student	Not known to student
Known to teacher	**1** Open area	**2** Teacher aware Student is blind
Not known to teacher	Student aware Teacher is blind **3**	Both unaware **4**

Figure 11. A model of person-to-person interaction: student—teacher.

what kinds of interaction help to enlarge the open area? Similar questions might be raised for Figs. 12, 13, and 14.

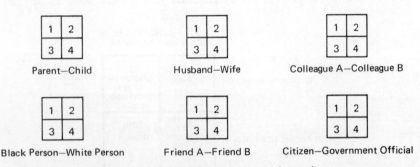

| 1 | 2 |
| 3 | 4 |
Parent—Child

| 1 | 2 |
| 3 | 4 |
Husband—Wife

| 1 | 2 |
| 3 | 4 |
Colleague A—Colleague B

| 1 | 2 |
| 3 | 4 |
Black Person—White Person

| 1 | 2 |
| 3 | 4 |
Friend A—Friend B

| 1 | 2 |
| 3 | 4 |
Citizen—Government Official

Figure 12. Other kinds of person-to-person interaction.

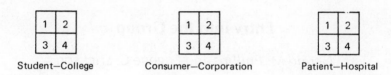

Figure 13. Interaction between individuals and organizations.

Figure 14. Interaction between organizations or groups.

Entry into the Group

Gerald M. Phillips and Eugene C. Erickson

Your personal behavior in a small group will be unlike that of any other person. You come to the group a unique person, and you adjust your uniqueness as far as you have to or care to in order to remain a member. The groups you choose to belong to will probably contain members who share your beliefs and behave much like you do. It is easy to feel comfortable in such a group and most of our socialization is carried on in groups of this type.

Sometimes, however, you may feel that membership in a particular group will elevate your status. In such a case it will be necessary for you to alter your behavior to fit the norms of the new group. This is particularly important in work groups, where your ability to conform to developed norms may well determine your progress in the organization.

But any small group you might belong to will have some effect on you personally. There is no question but that you will change as a result of your participation, because it is necessary to achieve a feeling of belonging. To feel a part of the group, some of your behaviors and values must be changed. This does not mean that groups tend to destroy the values of their members. Rather, groups will tend to strengthen and reinforce those values that you hold most strongly and will tend to reduce your commitment to values that are not so important to you. It is virtually impossible for you to belong to a group whose values conflict with your own. Even an occasional group in which your livelihood is at stake cannot compel you to change deep-seated values. It is not rare for a person to change jobs or even to quit without promise of another because of a value conflict between himself and the people with whom he works.

Apparently, people tend to seek membership in groups that best reflect their values. In this sense, we have an empirical test of our own values. To find out "who you are," an examination of the groups in which you hold membership and the people who belong to them, may well reflect back your own personality more effectively than solitary contemplation. For example, any number of people set out to pledge fraternities and sororities with a great deal of eagerness, only to discover that there is a fundamental difference in values between themselves and the members of the organizations, as a result of which it becomes necessary to withdraw. On the other hand there are those who pledge half-heartedly, and then find themselves making deeper and deeper commitments to the values of the group. A great social psychologist, George Herbert Mead, contends that you discover "yourself" by reflection from the people around you.

Joe Marks went off to the office anticipating another day of anguish. The merchandise planning committee had been meeting regularly all through the week and each meeting had ended with a flare-up between Joe and Tom Smith. It wasn't even clear what the issue was in these arguments. There just seemed to be something about the men that made it impossible for them to get along at all. There was no question that the work of the committee was seriously subverted by the hostility between the two men. Often members of the committee couldn't see why they fought. It seemed to these observers that Marks and Smith agreed on most issues. They could see no reason for conflict and they had told the men to "cool it."

Joe thought about this as he rode to the office and decided that this day would be different. He thought he knew what it was he didn't like about Tom Smith. It was that patronizing attitude, that aura of Anglo-Saxonism, that consistent display of superiority. It seemed to Joe that Tom picked up every one of his ideas and swallowed them and then came out with a slight modification, acting as though he had presented something original. Joe felt threatened, as though while Tom was around it would be impossible for the rest of the group to discover his own worth and merit. Furthermore, he experienced in each of these conflicts a fundamental value clash. Being the only Jew in an advertising agency was a difficult task, even though there was no blatant anti-Semitism. It seemed to Joe that underlying each of the disputes he had with his colleagues, particularly his conflict with Tom Smith, was some patronizing attitude, some demeaning of his worth. But this day was going to be different! This day would not be marked by conflict. This day would end the discussions and the program would be reported out. Win, lose, or draw, Joe resolved to himself that he would not dispute again with Tom Smith.

About ten minutes into the conference Joe had occasion to support an idea that appeared to be accepted by the entire group. As a matter of fact, the idea had been presented originally by Tom Smith. Joe had shown some resistance to it earlier, but in contemplation it had come clear to him that the reason he had resisted it was not the quality of the idea but simply because it had been presented by Smith. In order to show his goodwill, he asserted strong approval. Smith's response was quick and decisive. He shifted ground and began to mount an attack on his own idea, to the great confusion of the entire group. Joe Marks sat quietly for as long as he could and then took the floor to point out to Tom Smith that the idea had originally been his. Smith replied that there had to be something wrong with an idea "if your kind of person approves of it." All of Joe's firm resolve was forgotten. He launched into a vicious tirade against Tom Smith. All of the suppressed hostility came to the surface and within five minutes the two men were at each others' throats. Once again the group got nowhere but the issue was even more critical for the general chairman felt that the decision making could no longer proceed as long as the two men were in the group. The issue of which of them would remain with the company would be passed on to a higher authority.

Incidents similar to this occur in virtually all small group activity. It is impossible to tell how strongly a value operates until it is tested. In the case of Tom Smith, his opposition to Jews or at least to non-Anglo-Saxons did not appear to be a major force in his life, but the confrontation with Joe Marks revealed that he held the value more strongly than he thought, for it was impossible for him to function without referring to the one "outlander" in the group.

Joe Marks was lukewarm in his religious commitments, even neutral or mildly hostile in his religious behaviors, yet he felt compelled to respond to the attacks on his ethnic ancestry with considerable vigor. Apparently his sensitivity on this issue was deeper than he thought. It was impossible to get either man to commit to the group goal, even though each knew that his economic future was at stake to the point where both their livelihoods would be in jeopardy if they continued their antagonism. Their personal values transcended their economic values. Neither would have predicted this would have been the case. Both would have declared with vehemence that they were primarily dedicated to their career advancement and that their "petty biases" would not be permitted to interfere.

Much behavior people carry on in small groups can be tested against a model of this kind. It is very difficult to separate support and hostility to ideas from support and hostility to people. It is difficult for anyone to know whether his opinions are motivated by logical analysis of facts or by some deep-seated commitment that distorts the facts to permit the attitude to emerge. In the case of Joe Marks and Tom Smith it was possible for their supervisor to work with each of them separately and then together to make it clear to both men that they were permitting social values to interfere with their effectiveness in the organization. Through a painstaking examination of those values, followed by a direct confrontation between the two men, it was possible to train them to curb some of their hostilities. While the two never became fast friends, the examination of their behavior and what it meant made it possible for them to work together in the same organization. Their self-awareness had been expanded and since they were now consciously aware of how deep their value commitments were, they were in a much better position to prevent them from interfering with their careers.

It might be added that a situation like that between Joe Marks and Tom Smith is a good example of where "sensitivity training" was useful. The whole group need not be exposed to the confrontation. Work could be done with the two men privately and only in the context of the vocational group. No one tried to psychoanalyze them to discover the reasons for their commitments. It was assumed that they were there and they were entitled to be there. The difficulty was approached as a legitimate problem. The supervisor dealt with the questions, "How can these values be prevented from interfering with the business of the group?" not with "How can these values be eliminated?"

Furthermore, even after making a commitment to a small group, you cannot predict that its values become your own values and supersede those that you brought with you. Most of us live in a situation of ambiguity, where our beliefs and behaviors are controlled, to some extent, by the groups we belong to. We do not act or verbalize the same way at home with the family as we do on the street with friends or on the job with colleagues. This multiplicity of behaviors is what the sociologist calls "roles." Most of the time we have little difficulty reconciling conflicts, for we recognize the differing demands of the situations. However, when some belief we hold deeply is challenged or threatened, we discover the strength of the belief as we find ourselves acting counter to the demands of the group, and counter to our own expectations. The small group affords a fine arena for testing what we really believe in, for our real values will emerge in action and, more often than we expect, they will run counter to what we have been verbalizing. The following example illustrates this point:

> A recent study with small children indicated that children do not necessarily make choices in line with their verbalized values. The children in the study were asked to state whether they would prefer to use their free time to (1) watch a movie, (2) play a game on a playground, (3) play a "board" game with others, (4) do art or crafts alone. Each child made a choice. Then the children were put into groups to discuss the question, "Which of these activities will be the most fun?" After fifteen minutes of discussion, the children were moved back to their seats. They were then told that the next hour would be "free time" and were asked to go to the place where the movies were to be shown, or go out to the playground, or move to the tables where the games were, or go to the arts and crafts area. Very few children hesitated. Within three minutes all had made a choice. Interestingly enough, only about 50 percent of the children actually chose to do the thing they said they were going to do. The same results were obtained when the discussion step was omitted!

The implication here is that some values are suitable for verbalization because of understanding of social requirements about what can be said. Other values are designed for action because of what we, personally, hold to be important. Sometimes the two are in concord, but sometimes they are not, so that a man who wants to discover what he believes must test his belief again some active demand before he can be sure.

Entry Into the Group

It is not difficult for an individual, alone, to enter into the work and action of almost any group. While it would be moderately difficult for someone named Goldberg to participate well in the Sons of Italy or someone named O'Brien to become an officer of B'nai B'rith, for the most part task groups can accommodate individuals that come voluntarily or by assignment. On the other hand, entering a group with a block of others often stirs up considerable difficulty. An examination of some tendencies on college campuses might illustrate this point.

There appears to be, in the social interactions of college professors, groupings of people of similar rank and academic interest. In the case of large universities, those people who came in the same year seem to cleave together. In any case, the college is a fluid institution and each influx of new personnel represents a potential threat to the calm and serenity of the institution. An individual newcomer can easily be absorbed because he does not have sufficient strength to subvert the establishment, or if he attempts to do so the organization has sufficient strength to bring him back into line or see to it that he is ejected from the organization. Furthermore, there is small chance that an individual would feel sufficient confidence to make threatening gestures and the social pressures his colleagues could bring to bear would, in most cases, be sufficient to whip him into line, to compel him to suppress his antagonism to practices of the institution.

When more than one person enters an organization, however, it is possible for them to unify in programs and policies hostile to the status quo. The act of working to implement their ideas brings them closer together and that closeness reinforces the pressure they are able to exert on behalf of their programs. Particularly if the decision-making authority is remote, newcomers may gain access to the administration more readily than those who have been in the institution for a long period of time. There is a myth, which may be rooted in fact on some campuses, that newcomers have about three years to accomplish all they can in effecting change. After that, they fade back into the pack. Consequently a unified body of newcomers threatens the security of the older members who seek to protect themselves by purging hostile or antagonistic ideas. Indeed it may very well be that some organizations select their newcomers on the basis of how closely their ideas accord with those already in force. Assimilating acquiescent new members into a group does little to improve the group, or help it become more fit to face new problems. Organizations that restrict themselves to admitting only a few compliant new members often find themselves facing extreme crises and pressures for change and may well have to generate solutions from within the group. The challenge of new members who disagree often stimulates activity on the part of older members and is generally helpful to the organization.

A model of this kind of vitalizing activity may be found by observing the role that minority groups play in American society. The Anglo-Saxon heritage for American society was forceful, vigorous, and viable during the days when it was necessary to cope with a great many problems. By the late nineteenth century, however, many sectors of society were growing smug and highly contented. New sources of labor were needed to staff the industrial machine. Open immigration was encouraged. The people who availed themselves of open immigration, however, were not fully immersed in the value structure of the American society. Some who advocated open immigration had hoped that the immigration would come from Northern European countries. They were surprised to find that it was the Southern and Central Europeans, who differed drastically from established norms, that entered into society. The huge influx of immigrants mounted a number of threats to the established residents, who not only felt their economic survival threatened by the newcomers, but also their value system and life style. They felt it necessary to defend their values by excluding the newcomers from the mainstream of society. This they did with considerable vigor and "know-nothingism." Anti-Semitism and discrimination against the Irish and Italians flourished. This pattern of social rejection exists to this day. There is little anti-Semitism, for example, in parts of the country where there are few Jews. It is possible for one or two Jews to assimilate themselves into a town very nicely, but when the minority is sizeable people in the town begin to show signs of rejection. Only after the newcomer shows outward signs of accepting the mainstream of the culture does he find acceptance. If he is unable or unwilling to accept the main values of the culture, he finds himself rejected in a number of areas. Rejection of minority groups most often involves a stereotype. That is, a relatively simplistic classification of the person suffices as the basis of evaluation.

As in most cases where a simplistic rejection (or acceptance) is involved, one must be careful to recognize that the entire group (especially if that group is a community or a society) will not reject the individual or person or group. But whether all the members reject or accept is not particularly significant. The point only needs a large number acting alike to be sustained.

The people who do not reject members of a minority group are the ones who serve to bridge the two systems. They introduce new ideas, new practices from food to clothing which, eventually, are likely to meld the contrasting and rejecting systems.

The Negro today faces much the same problem. Most of the dominant white society find themselves able to accept an individual, successful Negro, whose life style very closely approximates their own. They are willing to overlook his blackness, recognizing that this is a matter about which he can do nothing, not recognizing that it might be a matter about which he wishes to do nothing. While there is an air of patronization it is possible for the individual, successful Negro to survive and prosper in white society. But the thought of millions of black people pouring out of the central city into the mainstream of American life fills the hearts of most Americans with uneasiness. The different appearance and the obvious disparity in values and life styles represents something akin to a threat to the main society. Riots and violence are the results of this kind of conflict and this macrocosm neatly recapitulates the microcosm of threat when newcomers enter a small group.

For the most part, however, people tend to select and form their small groups in such a way that they will reflect their values and biases or reinforce them. Within a small group people tend to show preference for members with similar life styles. In any small group there is a strong likelihood that cliques will develop. A clique is a small group of people inside the framework of a group whose values and behaviors so closely approximate each other that they can be counted upon to behave as a unit. These smaller units characterized by highly intense human relations represent a prime support for an individual as he functions in juxtaposition with others he does not know as well and consequently with whom there is some possibility of antagonism and conflict. While cliques may be individually supportive, they are potentially disruptive to small group activity, for clique members will tend to make decisions more on a basis of personal affiliation than on the potential for the decision in implementing the group's goal. Although there is much concern about how to dissolve cliques and broaden contact among members, it appears that cliques are necessary, for each individual has only limited capacity for close contacts. The zoologist Desmond Morris, writing in *The Naked Ape,* said we tend to select friends about to the extent that we could handle them in small tribal or herd units. There appears to be, in his opinion, a limitation on the capability of the human to make close friendships and consequently as the size of the group increases, we can expect more subgroups to be generated. Furthermore, as cliques develop, the style of their members tends to diversify, thus increasing the possibility of conflict within the groups.

Strategically, the individual seeking to exert influence on a small group must show considerable care. First, it is necessary to display caution when speaking in the early stages of group membership. A new man can't say too much, for he holds no status within the group and excessive talk on his part may be considered by others to be presumptive. He may, however, display solidarity and support for the ideas of others and, in doing this, cement bonds with other members. He will soon discover the "power" in the group and play to it or he may find himself admitted to membership in a clique. Until he has some influential member willing to give support to his remarks or has gotten three or four other members to back him, it will not be possible for him to exert very much influence, regardless of how good his rhetoric or how good his words. Even his most effective ideas will be largely ignored. Many people, newcomers to groups, are dismayed to find that the ideas they expressed on Monday are presented by someone else on Friday and adopted by the group even though they were rejected when originally expressed. While there may be considerable frustration associated with this kind of ostensible rejection it must be recognized that the group cannot afford to concede too much deference to a newcomer, for once people concede that a newcomer has ability it must be conceded that they might have disabilities. If several members enter a group at once, however, it is possible for them to exert considerable pressure by presenting a united front.

The pledge period in the typical fraternity or sorority exemplifies this kind of behavior. If a group of fifty or sixty members takes in ten or twelve new members all at one time there is a considerable potential for threat to the values of the organization. As a result, it is necessary to develop a format in which the new members can be acculturated to the values of the larger group. Those that resist acculturation can be dropped from potential membership or pressured to withdraw voluntarily. Those that survive the acculturation or pledge period can be moved into the group with confidence that they will not disrupt the existing value system. Furthermore, fraternities protect themselves by assigning specific duties and activities to pledges and new members to give them the feel of working for the order in such a way that they can learn to accept the prevailing values.

Similar kinds of "pledging" are often found operating informally in companies. A new employee has considerable difficulty gaining acceptance in a group. If the other employees have been together for a long time they will have developed a style of operation that accommodates their needs. The newcomer will find that dissidents and nonconformists will make the initial overtures to him. Those with some position in the social hierarchy will accept the new employee only to the extent that they do not perceive him as a threat to their position. Thus, he will have to demonstrate compliance and acceptance of norms and will have to seek a position not yet held by anyone else.

New entry is exceptionally difficult at the executive level. A new supervisor will often find himself threatened, particularly if he is brought in from the outside. The group he is to lead has habituated a problem-solving style with which they are comfortable, and they will attempt to defend it against infringements even if it is flagrantly ineffective. The new executive from the outside will take considerable time to understand the values and characteristic behavior of his group. Until he does, it is impossible for him to do much to change operations.

The situation may often be more difficult for the new leader coming up from the ranks, for if he is not the choice of the greater number of members, he will find himself leader in name only and will be forced to ratify and implement decisions made according to established procedures of the group.

It seems that the new member of a group must engage in a variety of self-effacing acts in order to demonstrate that he is willing to subordinate himself to the norms of the group. Only after he makes this clear does he begin to win acceptance. Newcomers to small towns find this graphically illustrated to them for they may be regarded as newcomers or interlopers even after they have been residents for ten or fifteen years. If, however, they move through accepted channels in the hierarchies of established organizations in the town they may achieve some status and aspire to positions of leadership. For the most part, however, in college towns, the academic community separates from the town community and develops its own set of values and rewards so that newcomers need not be too frustrated by the social customs they find around them.

There is no reason to believe that a small group of five is much different from a large group of five hundred or five thousand, except in degree of complexity. The essentials of interaction can be found in both. The member who seeks to exert control over a small group will need to use political and social techniques similar to those employed for the same ends in society. Unless he is willing to utilize strategies to achieve his goals, he will find himself being absorbed into the group, which will make of him an "ordinary" conforming member with little ability to alter the character of the group.

Bargaining: Communication and Process

Norman Page

Interdependence is the essence of complex society. Each social unit, whether the individual, the group or the organization, must rely on other individuals, groups, and organizations in order to satisfy both basic and higher needs. In situations where interdependent parties seek scarce resources those parties are said to be involved in a conflict of interests. Whether the situation is international trade negotiation, a labor-management dispute, or a disagreement between two people deciding how to spend an evening, the principles of conflict and conflict management apply. Traditionally, parties attempting to deal with conflict have used one or a combination of the following approaches: withdrawal, smoothing, forcing, compromise and problem-solving[1]

Withdrawal occurs when a party to the conflict assesses the cost/reward ratio of the conflict situation and revaluates his interest in the outcome; smoothing is similar to withdrawal but occurs when both parties reduce the intensity of their conflicting interests; forcing, like fighting, occurs when one party attempts to crush the other and claim all of the payoff for itself; compromise requires that both parties gain less than desired but more than if the interaction had not occurred; and problem-solving, in which the parties function jointly to combine their resources to generate new alternatives which serve to change the nature of the conflict by increasing the potential payoff to both. Bargaining is a process of conflict settlement incorporating aspects of forcing, compromise and problem-solving, and, on occasion, smoothing and withdrawal.

Five conditions must occur before the bargaining process can serve as a method of conflict settlement: a conflict of interests, interdependence among the parties, viability of the parties, divisibility of outcome, and "good faith."

Obviously, without a conflict of interests between the interdependent parties there would be no need for bargaining to occur. To be viable the parties must possess the flexibilities to make concessions to each other. Divisibility requires that the outcome must be capable of being divided, i.e., money, time, and material are divisible but status and prestige are not. Finally, bargaining in "good faith" refers to the willingness of both

---

1. Ronald Burke, "Methods of Resolving Interpersonal Conflict," *Personnel Administration* (July-August, 1969): 48:55.

parties to make concessions to each other and begin concession-making early enough to allow the situation to mature before time becomes a dominating factor.

Definition and Assumptions

Bargaining has been defined as . . . an occasion in which two or more representatives of two or more groups interact in an explicit attempt to reach a jointly-acceptable position on one or more issues which keep them apart.[2]

The assumptions underlying bargaining behavior make it a unique communication arena. Game theorists have isolated two basic types of interaction games: the zero-sum and the non-zero-sum game. The zero-sum game is one of pure competition in which one party takes all at the expense of the other; the net gain totals zero. This could be the "sudden death" playoff in a sporting event or a game of "matching pennies." The non-zero-sum game is one of pure cooperation and may have two different outcomes: the positive sum outcome in which both parties win (sometimes referred to as a win-win situation) and the negative sum outcome in which both parties lose (a lose-lose situation). The positive and negative outcomes of the non-zero-sum game could be illustrated by the benefits of education and the total destruction of nuclear war, respectively. Since bargaining involves motivations toward both cooperation and competition, it has been correctly labeled a "mixed-motive" game. It is true that the same motivations are present in small group process; the difference, however, occurs in the relative emphasis placed on cooperation and competition. In bargaining, the motive to compete is overt and dominates while cooperative behavior occurs only to facilitate the process. These motives often work as cross-purposes to each other, generating difficult dilemmas for the bargainers. This problem will be addressed in another section of this paper.

The terms "bargaining" and "negotiation" are often a source of confusion. Although Keltner provides an explanation of the theoretical distinctions,[3] for the most practical purposes the differences are minimal and refer primarily to the situational climate. "Negotiation" lends itself to a climate of cooperation and compromise while "bargaining" tends to make the power relationships between the parties more explicit. Negotiation is more aligned with the type of inquiry associated with joint problem solving while bargaining more closely resembles the inquiry of debate. The difference is

---

2. Joseph E. McGrath, "A Social Psychological Approach to the Study of Negotiation," Bowers, Raymond V. ed., *Studies on Behavior in Organizations* (Athens, Ga., University of Georgia Press, 1966), p. 101.

3. John W. Keltner, *Interpersonal Speech-Communication: Elements and Structures* (Belmont, Ca., Wadsworth Publishing Company, Inc., 1970), p. 238.

one of degree and not of kind. For simplicity, this essay will favor the use of the term "bargaining."

Bargaining Communication

Since bargaining is a framework for the symbolic settlement of conflict it is basically communication behavior. A successful bargaining effort is an apex of human accomplishment. A mark of civilized behavior is to settle conflict as a "symbolic" rather than a "real" level.

Because of the warfare aspect of bargaining one cannot expect bargaining communication to be always open and honest. It is here that we find the most telling difference between bargaining communication and small group communication.

Bargaining communication must accomplish several ends: to preserve and maintain the symbolic process, to modify the power perceptions of the parties, and provide a climate to insure subsequent bargaining success. To preserve and maintain the process each party must keep the other convinced that the situation is a non-zero-sum game of the positive sum type. A party perceiving a minimal or negative reward (or payoff) would likely withdraw, especially considering the costs of time, preparation, and emotional energy. Communication (as persuasion) serves to affect the perceptions of power which in turn governs the distribution of the mutual gains. It must be remembered that the only bargaining power a party has is the power that that party can get his opponent to perceive it has. Finally, the anticipation of profitable future bargaining encounters along with the often valuable interpersonal relationships which develop among bargainers helps to keep it a fair confrontation.

It is not surprising to realize that bargainers frequently withhold, distort, and misrepresent information in their efforts to arrive at a mutual satisfactory settlement. Ann Douglas articulates the obtuse nature of some aspects of bargaining communication.

> The fact that verbal strategems directed against the opponent can ricochet in bargaining has resulted in a spurious mutation of communications in this social area. In the whole of human discourse I question whether there is to be found anywhere else a more extraordinary hybrid of efforts both to clarify and to muddle . . . [4]

Strategies and Tactics

The terms "strategies" and "tactics" are often used synonomously. The following distinction, however, should serve to facilitate a clearer theoret-

---

4. Ann Douglas, "The Peaceful Settlement of Industrial and Intergroup Disputes," *Journal of Conflict Resolution* 6 (1975): 78.

ical discussion. A strategy is a general plan (or bargaining posture) whereas a tactic is a specific verbal or nonverbal communication behavior serving as part of a strategy.

Two basic strategies represent extreme bargaining postures while many functional strategies occur as a combination of the extremes. One extreme is the "hard" strategy—a "no concession" posture. Continued use of this strategy constitutes a lack of good faith, thus violating a condition necessary for bargaining to occur. When both parties bargain hard the process soon becomes dysfunctional as each misperceives the power in the situation. A hard strategy is successful only if one's opponent adopts a soft strategy. But even in the hard-soft situation the process is inclined to fail because the weaker party would tend to prefer a return to the problems of the status quo rather than to lose or gain relatively little. Functionally such extremes are rarely found.

Tactics are specific communication behaviors which serve to modify the power perceptions between the parties, to facilitate and maintain the process, and to provide a degree of showmanship for the constituency. "Power" tactics are threats, inflexibility, delay, surprise, and sidepayments, whereas "facilitation" tactics are promises, concessions, and face-saving.

A threat occurs when one party attempts to communicate its ability to inflict punishment (or non-reward) on the other without fear of retaliation. To be effective the threat must possess threat credibility. Threats, which lack sufficient perception of credibility will have one of the following outcomes; they may be challenged, forcing the threatener to either withdraw, or carry the threat out. The former would constitute a loss of face, the latter would reduce the symbolic nature of the warfare to a "real" situation, most likely resulting in a win-lose or a lose-lose outcome. An interesting question arises when one compares threat credibility with traditional concepts of credibility. In many cases, communication of a threat is most effective when the threatener expresses an attitude of ill will (rather than goodwill) toward the other. The power of the skyjacker serves to illustrate the point. It is not the place of this essay to analyze this issue, but it does raise an interesting question for the student of credibility research. In bargaining, threats should be implied rather than made explicit, mild rather than massive, and rational rather than emotional. The use of massive threat, labeled "brinkmanship," easily generates instability in the form of irrationality which may force the threat to be carried out or result in a severe loss of face by the one threatened.

A more commonly used tactic is "feigning inflexibility." It occurs when a bargainer claims the inability to make concessions through a lack of mandate by his constituency. To the extent that the bargainer is known as a leader of his constituency or as representing himself rather than as a delegate or representative, the tactic loses its effectiveness. One does not expect to bargain with the clerk at the local department store but could certainly expect pricing concessions from a sidewalk artist. Continued claims of inflexibility constitute a hard bargaining strategy and result in a violation of the good faith requirement. Inflexibility is also used as a delay tactic. The bargainer will use valuable bargaining time by constantly checking with his constituency knowing that the party with less time pressure holds a power advantage. The wise opponent, of course, will conceal all information about his time limitations.

When the power relationship is clearly one-sided the weaker party may withdraw from the process rather than accept a payoff moderately better than the status quo. This is labeled a "reactance effect," an emotional reaction caused by a loss of face in recognition of extreme power differences. The sensitive "victorious" party will reduce this potentiality by facilitating some form of face-saving behavior. This may consist of offering a minor concession for a major concession but not without portraying that offering as a "major sacrifice," or at least a tit-for-tat exchange. This is illustrated by a cursory analysis of the 1962 Cuban Missile Crisis in which President Kennedy, using the tactic of brinkmanship demanded that Chairman Khrushchev remove Russian missiles from Cuba. Submission to the threat would generate a severe loss of face for the Russian Premier. Consequently a "settlement" was made in which Kennedy agreed "not to invade Cuba," a concession which did not counter the intentions of the United States anyway. These "mutual concessions" permitted Mr. Khrushchev to save face, answer his critics, and even claim a "victory" by yielding to Kennedy's threat.[5]

The tactic of surprise constitutes informational power. It occurs when a bargainer withholds critical information until the most strategic time. The "turning point" in the Perry Mason dramas is often based on this tactic. It may also take the form of a change of mood, attitude, or strategy. This tactic also might generate an indictment of "bad faith" behavior.

The sidepayment is a tactic which allows one party to win a concession during the formal bargaining and return the concession "informally" or concede during a subsequent bargaining encounter. Sidepayments often facilitate a "show" for the constituency to generate a type of bargainer/constituency face-saving attempt.

Whereas a threat is designed to communicate punishment, a tactic of "promise" is designed to communicate rewards for future behavior. The promise is often used to communicate a climate of cooperation needed to maintain the bargaining process. Promises, like threats, require credibility and tend to become ineffective if not kept. The bargainer should establish a consistent image to aid in subsequent bargaining encounters.

---

5. Ann Douglas, "Backdown on Cuba; how Kruschchev explains it at home," *United States News and World Report* 53 (December 24, 1962): 36-37.

As indicated earlier, withdrawal is a choice always available but does not need to be a total withdrawal. More often it is used to feign dissatisfaction with the process as a means of testing the nature of the power relationship among the parties. More legitimately, withdrawal takes the form of the "caucus," where both parties temporarily withdraw from the confrontation to rebuild group unity and cohesion, consider proposals, modify strategic positions, or choose different tactics. Third-party consultation, to be discussed later, may also occur during the caucus.

Bargaining Process

Good faith is a very important condition for bargaining success. It demands that both parties make concessions to each other toward the facilitation of a settlement. Informal bargaining, sometimes called "mundane" bargaining, often deals with a single issue incorporating only a few tactics. One has only to attend a garage sale or a swap meet to observe such bargaining behavior. The issue is usually the price, and tactics range from surprise, delay, to threat of withdrawal. Formal bargaining is much more structured; like small group problem solving, it tends to progress through recognizable phases. Ann Douglas, observing a series of labor-management negotiations, isolated and labeled three distinct bargaining phases: "Establishing the Bargaining Range, Reconnoitering the 'Range,' and Precipitating and Decision-Making Crisis."[6]

Realizing that bargainers must participate in problem solving to create the payoff matrix, one might expect the first phase to be highly cooperative. But each party faces the dilemma of revealing information (needs, desires, capabilities, etc.) in the spirit of problem solving which reduces the effectiveness of tactics used later, i.e., threats, surprise, inflexibility. Experienced bargainers cope with this dilemma by participating in some extraordinary displays of behavior which serve to shield their underlying cooperative efforts. According to Douglas the first phase is characterized by long bombastic speeches expressing extreme demands seasoned with exaggerated claims of power. This behavior is largely ritualistic and serves two purposes. It serves to impress "the folks back home" and to establish the range of possible agreement. The bombast of this phase also serves to shadow the cooperation and problem-solving efforts taking place. The bargainers are coping with their difficult dilemma of revealing and concealing information at the same time. Perhaps now Ann Douglas' comment concerning " . . . a spurious mutation of communications" is more meaningful. One must remember that specific communication content expressed during this phase cannot be taken literally.

---

6. Douglas, passim.

The second phase, "Reconnoitering the 'Range,'" is marked by occasional soft spots in the verbal armor indicated by occasional exchanges of minor concessions and statements of agreement. One might observe the most artistic use of power tactics in this phase; it is here where " . . . each party . . . turns toward testing out its hypotheses about the other before it becomes fatally penalized by a blundering move."[7]

Phase three, "Precipitating the Decision-Making Crisis," occurs after the parties have sufficiently tried and tested each other both tactically and psychologically and have gathered information about their hypothesis about the other, i.e., needs, strengths, and weaknesses. It is here that a clearer perception of the situational power relationship is realized. Tangents are avoided and final offers are made. To renege from a concession or fail to keep a promise during this phase would severely jeopardize the delicate progress of the earlier phases. It is not uncommon to observe face-saving attempts during this phase. The reader familiar with the Johari Window model of self-disclosure[8] will be able to see its application to the phase sequence observed by Douglas. The model categorizes information that is "open" and shared with others, that is "hidden" from others, and that which is "blind," i.e., known to others but not to self. In phase one each party possesses a large portion of hidden information and consequently, each is blind to the information of the other which will affect the outcome. Information from both the blind and hidden areas must appear in the open area before effective problem solving and settlement can occur. So in phase two each side attempts to modify the situational power relationship and attempts to regulate the information revealed. Phase three occurs when sufficient information appears in the open area to facilitate a settlement.

A deadlock is a break in the bargaining process and may occur at any time. It may occur for a variety of reasons (e.g., frustration, delay, etc.) and consequently occurs in different forms. The mildest form of deadlock is the caucus and the most severe is the strike (or lockout). Although the deadlock eliminates communication between the parties, a form of indirect communication through the aid of disinterested third parties serves to preserve the bargaining process. Three forms of third party intervention are the conciliator, the mediator, and the arbitrator.

The conciliator is one who functions as a relay man to shuttle messages between the separated parties. His goal is to present information (e.g., concessions, arguments, promises, etc.) as clearly and unambiguously as possible. The mediator is academically involved in the issues under dispute. He functions in a creative mode and often attempts to persuade the parties to accept alternatives he has generated. The arbitrator is the most

---

7. Ibid., p. 77.

8. Joseph P. Zima, "Self-Analysis Inventory: An Interpersonal Communication Exercise," *Speech Teacher* 20 (March, 1971): 108-114.

powerful of the third party roles. He has the power of decision which has been granted by both sides. A common arbitration tactic is to solicit a "fairest final settlement" from each side from which he will select one. The desire to be selected generally motivates a sense of fairness and rationality by the parties which would not occur had they been left to their own devices. Surprisingly, the deadlocked parties often discover their "realistic" positions are not as far apart as they perceived them to be.

Contract Language

As mundane bargaining tends to result in a verbal settlement, collective bargaining and other forms of formal bargaining usually culminate in a written agreement, or contract. Contracts are then used as policy statements and are interpreted by persons other than those who write them. And often when negotiators are working under the stresses of the confrontation they tend to get caught up in the "snares" of language.[9] In addition, written language tends to lack the type of redundancy of the spoken in terms of the nonverbal vocal and situational climate.

A problem in contract writing is ambiguity. Language is said to be ambiguous when on simple reading it suggests several interpretations; conversely, language is unambiguous when on a simple reading it clearly and plainly suggests a single meaning or interpretation. The following statement might be found in a typical contract, "An employee who does not work the day before the holiday or the day after the holiday will not be paid for the holiday." This statement might later be interpreted as meaning the employee must work *both* days or only one of the days. Stronger coordinate structure would serve to add precision to the statement and reduce the ambiguity. More correctly, then, the statement might read, "An employee who does not work both the day before the holiday and the day after the holiday will not be paid for the holiday."

In summary, this essay has provided the reader with an overview of bargaining process as a communication arena. It has indicated the milieu appropriate for bargaining to occur, along with considerations necessary for it to function succcessfully. It is important to realize that bargaining, unlike many other communication arenas, does not always require or expect open, honest, or even clear communication. Bargaining communication uses strategies and tactics in order to generate perception of the power relationship among the parties. Ultimately, however, it is necessary that both parties participate in good faith and yield to the shared perceptions of the situation, then conclude a settlement which is more satisfying than had the process not occurred.

---

9. William V. Haney, *Communication and Organizational Behavior: Text and Cases,* 3d edition (Homewood, Ill., Richard D. Irwin, Inc., 1973).

Intercultural Small Group Communication

Richard E. Porter

Intercultural communication has become an issue of major concern, inquiry, and study during the past ten years.[1] This concern is prompted by a recognition that people no longer live in relative isolation but find themselves in situations where they are interacting with people from various cultural backgrounds. With rapid increases in transportation and communication capabilities, millions of people now visit many parts of the world or are introduced to a variety of cultures in their own living rooms. At the same time, here at home, racial and ethnic minorities have become both vocal and visible, peacefully, and sometimes violently, demanding their place in the mainstream of American life. Court decisions and legislative actions have forced increased intercultural contact through equal opportunity and affirmative action employment practices; desegregation and integration of public schools; and the establishment of minority quotas for admission to unions, colleges and universities, and graduate and professional schools. In almost every facet of our lives we increasingly are in the presence of and are more aware of others who are culturally different. We must learn to interact successfully with these people if our society is to be one of peace where all people have respect and dignity.

Successful interaction with culturally different people requires that we develop a facility for intercultural communication and learn to use it in a wide variety of communication contexts. One of these contexts, and the one we will examine, is the small group communication setting. Before we consider this, however, brief attention will be given to the basic natures of intercultural communication and to the relationship of culture to communication.

Intercultural Communication

Intercultural communication is defined here as a communication setting in which a source in one culture encodes a message which is to be decoded by a receiver in another culture. In other words, whenever a person who is a member of one culture sends a message—whether it be verbal

---

1. See, for example, Samovar and Porter (1972, 1976), Harms (1973), Prosser (1973), Smith (1973), Rich (1974), Brislin, Bochner and Lenner (1975), Condon and Yousef (1975), and Sitaram and Cogdell (1976).

or nonverbal, spoken or written—to someone who is a member of another culture, both are communicating interculturally.

Today in the United States we find many cultures. Some are based on race: black, Hispanic, Oriental, and the original American—the Indian. Others are based on ethnic differences: Jew, Italian, German, Pole, Irish, and Greek are but a few of the many ethnic cultures we find in the United States. There are also cultures based on socio-economic differences. The culture of a Rockefeller or a Kennedy is vastly different from that of a third-generation welfare family living in Denver. And, finally, cultures develop around ways of life and value systems. Members of the drug culture share perceptions of the world and values that are vastly different from those shared, for example, by members of the John Birch Society or the Ku Klux Klan. Or, there are followers of Reverend Moon, members of the gay community, or activists in the feminist movement who all have different perceptions and belief-value structures.

If we venture beyond our national boundaries, we find even greater differences in cultures. Religious, philosophical, political, economic, and social role views may differ greatly from our own, as may communities, modes of life, forms of work, degrees of industrialization, and social organization. In these cases, we find people are noticeably different from ourselves in their ways of life, customs, and traditions.

The major communication problem here is one of *cultural variance in social perception,* that is, differences in the ways people develop and attribute meaning to social objects and events. We are all aware that meaning resides in people and that people interpret symbols and messages according to their backgrounds and prior experiences. This problem is minimized when source and receiver are both in the same culture. When source and receiver are from different cultures, however, the problems of understanding and meaning attribution can be magnified many times. Unless interactors are aware of cultural influences on meaning and can act to compensate for this influence, communication attempts may be unsuccessful.

Although problems inherent in intercultural communication may be best solved by becoming what Adler (1976) has described as multicultural man, this is a long and difficult goal that many cannot attain. Most people, however, can become aware of and sensitize themselves to the effects, which culture imposes on communication, and through this awareness and sensitivity they become better able to communicate interculturally. Some of these effects will be described before we move into our discussion of intercultural small group communication.

Culture and Communication

Analysis of intercultural communication processes has revealed eight socio-cultural variables crucial to any intercultural event that are strongly influenced by culture: (1) attitudes, (2) social organization, (3) patterns of thought, (4) roles and role prescriptions, (5) language, (6) nonverbal expressive behavior, (7) use and organization of space, and (8) time conceptualization. As these variables are discussed in detail elsewhere (Porter, 1972; Porter and Samovar, 1976) only those most relevant to small group communication will receive attention here.

Attitudes

"Attitude" symbolizes an internal psychological state of readiness to respond that predisposes us to behave in rather specific and consistent ways when we come in contact with various social objects or events. As Fishbein and Ajzen (1975) point out, attitude formation is a function of our underlying belief and value structures. That is, our predispositions toward social objects and events are a function of the salient beliefs and values we hold. This concept of attitude formation is crucial to intercultural communication because the belief-value structures from which we form our attitudes are culturally determined. What we believe and how we evaluate our beliefs are deeply embedded in everyday experiences of interacting with our environment and culture. The culture in which we establish our beliefs and values in many ways influences (if not dictates) the content and extent of our beliefs as well as the direction and intensity of our values.[2] Our attitudes, then, influence both our overt behaviors and our perceptions. They lead us to interpret events according to our biases and sometimes to see things as we wish or believe them to be rather than as they are.

Four forms of attitudes exert the greatest influence on intercultural communication: *ethnocentrism, world view, absoluteness,* and *stereotypes and prejudices.* Ethnocentrism is a tendency for us to view others, using ourselves as the standard for all judgments; we place ourselves at the center of the universe and rate all others according to their distance from us. We rank one group above another, one element of society above another, one ethnic group, one race above another, and one country above another. We place our own groups, our own country, and our own culture above others; we see ourselves as best.

When ethnocentrism enters our social perceptions, intercultural communication effectiveness is reduced because we lose objectivity toward others. How much ethnocentrism interferes with intercultural communication cannot be predicted, but we do know it is strongest in moral and religious contexts where emotions often promote hostility that prevents effective communication. In the extreme, ethnocentrism robs us of willingness or desire to communicate interculturally.

---

2. A detailed discussion of cultural value systems may be found in Condon and Yousef (1975, 47-121).

Our view of the world in which we live is a function of culture. As Americans, we tend to have a man-centered view of the world. We see it as a vast space on which to carry out our desires; we build what we wish, seek to control nature, and when displeased tear it all down and start over again. Urban renewal is but one example of this world view transformed into action. Other cultures see the world differently. Orientals, for instance, are apt to view the human-universe relationship as one of balance in which people share a place between heaven and earth. Each thing a person does exerts some influence on the balance of that relationship. People must act carefully and not upset the balance because the nature of the universe is toward harmony.

World view gives us a perspective from which we shape and form our impressions of social objects and events. As we encounter people with differing world views, our communicative behavior may be hampered because we view events differently. We may use different frames of reference that seem vague or obscure to others, just as theirs may seem to us. Our perceptions become clouded and our attitudes interfere with our ability to communicate effectively with others.

Absoluteness is closely related to and often derived from ethnocentrism and world view. Absoluteness is reflected in culturally derived notions we have of right and wrong, good and bad, beautiful and ugly, true and false, positive and negative, and so on. Absoluteness influences social perception by providing us with a set of basic precepts from which we judge the behavior and beliefs of others. We take these notions to be absolute— to be "truth"—and do not or cannot realize these "absolutes" are not absolute but are subject to cultural variation. An absolute is meaningful to us only in the relative sense of what is accepted or believed within a given culture.

Stereotypes are attitudinal sets from which we assign attributes to another person solely on the basis of a class or category we believe that person belongs to. Stereotypes might lead us to believe, for example, that all Irish are red-headed and quick-tempered; that all Japanese are short and sly; that all Jews are shrewd and grasping; or that blacks are superstitious and that Mexicans are lazy. Although these generalizations are commonly held stereotypes, they are untrue! Prejudices, on the other hand, are attitudinal sets that predispose us to behave in certain ways toward people solely on the basis of their membership in some group. For example, because a person is an Oriental, a homosexual, or a black, we may deny him membership in a country club, force him to live in a ghetto or barrio, or restrict him to low-paying jobs and performance of menial tasks. Stereotypes and prejudices, obviously, are closely interrelated.

Stereotypes and prejudices work in various ways to affect our communication. By predisposing us to behave in specific ways when confronted by a particular stimulus and by causing us to attach generalized attributes to people whom we encounter, we can permit stereotypes and prejudices to interfere with our communicative experiences and to limit their effectiveness. We spend our time looking for whatever reinforces our prejudices and stereotypes and ignore what is contradictory.

Roles and Role Prescriptions

If we encounter members of other cultures and their behavior seems strange to us, it very well could be a matter of different role prescriptions. Roles and role prescriptions vary culturally, and although we might argue the value of a particular role prescription, we must realize—if we are to succeed in our task of communication—that for members of the culture we are communicating with, their behaviors are completely natural, normal, and ethical.

The problem here is one of value. We tend to value prescribed social role behavior, and when role behaviors fail to meet our expectations, conflict can result. In our American culture we sometimes find one segment of society that fulfills a role of social protector. This group has a value system that holds such things as nude sunbathing, homosexual acts, drug use, buying sex, or viewing pornographic materials as absolutely evil and to be prohibited under all circumstances. Yet, those who fulfill roles of nude sunbather, homosexual, drug user, pimp or prostitute, and explicit sex film producer or viewer value these acts differently. Their value systems permit and even approve these acts and hold they are not evil but are the exercise of free choice by mature people in a free society. Values held by various role groups within a culture or between cultures often conflict and can lead to ineffective communication and even violence.

Nonverbal Expression

It is a common experience among people who travel to find that it is difficult to interpret the facial expressions of people of cultures other than their own. This difficulty has frequently been voiced with reference to Oriental people whose modes of expression are found to differ from those of Caucasians (Vinacke, 1949, 407).

The form nonverbal messages take as well as the circumstances for their expression and the amount of expression permitted is culturally determined. Which emotion may be displayed, by whom it may be displayed, the circumstances under which it may be displayed, and the extent of its display are cultural norms that children learn very early. In this regard Klineberg (1954) has noted:

We find that cultures differ widely from one another in the amount of emotional expression which is permitted. We speak, for example, of the imperturbability of the American Indian, the inscrutability of the Oriental, the reserve of the Englishman, and at the other extreme of the expressiveness of the Negro or the Sicilian. Although there is always some exaggeration in such cliches, it is probable that they do correspond to an accepted cultural pattern, at least to some degree (p. 174).

The Japanese smile, for example, is a law of etiquette that has been elaborated and cultured from early times; it is not necessarily a spontaneous expression of amusement. This smile is a silent language often inexplicable to Westerners. Japanese children are taught to smile as a social duty so they will appear happy and avoid inflicting sorrow or grief upon their friends.

Cultural variance in nonverbal expression and its potential effect upon social perception and intercultural communication is well expressed by Sitaram (1972):

What is an affective communication symbol in one culture could be an obscene gesture in another culture. The communication technique that makes a person successful in New York could kill him in New Delhi (p. 19).

An example will serve as a case in point and demonstrate how harmful the use and misinterpretation of nonverbal behavior can be in an intercultural situation. A visiting British professor precipitated a student demonstration and riot at Ain Shams University in Cairo in 1952 when he leaned back in his chair and put his feet upon the desk while talking to his class. What he did not realize is in the Middle East it is extremely insulting to have to sit facing the soles of someone's shoes (Yousef, 1972).

Nonverbal aspects of intercultural communication are probably among the most difficult because of the reliance we place on the interpretation of nonverbal cues in the decoding of verbal cues. We have much to learn about how people from other cultures use nonverbal cues to express themselves. Until we gain this knowledge we will encounter trouble when communicating interculturally.

This discussion of intercultural communication has been extremely brief and has touched only upon the most striking aspects of culture as they influence the communication process. But, we have shown how our culture gives us different backgrounds and experiences not necessarily available to or known by others with whom we may communicate. Our ability to decode and to understand a message requires knowledge of the culture in which it was encoded. Ignorance can result in misinterpreting and misunderstanding, which can cause us to make inappropriate responses.

Intercultural Communication Within Small Groups

Small group communication settings involve intercultural communication when a group is composed of people from differing cultural backgrounds. This quite naturally occurs in international settings when people from various countries and cultures meet to discuss international politics, economics, and business. Or we may find it in domestic areas when civic bodies attempt to solve problems within their communities or when students representing various ethnic and racial backgrounds meet to recommend school policies and actions.

Small group communication is a complex process involving a highly complicated interrelationship of many dynamic elements. The sharing of common goals or purposes, a social organization, the establishment of communication channels, and the sharing of relevant beliefs and values are all recognized necessary ingredients for the emergence of a group and the development of an atmosphere suitable for small group communication. In general, a certain similarity between people is necessary for the creation of this atmosphere and the development of what Fisher (1964) calls "groupness." Successful small group formation and communication is difficult enough a task when group members are culturally similar, but when members are culturally dissimilar, the task may be formidable.

Since intercultural small group communication occurs in both international and domestic dimensions, we will examine each of these situations. Intercultural communication in any context is dependent upon both a desire to communicate interculturally and a recognition of cultural influences on communication processes. Since it is impossible to examine a wide variety of cultures and cultural contexts, we will limit our discussion to examining some of the problems that could arise in intercultural small group communication.

The international dimension of intercultural communication is confused at times by political and ideological issues that inhibit real communicative purposes. Some of these issues include secret agreements, treaties with other countries, hidden agendas, and image maintenance, to name but a few. We will assume a situation in which these influences are absent, an environment in which interested, earnest, and sincere people have gathered to seek consensus and agreement about a political issue, an economic issue, or a business issue. The actual topic does not matter; what is important here is the sociocultural environment in which communication takes place and the way culture influences, guides, and determines communicative behavior. All of the possible problems that could be encountered cannot even be imagined, let alone covered. Considering cultural differences in approaches to small group interaction, however, will give us an insight into difficulties that can arise.

As Americans, we tend to be task oriented, direct, and businesslike, immediately wanting to get at the heart of the matter. We depreciate what we consider to be irrelevant concerns, and urge immediate action to get the job done.

Other cultures are not like us; the small, seemingly trivial matters are very important. Until those matters are resolved, progress toward the task at hand cannot proceed. This was very apparent several years ago at the Paris Peace Conference where there was much controversy over table shape and seating arrangements. We Americans tended to react with a what-difference-does-it-make attitude; we wanted to get down to business, to start negotiating an end to the war. We had difficulty understanding how something as important as ending a war could be bogged down for weeks over something (to us) as silly as the shape of a conference table.

What we did not realize was the importance given to such nonverbal environmental factors as seating arrangement by the Vietnamese. In Oriental cultures social hierarchy is extremely important and before anything as important as peace negotiations can begin, the social hierarchies must be clearly established, understood, and stated in nonverbal terms. This is why table shape was so important. To have a square table would indicate equality of all participants. And, since, the government of South Vietnam claimed not to recognize the Viet Cong, to permit them to sit at a square table would imply they were of equal stature—clearly an inconsistency and a detriment to negotiation.

Another problem we may face in intercultural small group communication is the actual communication process itself. This is readily seen if we examine the differences in approach between Americans and Japanese.[3] We Americans want to talk to the top-man, the one in authority who can make tough decisions. We want to get down to business and drive a hard bargain, and we want answers now. We are busy; time is money, and we cannot fool around. The Japanese, however, are quite different in their approach. "If we were to place Japanese concepts of self and group at one end of a continuum it would be possible to produce an almost perfect paradigm by placing American concepts at the other" (Cathcart & Cathcart, 1976, 58). In other words, Japanese concepts of self and group are essentially the opposite of our own. Some distinctions between American and Japanese concepts will be discussed in order to see how different approaches to group interaction influence communication.

---

3. An excellent discussion of the underlying principles as they reflect Japanese culture may be found in Cathcart and Cathcart (1976), Doi (1976), Morsbach (1976), and Van Zandt (1976).

Americans tend to view groups as being composed of individuals where the role of the individual is paramount. This concern with the individual is reflected in the American culture through admiration of "rugged individualism" and the desire to interact with the responsible party. The Japanese, on the other hand, have a selfless view of groups. The group is the social entity; individual identity is submerged for group identity.

This distinction between concept of self in relation to groups is important in terms of decision making and the outcomes of intercultural negotiation. The American concept of individual importance leads to a notion of individual responsibility. A single, unique person is ultimately responsible for decisions and their consequences. This individual is also expected to accept blame for decisions that lead to bad consequences. In a sense, we Americans want to know whom to "hang" when things go wrong. The Japanese, however, operate in a group sense rather than an individual sense. Decisions result from group interaction and group consensus; the group, not the individual, is responsible for the consequences of its action, and when something goes wrong the group, not the individual, is held responsible. The extreme of this position is aptly described by Cathcart and Cathcart (1976):

> This embodiment of group can be carried to the point where, in the extreme circumstances, those persons at the top of the group hierarchy feel constrained to answer for the misdeeds of individual group members by committing *hara-kiri* (suicide) in order to erase the blot on the group's honor. This act of *hara-kiri* reflects a total denial of self and a complete loyalty to the group (pp. 59-60).

Contrast this, if you will, in your imagination. Can you imagine the president of a top U.S. corporation committing suicide because a machine shop supervisor made a poor decision that adversely affected profits and angered stockholders?

A further aspect of culture that can have a significant effect on intercultural small group communication is what Hall (1976) has identified as the context dimension. According to this view, cultures vary along a context dimension that ranges from low to high. What this refers to as far as communication is concerned is the amount of shared cultural knowledge and background the communicators possess. Hall (1976) succinctly states:

> Any transaction can be characterized as high-, low-, or middle context. HC transactions feature preprogrammed information that is in the receiver and in the setting, with only minimal information in the transmitted message. LC transactions are the reverse. Most of the information must be in the transmitted message in order to make up for what is missing in context (p. 101).

This notion of context poses problems when interactors are from cultures that differ in context. Oriental cultures tend to be high context while we Americans tend toward low context. When we meet with members of high context cultures, unless we have the requisite contextual preprogramming, we are liable to have difficulty in communicating because the high context messages do not contain sufficient information for us to gain true or complete meaning. What is worse, we may interpret a high context message according to our low context dispositions and reach entirely the wrong meaning.

The cultural preprogramming referred to here goes beyond mere information, but involves an entire cultural tradition. It includes the entire nonverbal environment in which a communication takes place. Misunderstanding of the nonverbal context of a high context culture is described by Morsbach (1976):

> An American professor at a Japanese university with an excellent command of Japanese language told me the following:
>
> One day he had attended a faculty meeting where he fully participated in the lengthy discussions, using Japanese throughout. On leaving the meeting, he remarked to a Japanese colleague that, in his opinion, the meeting had finally arrived at a particular conclusion. Had not Professor X spoken in favor? His Japanese colleague agreed. And other professors, too? (going down the list one by one). Again, his Japanese colleague agreed, but finally remarked "All this may be so, but you are still mistaken. The meeting arrived at the opposite conclusion: You have correctly understood all the words spoken, but you didn't understand the silences between them" (p. 258).

In discussing the international dimension of intercultural communication we have reviewed several gross cultural differences that might be found between participants in small group intercultural communication. The point here was to emphasize how culture may affect our participation in small group communication and how it may influence our behaviors and the meanings—both social and literal—we attribute to other people and to their messages. Much of what we have viewed may seem trivial. But, to others these matters are very important. If we are to be successful intercultural communicators, we must realize how seemingly insignificant matters can affect the dynamics of our intercultural groups.

When we shift our interest to the domestic dimension of intercultural communication we are still faced with the problems of cultural differences but in a way that mostly manifests itself in terms of values and expectations. This situation may result when small groups are formed in such a manner as to bring together people of wide diversity within our unifying cultural umbrella. By cultural umbrella, we refer to the fact that although people in a small group situation may represent a variety of cultural backgrounds, they are all mediated to some extent by the overall American culture.

Frequently, culturally diversified groups are found when civic bodies or panels are formed. In this case an often first effort is to empanel as members a priest, a minister, and a rabbi, a black, an Oriental, and a Hispanic as well as women and representatives of other diverse groups within the community such as gays, civil libertarians, youth, welfare recipients, and senior citizens. However admirable this may be in terms of democratic institutions, it can result in artificially created groups whose composition defies the formation of an atmosphere conducive to cohesiveness and member satisfaction which are necessary for the feeling of "groupness" mentioned earlier. This is especially the case when cultural differences represent variability of values, beliefs, and attitudes. Whereas a natural group—one formed through the ongoing process of group dynamics—is composed of members who share similar relevant values, beliefs, and attitudes, artificial groups—those we form by administrative action—may be composed of persons who have dissimilar value systems and who distrust or even dislike the cultural systems of each other. Toleration may be practiced, but it may not overcome differences in basic beliefs and values that influence the outcome of group interaction.

Domestic groups may also be burdened by a variety of expectations. Cultural background as well as intercultural experience lead to the formation of expectations about what a group can or cannot do and what it will or will not do in terms of interaction and task accomplishment. Further, expectational differences may lead to problems of interpersonal trust. In an ideal group situation everyone trusts each other; they do not feel that someone will try to do them harm. But, in many intercultural settings, the situation is different; some people, usually but not always minority members of the community, may sense that others cannot be trusted, that they will ultimately harm or cheat them. An example of how differences in expectations can influence group activity is seen in an exchange between students in an intercultural workshop. A discussion between black and white students about black-white relationships had been going on for about thirty minutes. The general trend of the discussion was that blacks did not trust or believe whites. Finally, a frustrated white student, who could not understand why this attitude prevailed, asked a black woman if he came to her and said that he would like to help blacks achieve equality, how would she respond. She answered by saying, "I wouldn't believe you." When asked to explain why she wouldn't believe him, she outlined the history of the white's relationship with the American Indian in which promises and treaties were made and later broken when it was to the advantage of the whites. After citing numerous instances of whites having broken promises and treaties and generally mistreating minorities, she queried the white student with, "Why should I believe you?"

One cannot argue that the majority's past behavior toward racial and ethnic minorities has been one that would result in minority distrust of the majority. What must be recognized, however, by both the minorities and the majority is that individuals cannot be judged by the behaviors of the group from which they come. There are very good grounds for blacks and other minorities to distrust some or many whites, but not all of them. Only through mediating individual expectations in intercultural situations can we learn who can and who cannot be trusted. Anyone who hopes to successfully interact in intercultural small groups must be prepared to show, even to prove, their worthiness of trust and belief.

The value systems of people engaged in small group communication at times get in the way of their achieving consensus or agreement on an issue. When group members are from different cultures this often amplifies the problem because of the influence culture has on the development of values. As cultural diversity increases, the chances of value conflict also increases. This aspect is especially a problem in final phases of discussion when decisions about issues are being made. An example of this can be seen in a group discussion class where a group had been formed at the beginning of the semester to discuss the common interest problem of divorce in the United States. For several weeks everything went well. During initial phases of the discussion, agreement was easily reached on the nature of the problem, its extent, its effects, and even its causes. But, when the solution phase of discussion began, difficulty soon developed. One member of the group of Latin origin was a deeply devout Catholic. To him the only possible solution was to make divorce illegal because it was an immoral act that should not be permitted. This was his only solution; he was adamantly opposed to any other possible solution. The result was an initial attempt by others members of the group to communicate with him and attempt to have him modify his position or at least listen to alternatives that could be available to non-Catholics. This effort met with no success, and when it became evident he would not alter his position or even listen to other views, he was banished from the group. He became a mere observer where he had once been an active participant. After a short time, he began to miss the discussions altogether. Here was a case where the prevailing belief-value system of the group was too different from his, and it soon became more rewarding for him not to be a member of the group than to continue his group membership. Consequently, he dropped out of the group.

Granted this example is an extreme event. But it does represent the situation where the value system of an individual derived from his cultural heritage was of sufficient strength to prevent him from interacting with his fellow students and to even consider their positions. We also must realize that although Catholicism transcends culture, it is mediated by various cultures. And, this was one case where the cultural tradition of this man's Latin origin maximized Catholic dogma and made it a very strong part of his value system.

This type of situation can easily crop up when we form groups that represent all views and interests within a community. Perhaps it will not always be so severe as to disrupt the group or lead to its disintegration, but it can lead to problems that must be understood and resolved before a group can form its identity and reach consensus. We must remember that some views just are not compatible with others as some interests are not compatible with others. When we force these views and interests to interact, the outcome may not be what we expect or desire, and frustrate our attempts to obtain representative views in the formulation of community policies.

Here we have emphasized the view that the chief problem in intercultural communication lies in social perception. We have suggested that culture strongly influences social perception which leads to errors in the interpretation of messages. If there is to be successful intercultural communication within small groups in both domestic and international arenas, we must be aware of the cultural factors which affect communication in both our own culture and the cultures of others. We must understand both cultural differences and cultural similarities. Understanding differences can help us recognize problems, and understanding similarities can help us become closer.

References

Adler, P. S. "Beyond Cultural Identity: Reflections of Culture and Multicultural Man" in L. Samovar and R. Porter (eds.), *Intercultural Communication: A Reader,* 2d ed. Belmont, California: Wadsworth, 1976.

Brislin, R. W., Bochner, S. and Lonner, W. J. (eds.). *Cross-Cultural Perspectives of Learning.* New York: Halsted Press, John Wiley & Sons, 1975.

Cathcart, D. and Cathcart, R. "Japanese Social Experience and Concepts of Group" in L. Samovar and R. Porter (eds.), *Intercultural Communication: A Reader,* 2d ed. Belmont, California: Wadsworth, 1976.

Condon, J. C. and Yousef, F. *An Introduction to Intercultural Communication.* Indianapolis: Bobbs-Merrill, 1975.

Doi, L. T. "The Japanese Patterns of Communication and the Concept of *Amae*" in L. Samovar and R. Porter (eds.), *Intercultural Communication: A Reader,* 2d ed. Belmont, California: Wadsworth, 1976.

Fishbein, M. and Ajzen, I. *Belief, Attitude, Intention and Behavior: An Introduction to Theory and Research.* Reading, Mass.: Addison-Wesley, 1975.

Fisher, B. A. *Small Group Decision Making: Communication and the Group Process.* New York: McGraw-Hill, 1974.

Hall, E. T. *Beyond Culture.* Garden City, New York: Doubleday, 1976.

Harms, L. S. *Intercultural Communication.* New York: Harper & Row, 1973.

Klineberg, O. *Social Psychology,* rev. ed. New York: Holt, Rinehart & Winston, 1954.

Morsbach, H. "Aspects of Nonverbal Communication in Japan" in L. Samovar and R. Porter (eds.), *Intercultural Communication: A Reader.* Belmont, California: Wadsworth, 1976.

Porter, R. E. "An Overview of Intercultural Communication in L. Samovar and R. Porter (eds.), *Intercultural Communication: A reader.* Belmont, California: Wadsworth, 1972.

Porter, R. E. and Samovar, L. A. "Communicating Interculturally" in L. Samovar and R. Porter (eds.), *Intercultural Communication: A Reader.* Belmont, California: Wadsworth, 1976.

Prosser, M. H. (ed.). *Intercommunication Among Nations and Peoples.* New York: Harper & Row, 1973.

Rich, A. L. *Interracial Communication.* New York: Harper & Row, 1974.

Samovar, L. A. and Porter, R. E. (eds.). *Intercultural Communication: A Reader.* Belmont, California: Wadsworth, 1972.

Samovar, L. A. and Porter, R. E. (eds.). *Intercultural Communication: A Reader,* 2d ed. Belmont, California: Wadsworth, 1976.

Sitaram, K. S. "What is Intercultural Communication?" in L. Samovar and R. Porter (eds.), *Intercultural Communication: A Reader.* Belmont, California: Wadsworth, 1972.

Sitaram, K. S. and Cogdell, R. T. *Foundations of Intercultural Communication.* Columbus, Ohio: Merrill, 1976.

Smith, A. L. *Transracial Communication.* Englewood Cliffs, New Jersey: Prentice-Hall, 1973.

Van Zandt, H. F. "How to Negotiate in Japan" in L. Samovar and R. Porter (eds.), *Intercultural Communication: A Reader,* 2d ed. Belmont, California: Wadsworth, 1976.

Vinacke, E. W. "The Judgment of Facial Expressions by Three National-Racial Groups in Hawaii: I. Caucasian Faces," *Journal of Personality,* 17, 1949, 407-429.

Yousef, F. "Intercultural Communication: Aspects of Contrastive Social Values Between North Americans and Middle Easterners." Unpublished manuscript. California State University, Long Beach, California, 1972.

SUGGESTED READINGS

Chapter 2

Altman, Irwin and Taylor, Dalmas. *Social Penetration: The Development of Interpersonal Relationships.* New York: Holt, Rinehart & Winston, 1973.

Austin-Lett, Genelle and Sprague, Jan. *Talk to Yourself: Experiencing Intrapersonal Communication.* Boston: Houghton-Mifflin Company, 1976.

Blatz, William E. "The Individual and the Group," *The American Journal of Sociology,* 44 (May, 1939), 820-38.

Buss, Allan R. and Poley, Wayne. *Individual Differences: Traits and Factors.* New York: Gardner Press (John Wiley & Sons), 1976.

Condon, John C. and Yousef, Fathi. *An Introduction to Intercultural Communication.* Indianapolis: The Bobbs-Merrill Company, Inc., 1975.

Deutsch, M. and Krauss, R. "Studies of Interpersonal Bargaining," *Journal of Conflict Resolution* 6 (1962): 52-76.

Egan, Gerard. *Interpersonal Living: A Skills/Contract Approach to Human Relations Training in Groups.* Monterey, CA: Brooks/Cole Publishing Company, 1976.

Goffman, Erving. *The Presentation of Self in Everyday Life.* New York: Doubleday & Company, Inc., 1959.

Jacobson, D. *Power and Interpersonal Relations.* Belmont, CA: Wadsworth Publishing Company, Inc., 1972.

Janis, Irving L. "Groupthink," *Psychology Today* 5 (November, 1971), 43-46, 74-76.

Kephart, William M. *Extraordinary Groups: The Sociology of Unconventional Life Styles*. New York: St. Martin's Press, 1976.

Kiefer, C. W. *Changing Cultures, Changing Times*. San Francisco: Jossey-Bass, 1974.

McFeat, T. *Small Group Cultures*. New York: Pergamon Press, 1974.

Palmer, Stuart. *Deviance and Conformity*. New Haven: College and University Press, 1970.

Porter, L. W., Lawler III, E.E. and Hackman, J. R. *Behavior in Organizations*. New York: McGraw-Hill Book Company, 1974.

Samovar, Larry A. and Porter, Richard E., eds. *Intercultural Communication: A Reader*. Belmont, CA: Wadsworth Publishing Co., 1976.

Young, O. R., ed. *Bargaining: Formal Theories of Negotiation*. Urbana, IL: University of Illinois Press, 1975.

GROUP OPERATIONS: TASK GROUPS, GROWTH GROUPS, EXPERIENCING AND EVALUATING

Sayings like, "two heads are better than one," express a folk wisdom which, according to Ivan Steiner in Chapter 1, reflect accumulated knowledge about human behavior in groups. All of us are aware that there are tasks which are more readily and effectively accomplished when we work through a group rather than alone. Our society is permeated with work groups wherein individuals join together to accomplish some task. Every business and industry is made up of one or more small groups, each with an assigned task. All governmental and academic institutions are dependent on departmental groups and committee groups to solve problems and formulate policy. In short, we all spend a great deal of our time in work groups or task groups, and therefore it behooves us to study the operations of such groups if we are to better understand group process.

As we pointed out in the Introduction to Section I, the modern study of small groups has been concentrated longer and more extensively on this phenomenon—the problem-solving small group and how to make it more effective—than on any other aspect of the small group. As early as 1910 academicians were applying John Dewey's "reflective thinking" pattern in small groups to improve their problem-solving. In the 1920's there was an upsurge of interest on the part of business and government in ways of turning workers into cooperative teams which would work more efficiently. By the 1930's almost all colleges and universities in the U.S. were offering courses in "group discussion" or "group problem-solving" designed to develop students' knowledge about and skill in performance in small groups. To date, this is still one of the prime areas of study of small groups, and there has been developed a whole body of literature about the task group.

Interestingly, it was this great interest in improving group operations in task groups that led to the so-called human potential movement of the

1960's and 1970's. Scholars studying small groups became aware, as discussed in Chapter 2, that the group is made up of individuals who remain unique no matter how tightly knit the group, and that if the group was going to be made to operate more efficiently individuals had to be "improved" also. It was recognized that not only did groups have to know how to accomplish a task cooperatively, they had to know how to "solve" the social interactional problems that existed among the individuals comprising the group. This led to a whole new area of group study—group dynamics—in which the main concern was to learn how and why *individuals* operate as they do in various small groups. It was established that there was a symbiotic relationship between the individual and the group. Not only could better organized, more cooperatively motivated individuals make a group more efficient, a well ordered group could create an atmosphere where the individual could improve his own self image and performance. Thus were born sensitivity training and group encounters. This meant the formation of groups designed not to solve problems or accomplish tasks external to the group, but groups established solely for the purpose of helping individuals grow as integrated personalities.

Growth groups, in the last fifteen years, have become the most pervasive form for dealing with individual psychological problems, and they provide thousands of people with a means of better understanding themselves in their relationships with other individuals. As such, growth groups are worthy of study as a special form of small group, and a knowledge of how such groups operate can be very useful to the student of small groups, both for an understanding of human potential and for insights into solving interpersonal problems in task groups.

In Section II we have brought together a number of readings selected for their usefulness in helping the reader understand the differences and similarities between task groups and growth groups and for their contribution to knowledge about how each type of group operates. In addition, we have included writings about activities, games, and simulations which can be performed in the classroom to heighten group experience and to sharpen the observation of group dynamics, and some checklists and observation forms that can be useful in evaluating both task groups and growth groups.

Chapter 3, which begins Section II, focuses on Task Groups and the problem-solving process. The five readings pertain to the small group that is concerned wth a task or problem external to the group. They describe how such groups are organized, the patterns most suited to problem-solving, and the kinds of communication which make it easier to accomplish the group's task. It should be emphasized, however, that task maintenance behavior cannot be totally separated from interpersonal behavior. It is important to keep in mind that a task group is one that has to overcome interaction difficulties as well as overcome task barriers.

We begin Chapter 3 with a selection from John Keltner's book,

Interpersonal Speech-Communication. Keltner examines some important issues in decision making, commitment, and problem solving. For Keltner, as for John Dewey, there is a direct relationship existing between individual and group decisions. He notes, "A group decision is a collection of common individual commitments." In reaching these decisions, groups arrange and organize their findings into a system or pattern that allows them the greatest usefulness and value. Keltner concludes his selection by suggesting that groups might find it helpful to place their issues into a goal-obstacle-encounter pattern.

The second selection deals with the organization and structured patterns found in the task group. Michael Burgoon, Judee Heston and James McCroskey claim that "organized groups tend to discover more possible solutions, to reach better decisions, and to be more satisfied generally with the decisions they reach." In their piece, "A Structure for Problem-solving," they describe a step-by-step structure for problem-solving and present a model of the decision-making process. Understanding their structure and process should be helpful in creating more organized groups.

Although most groups do use some structured approach to problem-solving, it is by no means the only format for effective task accomplishment. One recent form, often widely misunderstood and misused, is what Arthur Coon refers to as "brainstorming." In Coon's analysis of brainstorming, it is viewed as a technique for stimulating the generation of ideas and facilitating their expression. To this end, he adds, it may well contribute to a climate that is conducive to effective problem solving.

Peter Meirs approaches the task group from a business management viewpoint and finds that some of the theories about communication in work groups do not fit the practical problems of such groups. In his article, "Structuring Communication in a Working Group," he discusses the three most commonly used communication networks, the circle, the chain, and the wheel, and then by means of a case study demonstrates which networks perform best in business world task groups.

James H. Davis, a sociologist, has written extensively about the performance of task groups, and the excerpt from his book, *Group Performance,* presents some of the variables which inhere in groups and seem to exist apart from individual propensities. He calls these variables " group level concepts" and he discusses how the ones labeled *cohesiveness, cooperation,* and *norm* affect the performance of task groups.

In Chapter 4, Growth Groups, we examine the group activities most often associated with the Human Potential Movement. One need only reflect on the history of this movement to see its impact on our culture and on the study of small group communication. From its early beginnings in Bethel, Maine in 1947, to the countless groups that have been spawned as a result of its popularity, growth groups have become part of American Society. Chapter 4 presents some readings that help explain this popularity while at the same time explaining something about the workings of growth groups. More specifically, we have selected readings that not only reflect how these groups operate, but also discuss the stages and procedures found in most growth groups. We must, however remind the reader that each group is different and unique. Our sampling is only a small portion of a larger spectrum, and may not describe all the growth group experiences that the reader may encounter.

In recent years the intensive group experience has become part of our modern life. Perhaps of all growth group situations, the intensive group experience is the one that is most often misconstrued and maltreated. Carl Rogers, who is in the *avant-garde* of the Human Potential Movement, describes the intensive groups' goals and objectives. In his essay, "The Process of the Basic Encounter Group," Rogers explains the workings of this type of group, while indicating what the intensive group *is* and what it *is not*. He maintains that in an atmosphere of much freedom and little structure, the individual will gradually feel safe enough to drop some of his defenses and facades. One of his premises is that the correct use of this group process can aid an individual in both understanding himself and his relationships with others.

The second selection in Chapter 4, "The Experiential Group" by Lakin and Costanzo, looks at growth groups in general. For Lakin and Costanzo, what is important is that all these groups share a common goal, if not a common label. It is what they seek to do, and how they do it, that is the major concern of these authors. They believe that all growth groups, whatever they are called, attempt to provide group interactions where "personal disclosures and interpersonal reactions generated by those disclosures will repeatedly recur and stimulate progressive deeper inner experiencing." They hold that most groups move towards those experiences by engaging in certain "core processes," and that these are found in all growth groups. These processes are discussed in some detail as a means of showing their influence on interaction.

The conscious-raising group is yet another type of growth group that has become popular in the 1970's. Most often associated with the Women's Movement, these unique groups offer a group situation that allows women (and men) an opportunity to share and examine those life experiences common to all of them—despite differences in age, race, sexual preference, class, or marital status. Edith Folb looks at the conscious-raising group and presents a description of the structure, format, ground rules, procedures and processes that characterize these groups.

Assertive training groups are one of the newest group forms which appeared in recent years. Assertive training leaders often employ the group setting because it so closely parallels real life environments. Osborn and Harris note, "The group provides a laboratory for experimenting with and rehearsing new assertive behaviors and a broader base for social modeling than does a one-to-one interaction." In their essay on assertive training they suggest ways for practicing that social modeling by presenting the developmental phases found in most assertive groups. In addition, they discuss the five stages most groups go through—1) preaffiliation, 2) power and control, 3) intimacy, 4) differentiation, and 5) separation.

Chapter 5 combines two types of activities designed to enhance student performance in small group communication. The first is experimental activities or games, which, when properly carried out in the classroom, allow students to confront their own communication behavior. The second type of activity is that which is necessary to all learning—evaluation. All groups can profit from careful observation and skillful evaluation especially by the group's own members. We have drawn six readings from the literature in both of these areas; mainly from those who have focused their attention on developing and testing training techniques designed to provide a set of structured experiences that might lead a group into the realm of self-exploration and learning through experience.

The first reading in Chapter 5 is by Joan Ellen Zweben and Kalen Hamman, who give a theoretical perspective to the use of prescribed games in group situations. They go on to describe the strategies involved in their use.

The next reading is an original essay written especially for this chapter by Edward D. Rintye. In it he talks about how difficult it is for a person to drop old or undesirable communicative behaviors; about how often we are told how to adopt new behaviors but never how to get rid of the old unwanted ones. He goes on to describe in detail an exercise which will help group members cast off old behaviors while learning new ones. He calls it "behavioral rehearsal, the Cinderella skill."

The third selection is from a book called *Communication Games* by Karen R. Krupak. She describes four games which can be used in any classroom and will develop an awareness of how we appear to others in small groups. They also sensitize group members to the roles which make up all group behavior.

Turning to the act of observing and evaluating small group communication, we present a selection by John K. Brilhart who tells us what to look for in effective evaluation procedures. By knowing what to look for when evaluating a group, we can tell a great deal about the processes followed by that group. In addition, by evaluating the process itself we are able to improve our own behavior. Brilhart underscores this notion when he notes, "Unless practice is constantly evaluated, it may result in bad habits. The means to learning is practice with analysis and evaluation leading to change in future discussions."

In the next reading Gerard Egan presents an "Encounter Group Checklist" that can be used to evaluate what is happening in a growth group. A careful study of his list not only offers recommendations for areas of evaluation but also suggests the types of communication relationships, networks, and patterns useful in growth groups. For example, by knowing what to look for (tone, initiative, climate, trust, etc.) we can better understand the processes of the encounter growth group.

Our final reading in this section has the intriguing title, "PROANA 5: A Computerized Technique for the Analysis of Small Group Communication" and its authors, Edward Bodaken, William Lashbrook, and Marie Champagne bring us the latest in small group analysis—a computer program for the study and evaluation of group variables. They describe a computer program which has been tested and can be used by any group that has access to a standard computer.

Task Groups

. Decision-making, Commitment and Problem Solving

John W. Keltner

. . . When we become involved in a group, whether it is a staff group, a class group, an informal group, a family group, or any group of any kind, one of the decisions that we unconsciously make has to do with the amount of claim or control we will allow others to have on our actions; that is, how much effect we are going to allow others to have upon our own decision-making. We are seldom aware of the process of making this decision; but each time we associate with another person we must resolve a question in relation to that other person: *To what degree are we going to allow another person to control our behavior?*

Our choice of whom we will follow, our choice of leadership, involves interpersonal decisions. Interpersonal decisions of this type are also involved in decisions about whom we should try to lead. We have no desire to influence some people through our leadership; we very much want some others to follow our directions. As we relate to others, we are constantly making interpersonal decisions about following and leading.

Individual decisions, particularly interpersonal decisions, are often made quite rapidly. Within a short span of time, seconds or even fractions of seconds, a large number of conscious and unconscious decisions may be made.

From *Interpersonal Speech-Communication, Elements and Structures* by John W. Keltner. © 1970 by Wadsworth Publishing Company, Inc., Belmont, California 94002. Reprinted by permisssion of the publisher.

Group decision-making

Group decision-making is more complex and more involved than the interpersonal and the intrapersonal decision-making. *A group decision is a collection of common individual commitments.* It involves intrapersonal and interpersonal decisions. When several of us agree to perform a common act or to accept a common anticipation of action (that is, an attitude) through joint discussion, we are making a group decision. A unanimous, or consensus, decision occurs when all members of a group make the same commitment and proceed to perform similar behaviors.

Majority decisions represent something less than total group commitment in any given matter. In many groups, there are always some people who are not committed to any action that the majority of the group will follow. When unanimous, or consensus, procedure is used, no decision or commitment is made that is not followed by everyone in the group. Both types of group commitment have values and weaknesses, depending upon the demands of a given situation.

Interactions of the members of the group itself represent various kinds of commitment to each other. Each person responds to another person in a manner different from that of anyone else. In any group, each member chooses among the others those whom he likes and dislikes and those with whom he will and will not do certain things; and his pattern of choices usually will be different from the choices made by anyone else in the group. The interpersonal interactions that are apparent in any group are the result of a type of decision or commitment of the individual members with relation to each other.

True full commitment of a group to a common action, a common objective, or a common attitude is practically impossible in a complete sense because each one of the group members, as we have so often mentioned, sees the world differently. You and I may stand at the bottom of the steps of the east entrance of the United States Capitol in Washington, D.C., and by concurrent agreement we may decide to walk up those steps. Now, that is a simple decision, a simple commitment; but the decision *I* make to walk up those steps is not the same as the decision *you* make to walk up the steps. While we both have decided to walk up those steps, we may each be doing it for a different purpose. Neither of us can walk up exactly in the same way or in the same place as the other nor can we do it at the same time.

A social-action group decided that each member of the group would persuade five persons to come to the next meeting. This decision was unanimous and everyone left the meeting expressing conviction that things were really going to happen. Now, I don't know about the others, but in my own mind I'd accepted the *idea* of getting five people, although I knew I couldn't really *get* five people. My own private decision was that I would probably try for five and there were three prospects I would definitely approach. However, I was none too sure that I could persuade any of them to attend the meeting. My decision really was different from the group decision, and I'm sure that the decision of each individual in that group differed from our joint decision—and from the individual decision of every other member.

At a certain level of abstraction, a group may reach a joint commitment. *The more abstract the proposition under consideration, the greater the possibilities of joint agreement; and the more concrete the proposition under consideration, the less the opportunity for full agreement.* In the monthly meeting of a union local, there will be genuine full agreement about the highly abstract proposition that "in union there is strength"; but concrete details of planning the local's annual picnic will be determined by bare-majority vote. The level at which agreement can be reached must be sought by a group. Collective bargaining between labor and management or between any other groups presents a classic example of how the parties to a disagreement seek the level at which they might reach agreement.

In one typical instance, contract negotiations bogged down over a clause about hiring part-time employees. Before this clause could be acceptable to both parties, the term "part-time employee" had to be defined to mutual satisfaction. One proposed definition was "a part-time employee is one who works less than forty hours a week, on irregular schedules, and is not subject to the benefits of regular employees." Another was "anyone who works less than forty hours per week." Obviously, the latter definition would cover more people than would the first definition; it not only would cover more people but also would permit a wider range of interpretation. The union wanted a very specific definition so that it would include all part-time employees as dues-paying members of the union. The company wanted the broad definition so that it could, at its own discretion, decide on those persons who would secure the full benefits of the employment. In order to reach agreement, it was necessary for both parties to accept a definition more abstract than either wanted: "Part-time employees are all those employees who are not regular employees." Only on this could they agree. Application was left open, depending on circumstances of future specific cases.

The effectiveness of decision-making in groups depends largely on the degree of appropriateness of the alternatives that are available to a group. Suppose we are a committee on student discipline in a large university. One of the rules of the university is that no member of the university community shall interfere with the orderly conduct of classes and administrative business. We are called upon to decide upon the discipline of students who, during the course of a demonstration, caused disruption of classes and of the university administration.

If the regulations restrict us by spelling out in detail the choices we have and the conditions of each choice, we would be limited in the decisions we can make. Suppose we have only two alternatives: expulsion with denial of readmission or a one-semester suspension with readmission subject to review. There would be an immediate division within our group. But suppose instead of two possibilities, we have eight, ranging from a nonpunitive warning to summary expulsion. There would be six other alternatives between these two extremes; our decision-making would have greater possibility of common agreement. The more limited the alternatives, the greater the possibility that strong differences will arise. The appropriateness and inappropriateness of the alternatives that are available to the group will depend in part on the variety or range of choices available.

Appropriateness may also be related to the degree to which the choices available fit the particular situations. In this case, if we had no policy or precedent and were free to make the decision, the number of alternatives would be almost infinite at the beginning of our deliberations. Alternatives for consideration would then arise from each of us present as we submitted our ideas.

Problem-solving

We have said that decision-making and problem-solving are different processes. So they are; however, the two are closely related. Certainly, decisions are involved in the solving of problems. The existence of problems requires the making of decisions, and problem-solving activity is essential to human life. The distinguishing difference between the two processes lies in the manner in which problem-solving organizes the decisions. *Problem-solving is a system of arranging and organizing our decisions so that they will have the greatest usefulness or value.*

Effective problem-solving permits a person to cope with the conditions around him through an organized and rational system of related decisions. Some of the ways in which decisions are organized to solve problems are familiar to all of us.

We may let someone else tell us how to act to solve the problem. (Note that this is a decision.)

We may use an organized, rational procedure of studying and analyzing a problem and acting on our conclusions.

We may let the problem "incubate" in the unconscious until a solution occurs to us on which we can make a decision.

We may suddenly have a flash of insight that will reveal a solution to a problem on which we can act.

We may solicit the aid of others in a joint discussion of the problem and seek to get a joint decision.

In all these approaches, decisions play an integral part in the total process; but in problem-solving the decisions are fitted together in a particular manner.

Problems

All problems have certain elements. In any problem, there must be a goal, obstacles to achievement of that goal, and the point of encounter at which we become aware of the obstacles. Notice the identification of the following problems: I want an album recorded by a new jazz quartet (*goal*). I am in a record shop (*point of encounter*) and find that the record costs more than I have with me in cash (*obstacle*). In coping with the problem, I must deal with factors from all three of these aspects. The goal may be strong or weak; I may very much want the record right now or I may be only mildly interested in adding it to my collection. The degree of intensity of my desire to reach my goal will influence my attempts to solve the problem. The nature of the obstacle, my financial situation, is important; the cash in my pocket might be all I have till payday or I might have a checkbook and credit cards. If the record shop is a "cash only" establishment, the solution of my problem may be more difficult to find than if the management will accept a check or a credit card.

Practically all our human problems can be placed in the goal-obstacle-encounter context, which allows us to examine problems closely and provides an opportunity for us to find effective solutions.

Goals

First, no problem exists unless there is essentially some goal or target or desire that we strive to accomplish or reach. Our goals are simple and complex, rational and irrational, conscious and unconscious. Some are inherent in our physiological nature. The seeking for food, for elimination, and for maintaining the equilibrium or balance of our biological systems are almost purely physical in nature. Each of us also has psychological goals which serve to sustain and enhance ourselves. Our social and cultural conditioning sets up other goals of behavior which we are expected to follow. (The sociocultural goals are often interrelated with the physical and psychological goals.) Acceptance by others around us is a psychological goal related to the eventual self-realization objectives. Acquiring economic substance or becoming a leader are social goals.

In addition, goals may arise from a particular situation. In almost every situation in which we find ourselves, goals or objectives affect our behavior in that situation. When we start out in the morning, we have goals or objectives for the day. Some are not so clearly perceived, while others are very obvious; some are inherent in our bio-social-psychological existence, while others are developed from the situation facing us.

Likewise, goals may be developed jointly, to be shared by several persons. Persons who decide that they wish to form a corporation to produce lumber products have a common goal. In the venture, each person in the group also has specific goals of his own, but these are related to the group goal.

Our goals may have a quality of generality or specificity. A member of the track team may be trying to run a four-minute mile. In one sense, that would be a specific goal; but, in order to accomplish that four-minute mile, a number of more specific objectives must be met. He must be in condition; he must have a plan for the amount of time to be expended for each quarter of the mile. Thus, if he plans to run the first quarter in 53 seconds, the second in 60 seconds, the third in 67 seconds, and the last in 60 seconds, he is setting intermediate, or more specific, goals to accomplish. *To accomplish a major objective, we must reach certain subordinate or contributing objectives.* The more specific, intermediate, contributing goals to any of our objectives we are able to determine, the more likely we are to understand and develop ways to reach the larger target.

A student entering a university often has some general idea of purpose or goal of his education. The student who decides, for example, to become a lawyer soon discovers that there are some intermediate objectives which he will have to meet such as pre-law undergraduate courses, law school, and bar examination. Any student whose larger target is a degree must achieve many subordinate goals and must plan the intermediate steps for each year of his work. Certain school requirements must be met, required or desired courses have prerequisites that must be successfully met, and so forth (sometimes ad nauseam).

Obstacles

The second characteristic of a problem is that the goals are blocked, hindered, inhibited, resisted, opposed, obstructed, or restrained by some thing, person, idea, or combination. These barriers we call obstacles. Without obstacles, there are no real problems; were the goals reached with no form of obstacle, there would be no problem. *The existence of the obstacle to achievement of a goal creates the condition that we identify as a problem.*

Attainment of a college degree of itself presents no problem. However, between a high school senior and that degree there are many barriers; and these barriers create problems. There are entrance requirements. Classes may not be available when he needs them. He may have inadequate high school background in some subject areas. Funds may not be adequate for expenses. In four years or so, any student encounters a host of major and minor barriers; the route to a degree is beset by problems.

Point of encounter

The third characteristic of a problem is the point of encounter, when one becomes aware of obstacles between him and his goal. *The circumstances of time and place surrounding the point of encounter are important aspects of the problem itself.* A street blockade is certainly an obstacle for a driver who wishes to use that street. If he is on an errand that has no particular time restrictions and permits alternative routes, the point of encounter will not present him with a serious problem. If, however, he has selected the street as a shortcut to the airport where he must catch a plane to keep a vitally important appointment in another city, at the point of encounter he will become aware of problems of great moment to him.

If we can perceive and define our problems in terms of the goal-obstacle-encounter triad, we have taken the first rational step in the process of problem-solving. However, this first step is often quite difficult. Many times we perceive problems in terms of symptoms, and these do not necessarily relate to the nature of the goals we may have. The race riots that began in 1965 in Watts and the campus confrontations that started about the same time were symptoms of some very serious and very basic problems of our society. Few people calmly and carefully examined the nature of the goals of the people involved and the obstacles to these goals that existed in the affected communities. Nor did many examine the goals of the overall society to determine what obstacles became apparent at the points of encounter of the various civil disorders.

Actual differences in and conflict of goals may cause us to stalemate at this first step. Here decision-making becomes a part of problem-solving. Clear decisions must be made about what goals are to be sought as an essential aspect of the initial step of problem-solving.

Once the goals have been perceived or decided upon, it is reasonable to identify and to examine both the obstacles and the nature of the encounter. This process requires systematic investigation of these factors so that we may understand what they are and their relation to the eventual realization of our basic and total objectives. In the process of this examination, we often change our objectives (decisions again) or become more intense in our desire to reach the goals.

Criteria

In this examination we may discover certain conditions that must be met if we are to reach our ultimate objective. These conditions can be identified as the criteria by which we will judge any possible solution to the problem. We are not ready to explore possible solutions until these criteria have been established. The criteria help us to select (by decision again) the type of solutions that may be useful.

Alternatives and solution

The examination of possible solutions is of extreme importance. At the outset, there usually are several alternative possibilities available for the solution of a problem. The more alternatives, the greater the possibility of finding good solutions. Solution possibilities should include as wide a range of possible methods as we can create or discover. Of course, all the possible solutions must be in terms of the established criteria.

Having identified several solutions, our next step is to test each one. The testing is a rational process of making decisions as to the degree to which each of the possibilities does or does not satisfy the established criteria. For example, I am thinking of purchasing a new car. My examination of the obstacles and the encounter lead to the following:

Goal: New car.
Obstacles: Not enough money, resistance of wife.
Encounter: Service man reports, after attempting to tune engine, that major repairs on old car are essential.

So, in developing criteria for the solution, I find at least the following: (1) must satisfy wife, (2) must be able to finance without excess costs, and (3) must meet my needs for transportation.

With this sketchy analysis of the problem, I must then visit a number of car dealers (examination of possible solutions). With each one I review the criteria that have come out of my encounter with the problem. As I go from one to another, I may now and again re-examine my whole problem. My criteria may be modified; for example, I might add that I want a new car that will be consistent with my perceived status in the community. Eventually, I may make a decision about which new car I shall purchase. (Remember that the first decision was the result of an alternative issue that arose in the encounter; namely, whether I should buy a new car or repair the old one.)

The rational recognition that this decision may lead me to the goal does not necessarily mean that the problem is solved. The decision to act does not necessarily include the decision on *what* action should eventually be taken or exactly *how* that action should come about. I may decide to buy a new car offered by one dealer; but immediately the means of financing, the time of delivery, and the like become problems. These, in turn, are subject to problem-solving treatment.

Further, *the decision to act must emerge from the total "need-emotion-rational" condition that prevails when the decision must be made.* In other words, the decision on a solution is still not the action. After I have decided on the new car, I still must sign a contract, clear out the trunk and glove compartment of the old car, turn over its keys, and take delivery on the new one. The act itself requires additional pressure, which in this case, the salesman will provide—with suave alacrity.

We often reach general decisions about large or small problems, then find that decisions to perform specific acts required by that general decision are not so readily made. A general decision to lose weight in order to solve the problem of clothes that no longer fit does not assure consistent rejection of desserts. A decision to make better grades as a solution to the problem of a condition does not guarantee the act of studying day after day. The decisions to perform specific acts may not follow from the decisions of general nature.

The use of problem-solving

An organized approach to problems is not necessarily an inherent process; it can be learned. The approach can become an effective instrument with which to deal with personal problems as well as with group and social problems. First and foremost, each of us needs to understand himself and his goals. Further, we must be able to reveal ourselves so that others can help us to understand our problems.

Problem-solving is not a singular decision process, as we have seen. Such decisions as which goals are desirable, which obstacles are significant, which criteria should be used, which solutions are applicable and critical to the process. Throughout, a multitude of smaller decisions are made in relation to eventual behavior and action.

The process, as an organized method, can be applied by groups in dealing with their problems. Administrative staffs, organizations, work teams, committees, and other combinations of people on a less formal basis, such as the family, may find the use of an organized approach such as we have described most useful in dealing with problems or with tasks that become problems.

A Structure for Problem Solving

Michael Burgoon, Judee K. Heston and James McCroskey

Some groups are highly organized and structured, others have much less organization, and some are almost chaotic. For many groups, there is little or no need for organization of their communication. For example, a social group does not need to structure its communication. In fact, if structure were imposed on such a group, it might actually get in the way of accomplishing its objectives. Task groups, however, have a very great need for organization and structure if they are to accomplish their objectives.

Research concerned with task groups has consistently indicated the desirability of organization and structure. Organized groups tend to discover more possible solutions, to reach better decisions, and to be more satisfied generally with the decisions they reach. The organization and structure of small group communication may cause the group to take longer to accomplish their tasks. However, this is the only negative element and is usually not too important. One might ask, "Do you want it fast, or do you want it good?" A poorly structured group may reach a quick decision, but it is very unlikely that it will be a quality decision.

A wide variety of patterns have been observed in effective groups. It seems clear that there is no one pattern that is inherently superior to all the others. However, as we have indicated, *some* pattern is better than *no* pattern. In this chapter, we will describe some patterns that have been found to be particularly useful.

A Structure for Problem-Solving Tasks

Almost four decades ago, John Dewey published a book entitled *How We Think* in which he described a basic thought process that he believed was most commonly used by individuals when they were confronted with problem-solving tasks. Dewey's description has led to an organizational pattern that is recommended by many writers concerned with small group communication. This pattern has three essential steps: identification of the problem, analysis of the problem, and determination of possible solutions.

From *Small Group Communication: A Functional Approach* by Michael Burgoon, Judee K. Heston and James McCroskey. Copyright © 1974 by Holt, Rinehart and Winston. Reprinted by permisssion of Holt, Rinehart and Winston.

Problem Identification. The first step in problem solving is identification of the problem. The group must determine the essential nature of the problem itself. Is it a new problem? Is it a problem that is severe? Have attempts been made previously to solve the problem? What is likely to happen if nothing is done? Answering these questions permits the group to determine whether they are concerned with something vital or something more trivial.

Let us consider three groups that discussed the topic of "student participation in university governance" to see the different conclusions that groups can draw concerning the same problem. We will not attempt to evaluate or compare the groups' conclusions, but you may find it interesting to do so. Group A was composed of five university students, Group B was composed of five university faculty members from different departments, and Group C included two students, two faculty members, and one administrator, the vice-president of the university.

Group A: The basic problem is the students' lack of opportunity to influence their own environment. This has been a recent development that has occurred since the enrollment in the university has grown to its current large size. It is a very severe problem in that many students are alienated from the university. There have been no attempts to solve the problem; the administration has ignored all student requests. If the problem is not overcome, more students will become alienated, and our present poor-quality educational program will continue to exist.

Group B: The basic problem is student demands for control of the university. This is not a new problem, it has occurred throughout the history of the university from time to time. The problem is not severe because only a few students really care. There has been an attempt to solve it by putting some students on university committees. If nothing further is done, students will continue to complain for awhile and then forget the issue.

Group C: The basic problem is a lack of understanding and cooperation among students, faculty members, and the administration. It is a relatively new problem; when the university was smaller, there was a lot more interaction, understanding, and cooperation among the elements in the university. It is a very severe problem. There has been an attempt to solve it by instituting university committees composed of faculty members, administrators, and some students. If the problem is not solved, it is likely that the groups will become more alienated from one another and the possible benefits of cooperation among the groups will be lost.

Problem Analysis. After the problem has been defined, the group must seek to develop a thorough understanding of the problem. How long has the problem existed? Who or what is affected by the problem? Is it becoming more or less severe? What are the causes? What are people's attitudes towards it? Essentially, the problem-solving group has to confront the traditional journalist's questions: Who? What? When? Why? How? Where?

As we noted in the previous section, three different groups who are discussing the same question can identify an existing problem in very different ways. They can also develop very different analyses of the problem. Consider the conclusions arrived at by our groups.

Group A: This problem has existed ever since the enrollment underwent rapid growth in the 1960s. The people affected by the problem are the students, and the problem is getting more severe all the time. It has been caused by the faculty's and administration's lack of concern for the needs of students, who are very upset and concerned about the quality of the education they are receiving. They believe that they have more insight into what they need to learn than the administrators who are not even familiar with them.

Group B: The problem began about six months ago when a group of students who were dissatisfied with the military policy of the federal government began demonstrating on campus. This group sought to blame the University as a contributor to the nation's problems and started demanding change. Not very many people are affected by the problem at present, though some classes have been disrupted by demonstrators. The problem is becoming less severe since the government has withdrawn troops from Indo-China. The attitude of most students is apathy and most faculty members are completely unconcerned.

Group C: The problem has existed to some extent for almost ten years. As the university has grown, the various groups in the university have become more distant from one another and have had decreasing opportunities to interact. The primary cause of the problem is the size of the university enrollment. Most of the people in the university are aware of the problem and feel that something should be done to overcome it.

Research suggests that the group should not move on to consider any possible solution until the problem has been thoroughly analyzed. Otherwise, while talking about possible solutions, the group will discover elements of the problem that they do not understand and will have to return to the problem-analysis phase. This will lead to disorganization within the group and may interfere with rational thought processes.

Discovery of Possible Solutions. The final phase of the problem-solving process is the generation of possible solutions. Deciding which solution is the best of the possible ones is not part of this process, but belongs rather in the decision-making process. The group that handles this discovery phase effectively exhausts all possibilities of solutions. They leave no stone unturned.

Since our three groups have identified and analyzed the problem differently, it should come as no surprise that they will come up with different alternative solutions. Let us consider the results of their efforts.

Group A: Possible solutions:

1. Reorganize the university's senate so that it is composed of 50 percent students and 50 percent faculty.
2. Appoint four students and two faculty members to the nine-member board of regents.
3. Reduce the enrollment of the university to correspond with the level in 1957.
4. Fire the dean of students.
5. Fire the president.
6. Establish a curriculum committee for the university that includes a majority of students.
7. Abolish all regulations imposed on students except those directly related to academic matters.
8. Abolish required courses.

Group B: Possible solutions:

1. The administration should maintain a low profile until the demonstrations and complaints have run their course.

Group C: Possible solutions:

1. Form a university senate composed of all the various groups in the university, including students, faculty, administrators, and civil service employees.
2. Establish committees in the university that include elected faculty and student members.
3. Appoint a committee to investigate the possibility of limiting future enrollments.
4. Establish departmental curriculum committees at every level composed of both elected students and faculty members.
5. Elect students to serve as assistants to all administrators in the university.

The problem-solving process, therefore, should pass through three relatively discrete phases. First, the group must clearly identify the problem with which it is concerned. Then, the group must be certain that it develops a thorough understanding of the nature of the problem, its causes and effects. And, finally, the group must attempt to determine all the possible solutions that could be employed to solve the problem. If this simple process is followed, the probability of effective problem solving is greatly enhanced. We will take a closer look later at the behaviors of our three groups. . . .

Structuring the Decision-Making Process

As we have indicated previously, decision making must follow problem solving. A group may begin their interaction at the decision-making level if they, someone else, or some other group have already gone through the problem-solving process and have generated alternative solutions. In other circumstances, a group may move from the problem-solving process to the decision-making process during the same period of interaction. It is very imporant, however, to keep these two processes separate. If they are not carefully separated, the group is very likely to fall into disarray and unproductive communication.

Figure 1 presents a model of the decision-making process. Many other similar models have been suggested, and this model should not be considered the only procedure that a group can follow to reach effective decisions. However, this model is probably as good as any. Let us consider each of the steps in the model.

Recognition of Alternative Decisions. The first step in the decision-making process requires the group to be fully aware of all alternative decisions available. If it is not, the problem-solving process has been either inadequate or incomplete, and the group should return to it.

In the case of our three groups who were concerned with student participation in university governance, all three should return to the problem-solving phase. A comparison of the three individual lists of proposed solutions indicates that each of the groups failed to consider some alternatives generated by the other groups. If, however, the groups had been more diligent in their generation of possible solutions, they could now move on to the next step in the decision-making process.

Determination of Criteria for Acceptable Decisions. Once all the alternative decisions available are recognized, the group needs to establish criteria for evaluating them. Evaluation should never begin prior to the establishment of criteria. Otherwise, the group is very likely to be inconsistent in the criteria applied to different alternative decisions. The specific criteria that should be set depend on the topic of the discussion. Things such as cost, impact on the organization, and so forth provide the basis for appropriate criteria.

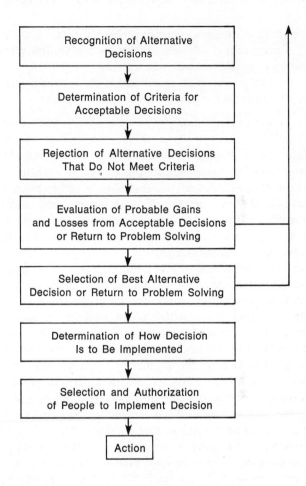

Figure 1. A Model of the Decision-Making Process

Let us see what kind of criteria our three university governance groups came up with.

Group A: Criteria for an acceptable solution:
1. Students must be able to veto irresponsible decisions of faculty or administrative committees.
2. Students must be able to determine their own curriculum.
3. No student should be required to take any particular course.
Group B: Criteria for an acceptable solution:
None.

Group C: Criteria for an acceptable solution:
1. It must provide an opportunity for the various groups within the university to interact with one another.
2. It must permit each group within the university to participate in all decisions that affect the group.
3. All people representing a group must be elected by the group involved.

Rejection of Alternative Decisions That Do Not Meet Criteria. The next step in the decision-making process is to evaluate the alternative decisions in terms of the criteria that have been established. During this decision-making phase, inappropriate, ineffective, and irrelevant decisions will be rejected. If the group finds that there are no alternatives remaining after they have completed this process, they must return to problem-solving to generate new alternatives.

Evaluation of Acceptable Alternative Decisions. During this phase of decision-making, the group should analyze intensively the probable impact of the alternative decisions. The group should consider all probable gains and all probable losses that could accrue from each alternative decision. This phase of decision-making is very similar to the problem analysis phase of the problem-solving process, since each alternative decision is examined only in terms of whether or not it will solve the problem but also in terms of whether or not it might create new problems.

Let us again consider our university governance groups. Only two are still functioning, Group B has already decided on its course of action.

Group A: The evaluation of alternatives. The first proposed solution was evaluated as a desirable alternative since it met the established criteria. It would provide student control over their environment. The second alternative was rejected because it did not meet the criteria on control. Students would still be in a minority. The third alternative was rejected because such a severe reduction in enrollment would adversely affect many current students. Alternatives four and five were rejected bcause they did not provide any assurance of overcoming the problem. The people appointed to replace the dean and the president might be worse than the present holders of the positions. Alternatives six, seven, and eight were all considered desirable, even though it was recognized that alternative seven did not meet the criteria for a solution to the problem.

Group C: The first and second alternatives were determined to be desirable since they met all the criteria established for an acceptable solution. The third alternative was rejected because it could have no immediate impact on the problem. The fourth alternative was considered desirable since it met all the criteria for a solution. The fifth alternative was rejected because it was decided that one student would not have the time to devote to such a task.

Selection of the Best Alternative Decision. After each of the alternative decisions has been carefully analyzed on the basis of probable gains and losses, the various alternatives must be compared in terms of their gains and losses. The group then must reach a decision on the basis of which alternative decision will provide the greatest gain with the minimum loss compared to other alternative decisions. If, among all the available alternatives, no alternative provides a probability of greater gain than loss, all alternative decisions should be rejected and the group should return to problem-solving.

Let us look again at our three groups, since each has now reached a decision.

Group A: It was decided that the university should reorganize the university senate so that it would be composed of 50 percent students and 50 percent faculty. This was believed to be the best decision because it would permit implementation of all the other solutions as well.

Group B: It was decided that the administration should maintain a low profile until the demonstrations and complaints had run their course. This decision was reached because it was felt that the problem was a minor one that would go away of its own accord if left alone.

Group C: It was decided to combine three alternative solutions into one. Thus, the group concluded that a representatively elected university senate including students, faculty, administrators, and civil service employees should be established. It was further decided that the senate should form committees concerned with all important university matters that would include both faculty and student members, and that the University Senate should direct each department to form curriculum committees composed of elected students and faculty members.

Determining Means of Implementation. Presuming that the group has been able to decide on an alternative that will probably provide more gains than losses and is superior to any other alternative, the group must now determine how this decision will be carried out. The concern here is not whether or not the decision that has already been determined is good or bad; it is how the group is to get the job done. During this phase of the group's communication, the group may be concerned with such matters as what committees are needed, whether or not new employees are needed, whether or not the group can divide the work up among themselves, and so forth.

Let us see how our three groups decided to implement their decisions.

Group A: It was decided that there was no way for the group to implement the decision they had reached since they had no power. Consequently, two members of the group indicated that they intended to organize a rally of students to demonstrate against the administration of the university.

Group B: It was decided that a letter to the university president should be drafted with the committee's recommendation and delivered to him.

Group C: It was decided that only the president of the university could actually begin implementation of the decision reached by the group. Consequently, the group decided that it was imperative that they schedule a meeting with the president as soon as possible.

Selection and Authorization of People to Implement Decision. The final step in the decision-making process is the selection and authorization of the people who will carry out the decision. At this point, the only concern that remains for the group is final implementation of the decision.

Group A did not have to concern itself with this step in the decision-making process, since its discussion was terminated a step previously. Group B appointed one of the members to write and deliver the letter to the president. Group C delegated the administrative member of the group to attempt to schedule a meeting with the president.

Action. The final outcome of the decision-making process is action; people designated by the group carry out the decision reached by the group. Of our three groups, which one(s), if any, do you think resulted in action?

We have intentionally used as our example three groups with different types of members who have different orientations, and who make some different errors in the problem-solving and decision-making processes. Many of these errors have little to do directly with the organizational pattern that was employed. However, the causes of these problems have been discussed extensively in the previous chapters in this book. Before going on to the next chapter, it would be useful for you to examine carefully the products of these three discussion groups in relation to what you have learned throughout the preceding . . . chapters. By diagnosing the problems of these groups, you may be able to avoid the same problems in groups of which you are a member.

Brainstorming — A Creative Problem-solving Technique

*Arthur M. Coon**

Simply put, brainstorming is a technique for stimulating the generation of ideas and facilitating their expression. To define further: brainstorming is an application of methods suggested by Alex F. Osborn for explicit stimulation of the imagination in the production of ideas. It usually involves cooperative thinking by groups and is usually directed to the solution of specific problems.

The technique has been so bandied about by Babbitts, so juggled by journalists, so pawned and promoted and perverted by proselytes that the above definition may come as a surprise to many. Such distortions are to be expected when some new process or attitude catches the fancy of the public. First the press celebrates it with awe, and its disciples and converts cannot say enough in its praise. Then a new crop of journalists have to write new stories. Since praise has been exhausted, they go to the other extreme (ironically using a device of brainstorming itself!) and condemn. Meanwhile rival "innovators" spring up to claim the new process is not so novel as theirs, or that it is not new at all, or that their model is a vast improvement over the original.

If the process or attitude has real merit, it will survive these superficial gusts and squalls. The almost universal testimony of those who have tried brainstorming, according to the suggestions of its inventor, is that it does have real merit. It stands the pragmatic test. It works.

Not that it is a cure-all, nor the only way to do creative thinking. But the results so far indicate that through its employment individuals produce more ideas than they would otherwise; in some cases two or three times as many as when they do their cerebrating solo. Further, they tend to retain this greater fluency of ideation. They also experience side- or after-effects which perhaps are even more important. (These will be referred to later.) Therefore, brainstorming—with whatever refinements and improvements are suggested by research and experiment—will probably be around for some time.

Reprinted with permission from *Journal Of Communication*, Vol. VII, No. 3 (Autumn, 1957), pp. 111-118.

I should like to conclude these prefatory remarks with the reminder that brainstorming is by no means all there is to Osborn's theory of creative thinking. It is simply one of a number of advocated techniques which happens to have caught the public fancy. As a result it has been ballyhooed out of all proportion in the public press. Those wishing to understand its relative and full significance are referred to Osborn's books which I shall shortly mention. . . .

In the course of his work [as a successful advertising man] Osborn found himself constantly confronted with the necessity of producing, or creating, new ideas that would help sell the products of his clients. In other words, he was in the business of using his imagination. He also found it incumbent upon him—to a small degree at first, more and more later—to supervise the similar creation of ideas in his assistants, and teach them, too, to be more creative.

At this point, for some reason difficult to explain, Osborn began to become interested in the processes of imagination: perhaps because he was more analytical than others, perhaps just because it was a way of getting a job done better. At any rate, he found that some things helped him think up ideas, and that others hindered or inhibited the process. He began to experiment— to try to find more things that helped, and things that helped more; at the same time trying to identify and avoid things that were inhibitive: times, places, attitudes, what-not. . . .

As usually practiced, brainstorming is engaged in by a group. The group may range from as many as several hundred to as few as three or four. But the optimum number averages ten or twelve. The group does not meet to *settle* a problem, but to get ideas on how to settle it, or at the very least (if the problem is intricate, or highly difficult or technical) to evolve fresh approaches to the problem. But here again Osborn frequently points out that a specific problem is not absolutely essential.

Therefore, it is not strictly correct to call brainstorming either a group technique or a problem-solving technique, although in practice it is usually both. Neither, though it involves discussion, is it exactly a discussion technique. It is best to think and speak of it simply as a device for stimulating the production of ideas.

With the above matters clarified, we come to the four "Brainstorming Rules" with which practitioners of the Osborn technique always preface their sessions, and which they constantly emphasize. These are of great importance, as they are the heart of the method:

1. Adverse criticism is taboo.
2. "Free-wheeling" is welcomed.
3. Quantity of ideas is desired.

4. Combination and improvement of ideas are sought.

It is difficult to say that one of these rules is more important than another. But if one had to be so designated, it would be the first. It is probably also the most misunderstood. Osborn observed that nothing had so inhibiting an effect on his production of ideas as concurrent criticism.

What causes some people to underrate the magnitude of Osborn's contribution to creative thinking is that most of us have observed the same thing. We have all been excited over some new idea, and are full of further thoughts upon it, only to have someone nip our enthusiasm in the bud by saying, "That won't work," or "It's too expensive," or "We tried that in 1943 and it was no good." The result was that we never expressed the further ideas.

But Osborn had the originality to do something about the fact that he and others had observed. He suggested that adverse criticism be held back for the time being. Therefore, at all Osbornian brainstorms there is a wielder of a bell, empowered and instructed to sound it at any manifestation of adverse judgment of ideas—even a derisive laugh.

Almost everyone is surprised at how freely ideas flow forth, once the critical attitude is suspended. Please note the word "suspended"—not "abandoned." This point is one that results in a good deal of misunderstanding, and it is often mistakenly said that Osborn underrates the importance of criticism. This is not the case. He only advocates postponing operations of the critical faculty until the creative faculty has had a chance to function. "Don't try to drive with your brakes on," is how he puts it. "Evaluation is important, essential, but it can and should come later."[1]

By "free-wheeling is welcomed" Osborn means to encourage the wild, implausible, even impossible flights of fancy without which the wings of imagination cannot be fledged. No one knows how the imagination works, but it certainly cannot soar if "cabined, cribb'd, confined."

A third objective in brainstorm sessions is to get as many ideas as possible, the theory being that if the number is great, the laws of probability will work in favor of the proportion of good ideas being larger than otherwise.

Finally, Osborn advocates building and improving upon ideas already expressed. This, indeed, is a key point, since everyone's experience is different, and that of one person in a group may well reinforce and supplement that of another. In practice, Osbornian Brainstormers use here what is called the "hitch-hike" technique. A person who thinks of an addition to an idea already expressed snaps his fingers to get attention. The moderator or leader of the session then recognizes him ahead of the person with the completely new idea.

---

1. Cf. the similar doctrine of Wadsworth and Coleridge that colored the whole romantic movement in English literature: "the willing suspension of disbelief."

Some observations may be offered here as to various other mechanical aspects of brainstorming. The moderator just referred to has the duty of recognizing participants with ideas. He announces the subject or problem, and gives necessary background information upon it, answering questions if necessary. He may offer a few suggestive ideas or solutions, as pump-primers, at the beginning. He should also keep the ideation moving, with an occasional priming suggestion if needed, such as, "Who else could help?" "How could color be used?" or "Can this be combined with that in some way?" It is important that he recognize speakers only when they raise their hands. Otherwise the less self-assured are left out, or some ideas lost.

To another person will also usually be assigned the function of writing the ideas down, reportorially. Such a person should be quick-witted to catch them all rapidly, and it is best that he write the ideas where all can see them, as on a large flip-chart or blackboard. In practice with actual problems, it has been found productive of best results to announce the subject to participants some little time in advance—several days, perhaps—so they can be thinking about it.

The statement of the problem also demands considerable thought. Time spent on getting it exact, specific, and clear is usually rewarded by a more productive brainstorm. A good beginning for a Brainstorm question is, "How many ways can we think of to. . . ?"

A relaxed yet alert attitude in participants produces the best results, and Osborn employs various techniques to secure this attitude. Brainstorm sessions in Batten, Barton, Durstine, and Osborn usually take place after a luncheon. Often it is found best to break large questions into smaller ones so that about half an hour can be spent on each.

Sometimes the best ideas emerge after the participants have been going for some time, and are even slightly weary. Osborn theorizes that at the beginning they are skimming the familiar and superficial ideas off the surfaces of their minds, and that only after these are gone do the brains really get busy and begin to think creatively.

At least two operations follow the actual brainstorm session. These are of great importance.

One is the evaluation of ideas. Here the critical faculty, suspended before, comes into its own. The evaluation is usually done by others than the brainstormers, though the moderator often participates, if only to interpret some of the ideas.

Before the ideas can be evaluated, they often have to be categorized. Here the discovery of a new or missing category often leads to further ideas.

Still further ideas may also occur to one or more of the participants after the brainstorm session. These ideas are often as good as or better than the original ones. For this reason Osborn places great emphasis on this part of the "follow-up." Sometimes, also, a new brainstorm session may be held after the follow-up, categorization, and evaluation.

It will be observed that each of these rules embodies the "horse sense" of which Osborn speaks, no doubt because each is the result of trial and error, selection, elimination, and all that this implies—in other words, is based upon successful pragmatic experience.

Many other aspects of Osborn's techniques deserve comment. For instance, one realizes after some experience with brainstorming that many of the reasons ideas are never born, or—once born—quickly stifled, have nothing to do with the value of the ideas themselves. A cartoon which showed a conference leader addressing his group well illustrated an aspect of this. The leader says "Those opposed will signify by clearing out their desks, putting on their hats, and saying: 'I resign.' "

Osborn observed in the advertising business what is equally true elsewhere, that fear, jealousy, pride, timidity, and other emotions and attitudes discourage the conception of ideas.

One result of this understanding is that the person with the problem is almost never invited to sit in on its brainstorming. He already knows too many ways in which the thing cannot be done, and is likely to inhibit the ideas of others by word, gesture, or even silence, and at best to contribute little to the discussion. In Osborn's method, the person closest to the problem presents it as clearly and specifically as he can to the brainstorm group: then leaves the room before brainstorming actually starts.

Connected is the fact that many of us spend most of our entire days critically evaluating ideas and saying "no." Such ingrained habits and attitudes are very difficult to shake off, and are apt to carry over into brainstorming. For this reason executives and others whose critical judgment is their stock in trade may have the most difficulty using the Brainstorm technique, and sometimes succeed only imperfectly even after training and practice.

It will be observed also that Osborn's technique sets up what the psychiatrists call a "permissive situation." In psychiatry, the patient is encouraged to feel that he need fear no punishment—of which critical and especially adverse judgment is of course a type—no matter what he says.

In this way he is encouraged to discharge all his troubles, just as by similar means the brainstormer is encouraged to pour out all his ideas—good, bad, or indifferent. I believe that this element of what Aristotle would call *katharsis* is an important aspect of the satisfaction people find in brainstorming, and in its consequent success.

One may also observe a parallel with education, in which many a successful teacher finds—by experience or through instruction—that the best way to encourage success and happiness in students is to create in the classroom this permissive situation. Probably it is not necessary here again to refer to the derivation of the word "education."

In fact, many feel that the importance of brainstorming for business, where it originated, or for any problem-solving situation, will be less than its importance for education generally. Some who have tried it in business, perhaps with a good deal of skepticism, report, "There are many worthwhile by-products of brainstorming beyond new solutions arrived at. We were amazed at the new attitudes encouraged among our employees. Many of them have gained self confidence at having their ideas listened to with respect for the first time. They are more willing to advance new ideas. And those to whom the new ideas are advanced seem to have a more receptive and tolerant attitude not only toward the ideas, but toward those who submit them."

I submit that if by practice with this technique educators can stimulate in students more creative and original thought along with a greater sympathy and tolerance for the ideas of others, they will have achieved something of major importance—whether or not the students reach any final conclusive solutions in their Brainstorm sessions.

Structuring Communication in a Working Group

Peter Mears

**Theories of task-oriented group communication have been tested
mostly in the laboratory. Here is their application to
industrial management, with some surprising results**

An organization's effectiveness depends upon the performance of
numerous small groups which function and interact within the overall
organizational system. Because of this dependence, much emphasis has
been placed on studies of subgroups, their cultures, status, and group
needs, in an attempt to determine the factors which are most likely to encourage group effectiveness. Since the activity of a small group depends to
a great extent upon its information flow, the communications act has been
studied as a means of influencing efficiency. Thus, research on communication networks has become increasingly important and promises better
understanding of the functioning of organizations.

One major criticism of past work in communication networks has
been directed at its lack of applicability to a business organization; experiments have been conducted primarily in nonorganizational environments
with student subjects. This kind of experimentation has resulted in a number of constraints which must be recognized in applying or "forcing" such
findings to a practical application in a real business setting. The purpose
of this article is to overcome these constraints by briefly presenting the
major research findings regarding communication networks, and then to
apply these research findings to a business situation.

**A communication network is the interaction required by a group
to accomplish a task**

Working groups tend to be composed of four, five, or six people.
Two people are not normally considered in a group; in a group of three
there is a danger that two of the people will tend to "gang up" on the third
person; and seven or more people in close proximity tend to split up into
smaller, more manageable working units.

An organization may be composed of hundreds of such small working
groups. This group idea is built into current management philosophy and

Reprinted from "Structuring Communication In A Working Group" by Peter Mears
in the *Journal Of Communication*, Vol. 24:1, pp. 71-79. Copyright © 1974 by The
Annenberg School of Communication.

is perhaps due to the notion that the managerial process involves the subdivision of brains as well as of labor. It is only natural for a business to try to increase the efficiency of these groups, and since the predominant activity of any group depends on the information flow, communications is one area in which the group may be made more efficient.

Three major types of small-group communication networks are shown in Figure 1. These are the circle, wheel, and chain networks. Each circle represents an individual in a working group, and the solid line connects the individual with the other members of the group he or she normally interacts with in performing a task.

Bavelas and Barrett performed some of the initial research on the effects of different communication networks. This work is summarized in Table 1.

Table 1
Performance of the Circle, Chain, and Wheel Communication Networks

	Circle	Chain	Wheel
SPEED	slow	fast	fast
ACCURACY	poor	good	good
ORGANIZATION	no stable form	slowly emerging but stable organization	almost immediate and stable organization
EMERGENCE OF LEADERSHIP	none	marked	very pronounced
MORALE	very good	poor	very poor

In the circle network an individual will normally converse with the person on his right or left, but not with any other members of the group. In the free circle group, all members converse frequently and equally with all other members of the group.

Appearances in these networks are deceptive. The wheel network on the left in Figure 1 is popularly referred to as an autocratic situation, and the wheel network on the right would be called a typical organizational setup. Both networks are the same; the only difference lies in the arrangement of the circles on the paper. The distinguishing characteristic of the wheel network is that the members do not normally communicate with one another. They interact with the hub of the wheel, the leader of the group.

The chain network has all the appearances of an organizational chain-of-command: A reports to B, who reports to C, and so on. In actual practice this network may appear within a working group whose members are all at the same organizational level or rank. The two end positions might be occupied by people who tend to be introverted and prefer normally to communicate with only one person. In the three middle positions, the normal interactions may be determined primarily by friendship.

This case study involves individuals interacting to solve a complex problem

The individuals are Systems and Procedure personnel who represent specific divisions in a large aerospace firm. Each of the representatives

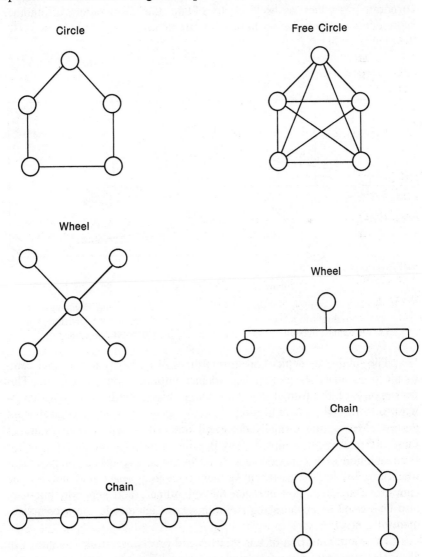

Figure 1. Communication networks

is in charge of a small, highly skilled, semitechnical group which develops unique systems and procedures for each of the firm's respective divisions (see Figure 2). It is the function of the division representative from "A" to coordinate the systems and procedures among divisions for consistency. To do this, A set up the working group of representatives whose communication structure is depicted in Figure 2. These division representatives communicate with each other in the interpretation and implementation of corporate directives as well as to obtain the cooperation of another representative to resolve an impending problem.

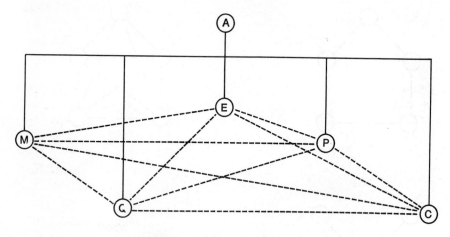

Figure 2. The initial organization

A	Administration Division	E	Engineering Division
M	Manufacturing Division	P	Procurement Division
Q	Quality Division	C	Contract Division

The solid lines depict both formal lines of authority and formal communication, while the dotted lines depict informal communication. This overlapping of the formal communication channel with an extensive network of informal communication channels occurs in many technical work groups. Mr. A, the formally delegated authority, may be well aware of these informal relationships as they pertain to the job, but interaction for the resolution of a common task is an accepted practice in management literature. In fact, the participative management approach may not only be viewed as an interaction between the subordinate and superior, but may also be viewed as encouraging subordinates to interact in the accomplishment of a task.

The communication of this systems and procedure group, as shown in Figure 2, was primarily a free circle network. Everyone in the group was free to utilize whatever channels of communication he desired, with the result that most of the group's time was spent in discussion, and very little work was accomplished. The morale of the group was very high; the only point of conflict occurred when a member felt obligated to agree with something he opposed in order that group consensus could be achieved. This result is consistent with the findings of Festinger, who states that "pressures toward uniformity may exist within a group; these pressures act toward making members of a group agree concerning some issue, or conform with respect to some behavior pattern." (8)

Each person's advice was appreciated and carefully evaluated. Because the individual group member was able to make a contribution on a complex issue, his involvement was high and there was a feeling of pride in his accomplishments. This fact is consistent with the findings of Shaw, who discovered that "morale is higher with greater independence because independence permits the gratification of the culturally supported needs for autonomy, recognition and achievement." (19)

Bales (1), Etzioni (7), and Davis (6) point out that in most groups, in addition to a formal leader, an informal leader, more commonly called the social leader, tends to emerge. The social leader restores and maintains group unity and satisfaction. In the group I am describing, the Contract division representative filled that role. This result may not be consistent with the findings of Kahn and Katz when they say that "pride or involvement in the work group and productivity are interacting variables and that an increase in one tends to bring about an increase in the other." (12) This was only true to a very limited point: in the Systems and Procedure group, because of the lack of specific channels of communication, too much time was spent in discussion and useless debate.

After several months the division representatives accomplished almost nothing. Management stepped in and disbanded the meetings

The group was reorganized by management as a wheel network. The new organization is shown in Figure 3. The change from an unrestricted network, the free circle, to a restricted network, the wheel, was essentially a change from a democratically-run group to an autocratically-run group. Under the free circle network, lengthy arguments and discussions sometimes extended well into the evenings after the formal group leader had left. Under the wheel network, in order to force all information to come through the wheel hub (the Administration representative), management issued a directive stating that any communication concerning procedures outside the individual's division was to be conducted only by the Administration division. This directive was ignored until one of the representatives was severely reprimanded for reaching an agreement with the Manufacturing representative without the concurrence of the Administration representative. After the reprimand, the group again became ineffective. Every representative lived up to the absolute letter of the directive. No opinion was voiced unless asked for, and then only the exact question asked would be answered.

Since only the representatives were competent to answer detailed questions about their divisions, information had to be relayed by the Ad-

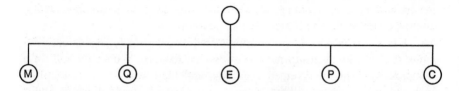

Figure 3. A wheel network

ministration division to each representative. Since each representative would protect his own interest by commenting only on what affected him, the number of errors grew astronomically. The same job would be redone several times; if it did not exactly suit the divisional representative's interests, it would be vetoed. A virtual boycott of any new system developed.

For all practical purposes, the installation of a wheel (autocratic) network decreased output

At first glance, this conclusion might seem inconsistent with the available literature. Bavelas and Barrett (2), Leavitt (15), and Guetzkow (11) quantitatively show the wheel as the fastest network for problem solution. Considering that their common conclusion was based on an experiment in which the participants had only to detect a missing symbol, their conclusion was justified. The actual solution of an industrial problem, however, may be very complex and quite often is based not purely on available facts but on a mixture of the facts available plus past experience on similar problems.

Mulder (17) indicates that the important element in group interactions may be the emergence of a decision structure. The decision structure determines the pattern of suggestion acceptance from one member to another. A change in the formal structure may disrupt the decision structure of the group, thus resulting in a loss of group efficiency.

When our group operated in a free circle network, what hurt efficiency was not the morale of the group, which was excellent, but the overabundance of communication channels available to each member. Shaw (19) would have stated that the saturation level of the individual was reached, that the total requirements placed on an individual in a network were excessive.

With the wheel network, the saturation level again accounted for the decrease in efficiency. The task was complex, and the individuals refused to accept the dictates of the central person without sufficient information. This forced the central person to handle more and more messages until he could do only one of two things: either state that he could not handle the job, or try to circumvent the group entirely by pointing out to management that the group was uncooperative. He took the second course.

Changing from democratic leadership to autocratic leadership had a disruptive effect on the group. People have a natural tendency to automatically develop a system for performing a task. Not having to think about how to go about doing a job reduces the uncertainty associated with the task; when people find themselves in a condition in which they again cannot automatically perform the required tasks, they center their attention on developing a system to accomplish the task. The wheel network demands an autocratic system, because its members cannot collectively interact, and the leader (hub) represents something that has introduced uncertainty. It is only natural that this uncertainty will be met with

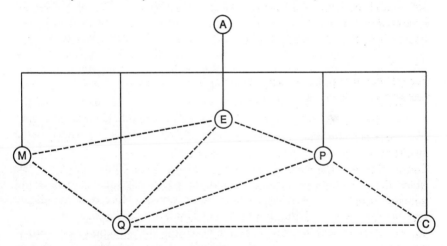

Figure 4. Modified circle network

hostility by workers who are accustomed to a more participative system.

Cohen and Bennis (5) hold the same viewpoint, and Lawson (13) points out that this knowledge holds a strong implication for training. If during a training period a group network is changed, then the individual's learning process will be disrupted; he will first concentrate on learning the new network and, after mastery, will then concentrate on the job.

After the disastrous effect of introducing a wheel network in the technical group, management recognized its error and carefully studied the interactions required by each group member. The Manufacturing division representative needed to communicate with Engineering and Quality division representatives. Analogously, since hardware under construction was ordered to Engineering specifications, problems with procured hardware should be discussed by Engineering and Procurement representatives. The addition of the Manufacturing representative would serve no useful purpose and would tend to slow the group down.

Each group member was requested to communicate only with the other members directly involved in the pertinent decision

As a result of this new communication restriction, the "A" division was relieved of having to make all decisions (as under the wheel network), and the other divisions did not waste time when decisions did not concern them (as under the free circle network). Figure 4 shows the communication patterns in this revised group organization.

The new system, in the long run, increased productivity and morale of the affected parties. But, just after the change in structure, there was a decrease in efficiency in the short run. The Contract members and the Procurement members had the lowest work load. Under the autocratic leadership their group morale had declined, and they had centered their attention on the problems internal to their own divisions. When the new network came into existence, they had to relearn the system, and it took several months for the members to obtain the satisfaction they had previously enjoyed under the free circle network. (In fact, they never fully reached the same high level of satisfaction.) Lawson (13) experienced the same conditions of disruptiveness, then increased efficiency and higher morale, when groups were changed from the more restrictive wheel to the freer circle.

In the business world, communication networks tend to be combinations of the prototypes depicted in Figure 1. Management should avoid getting too close to one of these extremes, or it may be forced to change the networks and create disruption and inefficiency in the work group.

Communication networks are not a theoretical abstraction from reality. The formal group is aware of the existence of the networks—informal as well as formal—and usually feels it must delegate the type of network in the interests of maximum efficiency. This may well be a desired practice, but network delegation must be done with respect to the complexity of the task, the desired morale, the desired efficiency, and the impact of the change. Omission of any of these factors from consideration will result in a network detrimental to the organization.

References

1. Bales, Robert F. "In Conference." *Harvard Business Review,* March-April 1954, pp. 44-50.
2. Bavelas, Alex, and Dermot Barrett. "An Experimental Approach to Organizational Communication," *Personnel* 27 (March 1951), 366-71.

3. Bello, Francis. "The Information Theory." *Fortune* 48 (December 1953), 137.
4. Blair, Elenn Myers, R. Stewart Jones, and Raymond H. Simpson. *Educational Psychology*, 3rd ed. New York: The Macmillan Company, 1965.
5. Cohen, Arthur M., and Warren G. Bennis. "Continuity of Leadership in Communication Networks." *Human Relations*, 1959, pp. 359-65.
6. Davis, Keith. *Human Relations at Work: The Dynamics of Organizational Behavior*, 3d ed. New York: McGraw-Hill, 1967.
7. Etzioni, Amitai. "Dual Leadership in Complex Organizations." *American Sociological Review*, October 1965, pp. 688-98.
8. Festinger, Leon. "Informal Social Communication," *Psychological Review* 57 (1950), 271-82.
9. Guetzkow, Harold. "Differentiation of Roles in Task-Oriented Groups." *Group Dynamics: Research and Theory*, 2d ed., edited by Doran Cartwright and Allen Zander. Evanston, Illinois: Row, Peterson & Company, 1960.
10. Guetzkow, Harold, and William R. Dill. "Factors in the Organizational Development of Task-oriented Groups." *Sociometry* 20 (1957), 175-204.
11. Guetzknow, Harold, and Herbert A. Simon. "The Impact of Certain Communication Networks upon Organization and Performance in Task-oriented Groups." *Management Science* 1 (1955), 233-50.
12. Kahn, Robert L., and Daniel Katz. "Leadership Practices in Relation to Productivity and Morale." In *Group Dynamics:* Research and Theory, 2d ed., edited by Doran Cartwright and Allen Zander. Evanston, Illinois: Row, Peterson & Company, 1960.
13. Lawson, Edwin D. "Changes in Communication Networks, Performance and Morale." *Human Relations*, May 1965, pp. 139-47.
14. Leavitt, Harold J. "Small Groups in Large Organizations." The *Journal of Business* 28-29 (January 1955), 8-17.
15. Leavitt, Harold J. "Some Effects of Certain Communication Patterns on Group Performance," *Journal of Abnormal Social Psychology*, 46 (1951), 38-50.
16. Lyle, Jack. "Communication, Group Atmosphere, Productivity, and Morale in Small Task-Groups." *Human Relations*, 1960, pp. 369-79.
17. Mulder, Mauk. *Group Structure, Motivation and Group Performance*. The Hague: Mouton & Co., 1963.
18. Rothschild, Gerard H., and Marvin E. Shaw. "Some Effects of Prolonged Experiences in Communication Nets." *Journal of Applied Psychology*, October 1956, 281-86.
19. Shaw, Marvin E. "Communication Networks." In *Advances in Experimental Social Psychology*, edited by Leonard Berkowitz. New York: Academic Press, 1964.
20. Shaw, Marvin E. "Some Effects of Problem Complexity upon Problem Solution Efficiency in Different Communication Nets." *Journal of Experimental Psychology* 48 (1954), 211-17.
21. Thayer, Lee O. *Administrative Communication*. Homewood, Illinois: Richard D. Irwin, 1961.
22. "The Number One Problem." *Personnel Journal* 45 (April 1965), 237-38.

The Effects of Task
Performance on Cohesiveness

James H. Davis

. . . For those tasks that permit feedback on progress, cohesiveness may produce a cyclic effect. It is often said about real-life groups that there is nothing like success to increase morale or group spirit. A near universal finding is that cohesiveness generally increases with success.

That success has the effect of increasing cohesiveness is illustrated in a famous study by Sherif and Sherif (1953), in which boys at a summer camp were first permitted to form freely in informal groups as they became acquainted. Subsequently they were placed in groups in which their friends (as revealed by earlier questionnaires) constituted only about one-third of the membership. At the end of five days, during which each group shared many pleasant experiences, a second questionnaire revealed that the friendship patterns had shifted so as to reflect the membership of the final group, and that these groups were highly cohesive. Cohesiveness could, in theory, thus be manipulated by a careful scheduling of success-failure experiences. In general, task failure or imperfect goal attainment tends to lower cohesiveness and thus break the performance-cohesiveness cycle (or perhaps initiate a reverse failure-low cohesiveness cycle).

Even the *method of attack* on the task can be a source of disagreement that lowers the level of interpersonal attraction. For example, when disagreement exists about the best means of constructing a solution to a problem, the result is a lowering of cohesiveness (Raven and Rietsema, 1957; French, 1941), sometimes to the point where members leave before a final product is proposed at all.

Interestingly enough, there are instances in which task failure does not result in a lowering of cohesiveness, but on the contrary may even result in its *increase*. One important case is that in which group failure can be attributed to an external threat or malevolent agency. In such cases group failure may be a special boon for flagging interest in the group. There are other exceptions as well (see Festinger, Riecken, and Schachter, 1956), but we shall not consider their peculiar significance at this time.

Another concept that has been considered rather similar to cohesiveness, in that it likewise focuses on the nature of the interdependence among group members, is that of cooperation-competition. This topic, to which we now turn, has a particular appeal in our culture.

Davis, *Group Performance,* © 1969, Addison-Wesley, Reading, Massachusetts.

Cooperation and Competition

Intergroup competition generally tends to increase cohesiveness within a group, while *intragroup* competition tends to decrease it. Deutsch (1968) has in fact demonstrated, both theoretically and empirically, that group members who are cooperatively interdependent in the service of some task tend to be friendlier and mutually more influential, and otherwise give evidence of higher cohesiveness, than do similar groups acting in a competitive manner.

We might ask at this point just what it is that affects or controls the emergence of a cooperative, as opposed to a competitive, style of interaction. Because of practical implications, the question is often given the form: "Which is superior in terms of performance—cooperation or competition?" This question is, of course, naive in much the same way as the question about individual or group superiority considered earlier. One may well choose to compete with others because he dislikes them, desires to appear in a certain light, or is responding to motives unconnected with the immediate task and interaction sequence. We should not forget that cooperation, like cohesiveness, is more accurately described as the name of a *class* of phenomena. Many behaviors are cooperative in one setting, but meaningless in another.

Most of our discussion about group performance has carried, at least implicitly, the assumption of a cooperative group. Any competitive behavior that arose was more a function of "interaction accidents" than of instructions from an experimenter or demands of the task. Aside from these interpersonal variables, there are, however, conditions associated with the task that foster cooperative or competitive behavior.

Let us consider the question of payoff or feedback associated with the quality of performance. If the task permits individual contributions to be recovered or graded in the final group product, then *individual members* may be selectively rewarded accordingly. Alternatively, the group may be paid off *as a whole*. The result, not very surprisingly, is that cooperative behavior is usually evident in the latter kind of group, while a competitive interaction style typically characterizes the former sort of group. Deutsch (1949) used these two kinds of payoff as a means of creating internally cooperative and competitive small groups that were required, over the course of several weeks, to work at a sequence of human relations problems and logical puzzles. He found a higher degree of productivity in cooperative groups: higher output of puzzle solutions per unit of time and a higher quality of proposals for the human relations problems. This performance elevation was apparently achieved by means of pressures toward productive work in the cooperative groups; these groups coordinated the division of labor and achieved better communication among members in order to utilize available resources. Observers also judged cooperative groups to invest more effort in maintenance, strengthening, or regulation of the group. Such pressures to attend to group-centered activities had the effect not only of increasing cohesiveness, but also of keeping the group functioning smoothly and productively.

The performance virtues of cooperative functioning, evident from this study, do not apply to all settings and tasks. The Deutsch investigation was centered at the group level, and some tasks, as we know from earlier sections on individual-group comparisons, are more efficiently attacked by isolated individuals. Competition, if not overwhelming, may actually foster helpful isolation while keeping motivation at a suitably high level; in this case the effects of cooperation and competition as described above might be reversed.

The possible variations on the cooperation-competition paradigm are numerous, especially if the many qualifying variables are taken into account. But we can see from Deutsch's account some of the ways in which cooperation affects interaction and ultimately group performance.

A second kind of task-group format in which the structure of the task and the accompanying social structure combine to intensify the interpersonal confrontation is illustrated by *bargaining situations*. Cooperation effects, like so many other interaction variables, are frequently difficult to study in a precise way at the level of four- or five-person groups. By focusing on a task that is cast as a game between two or more players (or between two or more teams), a more detailed study of mutual conflict and the manner of its resolution (cooperation, competition, withdrawal, etc.) is possible.

We shall not consider further these interdependence problems, but shall instead direct the reader to Gergen's (1969) thorough discussion of such behavior-exchange situations.

The final group-level concept that we shall consider is that of *norm*. Few concepts in social psychology have figured more prominently in explanations of collective behavior than has the idea of a social norm. It is thus somewhat surprising that it has so infrequently been treated directly as an independent or dependent variable in experimental studies of group performance. In its most general sense, a norm is a standard against which the appropriateness of a behavior is to be judged. Some norms are pervasive, in that they are widely shared by the bulk of the members of a culture; others are local, in the sense that they apply specifically to the members of a particular group.

Norms vary in a number of respects. Some norms (perhaps most) apply to overt behavior, while others seem to guide subjective states when the individual is faced with uncertainty. Some norms are formal, in that they are written or otherwise conspicuously and intentionally adopted by a group (rules or operating procedures). On the other hand, many norms are informal in their origin; they arise from the interaction of the group members over time. Working norms emerging in this way may even occasionally be in conflict with the formal group norms which ostensibly govern behavior in some particular case. Informal norms are not necessarily equally evident to all group members; but in most small groups that have existed for a time, there is little likelihood that norm violations occur frequently without the awareness of most of the members.

It is generally thought that long-term groups are more likely to display distinct norms than are the short-term groups typical of laboratory experiments on group performance. This is probably true, but some group norms have their origin less in the immediate performance-oriented interaction than in some *value*—a basic belief or assumption about what is good, right, or proper. The norm in this sense is a kind of "logical" consequence of a value that is shared by the members of an *ad hoc* group, who after all come from a common culture.

However, there is reason to believe that group norms do arise over a rather short time period. But just how rapidly and under what conditions do norms form—norms that are strong enough to guide behavior to a significant degree? This is a question that remains to be systematically explored. Most of the available experimental evidence on the way norms function in social behavior comes from studies of social conformity and interpersonal influence, where norms obviously play an important role (see Kiesler and Kiesler, 1969). We shall at this point consider only one line of evidence on the rapid evolution of a norm and its effects on individual performance—namely, the evidence concerning judgment tasks.

Sherif (1936) set out to determine whether, and how, a set of individuals would develop a common standard when faced with a judgment task that precluded the easy use of external, physical standards. The task made use of the *autokinetic effect,* which was known even before the rise of experimental psychology. A stationary point of light in a suitably darkened room appears to move, and a subject unaware of the actual physical situation is easily induced to estimate the extent of this movement. Sherif required some subjects to judge the distance the light moved while they were alone in the room, and others to do likewise in the presence of other judges (i.e., in a group). In some cases the individual subjects had judged in a group situation prior to performing alone; other subjects were inexperienced. Sherif found that the inexperienced individuals soon developed a reference point about which the light seemed to range in a consistent manner, and that this norm was peculiar to the individual subject, persisting without much change over time. When subjects who had established their personal norms in this way were grouped, and then continued to make judgments in each other's presence, the previously established standards began to converge. The convergence took place without any related conversation or formal decision by the group as to how the members should judge the movement. The experimental paradigm is thus the same as that for the coaction studies we discussed earlier, but in this case the nature of the coactor's performance is especially evident to the others.

When subjects made their first judgments in the presence of a group, Sherif found the convergence to a collective norm to be even more rapid. Moreover, the group norm was pervasive in individual judgments. When subjects with experience in a group subsequently made a series of judgments alone, the *group* norm was "carried along," for the new judgments by individuals complied with the norms of the previous membership group.

We shall not explore the many interesting properties of norms, but rather concentrate on the implications for performance. The focus of the norm is either (a) *direct,* in that group output (quality, rate, etc.) is itself regulated by the norm, or (b) *indirect,* in that interpersonal behavior is generally affected and task performance is derivatively dependent on that interaction. In either case, there are two major components of a norm whereby the regulatory function is carried out: (a) the *behavioral expectation or point of maximum appropriateness* along the behavioral continuum; and (b) the *limits of tolerable deviations* about this expectation. When the behavior to which the norm is applicable deviates "too far" in any direction, the deviant may expect negative sanctions (rejections, penalties, or disapproval). Although sometimes there may be *distinct* limits, as with formal norms, in practice it would seem that the deviations about the expected behavior are increasingly likely to incur some expression of group displeasure as they become more extreme. The severity of the negative sanctions may even be roughly proportional to the size of the deviation. Conversely, behaviors along the continuum that approach the expectation are increasingly likely to receive positive sanctions such as praise and other expressions of approval, although both negative and positive sanctions are in many cases quite subtle.

SUGGESTED READINGS

Chapter 3

Agyris, Chris. *Interpersonal Competence and Organization Effectiveness.* Homewood, Ill.: Dorsey Press, 1962.

Bavelos, Alex. "Communication Patterns in Task-oriented Groups." *Journal of the Acoustical Society of America,* 22 (1950): 725-30.

Bayless, Ovid. "An Alternative Pattern for Problem-Solving Discussion," *Journal of Communication,* 17 (1967), 188-197.

Baird, J. "A Comparison of Distributional and Sequential Structure in Cooperative and Competitive Group Discussions," *Speech Monographs* 41 (1974): 226-32.

Bales, R., and Slater, P. "Role Differentiation in Small Decision-Making Groups." In *The Family, Socialization, and Interaction Process,* eds. T. Parson, R. Bales, and P. Slater. New York: Free Press, 1955.

Bormann, Ernest G. *Discussion and Group Methods.* Second edition. New York: Harper & Row, 1975.

Brilhart, John K. and Jochem, Laurene M. "The Effects of Different Patterns on Outcomes of Problem-Solving Discussions." *Journal of Applied Psychology,* XXXI (June, 1964): 124-27.

Delbecq, A. L., *et. al. Group Techniques for Program Planning: A Guide to Normal and Delphi Processes.* Glenview, Ill.: Scott, Foresman and Co., 1975.

Fisher, B. A. "Decision Emergence: Phases in Group Decision-Making." *Speech Monographs,* 37 (1970): 53-66.

Fisher, B. *Small Group Decision Making: Communication and the Group Process.* New York: McGraw-Hill Book Co., 1974.

Gouran, Dennis S. *Discussion: The Process of Group Decision-Making.* New York: Harper & Row, 1974.

Gouran, D., and Baird, J. "An Analysis of Distributional and Sequential Structure in Problem-Solving and Informal Group Discussions," *Speech Monographs* 39 (1972): 16-22.

Jandt, F. E., ed. *Conflict Resolution Through Communication.* New York: Harper & Row, 1973.

Kaplan, M. F. and Schwartz, S., eds. *Human Judgment and Decision Processes.* New York: Academic Press, Inc., 1975.

Kindler, Herbert S. *Organizing the Technical Conference.* New York: Reinhold, 1960.

Larson, Carl. "Forms of Analysis and Small Group Problem Solving," *Speech Monographs,* 36 (1969), 452-55.

Mabry, Edward A. "Exploratory Analysis of a Developmental Model for Task-oriented Small Groups," *Human Communication Research,* 2 (Fall 1975), 66-74.

Maier, Norman R. F. *Problem Solving and Creativity: In Individuals and Groups.* Belmont, Calif.: Brooks/Cole Publishing Company, 1970.

Mausner, B. "The Effect of One Partner's Success in a Relevant Task on the Interaction of Observer Pairs," *Journal of Abnormal and Social Psychology* 49 (1954): 557-60.

Osborne, A. F. *Applied Imagination.* New York: Scribner, 1957.

Patton, Bobby R. and Griffin, Kim. *Problem-Solving Group Interaction.* New York: Harper & Row, Publishers, 1973.

Phillips, Gerald M. " 'PERT' as a Logical Adjunct to Group Process," *The Journal of Communication,* 15 (June, 1965): 89-99.

Robbins, R. "Brainstorming Re-Evaluated," *Journal of Communication* 10 (1960): 152.

Rubenstein, M. F. *Patterns of Problem Solving.* Englewood Cliffs, N.J.: Prentice-Hall, 1975.

Schoner, B., Rose, G. and Hoyt, G. "Quality of Decisions: Individuals Versus Real and Synthetic Groups," *Journal of Applied Psychology* 59 (1974): 424-32.

Shaw, Marvin E. "Communication Networks." In *Advances in Experimental Social Psychology,* edited by Leonard Berkowitz. New York: Academic Press, 1964.

Steiner, I. D. *Group Process and Productivity.* New York: Academic Press, 1972.

Wickelgren, W. A. *Howk to Solve Problems: Elements of a Theory of Problems and Problem Solving.* San Francisco: W. H. Freeman, 1974.

Growth Groups

The Process of the Basic Encounter Group

Carl R. Rogers

. . . I should like briefly to describe the many different forms and different labels under which the intensive group experience has become a part of our modern life. It has involved different kinds of individuals, and it has spawned various theories to account for its effects.

As to labels, the intensive group experience has at times been called the *T-group* or *lab group,* "T" standing for training laboratory in group dynamics. It has been termed *sensitivity training* in human relationships. The experience has sometimes been called a *basic encounter group* or a *workshop* —a workshop in human relationships, in leadership, in counseling, in education, in research, in psychotherapy. In dealing with one particular type of person—the drug addict—it has been called a *synanon.*

The intensive group experience has functioned in various settings. It has operated in industries, in universities, in church groups, and in resort settings which provide a retreat from everyday life. It has functioned in various educational institutions and in penitentiaries. . . .

The Group Process

As I consider the terribly complex interactions which arise during twenty, forty, sixty, or more hours of intensive sessions, I believe that I see some threads which weave in and out of the pattern. Some of these trends or tendencies are likely to appear early and some later in the group sessions, but there is no clear-cut sequence in which one ends and another begins. The interaction is best thought of, I believe, as a varied tapestry, differing from group to group, yet with certain kinds of trends evident in most of these intensive encounters and with certain patterns tending to precede and others to follow. Here are some of the process patterns which I see developing, briefly described in simple terms, illustrated from tape recordings and personal reports, and presented in roughly sequential order. I am not aiming at a high-level theory of group process but rather at a naturalistic observation out of which, I hope, true theory can be built.[1]

Milling Around

As the leader or facilitator makes clear at the outset that this is a group with unusual freedom, that it is not one for which he will take directional responsibility, there tends to develop a period of initial confusion, awkward silence, polite surface interaction, "cocktail-party talk," frustration, and great lack of continuity. The individuals come face-to-face with the fact that "there is no structure here except what we provide. We do not know our purposes; we do not even know one another, and we are committed to remain together over a considerable period of time." In this situation, confusion and frustration are natural. Particularly striking to the observer is the lack of continuity between personal expressions. Individual A will present some proposal or concern, clearly looking for a response from the group. Individual B has obviously been waiting for his turn and starts off on some completely different tangent as though he had never heard A. One member makes a simple suggestion such as, "I think we should introduce ourselves," and this may lead to several hours of highly involved discussion in which the underlying issues appear to be, "Who is the leader?" "Who is responsible for us?" "Who is a member of the group?" "What is the purpose of the group?"

---

1. Jack and Lorraine Gibb have long been working on an analysis of trust development as the essential theory of group process. Others who have contributed significantly to the theory of group process are Chris Argyris, Kenneth Benne, Warren Bennis, Dorwin Cartwright, Matthew Miles, and Robert Blake. Samples of the thinking of all these and others may be found in three recent books: Bradford, Gibb & Benne (1964): Bennis, Benne, & Chin (1961): and Bennis, Schein, Berlew & Steele (1964). Thus, there are many promising leads for theory construction involving a considerable degree of abstraction. This chapter has a more elementary aim—a naturalistic descriptive account of the process.

Resistance to Personal Expression or Exploration

During the milling period, some individuals are likely to reveal some rather personal attitudes. This tends to foster a very ambivalent reaction among other members of the group. One member, writing of his experience, says:

> There is a self which I present to the world and another one which I know more intimately. With others I try to appear able, knowing, un-ruffled, problem-free. To substantiate this image I will act in a way which at the time or later seems false or artificial or "not the real me." Or I will keep to myself thoughts which if expressed would reveal an imperfect me.
>
> My inner self, by contrast with the image I present to the world, is characterized by many doubts. The worth I attach to this inner self is subject to much fluctuation and is very dependent on how others are reacting to me. At times this private self can feel worthless.

It is the public self which members tend to reveal to one another, and only gradually, fearfully, and ambivalently do they take steps to reveal something of their inner world.

Early in one intensive workshop, the members were asked to write anonymously a statement of some feeling or feelings which they had which they were not willing to tell in the group. One man wrote:

> I don't relate easily to people. I have an almost impenetrable facade. Nothing gets in to hurt me, but nothing gets out. I have repressed so many emotions that I am close to emotional sterility. This situation doesn't make me happy, but I don't know what to do about it.

This individual is clearly living inside a private dungeon, but he does not even dare, except in this disguised fashion, to send out a call for help. . . .

Description of Past Feelings

In spite of ambivalence about the trustworthiness of the group and the risk of exposing oneself, expression of feelings does begin to assume a larger proportion of the discussion. The executive tells how frustrated he feels by certain situations in his industry, or the housewife relates problems she has experienced with her children. A tape-recorded exchange involving a Roman Catholic nun occurs early in a one-week workshop, when the discussion has turned to a rather intellectualized consideration of anger:

> *Bill:* What happens when you get mad, Sister, or don't you?
> *Sister:* Yes, I do—yes I do. And I find when I get mad, I, I almost get, well, the kind of person that antagonizes me is the person who seems so unfeeling toward people—now I take our dean as a per-

son in point because she is a very aggressive woman and has certain ideas about what the various rules in a college should be; and this woman can just send me into a high "G"; in an angry mood. *I mean this.* But then I find, I. . . .

Facil.:[2] But what, what do you do?

Sister: I find that when I'm in a situation like this, that I strike out in a very sharp, uh, *tone,* or else I just refuse to respond—"All right, this happens to be her way"—I don't think I've ever gone into a tantrum.

Joe: You just withdraw—no use to fight it.

Facil.: You say you use a sharp tone. To *her,* or to other people you're dealing with?

Sister: Oh, no. To *her.*

This is a typical example of a *description* of feelings which are obviously current in her in a sense but which she is placing in the past and which she describes as being outside the group in time and place. It is an example of feelings existing "there and then."

Expression of Negative Feelings

Curiously enough, the first expression of genuinely significant "here-and-now" feeling is apt to come out in negative attitudes toward other group members or toward the group leader. In one group in which members introduced themselves at some length, one woman refused, saying that she preferred to be known for what she was in the group and not in terms of her status outside. Very shortly after this, one of the men in the group attacked her vigorously and angrily for this stand, accusing her of failing to cooperate, of keeping herself aloof from the group, and so forth. It was the first *personal current feeling* which had been brought into the open in the group.

Frequently the leader is attacked for his failure to give proper guidance to the group. One vivid example of this comes from a recorded account of an early session with a group of delinquents, where one member shouts at the leader (Gordon, 1955, p. 214):

> You will be licked if you don't control us right at the start. You have to keep order here because you are older than us. That's what a teacher is supposed to do. If he doesn't do it we will cause a lot of trouble and won't get anything done. [Then, referring to two boys in the group who were scuffling, he continues.] Throw 'em out, throw 'em out! You've just *got* to make us behave! . . .

Why are negatively toned expressions the first current feelings to be expressed? Some speculative answers might be the following: This is one of

---

the best ways to test the freedom and trustworthiness of the group. "Is it really a place where I can be and express myself positively and negatively? Is this really a safe place, or will I be punished?" Another quite different reason is that deeply positive feelings are much more difficult and dangerous to express than negative ones. "If I say, 'I love you,' I am vulnerable and open to the most awful rejection. If I say, 'I hate you,' I am at best liable to attack, against which I can defend." Whatever the reasons, such negatively toned feelings tend to be the first here-and-now material to appear.

Expression and Exploration of Personally Meaningful Material

It may seem puzzling that following such negative experiences as the initial confusion, the resistance to personal expression, the focus on outside events, and the voicing of critical or angry feelings, the event most likely to occur next is for an individual to reveal himself to the group in a significant way. The reason for this no doubt is that the individual member has come to realize that this is in part *his group*. He can help to make of it what he wishes. He has also experienced the fact that negative feelings have been expressed and have usually been accepted or assimilated without any catastrophic results. He realizes there is freedom here, albeit a risky freedom. A climate of trust is beginning to develop. So he begins to take the chance and gamble of letting the group know some deeper facet of himself. One man tells of the trap in which he finds himself, feeling that communication between himself and his wife is hopeless. A priest tells of the anger which he has bottled up because of unreasonable treatment by one of his superiors. What should he have done? What might he do now? A scientist at the head of a large research department finds the courage to speak of his painful isolation, to tell the group that he has never had a single friend in his life. By the time he finishes telling of his situation he is letting loose some of the tears of sorrow for himself which I am sure he has held in for many years. A psychiatrist tells of the guilt he feels because of the suicide of one of his patients. A woman of forty tells of her absolute inability to free herself from the grip of her controlling mother. A process which one workshop member has called a "journey to the center of self," often a very painful process, has begun. . . .

The Expression of Immediate Interpersonal Feelings in the Group

Entering into the process sometimes earlier, sometimes later, is the explicit bringing into the open of the feelings experienced in the immediate moment by one member about another. These are sometimes positive and sometimes negative. Examples would be: "I feel threatened by your silence." "You remind me of my mother, with whom I had a tough time." "I took an instant dislike to you the first moment I saw you." "To me you're like a breath of fresh air in the group." "I like your warmth and your smile." "I dislike you more every time you speak up." Each of these attitudes can be, and usually is, explored in the increasing climate of trust.

The Development of a Healing Capacity in the Group

One of the most fascinating aspects of any intensive group experience is the manner in which a number of the group members show a natural and spontaneous capacity for dealing in a helpful, facilitative, and therapeutic fashion with the pain and suffering of others. As one rather extreme example of this, I think of a man in charge of maintenance in a large plant who was one of the low-status members of an industrial executive group. As he informed us, he had not been "contaminated by education." In the initial phases the group tended to look down on him. As members delved more deeply into themselves and began to express their own attitudes more fully, this man came forth as, without doubt, the most sensitive member of the group. He knew intuitively how to be understanding and acceptant. He was alert to things which had not yet been expressed but which were just below the surface. When the rest of us were paying attention to a member who was speaking, he would frequently spot another individual who was suffering silently and in need of help. He had a deeply perceptive and facilitating attitude. This kind of ability shows up so commonly in groups that it has led me to feel that the ability to be healing or therapeutic is far more common in human life than we might suppose. Often it needs only the permission granted by a freely flowing group experience to become evident. . . .

Self-acceptance and the Beginning of Change

Many people feel that self-acceptance must stand in the way of change. Actually, in these group experiences, as in psychotherapy, it is the *beginning* of change. Some examples of the kind of attitudes expressed would be these: "I *am* a dominating person who likes to control others. I do want to mold these individuals into the proper shape." Another person says, "I really have a hurt and overburdened little boy inside of me who feels very sorry for himself. I *am* that little boy, in addition to being a competent and responsible manager." . . .

In another group one man kept a diary of his reactions. Here is his account of an experience in which he came really to accept his almost abject desire for love, a self-acceptance which marked the beginning of a very significant experience of change. He says (Hall, 1965):

> During the break between the third and fourth sessions, I felt very droopy and tired. I had it in mind to take a nap, but instead I was almost compulsively going around to people starting a conversation. I had a begging kind of a feeling, like a very cowed little puppy hoping that he'll be patted but half afraid he'll be kicked. Finally, back in my room I lay down and began to know that I was sad. Several times I found myself wishing my roommate would come in and talk to me. Or, whenever someone walked by the door, I would come to attention inside, the way a dog pricks up his ears; and I would feel an immediate wish for that person to come in and talk to me. I realized my raw wish to receive kindness.

. . . Still another person reporting shortly after his workshop experience said "I came away from the workshop feeling much more deeply that 'It is all right to be me with all my strengths and weaknesses.' My wife has told me that I appear to be more authentic, more real, more genuine."

This feeling of greater realness and authenticity is a very common experience. It would appear that the individual is learning to accept and to *be* himself, and this is laying the foundation for change. He is closer to his own feelings, and hence they are no longer so rigidly organized and are more open to change.

The Cracking of Facades

As the sessions continue, so many things tend to occur together that it is difficult to know which to describe first. It should again be stressed that these different threads and stages interweave and overlap. One of these threads is the increasing impatience with defenses. As time goes on, the group finds it unbearable that any member should live behind a mask or a front. The polite words, the intellectual understanding of one another and of relationships, the smooth coin of tack and cover-up—amply satisfactory for interactions outside—are just not good enough. The expression of self by some members of the group has made it very clear that a deeper and more basic encounter is *possible,* and the group appears to strive, intuitively and unconsciously, toward this goal. Gently at times, almost savagely at others, the group *demands* that the individual be himself, that his current feelings not be hidden, that he remove the mask of ordinary social intercourse. In one group there was a highly intelligent and quite academic man who had been rather perceptive in his understanding of others but who had not revealed himself at all. The attitude of the group was finally expressed sharply by one member when he said, "Come out from behind that lectern, Doc. Stop giving us speeches. Take off your dark glasses. We want to know *you*." . . .

If I am indicating that the group at times is quite violent in tearing down a facade or a defense, this would be accurate. On the other hand, it can also be sensitive and gentle. The man who was accused of hiding behind a lectern was deeply hurt by this attack, and over the lunch hour looked very troubled, as though he might break into tears at any moment. When the group reconvened, the members sensed this and treated him very gently, enabling him to tell us his own tragic personal story, which accounted for his aloofness and his intellectual and academic approach to life.

The Individual Receives Feedback

In the process of this freely expressive interaction, the individual rapidly acquires a great deal of data as to how he appears to others. The "hail-fellow-well-met" discovers that others resent his exaggerated friendliness. The executive who weighs his words carefully and speaks with heavy precision may find that others regard him as stuffy. A woman who shows a somewhat excessive desire to be of help to others is told in no uncertain terms that some group members do not want her for a mother. All this can be decidedly upsetting, but as long as these various bits of information are fed back in the context of caring which is developing in the group, they seem highly constructive.

Feedback can at times be very warm and positive as the following recorded excerpt indicates:

> *Leo* (very softly and gently): I've been struck with this ever since she talked about her waking in the night, that she has a very delicate sensitivity. *(Turning to Mary and speaking almost caressingly.)* And somehow I perceive—even looking at you or in your eyes— a very—almost like a gentle touch and from this gentle touch you can tell many—things—you sense in—this manner.
> *Fred:* Leo, when you said that, that she has this kind of delicate sensitivity, I just felt, *Lord yes!* Look at her eyes.
> *Leo:* M-hm.

A much more extended instance of negative and positive feedback, triggering a significant new experience of self-understanding and encounter with the group, is taken from the diary of the young man mentioned before. He had been telling the group that he had no feeling for them, and felt they had no feeling for him (Hall, 1965):

> Then, a girl lost patience with me and she said she didn't feel she could give any more. She said I looked like a bottomless well, and she wondered how many times I had to be told that I *was* cared for. By this time I was

feeling panicky, and I was saying to myself, "My God, can it be true that I can't be satisfied and that I'm somehow compelled to pester people for attention until I drive them away!"

At this point while I was really worried, a nun in the group spoke up. She said that I had not alienated her with some negative things I had said to her. She said she liked me, and she couldn't understand why I couldn't see that. She said she felt concerned for me and wanted to help me. With that, something began to really dawn on me, and I voiced it somewhat like the following. "You mean you are sitting there, feeling for me what I say I want you to feel, and that somewhere down inside me I'm stopping it from touching me?" I relaxed appreciably and began really to wonder why I had shut their caring out so much. I couldn't find the answer, and one woman said: "It looks like you are trying to stay continuously as deep in your feelings as you were this afternoon. It would make sense to me for you to draw back and assimilate it. Maybe if you don't push so hard, you can rest awhile and then move back into your feelings more naturally."

Her making the last suggestion really took effect. I saw the sense in it, and almost immediately I settled back very relaxed with something of a feeling of a bright, warm day dawning inside me. In addition to taking the pressure off of myself, however, I was for the first time really warmed by the friendly feelings which I felt they had for me. It is difficult to say why I felt liked only just then, but as opposed to the earlier sessions, I really *believed* they cared for me. I never have fully understood why I stood their affection off for so long, but at that point I almost abruptly began to trust that they did care. The measure of the effectiveness of this change lies in what I said next. I said, "Well, that really takes care of me. I'm really ready to listen to someone else now." I *meant* that, too.

Confrontation

There are times when the term "feedback" is far too mild to describe the interactions which take place, when it is better said that one individual *confronts* another, directly "leveling" with him. Such confrontations can be positive, but frequently they are decidedly negative, as the following example will make abundantly clear. In one of the last sessions of a group, Alice had made some quite vulgar and contemptuous remarks to John, who was entering religious work. The next morning, Norma, who had been a very quiet person in the group, took the floor:

> *Norma (loud sigh):* Well, I don't have *any* respect for you, Alice. *None!* (*Pause.*) There's about a hundred things going through my mind I want to say to you, and by God I hope I get through 'em all! First of all, if you wanted us to respect you, then why couldn't you respect *John's* feelings last night? Why have you been on him today? Hmm? Last night—couldn't you—couldn't you accept—*couldn't you* comprehend in any way at all that—that *he felt* his unworthi-

ness in the service of God? Couldn't you accept this, or did you have to dig into it today to find something *else there?* And his respect for womanhood—he *loves* women—yes, he does, because he's a real person, but you—you're not a real woman—to me—and thank God, you're not my mother!!! I want to come over and beat the hell out of you!!! I want to slap you across the mouth so hard and—oh, and you're so, you're many years above me—and I respect age, and I respect people who are older than me, *but I don't respect you, Alice. At all!* And I was so *hurt* and *confused* because you were making someone else feel *hurt* and *confused*. . . .

It may relieve the reader to know that these two women came to accept each other, not completely, but much more understandingly, before the end of the session. But this *was* a confrontation! . . .

The Basic Encounter

Running through some of the trends I have just been describing is the fact that individuals come into much closer and more direct contact with one another than is customary in ordinary life. This appears to be one of the most central, intense, and change-producing aspects of such a group experience. To illustrate what I mean, I would like to draw an example from a recent workshop group. A man tells, through his tears, of the very tragic loss of his child, a grief which he is experiencing *fully,* for the first time, not holding back his feelings in any way. Another says to him, also with tears in his eyes, "I've never felt so close to another human being. I've never before felt a real physical hurt in me from the pain of another. I feel *completely* with you." This is a basic encounter.

One member, trying to sort out his experiences immediately after a workshop, speaks of the "commitment to relationship" which often developed on the part of two individuals, not necessarily individuals who had liked each other initially. He goes on to say:

> The incredible fact experienced over and over by members of the group was that when a negative feeling was fully expressed to another, the relationship grew and the negative feeling was replaced by a deep acceptance for the other. . . . Thus real change seemed to occur when feelings were experienced and expressed in the context of the relationship. "I can't *stand* the way you talk!" turned into a real understanding and affection for you the *way* you talk.

This statement seems to capture some of the more complex meanings of the term "basic encounter."

The Expression of Positive Feelings and Closeness

As indicated in the last section, an inevitable part of the group process seems to be that when feelings are expressed and can be accepted in a relationship, a great deal of closeness and positive feelings result. Thus as the sessions proceed, there is an increasing feeling of warmth and group spirit and trust built, not out of positive attitudes only, but out of a realness which includes both positive and negative feeling. One member tried to capture this in writing very shortly after the workshop by saying that if he were trying to sum it up, ". . . it would have to do with what I call confirmation—a kind of confirmation of myself, of the uniqueness and universal qualities of men, a confirmation that when we can be human together something positive can emerge." . . .

Behavior Changes in the Group

It would seem from observation that many changes in behavior occur in the group itself. Gestures change. The tone of voice changes, becoming sometimes stronger, sometimes softer, usually more spontaneous, less artificial, more feelingful. Individuals show an astonishing amount of thoughtfulness and helpfulness toward one another.

Our major concern, however, is with the behavior changes which occur following the group experience. It is this which constitutes the most significant question and on which we need much more study and research. One person gives a catalog of the changes which he sees in himself which may seem too "pat" but which is echoed in many other statements:

I am more open, spontaneous. I express myself more freely. I am more sympathetic, empathic, and tolerant. I am more confident. I am more religious in my own way. My relations with my family, friends, and co-workers are more honest, and I express my likes and dislikes and true feelings more openly. I admit ignorance more readily. I am more cheerful. I want to help others more.

Another says:

Since the workshop there has been a new relationship with my parents. It has been trying and hard. However, I have found a greater freedom in talking with them, especially my father. Steps have been made toward being closer to my mother than I have ever been in the last five years. . . .

Sometimes the changes which are described are very subtle. "The primary change is the more positive view of my ability to allow myself to *hear,* and to become involved with someone else's 'silent scream.' " . . .

Disadvantages and Risks

Thus far one might think that every aspect of the group process was positive. As far as the evidence at hand indicates, it appears that it nearly always is a positive process for a majority of the participants. There are, nevertheless, failures which result. Let me try to describe briefly some of the negative aspects of the group process as they sometimes occur.

The most obvious deficiency of the intensive group experience is that frequently the behavior changes, if any, which occur, are not lasting. This is often recognized by the participants. One says, "I wish I had the ability to hold permanently the 'openness' I left the conference with." Another says, "I experienced a lot of acceptance, warmth, and love at the workshop. I find it hard to carry the ability to share this in the same way with people outside the workshop. I find it easier to slip back into my old unemotional role than to do the work necessary to open relationships." . . .

Some Data on Outcomes

What is the extent of this "slippage"? In the past year, I have administered follow-up questionnaires to 481 individuals who have been in groups I have organized or conducted. The information has been obtained from two to twelve months following the group experience, but the greatest number were followed up after a three- to six-month period.[3] Of these individuals, two (i.e., less than one-half of 1 percent) felt it had changed their behavior in ways they did not like. Fourteen percent felt the experience had made no perceptible change in their behavior. Another fourteen percent felt that it had changed their behavior but that this change had disappeared or left only a small residual positive effect. Fifty-seven percent felt it had made a continuing positive difference in their behavior, a few feeling that it had made some negative changes along with the positive.

A second potential risk involved in the intensive group experience and one which is often mentioned in public discussion is the risk that the individual may become deeply involved in revealing himself and then be left with problems which are not worked through. There have been a number of reports of people who have felt, following an intensive group experience, that they must go to a therapist to work through the feelings which were opened up in the intensive experience of the workshop and which were left unresolved. It is obvious that, without knowing more about each individual situation, it is difficult to say whether there was a negative outcome or a partially or entirely positive one. There are also very occasional accounts, and I can testify to two in my own experience, where an individual has had a psychotic episode during or immediately following an intensive group experience. On the other side of the picture is the fact that individuals have also lived through what were clearly psychotic episodes, and lived through them very constructively,

---

3. The 481 respondents constituted 82 percent of those to whom the questionnaire had been sent.

in the context of a basic encounter group. My own tentative clinical judgment would be that the more positively the group process has been proceeding, the less likely it is that any individual would be psychologically damaged through membership in the group. It is obvious, however, that this is a serious issue and that much more needs to be known. . . .

Out of the 481 participants followed up by questionnaires, two felt that the overall impact of their intensive group experience was "mostly damaging." Six more said that it had been "more unhelpful than helpful." Twenty-one, or 4 percent, stated that it had been "mostly frustrating, annoying, or confusing." Three and one-half percent said that it had been neutral in its impact. Nineteen percent checked that it had been "more helpful than unhelpful," indicating some degree of ambivalence. But 30 percent saw it as "constructive in its results," and 45 percent checked it as a "deeply meaningful, positive experience."[4] Thus for three-fourths of the group, it was *very* helpful. These figures should help to set the problem in perspective. It is obviously a very serious matter if an intensive group experience is psychologically damaging to *anyone*. It seems clear, however, that such damage occurs only rarely, if we are to judge by the reaction of the participants.

Other Hazards of the Group Experience

There is another risk or deficiency in the basic encounter group. Until very recent years it has been unusual for a workshop to include both husband and wife. This can be a real problem if significant change has taken place in one spouse during or as a result of the workshop experience. One individual felt this risk clearly after attending a workshop. He said, "I think there is a great danger to a marriage when one spouse attends a group. It is too hard for the other spouse to compete with the group individually and collectively." One of the frequent aftereffects of the intensive group experience is that it brings out into the open for discussion marital tensions which have been kept under cover.

Another risk which has sometimes been a cause of real concern in mixed intensive workshops is that very positive warm, and loving feelings can develop between members of the encounter group, as has been evident from some of the preceding examples. Inevitably some of these feelings have a sexual component, and this can be a matter of great concern to the participants and a profound threat to their spouses if these feelings are not worked through satisfactorily in the workshop. Also the close and loving feelings which develop may become a source of threat and marital difficulty

---

4. These figures add up to more than 100 percent since quite a number of the respondents checked more than one answer.

when a wife, for example, has not been present, but projects many fears about the loss of her spouse—whether well founded or not—onto the workshop experience. . . .

It is of interest in this connection that there has been increasing experimentation in recent years with "couples workshops" and with workshops for industrial executives and their spouses.

Still another negative potential growing out of these groups has become evident in recent years. Some individuals who have participated in previous encounter groups may exert a stultifying influence on new workshops which they attend. They sometimes exhibit what I think of as the "old pro" phenomenon. They feel they have learned the "rules of the game," and they subtly or openly try to impose these rules on newcomers. Thus, instead of promoting true expressiveness and spontaneity, they endeavor to substitute new rules for old—to make members feel guilty if they are not expressing feelings, are reluctant to voice criticism or hostility, are talking about situations outside the group relationship, or are fearful of revealing themselves. These old pros seem to be attempting to substitute a new tyranny in interpersonal relationships in the place of older, conventional restrictions. To me this is a perversion of the true group process. We need to ask ourselves how this travesty on spontaneity comes about.

Implications

I have tried to describe both the positive and the negative aspects of this burgeoning new cultural development. I would like now to touch on its implications for our society.

In the first place, it is a highly potent experience and hence clearly deserving of scientific study. As a phenomenon it has been both praised and criticized, but few people who have participated would doubt that *something* significant happens in these groups. People do not react in a neutral fashion toward the intensive group experience. They regard it as either strikingly worthwhile or deeply questionable. All would agree, however, that it is *potent*. This fact makes it of particular interest to the behavioral sciences since science is usually advanced by studying potent and dynamic phenomena. This is one of the reasons why I personally am devoting more and more of my time to this whole enterprise. I feel that we can learn much about the ways in which constructive personality change comes about as we study this group process more deeply.

In a different dimension, the intensive group experience appears to be one cultural attempt to meet the isolation of contemporary life. The person who has experienced an I-Thou relationship, who has entered into the basic encounter, is no longer an isolated individual. One workshop member stated this in a deeply expressed way:

Workshops seem to be at least a partial answer to the loneliness of modern man and his search for new meanings for his life. In short, workshops seem very quickly to allow the individual to become that person he wants to be. The first few steps are taken there, in uncertainty, in fear, and in anxiety. We may or may not continue the journey. It is a gusty way to live. You trade many, many loose ends for one big knot in the middle of your stomach. It sure as hell isn't easy, but it is a *life* at least—not a hollow imitation of life. It has fear as well as hope, sorrow as well as joy, but I daily offer it to more people in the hope that they will join me. . . . Out from a no-man's land of *fog* into the more violent atmosphere of extremes of thunder, hail, rain, and sunshine. It is worth the trip.

Another implication which is partially expressed in the foregoing statement is that it is an avenue to fulfillment, In a day when more income, a larger car, and a better washing machine seem scarcely to be satisfying the deepest needs of man, individuals are turning to the psychological world, groping for a greater degree of authenticity and fulfillment. One workshop member expressed this extremely vividly:

[It] has revealed a completely new dimension of life and has opened an infinite number of possibilities for me in my relationship to myself and to everyone dear to me. I feel truly alive and so grateful and joyful and hopeful and healthy and giddy and sparkly. I feel as though my eyes and ears and heart and guts have been opened to see and hear and love and feel more deeply, more widely, more intensely—this glorious, mixed-up, fabulous existence of ours. My whole body and each of its systems seems freer and healthier. I want to feel hot and cold, tired and rested, soft and hard, energetic and lazy. With persons everywhere, but especially my family, I have found a new freedom to explore and communicate. I know the change in me automatically brings a change in them. A whole new exciting relationship has started for me with my husband and with each of my children—a freedom to speak and to hear them speak.

Though one may wish to discount the enthusiasm of this statement, it describes an enrichment of life for which many are seeking....

Conclusion

I have tried to give a naturalistic, observational picture of one of the most significant modern social inventions, the so-called intensive group experience, or basic encounter group. I have tried to indicate some of the common elements of the process which occur in the climate of freedom that is present in such a group. I have pointed out some of the risks and shortcomings of the group experience. I have tried to indicate some of the reasons why it deserves serious consideration, not only from a personal point of view, but also from a scientific and philosophical point of view. I also hope I have made it clear that this is an area in which an enormous amount of deeply perceptive study and research is needed.

References

Bennis, W. G., Benne, K. D., & Chin R. (eds.) *The Planning of Change*. New York: Holt, Rinehart and Winston, 1961.

Bennis, W. G., Schein, E. H., Berlew, D. E., & Steele, F. I. (eds.) *Interpersonal Dynamics*. Homewood, Ill.: Dorsey, 1964.

Bradford, L., Gibb, J. R., & Benne, K. D. (eds.) *T-group Theory and Laboratory Method*. New York: Wiley, 1964.

Casriel, D. *So Fair a House*. Englewood Cliffs, N.J.: Prentice-Hall, 1963.

Gibb, J. R. "Climate for Trust Formation." In L. Bradford, J. R. Gibb, & K. D. Benne (eds.), *T-group Theory and Laboratory Method*. New York: Wiley, 1964.

Gordon, T. *Group-Centered Leadership*. Boston: Houghton Mifflin, 1955.

Hall, G. F. "A Participant's Experience in a Basic Encounter Group." (Mimeographed) Western Behavioral Sciences Institute, 1965.

The Experiential Group

Martin Lakin and Philip R. Costanzo

. . . The theory of experiential groups is based on a central assumption: in unprogrammed group interactions where a shared expectation of personal and interpersonal learning exists, personal disclosures and interpersonal recations generated by those disclosures will repeatedly recur and stimulate progressively deeper inner experiencing. The dynamics of group interaction may be counted on to promote identification with the group through sharing of experiences with fellow members. The dynamics of the group may also be counted on to intensify the emotionality of self-disclosure. Thus, 'feedback' based on self-disclosure to one another should be especially impactful. It is a cardinal assumption of the theory that the feedback will be honest and responsible, assuming the group has developed appropriately. If successful, the results of the process should be a greater sense of community, an increased ability to share emotionally with others and improved insights into one's interpersonal style and its effects upon others.

It is because of their multiple goals that experiential groups have been thought to require a blend of didactic and therapeutic skills. A review of the developments in such groups over the past quarter century should provide some understanding of what leadership in them has been and what it is becoming.

The 'mixed-motive' therapeutic *and* educational group is largely a post-World-War-II phenomenon. Therapeutic groups and therapeutic discussion groups had been known and described since the early part of the century.* However, enormous rehabilitation needs for recently discharged soldiers in the U.S.A. and in Britain stimulated the use of groups as rehabilitative aids. The shortage of available professionally trained manpower made the obvious economies of multi-person treatment format a highly desirable alternative to relatively expensive dyadic therapies.

Closely following the revolutionary expansion in the employment of therapeutic groups was the emergence of the experiential group. Its

---

*The 'Symposium' of the ancient Greeks and Socrates' dialogues were mixed relationships involving general educational and frankly therapeutic elements; thus, in a sense experiential groups are no departure from an historic chain of social association for learning and mutual betterment.

serendipitous 'discovery' has been recounted elsewhere (Benne, 1964). In brief, an unscheduled 'post-mortem' between researchers and participants led to the regular use of here-and-now reflections by participants on inter-actions in all their emotional aspects. Thus begun experiential group learn-ing. Through its subsequent development in National Training Labora-tories at Bethel, Maine, where it was first called Human Relations Train-ing, this type of 'training' spread throughout the country and beyond under many different rubrics.

Experiential groups have become a feature of the social landscape. Although occasionally employed as 'heroic' measures to achieve integra-tion in school systems, confront law enforcement officers with irate citizens who felt oppressed by them, or to work through difficult intra-staff re-lationships in organizational systems, they are mainly offered to volunteer applicants who perceive them as opportunities for self-development or for therapy. Because they are so widely available, under so many varieties of sponsorship, and conducted at such diverse levels of sophistication, it has become increasingly complicated to categorize them. In fact the overlap between educational and therapeutic purposes frustrates both intentions because of the problem of spelling out appropriate selection criteria or specifying what constitutes adequate preparation for their leaders.

Revisionists of its original theoretical underpinnings—a blend of neo-Freudian psychoanalysis, experiential group dynamics and democratically based pragmatism—have spawned their own splinter versions of the educational and the therapeutic purposes of the groups. Some have sug-gested changes in basic procedures—i.e., the introduction of leader-structured activities which would serve to facilitate their version of group purposes—while others have virtually abandoned the group-as-primary-vehicle in favour of a more individual-centered approach.

Experiential groups characteristically develop an intense emotional ambience, whether confrontational or supportive, as the group develops over time. The emotional intensity generated is usually seen as a *sine qua non* of group success. The emotionality of these groups is in fact rejuve-native and recreational. They permit regressive trends and encourage a certain venture-someness and sense of excitement. The consequent tend-encies to disinhibit one another combine to create an atmosphere of fellow-ship and camaraderie reminiscent of a summer camp.

Most groups are usually minimally structured by their designated leaders (variously called 'facilitators,' 'trainers,' or simply 'leaders') and involve between 8-15 participants, although this as well as the degrees and kinds of structuring vary to some extent depending upon sponsorship and upon whether the intention is primarily educational or therapeutic. There are no 'pure types' so that considerable overlap exists among all experiential groups.

To list experiential group titles as they currently appear is to give only very general information regarding commonalities or differences among them. In this sense Human Relations Laboratories, sensitivity training ('T'-groups) and Organizational Development ('O.D.') groups share a programmatic aim of interpersonal and intra-organizational problem diagnosis and problem solving. On a learning-therapy continuum the weighting in them is toward learning goals—although therapeutic change is by no means devalued. However, as a general rule, these groups disavow an explicitly therapeutic intention, and they are not as concerned with achieving 'personal growth' for its own sake as for instrumental aims of becoming more productive, more effective or more helpful in a job role or in one's primary relationships.

By contrast, the 'Human Potential Movement' may be said to have grown from among a different ideological wing in the experiential group movement. For instance, encounter groups emerged in the mid-1960s touted as 'therapy for normals' through the evocation of increasing levels of emotional expressiveness and intimate self-disclosures. In fact, the recent history of the term 'encounter' itself reflects the vicissitudes of the experiential group movement. The term has increasingly become applied to any form of relatively unstructured group psychological experience from body awareness to explicit therapeutic groups. In view of the incorporation by 'encounter' of so many types of experiential groups, it seems clear that there has been a drift toward the explicitly therapeutic goals of personal change and away from other learning aims over the past decade.

Positive and negative evaluations of experiential groups are, at this time, based upon a polyglot assortment of methods of assessment and are rooted in contrasting assumptions regarding their social utility. Critics claim that they achieve only superficial, transitory gains if any; moreover, they view post-group good feelings as merely reflections of the emotionality of the group atmosphere, i.e. as essentially revivalistic. Consequently, they consider these group experiences as scientifically suspect because of their quasi-religious nature. Despite this understandable wariness by researchers, the positive effects routinely reported by the overwhelming majority of participants are deserving of continuing scrutiny. Among these effects are positive self concept changes, greater interpersonal awareness and accompanying willingness to listen to others as well as satisfactions in emotional sharing. Whether these positive effects are long lasting or simply reflect a hyperenthusiasm in the immediate afterglow of the group remains in doubt. The most recent study of outcomes by Lieberman, Yalom and Miles (1973) indicates success proportions quite similar to those of psychotherapy-outcome studies; one-third claiming sustained positive change, one-third unchanged and an equivalent portion either dropping out or claiming a negative experience. In some cases (in proportions varying from 7-14% depending upon the *type* of *leadership*) an adverse reaction was serious enough to warrant listing the participant as a 'casualty'. These latter findings in particular have gained much notoriety among mental-health specialists and lend a sense of urgency to the considerations of experiential group leadership.

Despite the concerns over unwanted negative effects, the majority of participants come away as 'satisfied customers' and continue to send their friends with enthusiasm. Thus, from a retrospective view over 25 years or so, experiential groups appear to have secured a firm foothold in this society. They remain generally popular therapeutic and educational experiences even in the face of frequent criticisms. Their adherents maintain with constantly increasing confidence that they are in fact an effective admixture of potent educational and therapeutic processes, responsive to deeply felt needs in a time of enormous social change and dislocation.

A mini-theory of the workings of experiential groups

We take the position that experiential groups are therapeutically useful as vehicles for effective learning in direct relationship to their resemblance to real-life interactions. This will sound strange to the reader who has some knowledge of the uniqueness of such groups, of their 'contrivedness' in terms of the disavowal of agendas and of the customary rules of procedure. Nevertheless, these are means for facilitating a rapid transition to the heart of the matter—the elicitations and dramatization of the problematic aspects of ordinary interpersonal interaction. Our position may be contrasted with one which holds that experiential groups are valuable contrasts with daily life, a relief and a release from the humdrum. Exciting they may be (and should be!), and they are seemingly at great variance with daily encounters. But their value lies in the evocation of just those universal, ordinary aspects of relationship. Thus, while our mini-theory tells about the special workings of experiential groups, the reader may consider how similar factors determine the qualities of the various real-life groups to which he belongs.

Experiential group processes should be understood in terms of both the group *and* individual personality and are facilitated by designated leaders. To the group that provides acceptance and fulfillment for personal needs, members give loyalty. As members they, in turn, provide the group with its unique spirit. A group viewed as a developing social system progresses, stabilizes stagnates or disintegrates with changes in member involvement and interest. Where membership is valued, a cohesive group 'aura' is created. The cohesiveness is valued for its own sake in terms of the good feelings generated, but it also makes possible effective group actions.

Paradoxically, group membership threatens one's autonomy at the same time that it seems to offer security of a kind. The wish to be warmly nurtured and supported is offset by the fantasy of being overwhelmed and stifled. In ordinary life one can discern a similar ambivalence in the individual's relationship to his family or some other social unit. Most persons experience real deprivation when excluded from groups they want to be part of. On the other hand, many people also *defend* against being enveloped by a group, especially when they fear they might be subject to its controls and denied the expressions of their own individualities.

One way of avoiding absorption is through personal recognition for talents or skills. This involves evaluation whether overt or covert, as is most frequently the case in the 'real world.' During the group experience, member evaluation of one another becomes increasingly explicit. (This is so despite disclaimers of a 'non-judgemental' atmosphere. Evaluation is, as a matter of fact, most explicit in the process termed 'feedback.') The impelling factors are two: an almost irresistible tendency to engage in social comparison (comparing oneself with everyone else), and a tendency to assess the effects each member has on every other member. A member can be valued by his group for a variety of reasons. One may be outstanding for his communicating abilities; another may be respected for his insights; a third appreciated for stimulating others or for getting things started just when people seem to need active direction. Credit accrues especially to those who practise effective altruism, i.e., who are able to extend help to others at the right time and without sign of immediate personal payoff. Generally there is an effort to have evaluations be of behavior effects rather than of motivations, of how one's actions made another feel rather than *why* one did what he did (although motivational speculations are almost compulsive and can therefore not be disallowed).

The transaction between member and group involves group acceptance in exchange for member commitment, intimacy in exchange for personal disclosure, and a role in the group for each member. As a matter of fact, some participants are so anxious to feel a sense of belonging that they complain at the very onset. 'I don't feel as though I'm really a part of this group.' Such individuals are usually expressing a lack of understanding of how, in fact, one becomes an effective part of the social organization through helping to build it. Such a seemingly simple learning may be an important one for their participation in other groups.

The conditions for membership in the groups are more or less the same for all members. They are as follows: (1) to contribute to the shaping and coherence of the group, (2) to invest in it emotionally, (3) to help move it toward a goal, (4) to help establish its rules and to obey them, (5) to take on specific roles in the group, (6) to strive for deeper levels of intimacy and (7) to give help to other participants. Groups may be distinguished by the conditions which are most salient for them, i.e., those which are most emphasized. A group which is high on conditions 2 and 6 would demand relatively high emotionality. Collaboration and co-operation would be most important for the group which stresses conditions 1, 3 and 7.

The experiential training group requires the exercise of reflection as well as emotional commitment. With *only* intellectual comprehension the process becomes sterile. Emotions and intellect are both needed for a balanced and meaningful experience. Group effects interact with individual needs. How these effects are experienced in a specific group is partly the result of the mix of the personalities in that group and partly due to the influence of its leader. The core processes themselves, however, occur regardless of the quality of members or leader. Let us consider some of these core processes and see how they might interact with personal responses. The general point should be made that these core processes take place in all types of experiential groups that permit the development of group processes. The reader should therefore keep in mind that the facilitation of these processes by the leader will influence the successes of his group.

A. *Achieving and maintaining cohesiveness*

Group cohesiveness is the collective expression of personal belonging-ness. It leads to deeper association and concern about one's fellow members. Demonstrably, group cohesion (1) binds members emotionally to the common task as well as to one another; (2) assures greater stability of the group even in the fact of frustrating circumstances; (3) develops a shared frame of reference which allows for more tolerance for diverse aims of group members.

A negative attitude toward one's group reduces one's participation in the group task, but valued membership in that group leads to a greater commitment to its values and to the tasks the group undertakes. When membership is highly valued, the productivity of the group may be expected to rise. In experiential groups, the wish to be accepted is especially strong and participants are anxious to assure themselves that all members have in fact been 'accepted,' i.e., the group's 'success' is measured in terms of cohesion. Concern over the degree of success is epitomized in the question, 'How successful are we in having become a group?'. The potency of this concern is evidenced in the fact that one can even censure one's fellow members by complaining, 'We haven't become a "real" group.'

B. *Behaving in conformity with group norms*

All experiential groups encourage emotional expressiveness, warmth, openness and the like. In fact, such attributes as these become standards by which to judge the progress the group makes. They may even become 'norms' which compel conformist behavior by participants. The real point is that norms exist in any group; the real problem is to make them understandable in their influence upon the participants. It is less important and even misleading to declare norms for the group—'We will be open'—than to follow the creation, vicissitudes and effects of norms on members. How various kinds of norms come to be important for the group and their relative compellingness for individuals is the important learning issue here.

C. *Consensual validation of personal perceptions*

Another group effect is a press toward agreement. Members continually compare interpretations of events in order to establish meanings of events for themselves. Tracing the consensus processes that develop among the members of the group is in itself an absorbing learning process for attenders. 'How did we come to agree on our feelings about Fran?' is one form of the question. 'Why do we all react the same way to Adam?' is another. 'Feedback' is often given as a type of consensual reaction summary. To discover how this consensus is achieved, and with what consequences for each participant, is the learning objective. Ideally, each participant should be able to see himself in the consensus and evaluate the part he plays in arriving at it. This self-conscious view of group consensus process offsets the tendency for consensus to become merely another mechanism for increasing or enforcing conformity.

D. *The expression of emotional immediacy*

Any experiential group generates emotional expressiveness in participants. Hostile or affectionate feelings are evoked with fewer inhibitions in them than in most other interpersonal situations. There are, however, factors which discourage emotional 'binges' such as the media often portray. Concern for one's standing in the group influences one to monitor personal outpourings. The rapid spread of emotionality among the members of the group *is* helpful in freeing up a participant who is constricted in his expressing of feelings and it is readily apparent that in such cases the unblocking of 'frozen' feelings is a desirable development. This does not mean, however, that any display of emotionality is necessarily helpful, so that there are constraints upon emotionality just as there are facilitating elements for its expression.

E. *Group perception of problem relationships*

In what sense is it appropriate to talk about the group as a problem-solving experience? Experiential groups deal supportively with problems of human relationships and investigate the mutual perceptions which determine their problematic status. For instance, to Phil's query, 'How am I perceived?' Simone tells him, 'You come on too strong' or 'Your pompousness turns us off.' Through general discussion of how his behavior affects his relationships with others, he is stimulated to try alternate ways of relating that could be more effective. The assumption is that problematic interpersonal behaviours are most effectively looked at from fresh vantage points provided by the views of other group members. While 'many heads' do not necessarily come up with solutions to problems, they provide alternative perspectives on them.

F.   *Dominance alignments*

In experiential groups, leadership and influence positions rarely remain static. This is because any member can legitimately try exercising power and influence. His efforts are at best ambivalently received because the other participants are also impelled to try to assume *their* habitual positions of power. With the help of the leader, experiential groups try to develop flexibility in power allocation or 'ownership.' Thus a number of persons, regardless of real life' position, simultaneously experiment in the roles of decision-makers or influencers, or are treated as objects of influence. This contrasts with fixed self-perceptions as 'boss' or power victim. Even the 'naturally' dominant member must, after all, garner support from others if he is to continue to exercise leadership. The group thus provides a multiple perspective on power and influence transactions.

G.   *Role differentiation*

A group stagnates where there is no diversity of functions and especially where members feel stuck in undesirable and unproductive roles. In experiential groups, the functions of initiating, clarifying, harmonizing, etc., are easily recognizable. Other roles emerge, depending on the people in the group and its purpose. This availability of roles does not mean, however, that role interchange is easily or effortlessly achieved. As in the uses of power, participants gravitate to accustomed roles, such as 'the blocker,' the 'group clown' or the group 'foul-up,' perhaps to provide some elements of constancy and predictability. This tendency is not productive of learning and change. Thus, from the point of view of the participant who gets stuck in them the aim must be to enable him to experiment with different ways of being in the group. In the absence of such experimentation, stereotypic role stabilizes without constructive change.

H.   *Movement toward intimate disclosure*

Objective 'change' indices following training routinely demonstrate increases in feelings of intimacy. Whether these represent only a temporary emotional state precipitated by the experience or something more enduring we cannot say at this point. Nevertheless, in expressiveness forms of experiential groups especially, members are enjoined to push toward greater intimacy on the assumption that it will have considerable 'carry-over' beyond the life of the group.

The interaction between group effects and personal responses is singular for each participant. The same group experience may have rewarding and punishing consequences for two different members. For example, a person with great needs for belongingness may experience the Cohesiveness of his group (group Effect 'A') with a positive response of relieved belongingness while another may have a negative feeling of being hemmed in. With respect to Effect 'B,' Conformity, one participant could respond by becoming more aware of the need to be accountable to his fellows; whereas another simply brings his behaviour into line with everyone else's by uncritical acceptance of group standards. With respect to Effect 'C,' Consensus, although its achievement feels satisfying, there is the risk that it may come about at the cost of denying real differences in order to achieve it. What is the range of possible responses to the group effect of 'Emotional Immediacy' (Effect 'D')? On the positive side, one is likely to feel freed up emotionally. On the negative side, one could be coerced to express group evoked emotions. Effect 'E' (Group Perception of Problems) may facilitate one's thinking about one's interactional problems and it stimulates different perspectives. On the other hand, pressured sharing of problems arouses defensiveness.

With respect to Dominance Alignments (Effect 'F'), the important thing is to endeavour that no one remain permanently at either extreme, i.e. feeling either constantly manipulated at one end or able to dominate the group at the other. Group Effect 'G' (Role Differentiation) stimulates the individual to try himself out in hitherto unaccustomed ways. The negative side is a tendency of the group to stereotype the individual or to 'pigeon-hole' him into a category in order to reduce the cognitive complexity of the group situation in one's mind. In regard to group Effect 'H' (Movement toward Intimate Disclosure), a desirable result is intimacy, when based on meaningful feedback. On the other hand, there is risk to self-esteem unavoidably associated with self-disclosure and the evaluative reactions from group-mates.

The group experience is theoretically self-regulating in the sense that belongingness needs and wishes impel members to share intimate experiences and feelings without excessive pressures. In practice, this 'self-regulation' is not completely reliable, and the leader may find it necessary to channel interactions to some extent—for example, away from excessive preoccupation with a personal historical narrative to here-and-now data in the group or to intervene where he perceives that a member is being confronted beyond his capacity to constructively absorb what is being offered. . . .

The Conscious-raising Group:
An Alternative Structure*

Edith Folb

> I believe increasingly that only the willingness to share private and
> sometimes painful experience can enable women to create a collec-
> tive description of the world which will be truly ours.
>
> —Adrienne Rich
> *Of Woman Born*

Since the late 60s, the Consciousness Raising group[1] (CR group)
has been a mainstay of the Women's Movement in this country. It is an
unique and potent small group experience—one that allows women to
share, look at and learn from those life situations common to all of us who
have 'come of age' in a patriarchal society.

The contemporary CR group grew out of a feminist need to insure
that personal growth kept pace with political and social activism.

> Since 1966, when the current resurgence of feminism got off the
> ground, women in the Movement had been working for the cause
> at such a furious pace that they never had time to really talk to each
> other. . . . When feminists met together to talk, it was about issues.
> . . . But the time came when . . . what bothered women personally
> about being female in a male-dominated society had to be discussed
> (Bonnetti, p. 2).

What began among New York feminists as an informal rap group in
which women began to look at social and political oppression in light of
their own personal experiences, soon grew beyond the bounds of New York
and the Radical Feminist community. By the end of the decade, the CR
group was a well-established and vital force in the Women's Movement and
beyond. Women from all parts of the country—from small towns and
suburbs—and from all walks of life were seeking information about CR
groups and forming their own.

The great grass roots appeal of the CR group is two-fold—it is
accessible and it is personal.

---

1. Throughout this article, I am indebted to the fine work done by the Los Angeles
chapter of the National Organization of Women (N.O.W.) CR Committee and the
Consciousness Raising Handbook they have painstakingly put together for all of us
to share.

> Because so many individuals have been alienated by political movements whose emphasis avoided self-recognition, CR . . . struck a responsive chord in thousands of potential feminists. . . . They like the idea of knowing the personal 'why' of rebellion (Dreifus 1973, p. 6).

What the CR experience brings home to each woman involved is that 'the personal is the political.' That is, the politics, sociology and economics of women's containment and oppression can be most graphically experienced in their daily lives. Instead of (or in addition to) reading socialist tracts on the abuses of the working class, women talk about the meaninglessness of the work they do each day. Or they explore the sociology of rape or the 'battered wife syndrome' or the sexual abuse of children, by revealing their own experiences as well as their feelings and fantasies about these issues.

What they find out from each other is the commonality of their experiences. They discover that they are not alone in their pain or privation. Nor are they 'crazy,' 'silly,' "neurotic' or 'bad' because they are disconnected from or discontent with the roles or life situations they have been told is their lot as women.

> Isolation is broken. They learn their experiences fit into a political pattern—a pattern best described as sexism. . . . CR fosters self-confidence among its participants. Often self-confidence leads to action—action against the institutions that oppress women, action against the individuals who act in the name of these institutions (Ibid, p. 5).

Therefore, the CR group is a potent instrument of both personal and political change. As one of my women students so graphically put it,

> I remember in grammar school, I used to draw female figures without arms or hands. I guess I felt a lot like those drawings—I couldn't reach out to anyone (especially other girls) and I had no power to do anything. My CR group really changed that. It gave me a lot. It really gave me my arms and hands back. Now, I feel like I can reach out to other people and I can do things to change my life—and other women's lives. I have real power!

What the CR Group is Not

Before discussing the structure, organization and leadership of the CR group, it is important to note what the CR group is *not*.

CR is not group therapy—or, for that matter, any type of therapy. Too often therapy views the individual as 'sick,' 'asocial' or 'maladjusted' and seeks to bring that person's feelings, behaviors and expectations in line with the society's norms. On the contrary, the CR process is grounded in the belief that it is not the woman who is 'sick.' If anything, it is the society within which she must struggle for personhood that is ailing. Rather than adjustment, CR encourages rebellion. Certainly the Human Potential movement has given us alternatives to the 'pathological' view of human behavior and a humanistic approach to therapy. Nonetheless, the CR group is not in the business of doing any kind of therapy, though the effects of being in a CR group may prove to be 'therapeutic' for many of the women involved.

CR groups are not 'encounter' groups. The CR group discourages rather than encourages confrontation, challenge or dispute with others. Women have too long been challenged and denied their personal perceptions, feelings and experiences. The CR experience does not seek to perpetuate this process—even when the intentions of the interaction are well meaning.

The CR group is not an informal 'rap group,' 'kaffee klatsch' or so-called 'bitch session.' Though these kinds of group interactions may be ways of ventilating feelings and getting out grievances, they often tend to be circular and innervating. White it is important to share problems and air grievances, it is not sufficient. Endless reiteration of one's plight may provide momentary release, but the problem still exists. The CR process is a structured experience that attempts to move women from discussion and awareness of shared problems to personal and political acts that attempt to alleviate the societal conditions that create the problems.

Finally, the CR group is not a personal "problem-solving' group. Women do not come together specifically to find solutions to their personal dilemmas or the 'shoulds' of their interactions with others—should Jane confront Barry on his infidelity, should Sally approach her boss for a raise, should Mary report her rape to the police? The CR group is certainly dedicated to change in a woman's life, but that change must come from a woman taking control over her own actions, not because others tell her she should effect this or that change.

These, then, are some of the things that the CR group is *not*. What follows is a discussion of what the CR experience *is*.

The CR Group Experience

The CR group structure is not a fixed or static form. That is, the organization, process, content and leadership or a particular group will reflect and accommodate the level of need, sophistication and expertise, vis-à-vis women's issues, of the participants. The following is a description of what I have experienced as a 'representative' CR group during my years as participant, leader and trainer. It is not the *only* structure, it is *a* structure that has worked for a large number of women.

The CR 'Contract'

Though the CR group is task-oriented in that it attempts to get women to effect change on a personal and political level, it is preeminently a person-centered experience. For this reason, certain 'ground rules' are usually observed and maintained throughout the group's life. In a very real sense, each woman 'contracts' with every other woman in the group to live up to the conditions of the contract—to observe the rules.

The bottom line of any effective CR group is *commitment.* If a woman contracts to be part of a CR group, she is saying to herself and her sister members that she takes the group seriously and that it is a significant experience in her life. In action terms, it means that she commits herself to regular attendance, being on time and staying for the duration of the session.[2]

Commitment also presumes that a woman will *share honestly* and in terms of her *personal experiences as a woman.* A disservice is done to oneself and the other woman in a CR group if one 'backs down' from the realities of her life as a woman in this society. Since personal growth and political action come from an awareness of how and why women are oppressed in a male-dominated society, it is imperative that a woman begin to honestly confront herself and begin to see how that self is also mirrored in the lives of other women.

If a woman is to speak honestly and deeply about her life, she must feel that she is safe. Therefore, *avoidance of confrontation* and *confidentiality* are two additional components of the CR contract. The whole CR experience is predicated on the belief that each woman's experience is valid. Her truth is just that—a statement of what it's like to be a woman *for her.* For many women, the CR group is the first and/or only place where they can openly share their personal truths without fear of being diminished, dishonored or disallowed. If she is called upon to explain, argue for or justify herself—if she must 'establish her credentials'—the chances for personal or political growth are severely retarded.

Emotional and even physical safety means not only freedom from intragroup challenges, but freedom from exposure beyond the group. What is said within the group, stays within the group. Neither lover or intimate friend nor close relative is expected to be privy to the group's shared confidences. What each woman chooses to share with outsiders of her own insights or experiences in relationship to herself is her choice. However, no woman is given license to speak for or about another woman.

---

2. The Los Angeles N.O.W. CR leadership makes attendance mandatory. A woman is dropped from the group after more than one absence. Though this act seems severe, it has proven over the years to be a positive decision. The 'sometimes' attender destroys group cohesion and intimacy.

The CR Group Structure

Although each CR group is structured somewhat differently, there are certain primary considerations each potential group must address before beginning.

Women only/men only

Limiting a CR group to women only—or men only—is not a sign of discrimination, but a mark of practicality, even necessity. Long and sometimes painful experience has demonstrated to this writer and to many others that mixed CR groups are generally limited and limiting for both sexes. For one, the process is different for female and male.

> Essentially, women have a need to discuss their oppression, while men have to face the painful fact that society is organized so that they, as a class, benefit from women's oppression. Where the recognition is [often] fast and emotionally positive for women, it is often slow and depressing for men. Confusion is inevitable if the processes are carried on simultaneously (Bonetti, p. 11).

From the female perspective, an all-woman CR group provides not only psychological safety, but emotional and literal 'space.' Women historically have been conditioned and rewarded by this society for giving over their space to men. This is very apparent in mixed CR groups. Women allow themselves to be interrupted by men, fall silent in their presence, defer to male opinion, focus attention on 'male problems' and generally restrict the content, length and quality of their utterances. In all these ways, women relinquish their space and, therefore, their ability to share fully their experiences as women—which is the basis of the CR experience.[3] As one woman saw it,

> I've been married for 22 years and this is the first time I've ever felt totally free about expressing my feelings. Harry always interrupted me and he'd talk for me—he never let me speak for myself! With my CR group, I got the space to talk. And I got respect for what I said.

Heterogeneity

Though opinion is divided about the degree to which CR group members should be different in terms of life styles, sexuality, class and race, feminist experiences and the like, I generally endorse heterogenous

---

3. Indeed separate CR groups for males have proven to be most effective. For many men, it is the first time they have shared their feelings with other men on such topics as homosexuality, fears around impotence, living up to the 'macho' image, woman loving and woman hating and a variety of other issues in mens' lives.

groups.[4] A significant aspect of the CR group experience is to discover and explore the *common* 'chains that bind'—however differently they may restrain us. For example, in a society that glorifies marriage and the nuclear family, a single mother or a lesbian or a childless woman or a wife and mother of four can all relate to questions like, 'How is marriage different for women than for men?' 'As a married or single woman, what is your biggest advantage/disadvantage?' 'Why did we fantasize, if we did, about marriage?'

Furthermore, heterogeneity, by its very nature, generates a level of liveliness, energy and exchange sometimes lacking in a homogeneous group. The differing life experiences and points of view related to a given topic expand and enrich the topic discussed and the insights of the women involved. At its very core, the CR experience is meant to be a process that brings women together around their oppression despite diversity of backgrounds.

Too often, political movements lose their vitality and creative impact because they begin to listen to and hear only one voice or one 'party line' or one set of political 'truths.' They begin to exclude and fragment rather than embrace and connect. To my mind, heterogeneity is the life blood of any viable political movement—and the Women's Movement is no exception.

Exclusion of close friends

Again, there is a difference of opinion over whether or not close friends can or should be in the same CR group. The arguments against their joint participation focus on freedom of expression and confidentiality. Though two women may be intimate friends, they may still find it difficult or painful to share some aspects of their life in each other's presence. My own experience has shown this to be more or less the case. Still another more potent argument is that close friends sometimes feel they have some special permission to talk about the group and its members outside the group, because they are mutually sharing the experience. This potential breach of confidentiality tends to restrict others' openness and honesty of expression. Finally, close friends, whether they intend to or not, sometimes band together inside the group and exclude others. This can undermine the intimate bonding that often occurs among all members, bonding that permits the group to function as a cohesive support system as well as a potential social action group.

I discourage rather than encourage sameness in the group itself— whether it be close friends or women with like backgrounds. However, no

---

4. On some occasions, women of 'like mind' may need or want to conduct a series of CR sessions specifically related to issues in their particular lives. For example, a group may form around such issues as single parenthood, aging and discrimination, black women's oppression, lesbianism and the like.

women should be excluded because transportation problems, child care arrangements or work schedules make coming separately impossible.

No alcohol, drugs, food or cigarettes

People may debate one or more of these restrictions, and finally the group itself will decide what is or is not permitted. The rationale for eliminating the above from the CR group setting is the belief (learned through experience) that all of them, in their own way, detract from a woman's concentration on the topic and her ability to involve herself deeply and fully in the process she is undergoing. Social events are one thing; CR groups are another. As one woman put it,

> When my CR group decided that we wouldn't smoke or drink or eat anything during our meetings, I wasn't sure I could do it—I'm a real smoker and *nosher* (nibbler)! But you know something? I did it and it taught me a lot about myself. I've always smoked and eaten when I'm nervous or scared or just to be doing something. It really made me look at my habits. I hide behind them. When I didn't, I could put more of myself into what I'm doing—like the CR. It was hard, but it was very good for me.

Number, size, time and place of CR group meetings

Experience conducting CR groups has shown that a minimum of 10 sessions is necessary if the CR experience is to have a lasting impact on the participants. For first-timers especially, there are a set of topics that are generally covered in those first ten meetings. Less time would severely curtail a woman's exposure to these 'basics' of women's shared experience. Many CR groups continue far beyond the 10 sessions. For example, my most recent CR group met every week for over a year.

Typically, a CR group meets once a week for approximately two hours. Though the time frame may differ from group to group, two hours usually allows the topic to be generally covered without emotionally and physically exhausting the members. As far as group size is concerned, the optimum number seems to be between seven and 10 women. Anything smaller reduces the range and diversity of the responses and reactions; anything larger limits the extent and quality of the participation.

Whatever the designated length of the sessions, it is important that they begin and end on time. Being on time and ending on time affects the group in a number of ways: it reinforces the seriousness of the CR experience; it honors the schedules of its participants—some of whom have made special arrangements to attend; it generates a more effective group process in relation to the topic (that is, members can expect to have a specified length of time in which to deal with the topic); it generally builds group cohesion and solidarity as women demonstrate their commitment to the group by respecting each other's time.

Finally, the location of the CR group is variable. Some groups rotate their meetings among members' homes from session to session; others meet regularly at one home or location for the duration of the CR group; still others, who are involved in a long-term CR group, periodically rotate the home or location in which they meet. The advantage of a regular, fixed meeting place is just that—everyone knows where it is, it is familiar and comfortable and, once agreed upon by the members, is known to be accessible to all—such as disabled women. Its major limitation is that one woman must volunteer her home for an extended period of time.

The overall structure of the CR group experience is finally a collective decision. Each group must ultimately determine what works for them. What the above discussion has attempted to do is present some of the considerations and problems that accompany various options.

The CR Group Process

The format

A representative CR group process is quite simple. Again, the major rationale for the process is to assure each woman equal space and time to be heard. Basically, the format is as follows. The CR group begins with a 'stroke'—a self-congratulatory 'pat on the back' for something done, said, not done or changed in one's life during the previous week. After each of the women has given herself a stroke, the designated leader will then turn to a specific topic. This topic has usually been chosen by the group at the end of the prior week's session. The leader is usually responsible for developing the questions on the topic. Going around the circle once again, each woman responds to the question—including the leader. In many CR groups, time constraints are placed on a woman's response. This may be anywhere from five to 10 minutes, depending on the size of the group, the needs of the members and the intensity of discussion generated.

If a woman chooses not to respond to a particular question, she 'passes.' After each person has had an opportunity for an initial response, the leader will return to the woman (or women) who has passed and ask her if she wants the chance to now speak. She may again choose to pass. At any time during the process, a woman may ask another woman to elaborate on or clarify some point if she doesn't understand what has been said.

At this juncture, the leader may ask for a second round of responses to the initial question or she may pose another question related to the topic, and once again go around the circle for responses. Depending on time constraints, perceived needs of the members and an overall sense of 'where the group is at,' the leader may choose to repeat the process with a second round of responses or move on to a third question.

At some point, the leader will move from specific questions to an open-ended group response to and analysis of the questions posed thus far. This aspect of the process may be delayed if women want to continue to explore the questions related to the topic. Whenever this period occurs, women are encouraged to express any impressions, observations or additional experiences related to the overall topic or specific questions. They are also asked to examine how these experiences collectively and individually oppress women and what options or avenues are open for change. The leader may choose, at this point, to summarize or synthesize what has been said so far and solicit any final remarks.

Before the meeting adjourns, the group decides whether or not they wish to continue exploration of the same topic or move on to another. If leadership is rotated among the members, a new leader takes responsibility for preparing questions for the coming week's topic. Usually, a leader continues to facilitate the meetings until the topic for which she is responsible is covered.

The stroke

The self-congratulatory stroke at the beginning of each session serves a number of purposes. For one, it breaks down social conditioning which encourages women to stroke, nurture, support (and live through) others rather than to focus attention or praise on themselves. It also serves to shift the focus of attention and importance from other to self. Strokes not only enhance self-worth and pride of accomplishment, but also tell the woman and others, 'I am a real person in the world.'

Though some women are initially shy or unsure about sharing a stroke, this reticence usually disappears after the first few meetings. Indeed, women look forward to sharing their 'pat on the back' for everything from refusing to be called a *chick,* to going back to school, to leaving an unbearable marriage. For many women, stroking at the beginning of the CR group may actually give them the courage or incentive to effect some change—large or small—in their lives. Like so much of the CR experience, stroking tells women they are important—and potentially powerful agents of change.

Usually strokes are brief—from one to two minutes for each women —since the primary focus of the group is on the selected topic. On occasion, though, a woman will have effected a major change in her life, and her stroke is given more time for the telling.

The option to pass

Just as every woman is assured her space to talk, everyone is allowed her time to be silent. For many a woman, the CR group is an experience totally unlike any she has had before. For some, it initially can be overwhelming. A woman who is timid or not used to sharing personal and many times painful experiences, may need to be silent on some questions, even some topics. Again, as with the stroke, women generally find their voices early on. Few women remain silent throughout the duration of the group.

Again, depending on the terms of the CR contract for a given group and the evolution of the group, a woman may be allowed her silence throughout (which is unlikely), or finally be asked to share the reasons for her silence. Continued silence on the part of a group member finally begins to inhibit other group participants and interferes with building group cohesiveness and trust. Since each woman's participation is crucial in order to build the collective life story of the group, the silent member begins to be seen as a detached, even hostile outsider, rather than an active participant—and can come to be resented as such. Ultimately, peer pressure (and support) moves even the most reluctant woman to take her space.[5]

Selection, Development and Treatment of the CR Topic

The selection, development and treatment of the CR topic is as important to the effectiveness of the CR experience as is the format. Earlier, I pointed out that the CR group is not an open-ended rap group but a highly structured small group experience aimed at making women more conscious of the ways in which the patriarchal system constrains them, so that they may begin to effect change in their lives and in that system.

Random discussion of a variety of issues or unstructured, desultory attention to a given topic may 'feel good,' but defeats the purpose of CR. Women may go away from the session feeling they're not so bad off after all—and do nothing to change the causes of the oppression in their lives. As one woman saw it, the rap group or sensitivity group approach to CR is like 'prescribing an aspirin for a brain tumor.'

The attempt always is to develop the questions related to the topic so as to move discussion from a personal level of exploration and understanding to a recognition of the political implications of the topic in women's lives—and an awareness of what can or must be done to change the personal, political and social conditions that confine us. For example, one

---

5. In the six years I have been involved in CR groups, I have only seen one woman remain totally silent throughout the time the group met—which was for 10 weeks. What she was unable to share with the group—but later shared with a few of the members—was the fact that she had been repeatedly raped and beaten by her father and she was terrified that she would 'break down' if she opened herself on *any* topic. She later joined another CR group and was not only an active participant but was able to share this painful experience with them.
She is presently a psychologist who works closely with rape victims.

of the basic topics treated in most every CR group is rape. In an unstructured group setting, women might rap about their experiences of rape, hear 'horror stories' more devastating than their own and go away from the group feeling their situation wasn't nearly as painful as Y's. Such a discussion makes no attempt to directly engage a women in terms of her attitudes or understanding around rape. Nor does it attempt to look at the political implications of the act of rape in our society.

Within the CR framework, the topic might be developed in the following manner.

(1)   A set of lead-off questions might ask, 'What are your feelings about rape or being raped?' 'Have you had an experience with rape or the attempted rape of someone you know?'

(2)   A second set of follow-up questions might begin to move women from a personal to a political level of awareness: 'How do women handle being raped (e.g., do they report it to the police as a crime, keep it totally secret or deny it ever happened)?' 'How does the fear of rape have an effect on your daily life?'

(3)   A third set of questions would attempt to bring to conscious awareness the specific political implications of rape: 'What comparison can you make between the rape of women and the lynching of blacks?' 'How is rape a political tool of the oppressor?' ('political' being the art of using power).[6]

A CR group might treat only one question or one question from each area in any given session; they may extend discussion of the questions over two or three meetings. However much time they give to a topic, they do so through a structured development of the topic.

Not all topics are grist for the mill. Some topics of and by themselves do little to raise consciousness. For example, I assign a paper in my women's communication class that deals with how the media see women—what image do they want us to 'buy'? As a CR topic, it has limitations—as one CR leader found out.

> Although women recognized the stereotype, they resisted analyzing how the situation affected them personally and then why it was a political issue (for one thing, it internalizes women's oppression), but instead got into an abstract discussion over whether or not the media reflects attitudes or whether it creates attitudes. While this is an interesting issue, it is irrelevant to how and why women might be conditioned to accept the stereotype that is already portrayed regardless of where it came from (Ibid, p. 22).

A topic must not only be specific enough to focus attention on the political ramifications in women's everyday lives, but it must provoke a real

---

6. The development of this topic is a highly abbreviated version of the treatment of the topic of rape found in the N.O.W. *CR Handbook,* pp. 38-39.

personal questioning of the degree and manner in which women have absorbed and integrated their oppression.

There are certain topics which, as mentioned, are considered to be 'basic' to any CR group. They are

(1) do women like other women?
(2) masculine/feminine
(3) women and the aging process
(4) women and anger
(5) mothers and daughters; fathers and daughters
(6) rape
(7) lesbianism
(8) sexual oppression
(9) life styles

Depending on the particular needs and interests of the CR group, additional topics might be

(1) women and work; what is 'women's work'?
(2) women and money
(3) women and power; do women fear success?
(4) women's relationship to their bodies
(5) do women oppress other women?

The development of a given topic is very much like the preparation that goes into a speech or an essay. The woman responsible for developing the week's topic will often set down the specific purpose of the upcoming CR session, e.g., to explore the personal and political implications of rape in women's lives. Next, the woman will 'research' the topic—both through an examination of her own and others' experience with the topic and through related readings on the topic. Out of this exploration will come the basic issues (both personal and political) that are to be addressed in relation to the topic. She may choose to jot down some pertinent quotes or points from her readings, which may later be phrased as questions.

After the woman writes down all those questions that seem relevant to the topic, she then attempts to order the questions so that they take the group deeper and deeper into an examination of the process by which we become socialized in terms of the topic. By the time a woman has 'done her homework,' she is well prepared to handle most questions or issues that may arise during the discussion and is able to focus the women's attention on the salient points to be explored.

The CR Group Leader

There are differences of opinion over who should take responsibility for CR group leadership. N.O.W., for example, favors a trained CR leader to head the group. In some circumstances, I would agree. When all of the women in the group are new to CR and/or the issues of the Women's Movement, a seasoned CR leader is a definite asset and important role model. However, the realities of the CR experience often mean that members come together out of a felt need—and often in faraway places—where a trained CR leader is non-existent. Though some women may have had prior CR group experience or have been active in the Women's Movement or have read about the CR group, few have been specifically trained as CR leaders. In such circumstances, leadership is learned 'on the job.'

Usually, the most 'experienced' person will take charge of the first few CR group meetings. After that, the group will often rotate leadership among its members. Often women will volunteer to lead a CR session that is closely related to events in their personal life—an older woman may choose to lead the CR session on aging, a particularly shy woman may wish to lead the group on the topic of anger. However the leader is selected, she is usually responsible for developing the questions on the upcoming topic.

The woman directing the group is more a facilitator than a leader. That is, she provides the necessary 'traffic direction' to ensure that the process moves smoothly. She is responsible for moving the group through the topic, while averting or disengaging women from 'roadblocks' such as confronting other women, advice-giving or seeking, talking beyond the allotted time or drifting off the subject. She may also provide necessary bridges when discussion bogs down or gets played out in relation to a particular question. She, along with others, synthesizes and/or summarizes where the group is at. But, always she is an active and equal participant in the group experience. One of the advantages of a rotating leadership is no woman gets fixed in the role of 'leader.' This avoids the potential schism between 'me' and 'thee.'

However, it is also important to acknowledge the appointed leader *as* leader. Otherwise, a diffusion of direction and purpose sets in. The CR experience is structured, and part of that structure provides for a designated leader. Long experience indicates that there is no such thing as a leaderless group—leaders always emerge—nor is it productive to the group process if the leader avoids her charge. The 'tyranny of structurelessness' is the kiss of death to the CR experience.

Because the trained leader is not available to most CR groups, the experience of leadership is often passed to women who have seldom been asked to assert themselves or take responsibility in such a public way. What the rotating leadership serves to do for many women is to de-mystify what leadership means (that is, to call into question the elitist model of 'the leader' as the ultimate authority). It also puts them in touch with their own sense of power and competence and thereby enhances their feelings of self-esteem. What the woman finds out is she, too, can lead.

What has been discussed above is how the CR experience might unfold in a given CR group. Again, I must remind the reader that the description represents one point of view. One of the most important aspects of the CR process is that it can respond to the particular needs of the participants without destroying the integrity of the experience.

The CR Group Experience as an Alternative Structure

In important ways, I feel the CR group experience alters, reinterprets or departs from more 'traditional' small group settings. And, in so doing, it interjects a new vitality into the small group process and provides a fresh perspective from which to view the possibilities of small group communication.

Probably one of the most significant features of the CR process is its attempt to build and reinforce a truly non-hierarchical, egalitarian structure and format. Not only is each member assured 'equal time' to speak (a level of participation seldom achieved in the most 'democratic' group setting), but each member is honored as an 'expert' in her own right. She need defer to no 'authority figure' in the group, since she, like the others, is an expert by virtue of her credentials as a woman in this society. That posture in the group setting is not apparent in many small groups—whether task or personal-centered.

Furthermore, the CR group process departs from traditional therapy or therapy-like groups in that a woman need not vie for space and attention, nor are therapeutic 'yardsticks of achievement' held up to her as some measure of her 'progress' or 'mental health.' Being assured one's space to be heard is itself an important departure from most small group settings. For women, this is particularly important, since studies indicate that they are allowed or take far less verbal space than males occupy in most small group interactions.

The rotation of leadership and leadership responsibilities among members, the expected and equal participation of all women, further serves to break down hierarchical or elitist structures within the group. In the best sense, the CR group is a 'peer group.'

In terms of group cohesiveness, the CR group experience operates in a potent way. Women have been rewarded by this society for competing against one another—for a man's favors, attention and protection. For many women, the CR group is the first time they have come together with other women for the purpose of serious and candid exploration and analysis of themselves as women. Rather than engaging in divisive competition, they find themselves cooperatively exploring their common ground and collectively reclaiming and rejoicing in their common heritage. They learn to take each other seriously.[7]

The bonding that takes place within the group is hard to describe on paper—it is a profound and intimate experience. It can be seen in the protectiveness that women begin to develop toward their CR group, in the longevity of many groups and in the maintenance of close friendships outside the group. Indeed, many groups have become the initiators of political and social action. For example, my CR group in San Diego helped to initiate the bumper sticker, 'Sisters share a ride.' We did this in response to our CR session on rape, during which two women recounted experiences of being sexually assaulted by male drivers who had picked them up—supposedly for a ride. The special sense of group solidarity and intimacy is expressed, for me, by one of my students. She said, 'I never knew what the word "sister" meant—not really—until I got into my CR group. Blood ties couldn't be any closer. This experience has made me closer to women outside the group too. I really feel like we're all sisters.' So, for many, the sense of group identity extends beyond the boundaries of the CR group to *women as a group*. For many women, this is a profound shift in self-identification and group allegiance.

Another important aspect of the CR group experience is the diversity of its goals. Most small groups are predominantly person-centered or task-centered in their orientation. The very nature of the CR experience makes the two goals inseparable. Because 'the personal is the political,' a woman is involved simultaneously in personal growth and development as well as political and social change—she takes control of her life, and thereby effects changes in the lives of those around her, by raising consciousness around issues such as marriage contracts, child-rearing practices and the like.

Finally, the CR group serves as an informational clearinghouse. Women not only give and get information, but transform the raw data of their lives into theories, inferences and suppositions about the nature of women's culture that have impact far beyond the confines of the group. Indeed, some of the best feminist thought and analysis has been inspired by participation in the CR group experience.

Certainly the CR group experience is not the be-all and end-all small group. It is an alternative structure that offers some options in terms of the way in which group members can relate to each other, the nature of leader-

---

7. It is my belief that a patriarchal society is not just contemptuous of female bonding, it is afraid of it. Therefore, it utilizes various means to discourage it—not the least of which is the devaluation of women's talk as 'empty,' 'silly,' 'unimportant' or 'irrelevant.' As Rysman (1977) has pointed out in his discussion of gossip and male devaluation of it as a female form, 'The negative effect applied to female gossiping . . . [is] a way of controlling female solidarity . . . a patriarchal society resents female solidarity' (p. 179).

ship in the small group and the kinds of 'ground rules' that might enhance group cohesion and identification in both task-centered and person-centered groups. The CR group doesn't always work. When it does, it is an extraordinary experience. At its core, it is a revolutionary venture that seeks to free women so that they may be 'free to be.'

References

Bonetti, Deborah, edit. *Consciousness Raising Handbook.* Los Angeles: L. A. N.O.W. Consciousness Raising Committee, 1976.

Dreifus, Claudia. *Woman's Fate: Raps from a feminist consciousness-raising group.* New York: Bantam Books, 1973.

Rysman, Alexander. 'How the "Gossip" Became a Woman.' *Journal of Communication,* vol. 27, no. 1 (Winter, 1977), pp. 176-180.

Assertive Training in Groups

Susan M. Osborn and Gloria H. Harris

Knowledge of group process is valuable because people rarely participate directly within society as individuals. They generally function in the arena of groups. The group is the medium through which socialization and social change are accomplished, and individual potentialities are maximized. Research on the effect of the group in changing individual attitudes and behavior has led to the important conclusion that group change is easier to bring about than is change of individuals separately and that its effects are more permanent.[1]

Research in group dynamics indicates that more effective methods for changing individual behaviors can be obtained through a better understanding of the group's influence on its members' behavior change.[2] An extensive study of encounter groups concluded that group dynamics do make a difference in personal learning *whether or not salient* attention is paid to them by trainers.[3] An understanding of group dynamics permits the possibility that desirable consequences from groups can be deliberately enhanced. Only the group trainer who is aware of their influence can maintain group cohesion as well as a reasonable and continued regularity of attendance and progressive changes in interactions.

Only a trainer who knows of group dynamics can evaluate whether a group proceeds at a reasonable rate from one group phase to another, from preaffiliation (Am I accepted?) to power and control (Dare I challenge the trainer and other group members?) and to intimacy (I like to give, not only to take).[4] A thorough knowledge of group dynamics enables a trainer to make better use of a group's potential to modify both human behavior and social institutions.[5]

Features of nondirective or humanistic group experiences can be incorporated into a behaviorally oriented approach to group change. For example, Gestalt therapy techniques, particularly the concept of the "here and now" which directs the focus of group activities to the feelings of group members about events occurring within the group, share with assertive training the hypothesis that patterns of behavior are a more productive focus for bringing about change than is insight into historical-determining factors.[6] We have utilized the incorporation of developments in humanistic approaches to group change in the innovative approach which is described in the following chapter.

Few systematic studies assessing the efficacy of conducting assertive training in groups have been reported. In one of the first published reports on group assertive training, Lomont and his colleagues compared group insight therapy and group assertive training in the treatment of hospitalized psychiatric patients. The results indicated that the assertive group showed a significantly greater total decrease on the clinical scales of the Minnesota Multiphasic Personality Inventory (MMPI) than the insight group.[7]

The effectiveness of group assertive training was also demonstrated in a study of socially anxious and unassertive college students.[8] The beneficial effects of this type of group treatment with sexually inadequate bachelors has been reported.[9] Rathus used group assertive training in two studies which employed groups of college women. [10, 11] In both of Rathus' studies, those exposed to assertive training reported significantly greater gains in assertive behavior than control subjects. Prior to these studies, the effectiveness of assertive training had been studied primarily through individual case histories.

We have found that assertive training is particularly well suited to a group setting. The group provides a laboratory for experimenting with and rehearsing new assertive behaviors and a broader base for social modeling than does a one-to-one interaction. Group members provide positive reinforcement and diversified feedback to each other in ways that one trainer working with a single trainee cannot. The numerous advantages of using a small group of eight to twelve participants as a setting for behavior change were discussed in detail in Chapter One.

Group Developmental Phases

The consensus of numerous systematic observations in the fields of social psychology, group psychotherapy, and group dynamics is that phases or cycle regularities exist in the developmental history of groups. Although the terminology varies, there appears to be considerable agreement among workers in the fields regarding the natural, optimal phases through which small groups progress.

It must be kept in mind, however, that the phases described represent general patterns, not ideal stages that ought to be neatly accomplished. In reality it is frequently difficult to determine the end of one phase and the beginning of another. Events and activities identified in a specific phase may be evident in other phases, and the trainer should avoid following a fixed timetable.[12] Nevertheless, certain predictable forces operate in all groups and broadly influence their course.

Various phases of group development have been identified. These include: (a) testing the leader; (b) beginning group-centered operations; and (c) group acceptance.[13] Another three-phase categorization of group development describes the process as: (a) candid self-revelation; (b) transforming personal problems into group problems; and (c) group interpretation.[14] Still another view has identified four distinct phases which are: (a) locating commonness; (b) creating exchange; (c) developing mutual identification; and (d) developing group identification.[15]

We have chosen a five-stage model for our purposes since many of the phases identified in the other models may be subsumed under it.[16] This model is solid in its theoretical underpinnings, is well articulated, and is derived from an analysis of group process records over a three-year period. It represents one of the most advanced statements in the literature concerning trainer focus at each of the various stages.[17]

This model identifies stages of group development in terms of the central theme characteristic of each. Since many models use similar, often synonomous language to describe the phases, we have placed frequently employed or synonomous terminology in parentheses for each stage. The five stages included in this model are:

1. Preaffiliation (orientation, milling): "closeness" of the members is the central theme of this stage. Ambivalence toward involvement is reflected in the members' vacillating responses to program activities and events. Relationships are usually non-intimate, and a good deal of use may be made of rather stereotypic activity as a means of getting acquainted;

2. Power and Control (conflict): after making the decision that the group is potentially rewarding, members move to a phase during which issues of power, control, status, skill, and decision making are the major issues. There is likely to be a testing of the leader and of the group members as well as an attempt to define a status hierarchy;

3. Intimacy (togetherness, affection, unity): a real group feeling develops and allows an honest exchange of feelings. There is growing awareness and mutual recognition of the significance of the group experience in terms of personality growth and change;

4. Differentiation (high cohesiveness, working group): in this stage, members begin to accept one another as distinct individuals and to see the group as providing a unique experience. The group experience achieves a functionally autonomous character in this stage. The group becomes its own frame of reference;

5. Separation (termination): the group experience has been completed, and the members may begin to move apart to find new resources for meeting their needs.

Stage I: Preaffiliation

Primary concerns of group members during this early stage center around the issues of group membership, acceptance, and approval. Preaffiliation is further characterized by a search for structure and goals, a great dependency on the leader, and a concern about the group boundaries. Many of the group members' comments are directed at or through the trainer. Surreptitious favor-seeking glances are cast at her as members demonstrate behavior which in the past has gained approval from authority. The trainer's early comments are carefully analyzed for directives about desirable and undesirable behavior.[18]

During this get acquainted phase, members are often engaged in the search for similarities. Trainees are intrigued by the idea that they are not unique, and many groups invest considerable energy in demonstrating the ways in which they resemble each other. For example, they may search for friends they have in common, experiences they have shared, books they have read, courses they have taken together. This process often provides part of the foundation for the third and fourth stages of increasing cohesion.

Simultaneously, members size up one another as well as the total group. They appear to search for a viable role for themselves while wondering if they will be liked and respected or, alternatively, ignored and rejected.[19]

Another dynamic of the early stages of group life is the presence of fear. Many factors in the new group increase the normal residual fear that all people share. Politeness, formality, and stereotyped behavior are early indications of this fear. Politeness wards off retaliation, keeps people at a safe distance, and discourages other persons from giving negative feedback.[20]

Still another response which frequently appears in the early stages of group life is the use of humor. It is ambiguous enough to serve as a relatively safe camouflage for negative feedback to another person. Humor at this stage may encourage people to keep things from getting too intense or too intimate.[21] Frequently, one or two women will be instantly liked by the other group members because they are witty. Often their moderately funny remarks elicit great bursts of nervous laughter because the group members are so tense.

During the preaffiliation stage the assertive trainer should provide an orientation to the group, outline its purpose, and establish a contract with the members. An initial contract includes an agreement on the part of the group members to attend regularly and to put their best effort into the group problem-solving process. Structuring the group in these ways provides opportunities for exploration among the group members and invites trust. The trainer may also point out to the group some common elements that bind them together as well as those factors that may separate them.[22]

The initial contract includes a commitment to continue in the group through the final session. This stabilizes the membership and resolves the issue of adding new members once the training has begun. On occasions when we have enrolled trainees after the preaffiliation stage, we have found that the group regresses temporarily until the new members have been assimilated into the group. We therefore refrain from adding latecomers.

Stage II: Power and Control

In this stage the group members deal with issues of interpersonal dominance and their relationship with authority. The group shifts from a preoccupation with acceptance, approval, and structure to a preoccupation with dominance, control, and power. Each member attempts to establish for herself her optimal amount of initiative and power, and gradually a control hierarchy is established. It is of interest to note that the assertive group trainer has no monopoly on authoritarianism. It is not at all uncommon for trainees to work on authoritarianism. It is not at all uncommon for trainees to work through problems of authority or of unassertiveness with other group members.[23]

One way in which the control issue often appears is through subtle comparisons among the group members of assessments about which trainees are more assertive than others. Or one trainee may covertly challenge the trainer to match her assertive skills. It is particularly important for the trainer to feel secure enough at this point about her own assertive abilities to be able to emphasize devising collective ways to increase assertive skills instead of encouraging competitive comparisons.

Communication jams and withholding of communications may arise in this stage of group life.[24] Members may be unable or unwilling to verbalize and communicate what they may clearly or vaguely sense as some state of frustration in the group situation that needs change and correction. When such a situation exists, assertive trainers have found it useful to use the psychodramatic techniques of identifying the negative feelings and encouraging members to express them. This technique appears to be useful only if it is followed by a task oriented discussion of concrete ways to alter the conditions which the members find annoying. Encouragement of negative statements should ultimately lead to evaluation of ongoing procedures and to a possible change in them.[25]

The emergence of anger directed toward the trainer is an inevitable occurrence in the developmental sequence of the group. This hostility usually has its roots not so much in what the trainer does or what she is in reality, but what she evokes in the fantasy of each group member. On the other hand, although disenchantment with the leader is an inevitable feature of small groups, by no means is the process the same in all groups. Those trainers who offer no guidelines for group members and who covertly make unfulfillable promises to the group early in its life appear to elicit greater negative response.[26] Assertive training groups, since they are more highly structured than more traditional group approaches, afford less opportunity for such failures on the part of group trainers. Also, the incidence of hostility appears to be minimal due to the trainer's interest in sharing the leadership with the trainees.

During this stage, however, it is recommended that the trainer act in her capacity as group executive and facilitator of membership roles in order to forestall the crystallization of any power takeover by a particular clique or subgroup which may want to use the group for purposes that are not relevant to assertive training. The trainer will want to strive to clarify the power struggle while attempting to focus attention on the function and goals of the group.[27]

Stage III: Intimacy

During this stage the group becomes increasingly concerned with intermember harmony, and differences are gradually submerged. There is an increase of morale, mutual trust, and self-disclosure.[28] The members respond to each other with behaviors that reflect recognition, interest, concern, sympathy, affection, assistance, and acceptance more frequently than do the members of a noncohesive group.

Specific examples of statements that may be viewed as signs of increasing intimacy or cohesiveness in a group are:
"I missed you last week."
"You gave me a lot of help when I was having trouble."
"Would you like to start a carpool for the rest of the sessions?"
"You won't let me detach myself from the group."
"We're all in the same boat."
"We do want to help you, if you will let us."
"If it's any consolation to you, I felt that way too."
The behavior presented in these examples includes those statements which tie one group member to another with positive feelings or which imply moving closer toegther.[29]

There are many reported advantages to the cohesive group. Included among these are: (a) one can expect its members to attend regularly; (b) there is greater likelihood of member conformance to group norms; and (c) there is greater likelihood of imitation of its models.[30] In an interesting study which compared a behavioral approach to group dynamics with a more conventional, intuitive, group-centered approach, it was found that members of the behaviorally oriented group showed a highly positive correlation between cohesiveness and early symptomatic improvement. This was not true for the comparison group. Furthermore, as cohesiveness increased the members of the behaviorally oriented group directed their actions increasingly toward other group members and away from the leader, thus demonstrating greater independence.[31]

Additional findings have been cited that lend support to the contention that group cohesiveness is an important determinant of positive therapeutic outcome.[32] There is evidence that individuals with positive outcome have had more mutually satisfying intermember relationships. Positive outcome is further correlated with individual attraction to the group and also to group popularity, a variable related to group support and acceptance.

Several other studies which have examined this stage show that members of a more cohesive group can readily exert influence on one another and are more readily influenced by one another. Other studies have shown that as cohesiveness increases, there is more frequent communication among members and a greater degree of participation in group activities. Finally, highly cohesive groups provide a source of security for members that serves to reduce anxiety and to heighten self-esteem.[33]

Certain properties of groups may serve to foster intimacy. Among those identified as possessing potential incentive value are:

1. *Similarities among members.* The total body of evidence indicates that similarity with respect to values, interests, attitudes, and beliefs important to the members of a group usually heightens attraction. Members of assertive training groups begin with this asset.

2. *Nature of group goals.* The goals of a group constitute another possible source of attractiveness. Having a distinct goal or purpose serves to facilitate the development of interpersonal bonds. This phenomenon is quite apparent in assertive training groups because the trainees enter the group with specific ideas about the behavior changes they want to make.

3. *Type of interdependence among members.* When the members of a group accept a common goal and agree on actions required to reach it, they become cooperatively interdependent. Each member gains satisfaction from the contributions made by others toward the attainment of their common goal.

4. *Style of leadership.* Studies indicate that a group's attractiveness is influenced by the nature of its leadership. A democratic form of organization that encourages widespread participation in decision making appears generally to induce more attraction to the group than does one in which decisions are centralized.[34]

A number of action strategies are suggested by the findings discussed in the intimacy-of-cohesiveness stage. The assertive trainer is required to support the group through the emotional phase of increased interdependency. She helps the members to sort out and to discuss the positive and negative aspects of increased closeness and works with them to clarify how this group is different from the others in which they participate. She is constantly on the lookout for opportunities to entrust the members with the responsibility that in the earlier stages she has reserved for herself.[35]

Furthermore, the selection of behaviors which might be reinforced for the benefit of members of an assertive training group is an additional strategy suggested. As the central and most valued figure in the group, the trainer acts as an effective agent of social reinforcement and prompting. A trainer who consciously and systematically reinforces cohesive group behavior can more quickly and thoroughly induce behavioral and attitudinal change in the realm of assertiveness than a leader who uses more intuitive and unplanned approaches.[36]

Stage IV: Differentiation

As a clarification of power relationships gives freedom for autonomy and intimacy, so clarification of and coming to terms with intimacy and mutual acceptance of personal needs bring freedom and ability to differentiate and to evaluate relationships and events in the group on a reality basis.[37] In this stage the group has resolved most of its power problems and has high mutual support among the members as well as good communication. The preconditions for a working group have been established.

Group members may become more spontaneous and less cautious. They learn to tolerate greater degrees of ambiguity and to make allowances for greater differences both in themselves and in others. Members are permitted to be themselves, to be unpredictable, and perhaps even to be disloyal. The boundaries of acceptance widen.[38] This acceptance also includes allowing for the emergence of occasional angry feelings. Only when all affect can be expressed and constructively accomplished in a cohesive assemblage does the group become a mature work group, a state lasting for the remainder of the group's life.[39]

The trainer now helps the group to run itself by encouraging individual members to take responsibility for achieving the group's objectives. With the increased cohesiveness and the heightened sense of the group's special identity as a separate, meaningful influence, the trainer can begin to direct the group toward situations in the larger community outside the group. The trainer aids the group in relating, while not necessarily adjusting, to the real-life environment and induces the members to begin evaluation of their experience in preparation for the separation phase.[40]

Stage V: Separation

The trainer helps the group through the process of separation by encouraging evaluation, recapitulation, and the formation of an action plan for the future. Traditionally, behavior therapy has viewed the relationship between the client and the behavior therapist as being of minor consequence, and as a result, most behavior therapy literature ignores the possibility of "separation anxiety" when the group is concluded. Insightists, on the other hand, view termination as one of the most critical phases of treatment.

Despite a lack of theoretical endorsement, our clinical observations and research support the view that near the close of their behavioral training groups, members do experience a sense of unresolved frustration about ending what has been a significant relationship. Therefore, even when the treatment has been predominantly behavioral, the anger and sadness of the members that they are losing in the group should be recognized if the experience is to have optimal success.[41]

References

1. Olmsted, Michael S.: *The Small Group.* New York, Random, 1959.
2. Bach, George R.: *Intensive Group Psychotherapy.* New York, Ronald, 1954.
3. Lieberman, Morton A., Yalom, Irvin, and Miles, Matthew: *Encounter Groups: First Facts.* New York, Basic, 1973.
4. Fried, E.: Basic concepts in group psychotherapy. In Sadock, B. J., and Kaplan, H. I. (Eds.): *The Evolution of Group Therapy.* New York, Jason Aronson, Inc., 1972.
5. Cartwright, Darwin, and Zander, Alvin F.: *Group Dynamics: Research and Theory.* New York, Har-Row, 1968.
6. Goldstein, Alan, and Wolpe, Joseph: Behavior therapy in groups. In Kaplan, H. I., and Sadock, B. I. (Eds.): *New Models for Group Therapy.* New York, Jason Aronson, Inc., 1972.
7. Lomont, James F., Gilner, Frank, Spector, Norman, and Skinner, Kathryn: Assertion training and group insight therapies. *Psychol Rep, 25:* 463-70, 1969.
8. Hedquist, Frances, and Weinhold, Barry: Behavioral group counseling with socially anxious and unassertive college students. *Journal of Counseling Psychology, 3:*237-42, 1970.
9. Fensterheim, Herbert: Behavior therapy: assertive training in groups. In Sager, Clifford J., and Kaplan, Helen Singer (Eds.): *Progress in Group and Family Therapy.* New York, Brunner/Mazel, 1972.
10. Rathus, Spencer: An experimental investigation of assertive training in a group setting. *Journal of Behavior Therapy and Experimental Psychiatry, 3:*81-86, 1972.
11. Rathus, Spencer: Instigation of assertive behavior through videotape mediated assertive models and directed practice. *Behav Res Ther, 2:*57-65, 1973.
12. Vintner, Robert: The Essential Components of Social Group Work Practice. Unpublished paper, School of Social Work, University of Michigan, September, 1959.
13. Thorpe, J. J., and Smith, B.: Phases in group development in the treatment of drug addiction. *Int J Group Psychoth, 3:*66-71, 1953.

14. Taylor, F. K.: The therapeutic factors of group analytic treatment. *Journal of Mental Science, 96:*976-80, 1950.
15. Maier, Henry W.: Application of psychological and sociological theory of teaching social work with the group. *Journal of Education for Social Work, 3:*29-41, 1967.
16. Garland, James, Jones, Hubert, and Kolodny, Ralph: A model for stages of development in social work groups. In Bernstein, S. (Ed.): *Explorations in Group Work.* Boston, Boston University School of Social Work, 1965.
17. Whittaker, James K.: Models of group development: implications for social group work practice. *The Social Service Review, 44,* 1970.
18. Yalom, Irvin: *The Theory and Practice of Group Psychotherapy.* New York, Basic, 1970.
19. Yalom: *Group Psychotherapy.*
20. Gibb, Jack, and Gibb, Lorraine: Humanistic elements in group growth. In Bugental, J. T. (Ed.): *Challenges of Humanistic Psychology.* New York, McGraw, 1967.
21. Gibb and Gibb: Humanistic elements.
22. Whittaker: Group development.
23. Yalom: *Group Psychotherapy.*
24. Bach: *Intensive Group Psychotherapy.*
25. Rose, Sheldon: *Treating Children in Groups.* San Francisco, Jossey-Bass, 1973.
26. Yalom: *Group Psychoterapy.*
27. Whittaker: Group development.
28. Yalom: *Group Psychotherapy.*
29. Liberman, Robert: A behavioral approach to group dynamics. *Behavior Therapy, 1:*141-75, 1970.
30. Cartwright, Dorwin: The nature of group cohesiveness. In Cartwright, Dorwin, and Zander, Alvin (Eds.): *Group Dynamics: Research and Theory.* New York, Har-Row, 1968.
31. Liberman: Behavioral approach.
32. Yalom: *Group Psychotherapy.*
33. Cartwright and Zander: *Group Dynamics.*
34. Cartwright and Zander: *Group Dynamics.*
35. Whittaker: Group development.
36. Liberman: Behavioral approach.
37. Garland: Stages of development.
38. Gibb and Gibb: Humanistic elements.
39. Yalom: *Group Psychotherapy.*
40. Whittaker: Group development.
41. Woody, Robert H.: *Psychobehavioral Counseling and Therapy.* New York, Appleton, 1971.

SUGGESTED READINGS

Chapter 4

Bradford, Leland R., Gibb, Jack R., and Benne, Kenneth D., eds. *T-Group Theory and Laboratory Method.* New York: John Wiley & Sons, Inc., 1964.

Burton, Arthur, ed. *Encounter: The Theory and Practice of Encounter Groups.* San Francisco: Jossey-Bass, Inc., 1969.

Cotter, B. and Guerra, J. *Assertion Training: A Humanistic-Behavioral Guide to Self-Dignity.* Champaign, Ill.: Research Press, 1976.

Egan, Gerard. *Face to Face: The Small-Group Experience and Interpersonal Growth.* Monterey, CA: Brooks/Cole Publishing Company, 1973.

Goldhaber, Gerald M. and Goldhaber, Marylynn B. *Transaction Analysis: Principles and Applications.* Boston: Allyn & Bacon, Inc., 1976.

Golembiewski, Robert T. and Blumberg, Arthur, *Sensitivity and the Laboratory Approach.* Itasca, Ill.: F. E. Peacock Publishers, Inc., 1970.

Guinan, James F. and Foulds, Melvin L. "The Marathon Group." *Journal of Counseling Psychology,* XIII (1963), 236-45.

Gunther, Bernard. *Sense Relaxation Below Your Mind.* New York: The Macmillan Co., 1968.

Moore, Lawrence J. and Clayton, Edward R. *Gert Modeling and Simulation Fundamentals and Applications.* New York: Petrocelli/Charter, 1976.

Pfeiffer, William J. and Jones, John E. *A Handbook of Structured Experiences for Human Relations Training, Vol. I.* Iowa City: University Associates Press, 1970.

O'Banion, Terry and O'Connell, April. *The Shared Journey.* Englewood Cliffs, N. J.: Prentice-Hall, Inc., 1970, Chapter 9.

Otto, Herbert A. *Group Methods to Actualize Human Potential.* Beverly Hills, CA: The Holistic Press, 1970.

Osborn, Alex F. *Applied Imagination.* New York: Charles Scribner's Sons, 1957.

Phillips, Donald J. "Report on Discussion 66." *Adult Education Journal,* 7 (1947): 181-82.

Rogers, Carl R. *Carl Rogers on Encounter Groups.* New York: Harper & Row, Publishers, 1970.

Schien, E. H. and Bennis, W. G. *Personal and Organizational Change Through Group Methods: The Laboratory Approach.* New York: John Wiley & Sons, Inc., 1965.

Schutz, William C. *Joy: Expanding Human Awareness.* New York: Grove Press, Inc., 1969.

Siroka, Robert W., Siroka, Ellen K., and Schloss, Gilbert A. *Sensitivity Training and Group Encounter: An Introduction.* New York: Grossett and Dunlap, 1971.

Experiencing and Evaluating

Prescribed Games: A Theoretical Perspective on the Use of Group Techniques[1]

Joan Ellen Zweben and Kalen Hammen

The past few years have seen a proliferation of ingenious techniques for encounter, sensitivity, and therapy groups. Unfortunately, such techniques often lack a broad conceptual rationale for their application; instead they are discussed as relatively isolated "things to try" with overly specific purposes. The following is a theoretical perspective on some of the techniques. First we shall discuss the place of rules in human interaction. Next, encounter groups and the like ("self-analytic groups") will be presented as structured situations in which the impact of rules can be explored. Finally, we shall present a rationale for "Prescribed Games" as techniques for such exploration within groups.

Rules and Roles in Human Interaction

Most human interaction is governed by implicit or explicit "rules" (Watzlawick, 1967) specifying what participants may and may not, must and must not do while they are together. Rules about behavior associated with some position in social space (father, leader, etc.) specify a "role;" a set of such roles constitute a "social system," and a social system typically involves an overarching set of rules ("norms") which apply to the behavior of all par-

From *Psychotherapy: Theory, Research and Practice*, 1970, 7 (1), pp. 22-27. Used with the permission of the publisher and the authors.
1. The authors wish to express their appreciation to Cora Bierman and Jessica Hammann for editorial assistance.

ticipants in the system. The rules each participant has for his own behavior are not limited to his own conceptions of his various roles.

In the initial encounters of a group (social system) the rules are tested out and defined by the participants. Later they become stabilized and relatively harder to alter as members become comfortable with established ways of interacting. People are generally unaware of this process and of the rules themselves, but if the rules are excessively constraining they may limit severely what sorts of persons participants can be with each other. Of crucial importance is the fact that the rules affect not only what people can do but also what they can experience. Hence changes in the rules both reflect preceding changes in experience and constrain or open new areas of future experience for those influenced by them.

The Link to Self-Analytic Groups

Despite their differences, therapy, sensitivity, and encounter groups provide opportunities to (1) experience the effects of rules by which they habitually limit their interaction with others, (2) become aware of how such rules are established and changed, and (3) experience what it is like to live under rules allowing greater freedom. It seems likely that such groups are more effective (lead to greater insight, behavior change, etc.) when they focus more directly on these kinds of rule-exploration.[2] How does such exploration take place?

Much of a leader's energy in this sort of group goes into explicitly or intuitively diagnosing the existing rules. He may focus more on the rules individuals have for themselves, as psychotherapists typically do, or on the rules the group is establishing for all members, but in either case he is likely to come across some rules that are quite constraining. He may then attempt to change such constraining rules in one of several ways.[3] A common approach is to point them out or to make an interpretation and hope group members will alter their behavior in appropriate ways.

For example, group members often initially express their feelings in the form of questions instead of statements, as if they had a rule against the open expression of feelings. Questions beginning with "Why . . ." (e.g., "Why did you do a crazy thing like that?") illustrate the functions such a rule performs. These questions lend themselves well to being employed as double binds, since it is impossible to pin down what the asker intends by his communication. Consider the question (asked tensely), "Why are you so angry with

---

2. For example, though he conceptualizes it somewhat differently, this seems to be much of what Eric Berne is doing through "transactional analysis." His thesaurus of *Games People Play* represents a significant, though not usefully organized, compendium of the relatively constraining sets of rules which form the basis of many relationships.

3. Whitaker and Lieberman (1964) have spelled out this notion that a group therapist's main function is to help a group establish "enabling" rather than "restrictive" rules.

him?" Responding to the affect by saying something like "You seem to object to my being angry with him" can evoke the reply, "Oh no, I was just curious." Responding to the question as if it were indeed a request for information is likely to evoke further angry questioning or accusations, since not dealing with the affect leaves unfinished business. "Why . . ." questions, then, are very well suited to evasion of responsibility for one's own "negative" reactions. Their appearance is therefore likely to signify that people are operating as if there were a rule against expressing negative affect directly or "unreasonably" and are seeking to avoid being blamed for such expression. Such a rule may, of course, be an internal one: a person may feel guilty if he allows himself to express anger directly "without a good reason."

In order to help group members become aware of the consequences of such a rule, the leader might focus their attention on the group's communication pattern by saying: "We seem to be expressing our feelings in the form of questions instead of statements; perhaps we're developing a norm against the open expression of (negative) feelings."

Prescribed Games

An alternative and, in our view, a more useful approach is the use of a "Prescribed Game."[4] The techniques subsumed under "Prescribed Games" go one step further than interpretations such as the above in that they permit participants to translate these interpretations directly into their own immediate experience. In a Prescribed Game the group leader structures interaction for a delimited period by prescribing what the norms and, sometimes, the roles for participants and the task will be during that time. Afterward, members discuss what they experienced during the game: what they saw, became aware of, and felt while interaction was governed by the rules the leader set up. In prescribing a game the leader may be following either or both of two main strategies: that of Caricature and that of Set-Breaking.

The Strategy of Caricature, or
More of the Same

In the strategy of Caricature (also referred to as symptom scheduling, negative practice, reactive inhibition, and therapeutic paradox or paradoxical intention), the essence is to ask group members to behave deliberately in accordance with a rule they were already following implicitly, under condi-

---

4. We are using "game" here in the sense of "rule-governed interaction." We regret the additional connotations the word "game" may carry for the reader, from "frivolous competition" to "(un)conscious manipulation" to mathematical "Game Theory," but no other word seems to serve as well. We hope our addition of the adjective "prescribed" will help in this regard: it seems to us to connote serious purpose and conscious participation, as well as a pleasing sense of being "just what the doctor ordered."

tions which allow its experiential impact to be heightened. To foster this heightening, the leader may ask members to exaggerate the behavior. For example, a member who seems to allow himself only ingratiating, self-dep-recating behavior may be requested to "Get on your hands and knees and apologize for yourself to every member of the group." Or he may be asked to, "Get a compliment from each member of the group and immediately find some way to refute or disqualify each one." Alternatively, the leader may request members to translate the behavior into another modality (e.g., two members who are using words to keep one another at a distance may be asked to push each other away physically). This exaggeration or translation allows the members to experience more fully the impact of what they are doing, both on themselves and on others, and to decide for or against change on the basis of this experiential understanding. In addition, the experience of doing de-liberately something which they may previously have been doing uncon-sciously or involuntarily can help members gain both awareness of and con-trol over the behavior. (Cf. control of muscular tics gained by practicing them, and Jackson's "prescribing the symptom" to help a patient learn to eliminate it.)

Other Examples:

1. In a situation like that described above in which members seem to be expressing their feelings in the form of questions rather than as statements, the leader might prescribe a game such as the following to bring it to members' attention through the strategy of Caricature:

> Members may communicate for the next five minutes *only* by asking questions. Once you have been asked a question, you may ask one to someone else in the group, but no one may answer any questions during the Game. You may not question the person who questions you more than twice in succession (so that the interaction will not focus on two people for very long).

This exercise very rapidly elevates the tension level and may reveal many content issues previously hidden as it becomes obvious to participants that questions are also statements. In addition, members become attuned to the affect-laden nature of questions in general and particularly to the accusatory quality of "Why . . ." questions.

2. Almost anything members are doing verbally can be highlighted by asking them to do it nonverbally. For example, a member who is seeking to dominate others may be asked to push them to the floor and stand trium-phantly over them, a group of newcomers who have been trying vainly to become full members of the group may be asked to break into a circle of old members, etc. In nearly all such cases, the impact of rules by which people were seeking to limit the range of their own or others' behavior is clearly demonstrated.

The Set-Breaking Strategy, or
Highlighting by Contrast

The second strategy a leader may use involves prescribing a game which gives group members a taste of interacting under very different rules. The sudden change in what participants experience may then demonstrate the effects of the previous rules quite clearly by contrast. For example, members may be asked to do exactly the opposite of what they have been doing. If they have been expressing their feelings in the form of questions, as above, the leader may prescribe a game with the rule that no one may ask a question until he has made a statement committing himself to a position. Members often find that once they have made the statement, there is no need for a question after all. They can then use their experiences to explore the use of questions to evade responsibility for feelings.

Other Examples:

1. Even if they do not hide behind questions, many group members initially communicate in highly tentative ways, surrounding all expressions of feeling with immense amounts of protective and distancing verbiage. Such verbiage helps them to disown controversial remarks, and hence reduces the risk of their being criticized or devalued for expressions of feeling or ideas which others cannot accept. Often such members seem to believe that only the most cautious kinds of approach and the most limited sorts of vulnerability to others will be safe for them to risk. The leader may help them explore the degree of reality in these assumptions through a Set-Breaking game such as the following:

> "Pair up, and carry on a dialogue in which each of you speaks only one sentence at a time before the other responds." (After members have done so for a short time:) "Now communicate using only one phrase before the other responds." . . . "Continue your dialogue using only one word before the other responds." . . . "Now use only gibberish." . . . "Now communicate nonverbally."

Members typically experience a heightening of emotional intensity in the interaction and greater contact with the other person as the game proceeds. Those who find this game extremely anxiety arousing are often able to gain meaningful insight into their reliance on words for distancing and control.

2. Gestalt therapists often make a rule "No Why-Because games" ("Why did you do that?" "Because I'm hung up on my mother, I guess." . . .). This rule has the effect of discouraging members from relating to one another through a detailed examination of how their psyches work. Such a rule is often particularly effective in enhancing professional therapists' capacity to relate! (Levitsky and Perls). For groups without a great tendency to intellectualize, one may prefer to allow or even prescribe why-because games in order to

facilitate intellectual understanding. The rule against them can always be invoked as a Set-Breaking game if the group becomes too involved in amateur psychoanalysis.[5]

An Example of Mixed Strategies:
The "Systems Games"

Other, more complicated Prescribed Games can be used for working with various dimensions of interpersonal style. Among the most powerful of these are the "systems games" (Satir, 1966; Zweben and Miller, 1968). They are based on the notion that the rules for interaction (norms) which characterize a social system depend in important ways on the set of roles which make up the system.

The systems games are efficiently played in subgroups of four, three participants and an observer. Participants suggest one of four interactional rules for their own behavior (roles). These are: # 1—agree to placate. All negotiations or expressions of feeling must be cast in these terms. Actor behaves as though his feelings are not worth considering. E.g., "Whatever you want is fine with me." "Don't you think we could do it better another way?" or "Let's not get upset about it; I'm sure you two can get along without fighting." # 2—blame or attack. Others are treated as though their feelings did not matter. E.g., "You *always* change the subject whenever we try to talk about sex." or "If you would only stop doing that, we could begin to accomplish something around here." # 3—be correct or reasonable. All disagreements are decided on the basis of pronouncements about what "authorities" (such as the *Bible* or a psychology text) say; the actor behaves as though neither he nor others have feelings worth considering. E.g., "It's not appropriate for a girl your age to wear lipstick. All the child-care manuals agree." or "I understand it is good to ventilate one's feelings. You seem upset; perhaps you should shout at me. (Of course, it will not touch me, but) it may prove therapeutic for you." # 4—being irrelevant. All significant interactions are disrupted by changing the subject or being in some way inappropriate or incongruous, making jokes, or diverting attention by nonverbal means. E.g., "(Argument? What argument?) I'm just sitting here, groovin' on the lights." Or "We've had spaghetti at our house four times this week." # 5—commit self to a position and include the other person. E.g., "I would like to do this; what would you like to do?" This way of relating is also characterized by congruence between what the person expressed verbally and in other modalities, i.e. there are no mixed or hidden messages.

---

5. Or what Gestalt therapists describe somewhat more colorfully as "mindfucking." Another useful bit of Gestalt argot is "mindbending," which refers to behavior aimed at getting someone to invalidate his own perceptions. E.g., "Don't say that. You're not *really* angry with your sister. Tell her how you love her. Tell her you're sorry."

Each participant in a group of four plays one role at a time, in combinations chosen at random or prescribed by the leader. (Rule # 5 is usually saved for later, as one purpose of the games is to bring the hidden rules into awareness and under conscious control.) Participants are then encouraged while taking the roles to make a decision of some sort or to discuss a controversial issue. The observer helps the participants in his group of four stick to the role they select and also comments on the interaction as an onlooker. Non-verbal means, such as voice tone, gestures, posture, and expression can and should be used to enact each role. Participants are asked to play until they have a sense of the payoffs and the constraints and frustrations of both the role they are enacting and the social system that is evolving. Everyone is then encouraged to comment on what he experienced. Both the Caricature and the Set-Breaking strategies can be employed by instructing participants to be sure to try the role they think they usually play and also the one that comes hardest for them. The leader can also use the games to highlight a group pattern by assigning a particular combination of roles. For example, if the group members are dealing with each other in a very gingerly fashion, having all members play the placator simultaneously usually effects a very rapid transformation.

An Additional Use for Prescribed Games: Finding Out What the Rules Are

In addition to those already mentioned, group leaders occasionally use prescribed games of a third type. These are games aimed at bringing out the effects not of one specific rule or cluster of rules, but rather of the whole pattern of rules by which interaction in the group is governed at a given point in time. They can also be used to help clarify for the members or the leader just what the rules are at that point. For example, the leader may ask members to think of things they would like to say to other members which they do not feel it is "appropriate" to say, or of things which previously seemed inappropriate but which could be said now. A discussion of what sorts of things these were can help clarify both what "autistic" rules individuals are using to limit their own behavior and what the norms of the group are perceived to be.

Other Examples:

Secrets: In a variant of the game just presented, the leader may request members to think of a secret they would not wish to tell at this time, to imagine telling it, and to then share their fantasies of what it was like to tell their secrets. This process may bring out clearly the nature of the rules (and attendant fears) which are currently making it difficult for members to share certain kinds of thoughts or feelings.

Group fantasy: The leader may begin a fantasy about the group and different members' roles in it, then suggest the rule that people add to the fantasy by saying whatever comes into their mind when another person finishes speaking. As in psychoanalytic "free association," such a rule may help members to talk about constraints or conflicts about what to do which they had not previously acknowledged.

Ranking: The leader may ask members to stand in a line representing their rank order on some dimension such as "influence in the group," "frankness," etc. How they place themselves may provide a rich source of data not only about perceptions of influence but also about rules concerning competition (Do people fight freely for the top spot? Do they fight politely for the bottom spot?), how much influence is it acceptable for people to suggest that they have (Do people seem to assume that only men can legitimately have the top spots?), and the like. The leader may then suggest that anyone who believes someone else is incorrectly placed can move him to another place in the line. This phase can similarly bring out rules about what parts of the dimension are seen as "legitimate" for men, older members, etc. to be in (e.g., are all the older members moved to the top?). In addition, it may bring out such rules as "It is all right to suggest that a person has more influence (is better) than he thinks, but not that he has less (is worse) than he thinks," or that "One must accept the leader's estimate of a member's position," etc. (This game can also be prescribed as a Set-Breaker if the group seems to be operating on the rule that all members are to be treated exactly alike, as if there were no important differences among people.)

Leaders seem to use fewer prescribed games of this last type than of the Caricature or Set-Breaking types. This may be in large part because the whole format of a self-analytic group often amounts to a prescribed game of this type writ large: members are presented with a relatively unstructured situation (on which they tend to impose their habitual rules for dealing with others) and with rules for their interaction (either explicit or implicit in what the leader says) such as "limit your discussion to what is occurring Here and Now" and "Talk about what you are feeling." Talking about "the Here and Now" often leads to identification of patterns of rules as they are established; talking about feelings supplies a constant stream of data about the effects of those rules as they form and change.

Summary and a Look Ahead

We have attempted to provide a theoretical perspective within which can be placed many of the growing number of exercises, "nonverbals," etc. used by leaders of self-analytic groups. We have pointed to the central importance of implicit and explicit group rules, both for individuals (roles) and for group interaction (norms), in determining what happens when people come together. We have suggested that exploration of these rules and their effects provides a central task for groups which hope to help individuals become aware of and change maladaptive or unnecessarily constraining ways of relating to others.

We see two main needs for the future in this area, a conceptual one and a practical one. The conceptual need we see is for a useable typology of the rules people use to structure their relationships. Such a typology would help practitioners think more clearly about the situations they encounter in groups and devise appropriate prescribed games to clarify these situations for participants. The practical need is for a compendium of prescribed games which are useful in the ways we have suggested. (The authors would be glad to serve as a clearing house for such games: readers who send descriptions of innovations they run across or originate will receive collections, brought up to date occasionally, of all prescribed games we have received.)

It may be that groups aimed at fostering human growth are on the verge of moving beyond a dependence for their methods on the intuitive flashes of brilliant artists, into an era of techniques firmly based on tested theories of human interaction. If this is true, a rich and exciting time lies just ahead.

References

Berne, Eric, *Transactional Analysis in Psychotherapy*. New York: Grove Press, Inc., 1961.

Berne, Eric, *Games People Play*. New York: Grove Press, 1964.

Garfinkle, Harold, *Studies in Ethnomethodology*. Englewood Cliffs, New Jersey: Prentice Hall, 1967.

Levitsky, Abraham, & Perls, Frederick, "The Rules and Games of Gestalt Therapy." Available from the San Francisco Gestalt Therapy Institute, 3701 Sacramento St., San Francisco, California 94118.

Satir, Virginia. Paper presented at the American Psychological Association Convention, New York City, 1966.

Watzlawick, Paul, Beavin, Janet, & Jackson, Don D., *Pragmatics of Human Communication*. New York: W. W. Norton, 1967.

Whitaker, Dorothy Stock & Lieberman, Morton A., *Psychotherapy through the Group Process*. New York: Atherton Press, 1964.

Zweben, Joan Ellen & Miller, Richard Louis, "The Systems Games: Teaching, Training, Psychotherapy." *Psychotherapy: Theory, Research and Practice*, June 1968, 5(2), pp. 73–76.

A Cinderella Skill: Behavior Rehearsal for Personal Change

Edward Rintye

I think Cinderella would have done well today.

She was adaptable, flexible, a survivor.

Remember how quickly she changed her old behaviors when reality called for new responses? She didn't hesitate a moment when her pumpkin changed into a splendid coach: she just climbed aboard. Remember how she dropped her servant act and put on her ballroom act? And how firmly she asserted her right to try on the glass slipper? That prince was no fool. He knew a quality lady when he saw one.

She dealt with reality. She handled it. She changed.

I find that skill important in my life, too. Especially is it important to me in my interpersonal relationships. Check this out from your own experience. What I get in life seems to depend on how I live—how I behave. And that means sometimes I need to drop old ways of doing my act and learn new ways. Behave in different ways to get better results.

The truth is that I became a teacher of communication in order to find out how to do it. I discovered how to communicate, alright, but no one seemed to know much about how to go about dropping old behaviors and assuming the workable new behaviors. I was in a place of knowing what to do but not knowing how to get there from where I was. Does that make any sense? I found it almost impossible to drop old communication habits and adopt new ones. I found it almost impossible to give up old attitudes and adopt new ones. In short, I needed some Cinderella skills.

Well . . . I found some.

In this brief essay I want to share with you a very useful and easy skill for changing behavior—"behavior rehearsal." It's called that because its essence is that you mentally or physically rehearse the new behavior you want to acquire. I'll get into that in a moment. Most of the research I'm aware of has been done by clinical psychologists or in extremely small experimental group settings.[1] Some of the leading authorities in that field are very encouraged about the size of behavior rehearsal in groups.[2] I have

1. Edward D. Rintye, "The Combined Effect of Overt and Covert Behavior Rehearsal on Student Self-Concept in a Community College Course in Interpersonal Communication" (Unpublished Ph.D. dissertation, School of Human Behavior, United States International University, 1976), pp. 32-49.

2. Ibid., pp. 32-41.

personally taught the skill quite successfully (if I can believe my eyes and my students) in a classroom setting with up to thirty people.[3]

The nice thing about behavior rehearsal is that once the skill is acquired by someone a teacher is unnecessary. The learner then has a tool which can be used independently whenever desired. The learner does not have to come back to the teacher to acquire new behaviors.

When I use the phrase "behavior rehearsal" I am referring to either a physical or a mental *simulation* of the new way a person wants to act in a given situation. Physical or overt behavior rehearsal is *role-playing* of the words and body actions which make up the desired behavior. The learner rehearses just as if she were an actress rehearsing for a play—which, in fact, is the case. In non-technical terms it is a "dry run" of actual behavior. Mental or covert behavior rehearsal is the *imaginary fantasy* rehearsal of the words and body actions which make up the desired behavior. Here the learner imagines or mentally visualizes the situation and sees himself speaking and acting in the new way. I was surprised to learn when I first began to get into behavior rehearsal that imaginary rehearsal produces the same significant changes in real behavior as does physical rehearsal.[4] When I teach them I insist that people use both forms, just to cover all the bases.

People use such rehearsal in much of their daily life. They physically rehearse as they try on new clothing, look into the mirror, talk to themselves in their car. The Army rehearses combat. Industry and education rehearse job performance (vocational training). Athletes rehearse competing. Your local DMV encourages rehearsal of auto driving. Can you think of any other examples? People use imaginary rehearsal before asking for that raise, as the traffic officer pulls them off the road, on the way home at 3:00 a.m., before calling in sick to work, as they raise their hand to ask a question in class, as they choose their costume for that special date, before they move that chess piece. You know still other cases, don't you? The list is endless.

The problem is that most individuals are unconscious about using the technique. They don't deliberately use rehearsal to change unsatisfactory behavior or add to their behavior repertoire. And that is a shame, since the method works so well and costs so little. My goal in writing this article is to help raise your awareness of the value of *deliberate use of something you already know how to do,* so that you can more consciously fill your needs.

O.K. Let's get to it.

I'm going to describe how I teach the technique in the classroom and I want you to make whatever adjustments are needed to fit your circum-

---

3. David C. Rimm and John C. Masters, *Behavior Therapy: Techniques and Empirical Findings* (New York: Academic Press, 1974), pp. 160-161.

4. Op cit., pp. 41-49.

stances. The basic steps are sound, so you needn't worry about goofing it up. It's "goof proof" if you follow the basics.

Step one: Be clear on the new behavior you wish to develop. Building new behaviors is as real and as concrete as building a bridge. You have to know what you want *before* you begin the process. To the degree you are fuzzy about what specific behavior you desire to learn, you will be unsatisfied with the results. Imagine building a bridge without a blueprint. It doesn't work. Of course this first step assumes that you are highly motivated to develop new behavior, for change takes energy. If you think that the target behavior will only be "nice to have" then you probably shouldn't waste your time rehearsing, because there is not enough energy behind that lack of commitment. Assuming that you do want the new behavior (and the results it will get for you), I suggest that you write out a detailed description of the behavior—in the specific situation you wish to use it. Think it through, tighten up the sloppy or fuzzy edges of your images, and write down the behavior you intend to achieve in *concrete* language. In my classroom I work with students to direct me as I try to act out the behavior they refer to. They correct me until the behavior appears to be what they want. At that point they have a concrete and specific model of the new behavior.

Step two: Role-play or act out the desired behavior. Once a model is clear in your mind, and you know how you want to sound, hold your body, what to say (keep three or four phrases in reserve), then it's time to practice the behavior. In private it is often useful to role-play before a mirror. Some students have even used a tape recorder or video tape. It may be useful to have a friend observe and make comments—once you are satisfied that he or she is absolutely clear on the model you wish to achieve. In the classroom I act out the role of the "other" and the student acts out the new behavior in response. This way the student gets to use the new behavior with someone who actually is a problem in real life, and the transfer to the real life of the student is therefore relatively easy and direct. We practice what will be with the people we will confront. Of course the more realistic the role-playing and the setting, the better the results will be and the more quickly they will occur. I've also found that the gestalt technique of using two empty chairs is useful here. The student sits in one of the chairs and acts out the behavior of the "other" person in the situation, then switches chairs and acts out the new, desired behavior as response. Back to the first chair for the response and so on, until the new behavior is shaped to handle most of the difficult communications with which the student thinks she will have to deal. This rehearsal technique is very productive and can be used by students in private once they have clearly defined the new behavior for themselves.

Step three: Conduct a fantasy rehearsal of the desired behavior. With a relaxed body, seated, and eyes lightly closed, the student creates a sharp mental picture of the situation in question. Then the sequence of new behavior is imagined, move by move, stimulus and response. As with physical rehearsal, this fantasy rehearsal deals with the broad range of possible difficult responses the student feels he could encounter. Again all bases are covered. Since research suggests that better results occur when the mental pictures are sharp and clear, it is often wise for students to practice forming mental images as an entirely separate exercise. This third step of imaginary rehearsal is not hurried in any way. In my classroom I often give about ten minutes for this. The students are on their own here, but note that this rehearsal has been preceded by the physical role-playing so that what is to be imagined has been pinned down solidly.

Step four: Clean up the act. When we first begin learning new behaviors and have only begun to rehearse them, I ask students for feedback on rehearsal problems. A variety of minor difficulties usually are voiced. They range from nervousness and difficulty in relaxing to trouble forming images and concentrating. Often I request feedback immediately after role-playing and then again after imaginary rehearsal. Other times I wait until both sequences are completed. Once a behavior has been rehearsed for a while, students are asked to begin acting it out in their daily living. The connection between classroom and out-of-class living becomes immediate and obvious, and at this point I start using feedback sessions to begin each rehearsal so that we can adjust our model as necessary. I find that as students tell of their experiences using the new behaviors, it is important to provide support and positive reinforcement for continuing to use the behaviors. It is here that the small group context is so helpful, because much positive and creative material is shared by various group members. Everyone is in the same boat trying to float on the same ocean, so they pull together.

Step five: Follow through with review. After these first four steps have been completed, the physical role-playing and the imaginary rehearsal should be done once each day until the new behavior is firmly established in daily living out-of-classroom. The student conducts this rehearsal entirely on his own, although in the classroom I do schedule sharing times throughout the semester for progress reports. My experience has been that change in behavior is very rapid when the student *genuinely wants* that change. It sometimes happens that students find themselves confronted by their own insincerity or lack of commitment to improving their lives as they resist maintaining their own rehearsal schedules. This discovery can be very productive, and I maintain a close relationship with the counseling department in order to refer students who want to look into what's behind such self-defeating action. I emphasize that no skill or magic wand can be effective unless the person using it *wants* it to be and willingly accepts the effort necessary to make it happen. Cinderella did not resist going to the ball.

These five steps, then, are the walkway to changing behavior. At least one path I have discovered. It may seem overly dramatic to call behavior rehearsal a "Cinderella skill," but this technique has such a definite impact and the results are so immediate that I am comfortable with the drama. Furthermore, these steps are so basic that they are easily adapted to your own fairy tale—your life—and can be used not only for communication skill development but also for study skills, driving skills, swimming skills, other social skills, and so on. Behavior is behavior is behavior.

You can get greater satisfaction and rewards in your life by changing your behavior. It's that simple, though it takes work.

The fairy godmother knew it.

Cinderella knew it.

And you know it.

So I suggest that you make your fairy tale a success story. You certainly deserve it as much as Cinderella, even if you don't wash the castle steps and mend your wicked step-mother's clothing.

Small Group Communication Games

Karen R. Krupar

People are not animals or machines, nor do they relate in configurations. They relate as actors playing roles to achieve satisfactions of the self which only other human actors can give them. They do so through communication, which, like struggle in the drama, involves both competition and cooperation.[1]

We are group-centered, we define ourselves by the groups to which we belong or do not belong. For example, the author of this book is white, from the middle-class, a professional educator and a female. She is not wealthy, a male or illiterate.

We belong to groups because we need to commune with each other. The act of communion serves to describe and reinforce our descriptions of ourselves, for we are defined in large part by what other group members say about us and how they act toward us.

The exercises in this section are designed to develop our awareness of how we appear to others in small groups. As objects of group evaluation, we become not only conscious but *self*-conscious. String Along, Cooperative Squares and the Coin Game stimulate our awareness of the roles we play in small groups. The Power Game sensitizes us to the authority roles upon which all group behavior depends.

String Along

We all have days when we feel put out and grouchy. Angry, frustrated, tired, we look at the world with a jaundiced eye, and if anyone so much as says hello—well, he regrets it!

Sure enough, sooner or later someone asks us the wrong question or makes the wrong comment. We leap up and verbally begin swinging. Before we realize how it happened, we have a real battle going. What began as a way for us to let off tension develops instead into a real communication conflict. The conflict may be so intense that it threatens to dissolve our relationship.

This situation is not an isolated case of interpersonal conflict. On the contrary, such typical communication conflicts develop whenever we try to relate to each other. Communication is a reciprocal exchange of feelings and ideas which requires cooperative understanding and awareness of self. If the cooperative element is not sufficient, conflict results.

1. Kenneth Burke, "The Seven Offices," *Diogenes*, No. 21, Spring 1958, p. 68.

To demonstrate the need for cooperative communication in class, pair off and sit facing your partner across a table. Draw a straight boundary line slightly in front of you. Between your boundary line and your partner's, mark another horizontal line to divide the space in half.

Each partner should stick a finger through the loop on his end of a thread. The object of the game is to move the thread to your boundary line without breaking the thread. The game is terminated if the thread is broken; there are no ties. If neither of you succeeds in moving the thread to your boundary line within ten minutes, the game ends.

Remember that breaking the thread is like breaking the communication or relationship.

Then join two other couples to form groups of six members. Discuss the following questions:

1. How did you feel playing this game? Why?
2. What happened? Why?
3. Would knowing your partner have affected your behavior? Why? Why not?
4. What implications does this game have outside the classroom?

Cooperative Squares

As we have seen, cooperative effort is needed in the communicative process. To demonstrate further our problem-solving behavior when faced with group pressure in a cooperative task, divide into groups of five.

Group I sits in an X with members A, B, C, D and E in the following positions:

Group II sits in a straight line with members A, B, C, D and E in the following positions:

Group III sits in a circle with members A, B, C, D and E in the following positions:

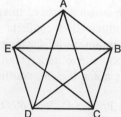

All group members have a number of puzzle pieces which have been distributed by your instructor in random order among the group. Each of you individually is to assemble a square of exactly the same size from the puzzle pieces. All the pieces in the group must be used.

No member of your group may speak to any other member nor may he indicate approval or disapproval of another group member's efforts by any nonverbal means.

No member of your group may take a puzzle piece from another group member or signal in any way that he wants it. However, any group member may give one or more of his pieces to another member, placing the piece into the other person's hand. But you may not help another group member form his square.

Group I: Members A, B, D and E must pass pieces through C.

Group II: Member A may pass to B; B may pass to A or C; C to B or D; D may pass pieces to C or E; E may pass only to D.

Group III: Any group member may pass pieces freely to any other group member.

When all your group members each have a square of equal size, raise your hands to signal the end of the game. The group to finish first receives ten points. For each correctly constructed square in a group, one point is awarded. The group with the highest score wins.

Redivide into new groups, each with a representative of I, II and III, and discuss the following questions:

1.   How did you feel while playing this game? Were you able to act as observer and player at the same time—both constructing your own square and contributing pieces to other members?

2.   What inferences did you make about the instructions? How did you communicate your inferences to other members in the group?

3.   How were you affected by the lack of verbal communication?

4.   What important principles did you derive from the communication exercise?

5.   Which group completed its squares first? Why?

Form A: Patterns for Jigsaw Pieces

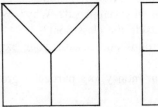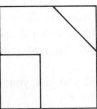

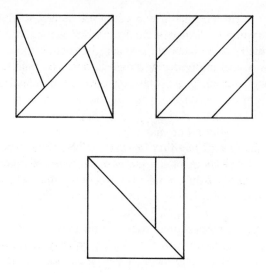

Coin Game

Before the next class meeting, write down the names of your family members and jot down a few observations about each individual's personality and contributions to the family. How willing is each member to share responsibilities for decisions and goals? How giving or taking, cooperative or uncooperative is each member? Include observations of your own personality and cooperative group efforts. In class we will explore our cooperative behavior by dividing into groups. Be sure to bring a dollar's worth of change to class.

Divide into groups of six members and sit together in a circle. Place your dollar's worth of change in front of you. You may *give* as little or as much of your change to as many or as few of the other group members as you wish.

After five minutes, discuss the following questions: What happened? Why? What implications did you see about your behavior outside this game?

Next, *take* as much or as little change from as many or as few of the other group members as you wish. After five minutes, discuss what happened. How did you feel about what happened? Why? What implications are there for your behavior outside the classroom?

Redivide into different groups and discuss your experiences during the exercise:

1. Why did you give your money to a particular group member and not to another?
2. What determined how much you gave? Why?

3. How might the giving and taking of money relate to the giving and taking in an interpersonal relationship?

4. How do you feel about your own behavior?

5. How was your behavior in this exercise compatible with the perceptions of yourself that you jotted down before class?

Power Game

Most of the groups to which we belong have some type of leadership and decision-making authority. How are we persuaded to entrust other people with leadership? How do these people react when they acquire leadership power? How do we feel about them once they have acquired such power?

To answer these questions, let us try an experiment in class. Divide into groups of seven, each member with an equal amount of play money. Discuss what you feel a leader should be and do and what his obligations should be within a group.

Choose a group member that you feel would best represent your group. This can be done by redistributing the money any way the group feels it should be distributed. Or, as in an anarchy, you may take the money from others for yourself, hoard it, or give it away.

After ten minutes of redistribution, the member with the most money is the group leader. Entrust him with all your group's money. Discuss how you feel about this person being chosen leader. Is he the best representative of the group? Why?

Those of you who have been chosen leaders meet together. You are the chosen elite: you have all the money and are holders of full power. You have fifteen minutes in which to decide whether to redistribute your wealth or keep it among yourselves.

After the time has elapsed, regardless of whether or not you have reached a decision, return to your group and discuss the following questions:

1. How do particular members in your group react to power?

2. Was the use of money realistic and meaningful as a source of power? Why? Why not?

3. How do people persuade others to entrust them with power?

4. How do the group members feel about those who have gained power?

Observing and Evaluating Discussions

John K. Brilhart

As many writers have pointed out, the old motto "practice makes perfect" should be revised to read "practice makes permanent." So it is in discussion. Unless practice is constantly evaluated, it may result in bad habits. The means to learning is practice with analysis and evaluation leading to change in future discussions.

Constructive evaluation depends on observation and feedback of information about how a discussion group is doing. Through reading this book, listening to your instructor, and classroom practice you are developing a participant-observer orientation. Even while you are participating in discussion, a part of your attention is given to observing how you and your group are proceeding. One cannot both observe and participate in the same instant, so attention must be shifted rapidly from the content of the discussion to the processes of the group. As skill is developed in being a participant-observer, a discussant becomes more and more able to supply both the functional roles needed by the group and feedback about what is going on. Evaluative feedback can be used by the group to change or correct any lack of information, attitudes, norms or procedures which keep the group from being as productive as it might be.

Skillful as one may become at maintaining a participant-observer orientation, he will sometimes become so involved in the interaction over an important issue that he will lose perspective. Then a nonparticipating observer will be helpful. Any group learning the skills and attitudes of discussion (such as in a speech class) will benefit from the feedback of a nonparticipating observer. The first part of this chapter describes the role of the observer, suggests how he can make himself most useful to a group and supplies him with some forms for guiding his observations. Some of these techniques and forms can be used by leaders and members, even when a nonparticipating observer is not present. The final part of the chapter considers interpersonal feedback and confrontation as a means to developing personal insight and proficiency in discussion.

As a result of studying this chapter and practice in applying its content, you should:

1. Be able to describe the role of a reminder-observer and a critic-observer;

From John K. Brilhart, "Observing and Evaluating Discussions," *Effective Group Discussion* (Wm. C. Brown Company Publishers: Dubuque, Iowa, 1967, pp. 163-187: 2nd Edition, 1974.)

2. Be able to prepare a specific set of questions which you would seek to answer as observer of any specific group to which you are assigned;
3. Be able to explain how to reduce defensive reactions to your observations;
4. Distinguish between process and content observations;
5. Be able to devise postmeeting reaction forms appropriate to any group of which you are a member, chart the flow and frequency of verbal interaction, diagram role functions of members, and use group, member, and leader rating scales;
6. Give direct interpersonal feedback that will be honest and helpful to fellow group members;
7. Describe how you are perceived as a discussant by your classmates.

The Role of the Observer

Every student of discussion and group processes needs the experience of observing discussion groups at work. As students have remarked countless times, "It looks different when you are sitting outside the discussion." The observer can see clearly what he was only vaguely aware of while discussing. After observing other discussants, he may be motivated to change his own conduct as a discussant. It is therefore suggested that you observe as many discussions as possible. In the speech classroom, it is wise for you to change frequently from being a discussant in one group to being an observer of another.

A very useful technique is the "fishbowl" arrangement in which a discussion group is surrounded by a circle of nonparticipating observers. These observers may all be focusing on the same aspects of group process and/or content, or may be assigned to observe, evaluate, and report on different factors (e.g., leadership, patterns of group problem solving, use of information, roles of members, verbal and nonverbal communication). Observers can be assigned on a one-to-one basis to participants as "alter egos" who make whispered suggestions to the discussant behind whom they sit, or when asked to do so indicate how they think their discussant feels or what he or she means by some action or comment.

Do not try to observe everything at once. Limit your focus to a few aspects of the discussion, perhaps at first to only one. Later, with experience, confidence, and increased awareness of the dynamics of a group, you will be ready to observe without a definite focus. You will then be able to decide as you watch which characteristics of the group are most important to assess in detail. No observer can simultaneously chronicle the content and flow of interaction, take notice of various group and individual objectives, judge the information and logic of remarks, assess the atmosphere and note the organization of the discussion. If the observer tries to do so, the result is sure to be confusion which will reduce both his personal learning and his ability to give feedback to the group.

The nonparticipating observer can do three types of things, sometimes all during a single discussion: learn from the example of others; remind the group of techniques or principles of discussion they have overlooked; supply critical evaluations of the discussion. Responsibilities as reminder and critic to the group will be discussed in the following pages.

The Reminder-Observer

Often group members need to be reminded of what they already know. During interaction they may fail to notice what has been happening or to remember useful attitudes and techniques. To help them, a type of reminder-observer role has been developed. The reminder helps the group without offering any criticism. Many of your classroom discussions will be improved by having one member participate only as a reminder-observer. The reminder role should be changed from one discussion to another in order to give everyone a chance to remind without depriving anyone for a long time of the chance to practice discussion skills. Once you have developed skill in maintaining a participant-observer orientation, you will be able to act as a reminder to nonclassroom discussion groups in which you are a participant. If you serve as a model, gradually you will notice that all members of a continuing group begin to remind.

Before serving as a reminder, the following guidelines for reminder-observers should be studied carefully. They are designed to reduce defensive reactions to your observations.

DO:

1. Stress the positive, pointing out what a group is doing well.
2. Emphasize what is most important, rather than commenting on everything you may have observed.
3. Focus on the processes of the group rather than on the content and issues per se.
4. Put most of your remarks in the form of questions, keeping in mind that all authority for change rests with the group. You have no authority except to remind, report, and raise questions.
5. Remain completely neutral, out of any controversy about either content or procedure. You can do this by asking questions in a dead-pan manner, such as, "I wonder if the group realizes that we have discussed _____, _____ and _____ in the space of five minutes?" "Are we ready for the consideration of possible solutions?" "I wonder if John and Amy understand each other's points of view?" "I wonder if we all understand the purpose of our committee?" "Is everyone getting an equal chance to participate?" Such questions remind the group of principles of good discussion without leveling specific criticisms.

6. Show trends and group characteristics rather than singling out individual discussants for comment (unless absolutely necessary).
7. Interrupt the discussion only when you believe the group is unlikely to become aware of what is troubling it. First give the group enough time to correct itself.

DON'T:

1. Play the critic-umpire, telling anyone he is wrong.
2. Argue with a member or the group. If your question is ignored, drop it.
3. Tell the group what they should do. You are not playing expert or consultant: your only job is to remind the group members of what they know but have overlooked.

When serving as observer, there are many things you might look for. The content of this book can provide you with a sort of checklist for observing. Some specific things you might notice when serving as reminder are suggested by the following questions:

1. Are the group goals clear? What helped or hindered in clarifying them?
2. Are all members aware of their area of freedom?
3. Is the group gathering information to define the problem fully, or has it become solution-centered too soon?
4. Do members seem to be well prepared for discussing the topic?
5. Is information being accepted at face value or tested for dependability?
6. Has a plan for the discussion been worked out and accepted by the group?
7. Does the discussion seem to be orderly and organized?
8. Do discussants display attitudes of inquiry and objectivity toward information, issues, and the subject as a whole?
9. To what degree does the group climate seem to be one of mutual respect, trust, and cohesiveness?
10. Do all members have an equal opportunity to participate?
11. Is the pattern of interaction open, or unduly restricted?
12. How sound is the reasoning being done by the group?
13. How creative is the group in finding potential solutions?
14. Is judgment deferred until all possible solutions can be listed and understood?
15. Does the group have a list of specific and useful criteria, and is it applying them to possible solutions?
16. While evaluating ideas, is the group making use of information from earlier parts of the discussion?
17. Are periodic summaries being used to help members recall and move on to new issues without undue redundancy?
18. Are there any hidden agendas hampering the group?

19. Are any norms or procedures hampering the group?
20. Are there any breakdowns in communication due to poor listening, by-passing or stoppers?
21. Is the style of leadership appropriate to the group?
22. If a designated leader is present, is he or she encouraging the sharing of leadership by other members?
23. Is the discussion being recorded and charted accurately?
24. Is the degree of formality appropriate to the group size and task?
25. What else seems to be affecting the group's attempts to achieve a goal?

In addition to serving as reminder during the discussion, afterward a reminder-observer may be able to help the group by leading a discussion of the discussion or by making a detailed report of his observations. At this point he can take either of two approaches, depending on what the group wants from him and his degree of expertise:

1. a reporter, who describes the meeting without judgment, diagnosis or suggestions for future meetings;
2. an interpreter, who in addition to reporting also offers explanations for the behavior of the group as seen from an impartial vantage point.

The Critic-Observer

A critic-observer may do considerable reminding, but his or her primary function is as a critic. Such an observer belongs only in the classroom or training group. In some cases the critic-observer is primarily an advisor, either to the group as a whole or to a designated leader. For example, your instructor may interrupt a discussion to point out what he feels is going wrong and to suggest a different technique or procedure. After you have become a proficient observer, you might take the role of critic-advisor for a small discussion group in another speech class or perhaps even for a group in your own class.

The critic-observer usually makes a more detailed report after the discussion than does the reminder-observer. In addition to describing and interpreting important aspects of the discussion, the critic will express opinions about weak and strong points of it. He or she may compliment the group, point out where and how it got into trouble, and even place blame or take an individual member to task. This must be done cautiously and with tact. Many students hesitate to criticize the participation of others, and some balk at accepting criticism leveled at them. Discussants can be helped to give and accept criticism by reminding them of two points: (1) All criticism should be constructive, objective, sincere, and designed to help. (2) All critiques should include both positive and negative comments, with the good points being presented first.

The critic-observer, of course, will look for the same kinds of group behavior as will the reminder. In general, judgments should cover at least four basic general aspects of the discussion: (1) the group product, including how well it has been assessed, how appropriate it seems to be to the problem, and how well group members support it; (2) the group process, including patterns of interaction, decision making, problem solving, and communication; (3) the contributions and functional roles of individual members; and (4) leadership, especially if a designated leader is present. Different criteria will be needed for public and private groups, learning and problem-solving groups, advisory and action groups. Observation and rating forms can be developed by the student of small groups for various types of discussions and groups. The forms included in this chapter are suggestive general models which should be modified or used as guides for the preparation of specific forms and rating scales adapted to specific situations in your class or natural groups.

Tools for Observing and Evaluating

Any group can improve its efficiency and atmosphere by taking time out for unstructured evaluation. The designated leader is in the best position to initiate such a bootstrap operation by suggesting the group take some time to study and discuss its activity. If this is not done on some periodic basis, there is danger of its being neglected. For this reason, regular times for assessment have been built into the operations of many business, government and military groups. Also, a systematic review is likely to be more objective than one which is undertaken during a crisis. However, if group evaluation is limited to regular periods following scheduled meetings, much of importance may be forgotten. Also, taking a break for an unplanned evaluation may correct a damaging attitude or procedure before a serious breakdown can occur within the group; therefore, it seems advisable for a continuing discussion group to use both routine and spontaneous discussions of discussion (unstructured evaluation sessions).

Many tools for more formal observation and evaluation of both groups and individual discussants have been developed and reported elsewhere. In this book a few of the more important tools are reported, especially those likely to be helpful for a class in discussion or fundamentals of speech. Instruments for assessing a group are presented first, followed by those for evaluating individual participants and designated leaders.

Evaluating the Group

Postmeeting Reaction Sheets, or PMR's as they are called for short, are frequently used to get objective reactions from discussants. Since

PMR's are anonymous, a participant can report personal evaluations without any threat to self. A PMR may be planned by a chairperson or other designated leader, by an instructor, by a group or by the organizers of a large conference. The PMR's are distributed, completed and collected immediately following the discussion. Figures 1, 2 and 3.

A PMR sheet consists of a simple questionnaire designated to elicit frank comments about important aspects of the group and the discussion. Questions should be tailored to fit the purposes and needs of the person preparing the questionnaire. Sometimes the questions concern substantive items, sometimes interpersonal matters and sometimes matters of technique and procedure. Two or more types of questions may be mixed on a PMR.

The results of the questionnaires should be tallied and reported back to the group as soon as possible, either in printed form or by posting on a blackboard or chart. The results then become a guide for review of past practice and for planning new practices. The questions must be designed to produce data which can readily be tabulated, summarized and reported.

Interaction Diagrams

A diagram of interaction made by an observer will reveal a lot about the relationships among members of a group. The diagram can reveal who is talking to whom, how often each member participates orally, and any dominating persons. A model interaction diagram is shown in Figure 4. Notice the data at the top of the sheet; the names of all participants are located around the circle in the same order in which they sat during the discussion. Each time a person speaks an arrow is drawn from his or her position toward the person to whom the remark was addressed. If a member speaks to the entire group, a longer arrow points towards the center of the circle. Subsequent remarks in the same direction are indicated by short cross marks on the base of the arrow.

Rating Scales

Rating scales can be used by critic-observers to record their judgments about any aspect of the group and its discussion, including group climate, cohesiveness, efficiency, satisfaction, degree of mutual respect, organization of discussion, adequacy of information and the like. A five-point scale is adequate for most purposes. A discussion class can profitably prepare and use its own scales to evaluate a variety of group characteristics. Two or more observers working independently of each other can rate each group and then check the similarity of their ratings. Whenever ratings on the same scale are more than one point apart, the observers can learn by discussing the reasons for their different ratings. Sample scales are shown in Figure 5, illustrating how you can construct your own.

POSTMEETING REACTION SHEET

Instructions: Check the point on each scale that best represents your honest judgment. Add any comments you wish to make which are not covered by the questionnaires. Do *not* sign your name.

1. How satisfied are you with the *results* of the discussion?

_____

very satisfied   moderately   very dissatisfied
                    satisfied

2. How well *organized and systematic* was the discussion?

_____

disorderly   just right   too rigid

3. How do you feel about the *style of leadership* supplied by the chairperson?

_____

too autocratic   democratic   weak

4. *Preparation for this meeting* was

_____

thorough   adequate   poor

5. Did you find yourself *wanting to speak* when you didn't get a chance?

_____

almost never   occasionally   often

6. How do you feel about *working again* with this same group?

_____

eager   I will   reluctant

Comments:

Figure 1

POSTMEETING REACTION SHEET

1. How do you feel about today's discussion?
   excellent ____ good ____ all right ____ so-so ____ bad ____

2. What were the strong points of the discussion?

3. What were the weaknesses?

4. What changes would you suggest for future meetings?

(you need not sign your name)

Figure 2

Evaluating Individual Participants

Almost any aspect of individual participation can be evaluated by preparing appropriate forms. An analysis of roles of members can be made by listing the names of all members in separate columns on a sheet on which the various functions described in Chapter 2 [Brilhart text] are listed in a vertical column at the left side of the sheet (Figure 6). Each time a participant speaks, a tally is made in the column after the role function just performed. If a member performs more than one function in a single speech, two or more tallies are made. The completed observation form will indicate what functions were supplied adequately, who took harmful roles, what was the degree of role flexibility of each participant in the discussion and so forth.

Figure 7 shows a simple rating form which can be completed by a critic-observer for each participant. The forms can be filled in near the end of the discussion and then handed to the participants. This form was prepared by a group of students and has been used extensively to rate students engaged in practice discussions. Although only illustrative of many types of scales and forms which could be used, it has the virtue of being simple and brief, yet focuses on some of the most important aspects of participation. A somewhat more detailed rating scale for individual participants is shown in Figure 8. Each form could be filled out by an observer, or each participant in a small group might prepare one for every other member of the group.

All of the previously described observation forms and rating scales can be used to analyze and appraise functional leadership.

Reaction Questionnaire

Instruction: Circle the number which best indicates your reactions to the following questions about the discussion in which you participated:

1. *Adequacy of Communication:* To what extent do you feel members were understanding each others' statements and positions?

   0   1   2   3   · 4   5   6   7   8   9   10

   Much talking past each other, misunderstanding   Communicated directly with each other, understanding well

2. *Opportunity to Speak:* To what extent did you feel free to speak?

   0   1   2   3   4   5   6   7   8   9   10

   Never had a chance to speak   All the opportunity to talk I wanted

3. *Climate of Acceptance:* How well did members support each other, show acceptance of individuals?

   0   1   2   3   4   5   6   7   8   9   10

   Highly critical and punishing   Supportive and receptive

4. *Interpersonal relations:* How pleasant and concerned were interpersonal relations?

   0   1   2   3   4   5   6   7   8   9   10

   Quarrelsome, status differences emphasized   Pleasant, empathic, concerned with persons

5. *Leadership:* How adequate was the leader (or leadership) of the group?

   0   1   2   3   4   5   6   7   8   9   10

   Too weak ( ) or dominating ( )   Shared, group-centered, and sufficient

6. *Satisfaction with role:* How satisfied are you with your personal participation in the discussion?

   0   1   2   3   4   5   6   7   8   9   10

   Very dissatisfied   Very satisfied

7. *Quality of product:* How satisfied are you with the decisions, solutions, or learnings that came out of this discussion?

   0   1   2   3   4   5   6   7   8   9   10

   Very displeased   Very satisfied

8. *Overall:* How do you rate the discussion as a whole apart from any specific aspect of it?

   0   1   2   3   4   5   6   7   8   9   10

   Awful, waste of time   Superb, time well spent

Figure 3

INTERACTION DIAGRAM

frequency and direction of
participation

Group _____

Time _____

     Begin _____

      End _____

Place _____

Observer _____

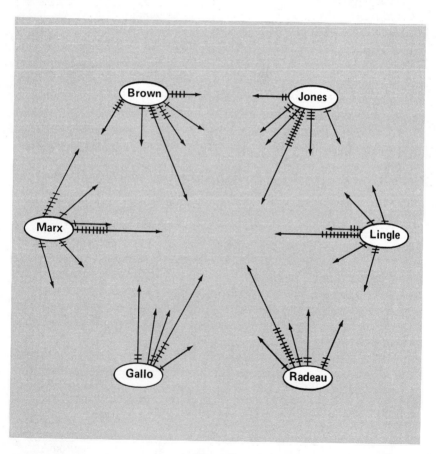

Figure 4

DISCUSSION EVALUATION

Date _____   Group _____

Time _____   Observer _____

Group Characteristic	5 excellent	4 good	3 average	2 fair	1 poor
Organization of discussion					
Equality of opportunity to speak					
Group orientation, mutual respect					
Listening to understand					
Evaluation of ideas					

Comments:

Figure 5

DISCUSSANT FUNCTIONS

Date _____   Group _____

Time _____   Observer _____

Participants' Names

Role Functions					
1. Idea initiating					
2. Information seeking					
3. Information giving					
4. Opinion seeking					
5. Opinion giving					
6. Elaborating					
7. Coordinating					
8. Orienting					
9. Energizing					
10. Recording					
11. Supporting					
12. Harmonizing					
13. Tension relieving					
14. Gatekeeping					
15. Norming					
16. Blocking					
17. Attacking					
18. Recognition seeking					
19. Horseplaying					
20. Dominating					
21. Advocating					

(Left margin labels: Group Task — functions 1–10; Maintenance — functions 11–15; Self-Centered — functions 16–21)

Figure 6

PARTICIPANT RATING SCALE

PARTICIPANT RATING SCALE

for   Date _____

_____

(name)   Observer _____

1. Did he make useful *substantive contributions to the discussion?* (well prepared, supplied information, adequate reasoning, etc.)

5	4	3	2	1
Outstanding in quality and quantity		Fair Share		Few or none

2. Did he contribute to *efficient group procedures?* (agenda planning, relevant comments, summaries, self-discipline)

5	4	3	2	1
Always relevant, aided organization		Relevant, no aid in order		Sidetracked, confused group

3. How constructive and cooperative was his *attitude?* (listen to understand, responsible, agreeable, group centered, open-minded)

5	4	3	2	1
Very responsible and constructive				Self-centered, stigmas

4. Did he *speak* well? (clear, to group, one point at a time, consise)

5	4	3	2	1
Brief, clear, to group				Vague, indirect, wordy

5. How *valuable* was he to the group? (overall rating)

5	4	3	2	1
Most valuable				Least Valuable

Suggestions:

Figure 7

DISCUSSION PARTICIPATION EVALUATION

For _____

Instructions: Circle the number which best reflects your evaluation of the
discussant's participation on each scale.

Superior   Poor

1	2	3	4	5	1.	Was prepared and informed.
1	2	3	4	5	2.	Contributions were brief and clear.
1	2	3	4	5	3.	Comments relevant and well timed.
1	2	3	4	5	4.	Spoke distinctly and audibly to all.
1	2	3	4	5	5.	Contributions made readily and voluntarily.
1	2	3	4	5	6.	Frequency of participation (if poor, too low ( )or high ( ).
1	2	3	4	5	7.	Nonverbal responses were clear and constant.
1	2	3	4	5	8.	Listened to understand and follow discussion.
1	2	3	4	5	9.	Openminded.
1	2	3	4	5	10.	Cooperative and constructive.
1	2	3	4	5	11.	Helped keep discussion organized, following outline
1	2	3	4	5	12.	Contributed to evaluation of information and ideas.
1	2	3	4	5	13.	Respectful and tactful with others.
1	2	3	4	5	14.	Encouraged others to participate.
1	2	3	4	5	15.	Assisted in leadership functions.
1	2	3	4	5	16.	Overall rating in relation to other discussants.

Comments:

Evaluator_____

Figure 8

Encounter Group Checklist

Gerard Egan

Use the following checklist to assess your participation in the group and the quality of the group interaction. This checklist will probably be more helpful after a few meetings when you get an experiential feeling for the contract.

1. *Tone.* What is the tone of the group (spontaneous, dead, cautious)?
2. *Commitment to goals.* Answer the following questions in view of the general procedural goal: that each member is to attempt to establish and develop a relationship of some intimacy with each of the other members.
   a. Are members working at establishing relationships with one another?
   b. Have a number of significant relationships emerged?
   c. Are relationships becoming deeper or remaining superficial?
   d. Is there consensus that the group is moving forward?
3. *Initiative*
   a. Do members actively reach out and contact one another or do they have to be pushed into it?
   b. Is there some risk-taking behavior in the group?
4. *A climate of immediacy*
   a. Do members deal with the here-and-now rather than the there-and-then?
   b. Are there a large number of one-to-one conversations as opposed to speeches to the group?
   c. Is the content of interactions concrete and specific rather than general and abstract?
   d. Do members use "I" when they *mean* I instead of substitutes (one, you?
   e. Do members avoid speaking for the group, using the pronoun "we"?
5. *Cooperation*
   a. *Cooperation.* Is there a climate of cooperation rather than one of antagonism, passivity or competition?
   b. *Polarizations.* Are there polarizations in the group that affect the quality of interactions (for example, leader versus members, active members versus passive members)?

   c. *Owning interactions.* Do members tend to "own" the dyadic interactions that take place in the group? When two members are having difficulty talking to each other, do other group members help them? Do those having difficulty seek the help of others?

   d. *Check it out.* Do the members, when they confront one another, check out their feelings and evaluations with other members?

   e. *Hostility.* Is there any degree of hostility in the group? Does the group or do individual members wallow in it or do they seek to resolve it? Is there covert hostility? If so, what is done to bring it out into the open?

6. *The principal modes of interaction*
   a. *Self-disclosure*
     (1) Was it appropriate, that is, geared to establishing here-and-now relationships of some intimacy?
     (2) Was then-and-there disclosure related to the here-and-now—that is, specifically to this group or one's relationship to this group?
     (3) Was it related to the process of encountering (establishing relationships) rather than counseling (dealing with there-and-then problems)?
     (4) Was it meaningful disclosure or superficial?
   b. *Expression of feeling*
     (1) Did people deal with feelings and emotions?
     (2) Did expression of feeling help establish and develop relationships?
     (3) Were feelings authentic or forced?
     (4) Are participants able to express themselves spontaneously?
   c. *Support*
     (1) Was there an adequate climate of respect, acceptance, support?
     (2) Were members active in giving support or is the climate of support principally a permissive, passive thing?
     (3) Did the group prevent any member from clawing at anyone?
   d. *Confrontation*
     (1) Were people willing to challenge one another?
     (2) Did members confront one another because they cared about one another and wanted to get involved?
     (3) Was there any degree of merely punitive confrontation?
     (4) Is conflict allowed in the group? Is it dealt with creatively or merely allowed to degenerate into hostility?
     (5) Is confrontation really an invitation to another to move into the group in a more fruitful way? Do the members take the initiative to invite one another into the group in various ways?

    e. *Response to confrontation*
      (1) Did members reply to responsible confrontation by self-explora-
         tion rather than defensiveness or counterattack?
      (2) If the person confronted found it difficult to accept what he
         heard, did he check it out with other members of the group?
         Did the other members take the initiative to confirm confronta-
         tion without "ganging up" on the one being confronted?

7. *Trust*
    a. Is the level of trust deepening in the group?
    b. Do members say in the group what they say outside?
    c. If there are problems with trust, do the members deal with them
       openly?

8. *Nonverbal communication.* What do members say nonverbally that they
    don't say verbally (concerning their anxiety, boredom, withdrawal, and
    so on)?

9. *Leadership*
    a. Does the facilitator model contractual behavior?
    b. Was the facilitator acting too much like a leader—that is, trying to get
       others to do things rather than doing things with others?
    c. Is leadership becoming diffused in the group? Or are the members
       sitting back and leaving most of the initiating to the facilitator? Who
       are those who are exercising leadership?
    d. If necessary, did the facilitator see to it that no one became the object
       of destructive behavior on the part of others?

10. *Exercises* (if any)
    a. If used, were they appropriate? Did they fit into what was happening?
    b. Were they well introduced? Were the instructions clear?
    c. Were they forced upon an unwilling group?
    d. Is there too much dependence on exercises?
    e. Does the group always flee exercises even though they might be
       helpful?
    f. Did the exercises used accomplish their goals?

11. *Anxiety*
    a. What is the anxiety level of the group? Too high? Too low?
    b. Is there always some motivating tension or is the group too com-
       fortable?

12. *Modes of flight and problematic interactions*
    a. What are the principal ways in which the group as a whole took flight?
    b. In what ways are individuals resisting the process of the group?
    c. Do members continue to claim that "they don't know what to do"?
    d. *Analysis.* Do members spend a great deal of time analyzing past inter-
       actions (an ounce of interaction followed by a pound of analysis)?

e. *Interpretation.* Do members tend to interpret and hypothesize about one another's behavior instead of meeting one another directly?

f. *Quiet members.* Did quieter members move into the group on their own initiative? If not, how was the problem handled? Do individuals or the group rationalize nonparticipation?

g. *Control.* Are there members who control the group by specific behaviors (by always having the focus of attention on themselves, by cynicism, by hostility, by silence, or by some other behavior)?

h. *Pairing.* Were coalitions formed that impeded the progress of the group?

i. *Tacit decisions.* Has the group made any tacit decisions (such as not to discuss certain subjects, not to allow conflict, not to get too close) that affect the quality of the interaction?

j. *Dealing-with-one*
   (1) Does the group tend to deal with one person at a time?
   (2) If so, is that person usually consulted about being the center of attention for an extended period of time?
   (3) Does dealing-with-one mean that others may not contact one another until the person in the focus of attention is "finished"?
   (4) Do some people withdraw from the interaction when one person is dealt with for an extended period of time?
   (5) If this is a problem for the group, is it dealt with openly?

13. What is needed to improve the quality of the group?

Obviously other kinds of checklists could be drawn up for different kinds of groups. The checklist should be related to the goals—overriding, procedural, and interactional—of the group.

PROANA 5: A Computerized Technique for the Analysis of Small Group Interaction

Edward M. Bodaken, William B. Lashbrook and Marie Champagne

During the summer and fall terms of 1966 a computerized technique for the analysis and interpretation of small group interaction was introduced into the basic course in group discussion at Michigan State University. The technique evolved initially from the principles of sociometrics used in conjunction with the definition of a small group developed by Robert Bales,[1] and was programmed for administration by the Michigan State University 3600 Control Data Corporation Computer. The program was titled PROANA5—PROANA short for process analysis, and 5 standing for the size of the group to be analyzed.

Input data consist of patterned and non-patterned interaction. Patterned interaction is operationally defined as a message which is relevant to the message just before it, and does not exceed 45 seconds. A message is classified as non-patterned interaction if it has low relevance to the message just before it and/or exceeds 45 seconds in duration. The determination of whether two bits of communication are relevant to the same topic is made by the PROANA5 coder.[2]

Although the input data consist simply of frequency and direction of interaction, the computer printout provides a detailed analysis of the discussion adapted from relevant communication variables explicated by Collins and Guetzkow.[3] Those variables are:

E. M. Bodaken, W. B. Lashbrook, M. Champagne, "PROANA5: A Computerized Technique for the Analysis of Small Group Interaction," *"Western Journal Of Speech Communication* (Spring, 1971), 112-115.

1. Robert F. Bales, *Interaction Process Analysis: A Method for the Study of Small Groups* (Cambridge, Massachusetts, 1950), p. 7.

2. For a more technical description of the program see: William B. Lashbrook, *PROANA5 A Computerized Technique for the Analysis of Small Group Interaction*, Report 3-67, Speech Communication Research Laboratory, Michigan State University, 1967; and William B. Lashbrook and Edward M. Bodaken, "PROANA5: A Venture in Computer Assisted Instruction in Small Group Communication," *Computer Studies in the Humanities and Verbal Behavior*, 2 (1969), 98-101.

3. Barry E. Collins and Harold Guetzkow, *A Social Psychology of Group Processes for Decision-Making* (New York, 1964), pp. 166-87.

1. The degree of *balance of participation* is based on the hypothesis that an effective interacting group tends to begin deliberation with the least amount of interaction, shows an increase in the middle period, and tapers off in the final period.

2. The degree of *communication line usage* between individual members of the group is derived from the hypothesis that group interaction is most effective when all the lines of communication are used at least once during each period of discussion.

3. The degree to which *clique groups* (subgroups within the group) are formed is based on an operational definition of a clique; namely, that such a group is formed when the total interactive communication between two members of the group exceeds that of the remaining members for any given period of discussion.

4. The degree to which *detrimental clique groups* interfere with the total interaction of the discussion is formulated from the hypothesis that a clique will have a detrimental effect on group interaction if it extends over a long period of time without interruption. For the purposes of PROANA5 analysis, detrimental clique groups are formed when they involve the same lines of communication for two consecutive periods of discussion.

5. The degree of *communication propensity* within a given period of discussion is manifested in the selection of one member of a group by a majority as a receiver for their communication. Propensity can reflect leadership or deviant behavior with the distinction based on the interaction of this variable with others contained in the program.

6. The degree of *leadership* reflected in the group is based on the definition that the perceived leader of a group is that person with whom a majority of the functioning members of that group seems to communicate most, while leadership *types* are determined by the amount of nonpatterned interaction exhibited by the person. This is derived from the hypothesis that some procedural leadership functions take the form of non-patterned interaction. Operationally, the "procedural leader" of the group must have at least five non-patterned interactions over the entire discussion and a minimum of one such communication during each period. An individual with a high amount of patterned interaction is designated as the "emergent leader" or "social emotional leader" of the group. If no individual can be designated, PROANA5 suggests that the role of leadership was shared by two or more group members.

7. The degree of *isolation* of any one member of the group by the remaining membership is dependent upon the hypothesis that isolation will be indicated by a definite and consistent reduction of involvement between that individual and the remaining group members. In order to distinguish the person being isolated from the person merely reducing his involvement in the discussion, PROANA5 considers non-patterned interaction. Since

an isolated individual is not allowed to interact with the membership, he must participate on a non-patterned interaction basis. Such an increase in non-patterned interaction is operationally defined as equal to or greater than 50 per cent over the preceding time period and the measure of consistency is stated in terms of two consecutive periods of discussion.

8. The degree of *dominance* of any one member of the group is based on the hypothesis that an individual member of a small group may be said to dominate a given period of discussion when his total amount of communication (both patterned and non-patterned) exceeds that of the combination of any two of the remaining members. If domination is detected, an attempt is made to find a possible explanation. PROANA5 scans the leadership sub-routine (variable 5) to determine whether the domination can be explained in terms of perceived leadership, and the clique group variable to determine whether domination has its roots in clique group membership. Finally, if dominance is primarily a function of a considerable amount of non-patterned interaction, PROANA5 suggests that the individual might well be advocating rather than discussing.

The computer program is employed in three ways: the data derived from classroom discussions are processed in such a manner that the output from PROANA5 serves as the critique for the activity; contrived data are processed so as to provide students in the class with a printed simulation of the effects of the previously identified variables; and data are submitted by the students to represent the effects of the variables discussed in class as related to small group interaction.

As each discussion takes place the instructor keeps a record of the patterned and non-patterned interaction for each time period. This information, along with instructor comments, is then subjected to the PROANA5 computer analysis. Each class member receives a copy of the analysis.

Also, PROANA5 is employed as a simulation device to study the effects of certain variables on small group behavior. Data are contrived as an illustration of class discussion material and submitted for analysis. For instance, a lecture on the effects of competition on group interaction may be presented to the class by integrating data from PROANA5. This particular use of PROANA5, as a supplement to materials provided by textbooks and class lectures, appears to be highly stimulating to the students in the course.

Finally, students are assigned the task of creating data which illustrates the effects of variables of group discussion, in a form suitable for analysis by PROANA5. The students are provided with a set of instructions for using PROANA5 and with a FORTRAN coding form. Data from this form are then punched on cards by the administrative staff of the course and submitted to the computer for analysis.

PROANA5 and its use in the discussion classroom is advanced as but one example of the way in which a computer may be of assistance to both students and their instructor. Major revisions are currently being made in PROANA5 to allow for generalization of the analysis from four to seven member groups and to incorporate VAIOS (a voice actuated input device which can be used in conjunction with an IBM 1230 optical scanner). VAIOS will eliminate the need for an observer by providing direct input of the occurrence of a particular bit of communication as well as an accurate measure of the time associated with the participation. This technique will also allow for an analysis of such things as time delays, the ratio of time for stimulus and response, and a finer distinction between patterned and non-patterned interaction. The fact that PROANA5 is being used in the classroom situation and will soon be incorporated into group therapy sessions in the fields of Speech Pathology and Audiology points to its potential use as a vital research tool.

SUGGESTED READINGS

Chapter 5

Bales, Robert. *Interaction Process Analysis*. Cambridge: Addison-Wesley Press, Inc., 1951.

Bavelos, Alex. "Role Playing in Management Training," *Sociometry* 1 (1952), 183-91.

Boocock, Sarance and Schild, E. O. *Simulation Games in Learning*. Beverly Hills, CA: Sage Publications, Inc., 1968.

Buchanan, P. C. "Evaluating the Effectiveness of Laboratory Training in Industry," *Explorations in Human Relations Training and Research, No. 1*. Washington, D.C.: NTL Institute for Applied Behavioral Science—National Education Association, 1965.

Chester, Mark and Fox, Robert. *Role Playing Methods in the Classroom*. San Francisco: Science Research Associates, 1966.

Giffin, K. "Interpersonal Trust in Small-Group Communication," *Quarterly Journal of Speech* 53 (1967); 224-34.

Grove, Theodore G. *Experiences in Interpersonal Communication*. Englewood Cliffs, N.J.: Prentice-Hall, Inc., 1976.

Gulley, Halbert E. and Leathers, Dale G. *Communication and Group Process*. New York: Holt, Rinehart and Winston, 1977.

Howard, Jane. *Please Touch*. New York: McGraw-Hill Book Company, 1970.

Johnson, David W. *Reaching Out: Interpersonal Effectiveness and Self-Actualization*. Englewood Cliffs, N.J.: Prentice-Hall, Inc., 1972.

Johnson, Kenneth G., *et. al. Nothing Never Happens*. Beverly Hills, CA: Glencoe Press, 1974.

Kline, J. and Hullinger, J. "Redundancy, Self Orientation, and Group Consensus," *Speech Monographs* 40 (1973): 72-74.

Krupar, Karen R. *Communication Games*. New York: The Free Press, 1973.

Leathers, D. "The Feedback Rating Instrument: A New Means of Evaluating Discussion," *Central States Speech Journal* 22 (1971): 32-42.

Leathers, D. "The Process Effects of Trust-Destroying Behavior in the Small Group," *Speech Monographs* 37 (1970): 180-87.

Leth, Pamela and Vandemark, Jo Ann F. *Small Group Communication.* Menlo Park, CA: Cummings Publishing Company, 1977.

McCroskey, James and Wright, D. "The Development of an Instrument for Measuring Interaction Behavior in Small Groups," *Speech Monographs* 38 (1971), 335-40.

Middleman, R. R. *The Non-Verbal Method in Working With Groups.* New York: Associated Press, 1968.

Moreno, J. L. "Psychodramatic Rules, Techniques and Adjunctive Methods," *Group Psychotherapy* 18 (March-June, 1965), 73-90.

Morris, Kenneth T. and Cinnamon, Kenneth M. *A Handbook of Verbal Group Exercises.* Springfield: Charles C. Thomas, Publishers, 1974.

Prentice, E. "The Effect of Trust-Destroying Communication on Verbal Fluency in the Small Group," *Speech Monographs* 42 (1975): 262-70.

Richard, Michael P. and Mann *Exploring Social Space: Exercises and Readings.* New York: The Free Press, 1973.

Ruben, Brent D. and Budd, Richard W. *Human Communication Handbook: Simulations and Games.* Rochelle Park,, N. J.: Hayden Book Company, Inc., 1975.

Watson, Goodwin. "Non Verbal Activities," in *Modern Theory and Method in Group Training,* edited by William G. Dyer. New York: Van Nostrand, Reinhold Co., 1972.

Section 3

SMALL GROUP COMMUNICATION: THEORY AND PRACTICE

The need to accentuate the importance of communication seems truly unnecessary in a decade that is undergoing a "communication explosion." From all areas and from every direction we are being confronted with personal examples of how crucial communication is to our existence. Although much of the emphasis is on communication "hardware," such as satellites, television, computers, and the like, we need only glance at our daily environments to see the role communication plays in the numerous group situations in which we find ourselves daily.

It can be generalized that the prevalence of communication in our many group activities can be considered the most significant structural property of a group as well as the most readily observable phenomenon of group life.[1]

If we are going to be able to perform effectively in small groups, we must be able to communicate. Social psychologist Soloman Asch states:

> We have good reason to suppose that conditions from the wider social field reach individuals from their everyday contacts with family, friends, companions. It is in these concrete contacts that communication and discussion takes place and that decisions are reached and pressures exerted to act in given ways.[2]

Just as most organizations are initiated, perpetuated, and held together by communication, so, too, this postulate is true in the life cycle of any group. It is through communication that we form the links that eventually fuse the individuals into what, by definition, can be called a "group." Without this highly complex phenomenon we would indeed be forced into total seclusion, conscripted into isolation that would set each of us apart from our fellow human beings. In a very real sense it is communication that enables us to tell and to be told; to share our innermost feelings and ideas; to exercise some control

---

1. Abraham Zaleznik and David Moment, *The Dynamics of Interpersonal Behavior* (New York: John Wiley and Sons, Inc., 1964), p. 71.
2. Soloman E. Asch, *Social Psychology* (New York: Prentice-Hall, Inc., 1952), p. 502.

over our environments; and to form into the countless groups that offer us the support of others, as well as the opportunity to interact and solve problems with those of similar and divergent views.

What is crucial in our view of the relationship existing between discussion and communication is the notion that man must be aware of how he influences and affects himself, as well as a knowledge of how, by his manipulation of both verbal and nonverbal symbols, he willingly or unwillingly affects others. His abilities to communicate with, and to be communicated with, are both cause and consequence of his unique competencies and his desires to manage himself and his interpersonal relationships in the organizations and groups, both formal and informal, to which he has some allegiance and responsibility. If man is to be successful in the many groups to which he belongs, including those that are highly structured as well as those that are inconspicuous and subtle, he must understand himself—how he communicates with himself, how he communicates with others, how he acts and reacts in groups—and something of the dynamics of each of these groups. In short, man must understand about communication if he is to operate to his full potential. We must know how communication works and something of the impact and influence we have over its workings. It is the intent of this section to contribute to that understanding. It is hoped that an appreciation of the communication process will evolve from this understanding.

In addition to a knowledge of some of the theory of communication we must be able to have that theory reflected in our communication behavior. Practice as well as theory should truly be the aim of each discussion participant. Being able to locate and isolate potential communication problems, and the eventual resolution of those problems, is, in part, an important ingredient of successful small group communication. For if effective communication is not practiced within the group, the final product might well be distrust, misunderstanding, apathy, and the like.

This section seeks to bring together both theory and practice. Under two interrelated headings, this fusion is discussed and explained. Chapter Six attempts to offer readings that discuss interpersonal and small group communication from a theoretical point of view. The main emphasis of these six selections centers on how communication, and all of its intricate variables, operate and function. In the second portion, the book seeks to set forth some selections that have the practice of communication as their main emphasis. They offer the reader some suggestions for improving his communication habit within the small group.

In the first selection, Wendell Johnson suggests that to understand a process as complex as communication we must look at that process and try to discover what difficulties and disorders "beset us in our efforts to communicate with one another." In this popular essay, "The Fateful Process of Mr. A

Talking to Mr. B," Johnson maintains that one way to examine this process (communication) is to diagram it. His contention is that "if you can't diagram it, you can't understand it." What he is proposing is the construction of a communication model as a means of discussing and describing the actions and reactions during each stage of the communication act.

Because of the ubiquitous nature of human communication scholars have, for a long time, been faced with the difficult task of trying to decide what is and what is not communication. Stephen King attempts to deal with this very question in an essay that both defines and explains interaction. He defines communication as "a process whereby symbols generated by people are received and responded to by people." He then examines five characteristics that grow out of this definition. In addition, he offers a discussion of some of the common myths most often associated with communication.

While Johnson and King looked at communication theory in general, our third selection focuses on human communication as it is reflected in a small group setting. In an article called "Elements of Group Communication," Baird and Weinberg examine three categories of communication: verbal, paraverbal and nonverbal. By placing each of these categories in a small group context the authors are able to analyze the interrelationship existing between communication and the environment in which that communication transpires.

In recent years teachers and students of human communication have become aware of the fact that we communicate with more than words. Many of our actions are, indeed, nonverbal, yet people attach meaning to them and make them part of the communication experience. In an essay by Laurence Rosenfeld, the issue of nonverbal communication is examined within the context of the small group. The importance of this examination becomes apparent when we realize that nonverbal cues, if interpreted correctly, can provide a means for successful group interaction. In addition, many of our feelings and attitudes are projected to other group members by our nonverbal behavior. Being able to understand our own behavior, as well as the behavior of others, will greatly facilitate the group process. As a means of contributing to that understanding, Rosenfeld investigates the influence and impact of the following nonverbal cues on the individual and the group: apparel, facial expression, posture, vocal cues, territoriality, personal space, environment, and body rhythms.

Whether in a small group or in a face-to-face situation, it is crucial to know all you can about your communication partner(s). Knowing who you are interacting with not only helps you formulate your messages but it also enables you to more accurately judge the responses those messages are producing. Empathy is one of the most effective ways to accomplish those two objectives, for it allows you an opportunity to both understand and predict the behavior of others. For when we experience empathy, Miller and Steinberg suggest that "we feel as if we were experiencing someone else's feelings as our own." As a means of further understanding the importance and workings of empathy, they discuss empathy from a variety of perspectives. They talk about what it is, how it operates, and how it can be improved.

It has long been granted that one's self-concept is directly related to how messages are both sent and received. This important topic is developed in detail by Bruce Eckman in an essay written specifically for this volume. In his article he traces how self-concept is developed initially and how it can further develop through confirming and disconfirming, feedback, risk-taking, self-disclosure and self awareness in the small group setting.

Thus far we have been talking about those selections in this portion of the book that views communication from a theoretical perspective. But anyone who has been engaged in small group activity realizes that it is the implementation of theory that accounts for the success or failure of the group, and hence, our personal success or failure as well. In Chapter 7, we offer six readings that have as their central aim the improving of personal communication skills in the small group.

In the first selection of this chapter, John Stewart presents some interesting information concerning how to communicate accurately and clearly. As one might suspect, accuracy and clarity are some of the essential ingredients needed for successful small-group communication. Stewart tells us that this success is fostered by 1) being aware of distortions introduced by positive or negative attitudes towards the topic or the persons involved, 2) trying to put yourself in the psychological frame of reference of the others communicating, 3) trying to reduce noise in the system, and 4) trying to increase clarity by being as succinct as possible. In his essay, Stewart explains these four aspects in detail and suggests ways to improve communication.

Students of communication have long agreed with the obvious observation that communication is a two-way process—with speaker and listener sharing an equal role in this transaction. Yet even with this much stated principle appearing throughout the writings in communication, the literature seems to reveal an uneven distribution in favor of the speaker. One possible reason for this unevenness might be that scholars have long either avoided any discussion as to the nature of listening or clearly indicated their uncertainty as to the ingredients of listening. Granting the importance of listening, Charles Kelly attempts to define and examine listening, and to offer an analysis of what he refers to as "empathic listening." In his essay, written specifically for this book, Kelly not only indicates what listening is and what it is not, but he also presents some suggestions for developing those empathic listening skills that might be helpful in small group communication.

Elliot Aronson's selection, "Characteristics of Effective Feedback," probes still another important element of successful small group communication—feedback. As you fully realize, the quality and quantity of the responses we give to others will greatly influence the relationship and rapport we have with them. It is these responses to the messages we get from other people that Aronson is talking about. Although he specifically deals with T-groups, his information and counsel can apply to all communication situations; for what he is telling us is that feedback expressed directly and openly enables us to gain insight into the impact that our actions and statements have on other people.

The title of our next selection, "Conflict and Its Resolution," is a rather concise summary of the entire Patton and Giffin article. The major premise behind this piece is that conflict does exist in the small group setting, and that this conflict must be treated in a rational manner. As a means of resolving the conflicts that do arise within and between groups, the authors discuss the levels of conflict, the differences in competitive and cooperative orientations, and the methods of handling conflict.

Jack R. Gibb suggests that one way to understand communication is to view it as a "people" process. In analyzing communication from this orientation, Gibb recommends we begin with "defensive behavior." For Gibb, defensive behavior is that behavior which occurs when an individual perceives threat, or anticipates threat, in the group. If a group is going to work effectively, and engage in meaningful communication, it must work to eliminate those factors that contribute to defensive behavior. He notes that a defensive climate within a group is characterized by individual attitudes and actions that reflect evaluation, control, strategy, neutrality, superiority, and certainty. In his selection, Gibb also offers a description of those elements which give rise to a supportive climate within a group. In this kind of group, the members mirror attitudes of description, problem orientation, spontaneity, empathy, equality, and provisionalism.

A somewhat unique approach to the topic of effective interpersonal communication is put forth by Erving Goffman. In his essay, "Alienation From Interaction," Goffman is concerned with those encounters where people *are not* spontaneous and involved. More specifically, he examines how and why involvement can fail to occur and the consequences of this failure. In addition, he considers the ways in which the individual can become alienated from a communication encounter and the consequence of this alienation and uneasiness upon interaction.

Chapter 6

Theory

The Fateful Process of Mr. A Talking to Mr. B

Wendell Johnson

It is a source of never-ending astonishment to me that there are so few men who possess in high degree the peculiar pattern of abilities required for administrative success. There are hundreds who can "meet people well" for every one who can gain the confidence, goodwill, and deep esteem of his fellows. There are thousands who can speak fluently and pleasantly for every one who can make statements of clear significance. There are tens of thousands who are cunning and clever for every one who is wise and creative.

Why is this so? The two stock answers which I have heard so often in so many different contexts are: (1) administrators are born, and (2) administrators are made.

The trouble with the first explanation—entirely apart from the fact that it contradicts the second—is that those who insist that only God can make a chairman of the board usually think themselves into unimaginative acceptance of men as they find them. Hence any attempt at improving men for leadership is automatically ruled out.

Meanwhile, those who contend that administrators can be tailor-made are far from omniscient in their varied approaches to the practical job of transforming bright young men into the inspired leaders without which our national economy could not long survive. Nevertheless, it is in the self-acknowledged but earnest fumblings of those who would seek out and train

Authors Note: Portions of the present article are adopted from a talk I gave before a conference of the American Management Association, Chicago, Illinois, February 18, 1952. Reprinted with permission from *Harvard Business Review*, XXXI No. 1 (January-February, 1953) pp. 49-56: 1969 by the President and Fellows of Harvard College. All rights reserved.

our future executives and administrators that we may find our finest hopes and possibilities.

This article does not propose to wrap up the problem of what will make men better administrators. Such an attempt would be presumptuous and foolhardy on anyone's part; there are too many side issues, too many far-reaching ramifications. Rather, this is simply an exploration into one of the relatively uncharted areas of the subject, made with the thought that the observations presented may help others to find their way a little better. At the same time, the objective of our exploration can perhaps be described as an oasis of insight in what otherwise is a rather frightening expanse of doubt and confusion.

The ability to respond to and with symbols would seem to be the single most important attribute of great administrators. Adroitness in reading and listening, in speaking and writing, in figuring, in drawing designs and diagrams, in smoothing the skin to conceal and wrinkling it to express inner feelings, and in making the pictures inside the head by means of which thinking, imagining, pondering, and evaluating are carried on—these are the fundamental skills without which no man may adequately exercise administrative responsibilities.

Many of the more significant aspects of these administrative prerequisites may be brought into focus by means of a consideration of what is probably the most fateful of all human functions, and certainly the one function indispensable to our economic life: communication. So let us go on, now, to look at the process of communication and to try to understand the difficulties and disorders that beset us in our efforts to communicate with one another.

The Process Diagramed

Several years ago I spent five weeks as a member of a group of university professors who had the job of setting up a project concerned with the study of speech. In the course of this academic exploring party we spent a major part of our time talking—or at least making noises—about "communication." By the second or third day it had become plain, and each day thereafter it became plainer, that we had no common and clear notion of just what the word "communication" meant.

After several days of deepening bewilderment, I recalled an old saying: "If you can't diagram it, you don't understand it." The next day I made a modest attempt to bring order out of the chaos—for myself, at least—by drawing on the blackboard a simple diagram representing what seemed to me to be the main steps in the curious process of Mr. A talking to Mr. B. Then I tried to discuss communication by describing what goes on at each step—

and what might go wrong. Since sketching that first diagram on the blackboard eight or nine years ago, I have refined and elaborated it, and I have tried from time to time, as I shall again here, to discuss the process of communication in terms of it (see Figure 1)[1].

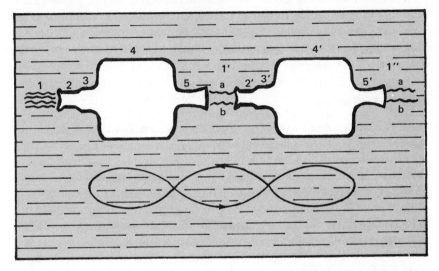

Key: Stage 1, event, or source of stimulation, external to the sensory end organs of the speaker; Stage 2, sensory stimulation; Stage 3, pre-verbal neurophysiological state; Stage 4, transformation of pre-verbal into symbolic forms; Stage 5, verbal formulations in "final draft" for overt expression; Stage 1', transformation of verbal formulations into (a) air waves and (b) light waves, which serve as sources of stimulation for the listener (who may be either the speaker himself or another person); Stages 2' through 1" correspond, in the listener, to Stages 2 through 1'. The arrowed loops represent the functional interrelationships of the stages in the process as a whole.

Figure 1 The process of communication.

Inside Mr. A

What appears to take place when Mr. A talks to Mr. B is that first of all, at Stage 1, some event occurs which is external to Mr. A's eyes, ears, taste buds, or other sensory organs. This event arouses the sensory stimulation that

---

1. The diagram, with a discussion of it, was first published in my book *People in Quandaries* (New York, Harper & Brothers, 1946), Chapter 18, "The Urgency of Paradise." I developed it further in *The Communication of Ideas*, edited by Lyman Bryson (New York: Harper & Brothers, 1948), Chapter 5, "Speech and Personality." It was also reproduced in *Mass Communications*, edited by Wilbur Schramm (Urbana: University of Illinois Press, 1949), pp. 261–274. The most recent statement is to be found in my article, "The Spoken Word and the Great Unsaid," *Quarterly Journal of Speech*, December, 1951, pp. 419–429. The form of the diagram reproduced here, together with a substantial portion of the text, are used by permission of the *Quarterly Journal of Speech*.

occurs at Stage 2. The dotted lines are intended to represent the fact that the process of communication takes place in a "field of reality," a context of energy manifestations external to the communication process and in major part external to both the speaker and the listener.

The importance of this fact is evident in relation to Stage 2 (or Stage 2′). The small size of the "opening" to Stage 2 in relation to the magnitude of the "channel" of Stage 1 represents the fact that our sensory receptors are capable of responding only to relatively small segments of the total ranges of energy radiations.

Sensory Limitations

The wave lengths to which the eye responds are but a small part of the total spectrum of such wave lengths. We register a sound only a narrow band of the full range of air vibrations. Noiseless dog whistles, "electronic eyes," and radar mechanisms—to say nothing of homing pigeons—underscore the primitive character of man's sensory equipment. Indeed, we seem little more than barely capable of tasting and smelling, and the narrowness of the temperature range we can tolerate is downright sobering to anyone dispassionately concerned with the efficiency of survival mechanisms.

The situation with regard to the normal individual may appear to be sufficiently dismal; let us not forget, however, how few of us are wholly normal in sensory acuity. We are familiar with the blind and partially sighted, the deaf and hard of hearing; we notice less the equally if not more numerous individuals who cannot taste the difference between peaches and strawberries, who cannot smell a distraught civet cat or feel a fly bite.

All in all, the degree to which we can know directly, through sensory avenues, the world outside (and this includes the world outside the sensory receptors but inside the body) is impressively restricted.

Any speaker is correspondingly limited in his physical ability to know what he is talking about. Relatively sophisticated listeners are likely to judge a speaker's dependability as a communicating agent by the degree to which he discloses his awareness of this limitation. The executive who demonstrates a realistic awareness of his own ignorance will in the long run acquire among his peers and subordinates a far better reputation for good judgment than the one who reveals his limitations by refusing to acknowledge them.

Pre-Verbal State

Once a sensory receptor has been stimulated, nerve currents travel quickly into the spinal cord and normally up through the base of the brain to the higher reaches of the cortex, out again along return tracts to the muscles and glands. The contractions and secretions they cause bring about new sensory stimulations which are "fed back" into the cord and brain and effect still further changes. The resulting reverberations of stimulation and response define what we may call a pre-verbal state of affairs within the organism. This state is represented at Stage 3 of the diagram.

Two statements about this pre-verbal state are fundamental: (1) we need to realize that our direct knowledge of this state is slight: (2) at the same time we are justified in assuming that it does occur.

No one has ever trudged through the spinal cord and brain with gun and camera, at least not while the owner of those organs was alive. Nevertheless, we are reasonably sure of certain facts about the nervous system. Observations have been reported by neurosurgeons, electroencephalographers, nerve physiologists, and anatomists. Thousands of laboratory animals have been sacrificed on the altars of scientific inquiry. We know that there are nerve currents, that they travel at known rates of speed, exhibit certain electrical properties, and are functionally related to specified kinds and loci of stimulation and to specified kinds and loci of response.

Thus, though our factual information is meager as yet, certainly it is sufficient to demonstrate that the nervous system is not merely a hypothetical construct. We can say with practical assurance that stimulation of our sensory end organs is normally followed by the transmission of nerve currents into the central nervous system, with a consequent reverberation effect, as described above, and the resulting state of affairs within the organism.

Two specific observations about this state of affairs are crucial: (1) it is truly pre-verbal, or silent; (2) it is this noiseless bodily state that gets transformed into words (or other symbols). Therefore—and these next few words should be read at a snail's pace and pondered long and fretfully—besides talking always to ourselves (although others may be listening more or less too), and whatever else we may also be striving to symbolize, *we inevitably talk about ourselves.*

The Individual's Filter

What the speaker—whether he be a junior executive or the general manager—directly symbolizes, *what he turns into words,* are physiological or electrochemical goings-on inside his body. His organism, in this sense, operates constantly as a kind of filter through which facts (in the sense of things that arouse sensory impulses) must pass before they can become known to him and before they can be *communicated* by him to others in some symbolic form, such as standard English speech.

It follows, to present a single, seemingly trivial, but quite representative example, that when the junior executive says to the general manager, "It's certainly a fine day," he is exhibiting an elaborate variety of confusion; indeed, he appears literally not to know what he is talking about. In the meantime, he is talking about himself—or at least about the weather only as "filtered" by himself. He is symbolizing an inner state, first of all. In this he is the brother of all of us who speak.

I do not mean to imply that we talk solely about our inner states. We often talk about the world outside; but when we do, we filter it through our inner states. To the degree that our individual filters are standardized and alike, we will agree in the statements we make about the world outside—allowing, of course, for differences in time, place, observational set, equipment, sensory acuity, perceptive skill, and manner of making verbal reports.

The existence of the filter at Stage 3 of the process of communication is the basic fact. We may differ in our manner of appreciating and interpreting the significance of the filter, and in so doing make ourselves interesting to each other. But when the administrator—when anyone at all—simply never learns that the filter is there, or forgets or disregards it, he becomes, as a speaker, a threat to his own sanity and a potential or actual menace in a public sense.

Self-Projection

Because the filter is there in each of us, self-projection is a basic bodily process that operates not only in all our speaking but in other kinds of communicative behavior. To claim to speak literally, then, a person must always say "as I see it," or "as I interpret the facts," or "as I filter the world" if you please, or simply "to me."

An administrator whose language becomes too "is"-y tends to persuade himself that what he says the facts are is the same thing as the facts, and under the numbing spell of this illusion he may become quite incapable of evaluating his own judgments. If he is aware of projection, he must make clear, first of all to himself that he is not speaking about reality in some utterly impersonal or disembodied and "revealed" sense, but only about reality as the prism of his own nervous system projects it upon the gray screen of his own language—and he must realize that this projection, however trustworthy or untrustworthy, must still be received, filtered, and reprojected by each of his listeners.

Sufficient contemplation of this curious engineering scheme renders one sensitive to the hazards involved in its use. As with any other possibility of miracle, one is well advised not to expect too much of it.

Patterns and Symbols

Stage 4, the first stage of symbolization, is represented in our diagram as a great enlargement in the tunnel through which "the world" passes from

Stage 1 to Stage 1′. The words ultimately selected for utterance (at Stage 5) are a very small part of the lush abundance of possible verbalizations from which they are abstracted. Moreover, the bulge is intended to suggest that the state of affairs at Stage 3 becomes in a peculiarly human way much more significant by virtue of its symbolization at Stage 4.

At Stage 4 the individual's symbolic system and the pattern of evaluation reflected in its use come into play. The evaluative processes represented at this stage have been the object of much and varied study and speculation:

Freud. Here, it would appear, was the location of Freud's chief pre-occupations, as he attempted to explain them in terms of the so-called unconscious depths of the person, the struggle between the Id and the Super-Ego from which the Ego evolves, the ceaseless brewing of dreamstuff, wish and counterwish, the fabulous symbolism of the drama that we call the human personality.[2] Indeed, at this stage there is more than meets the eye—incredibly more, so far as we may dimly but compellingly surmise.

Korzybski. Here, too, were the major preoccupations of the founder of general semantics, Alfred Korzybski: the symbol; the creation of symbols and of systems of symbols; the appalling distortions of experience wrought by the culturally imposed semantic crippling of the young through the witless and artful indoctrination of each new generation by the fateful words of the elders—the words which are the carriers of prejudice, unreasoning aspiration, delusional absolutes, and the resulting attitudes of self-abandonment. But also here we find the unencompassable promise of all that *human* can suggest, and this Korzybski called upon all men to see, to cherish, and to cultivate with fierce tenderness.[3]

Pavlov. The father of the modern science of behavior, Pavlov, also busied himself with ingenious explanations of occurrences at what we have called Stage 4.[4] In human beings, at least, the leading processes, as well as the drives and goals that power and direct them, appear to function at this stage of incipient symbolization.

It seems useful to conjecture that perhaps the general *patterns* of symbolic conditioning are formed at Stage 4 in contrast to the conditioning of specific symbolic responses (i.e., particular statements) produced at Stage 5. We may put it this way: at Stage 4 the syllogism, for example, as a *pattern* or *form* of possible symbolic response, is laid down, while at Stage 5 there occur the specific verbal responses patterned in this syllogistic mold.

2. Sigmund Freud, *A General Introduction to Psychoanalysis,* translated by Joan Riviere (New York: Liveright Publishing Corporation, 1935).

3. Alfred Korzybski, *Science and Sanity: An Introduction to Non-Aristotelian Systems and General Semantics* 3rd ed. (Lancaster, Pennsylvania: Science Press, 1948).

4. I. P. Pavlov, *Conditioned Reflexes: An Investigation of the Psychological Activity of the Cerebral Cortex,* translated and edited by G. V. Anrep (London: Oxford University Press, 1927).

Again, at Stage 4 we find the general form, "X affects Y"; at Stage 5 we see its specific progeny in such statements as "John loves Mary," "germs cause disease," "clothes make the man," and so on. In this relationship between general forms or patterns at Stage 4 and the corresponding specific utterances at Stage 5 we find the substantial sense of the proposition that our language does our thinking for us.

In fact, one of the grave disorders that we may usefully locate at Stage 4 consists in a lack of awareness of the influence on one's overt speech of the general symbolic forms operating at Stage 4. The more the individual knows about these forms, the more different forms he knows—or originates—and the more adroit he is in the selective and systematic use of them in patterning specific statements at Stage 5, the more control he exercises over "the language that does his thinking for him." The degree of such control exercised over the verbal responses at Stage 5 represents one of the important dimensions along which speakers range themselves, all the way from the naivete of the irresponsible robot—or compulsive schizophrenic patient—to the culture-shaping symbolic sophistication of the creative genius.

(Generally speaking, most of the disorders of abstracting described and emphasized by the general semantics are to be most usefully thought of as operating chiefly at Stage 4. These disorders include those involving identification or lack of effective discrimination for purposes of sound evaluation.)[5]

The Final Draft

The fact has been mentioned, and should be emphasized, that the "final draft" formulated at Stage 5, the words that come to be spoken, represents as a rule a highly condensed abstract of all that might have been spoken. What enters into this final draft is determined, in a positive sense, by the speaker's available knowledge of fact and relationship, his vocabulary, and his flexibility in using it, his purposes, and (to use the term in a broad sense) his habits. What enters into it is determined negatively by the repressions, inhibitions, taboos, semantic blockages, and ignorances, as well as the limiting symbolic forms, operating at Stage 4.

Mr. A to Mr. B

As the communication process moves from Stage 5 to Stage 1', it undergoes another of the incredible transformations which give it a unique and altogether remarkable character: the words, phrases, and sentences at Stage 5 are changed into air waves (and light waves) at Stage 1'. At close

---

5. See Alfred Korzybski, *Science and Sanity,* and Wendell Johnson, *People in Quandaries,* particularly Chapters 5 through 10.

quarters, Mr. A may at times pat the listener's shoulder, tug at his coat lapels, or in some other way try to inject his meaning into Mr. B by hand, as it were, but this transmission of meaning through mechanical pressure may be disregarded for present purposes.

Inefficiency of Air Waves

In general, it seems a valid observation that we place an unwarranted trust in spoken words partly because we disregard, or do not appreciate, the inefficiency of air waves as carriers of information and evaluation. The reasons for this inefficiency lie both in the speaker and in the listener, of course, as well as in the air waves themselves. What the listener ends up with is necessarily a highly abstracted version of what the speaker intends to convey.

The speaker who sufficiently understands this—the wise administrator —expects to be misunderstood and, as a matter of fact, predicts quite well the particular misunderstandings with which he will need to contend. Consequently, he is able not only to forestall confusion to some extent, but also to give himself a chance to meet misunderstanding with the poise essential to an intelligent handling of the relationships arising out of it. A minimal requirement for the handling of such relationships is that either the speaker or the listener (or, better, both) recognize that the fault lies not so much in either one of them as in the process of communication itself—including particularly the fragile and tenuous air waves, whose cargo of meaning, whether too light to be retained or too heavy to be borne, is so often lost in transit.

Such an executive takes sufficiently into account the fact that words, whether spoken or written, are not foolproof. He will do all he can, within reason, to find out how his statements, his letters and press releases, his instructions to subordinates, and so on are received and interpreted. He will not take for granted that anyone else thinks he means what he himself thinks he means. And when he discovers the misunderstandings and confusions he has learned to expect, he reacts with disarming and constructive forbearance to the resentments and disturbed human relationships that he recognizes as being due, not to men, but to the far from perfect communications by means of which men try to work and live together.

Inside Mr. B

The air waves (and light waves) that arrive at Stage 2'—that is, at the ears and eyes of the listener—serve to trigger the complex abstracting process which we have just examined, except that now it moves from 2' through 5' instead of 2 through 5. That is, the various stages sketched in the speaker are now repeated in the listener. To understand speech, or the communication process in general, is to be aware of the various functions and the disorders operating at each stage in the process—and to be conscious of the complex pattern of relationships among the various stages, as represented schematically by the double-arrowed loops in the diagram.

Effect of Feedback

Always important, these relationships become particularly significant when the speaker and listener are one and the same individual. And this, of course, is always the case, even when there are other listeners. The speaker is always affected by "feedback": he hears himself. What is significant is precisely the degree to which he is affected by feedback. It may, in fact, be ventured as a basic principle that the speaker's responsiveness to feedback— or, particularly important, the *administrator's* responsiveness to feedback—is crucial in determining the soundness of his spoken evaluations. It is crucial also, in determining his effectiveness in maintaining good working relationships with his associates.

Application to Problems

This view of the process of Mr. A speaking to Mr. B may be applied to any one of a great many specific problems and purposes. The diagram can be used especially well as a means of directing attention to the disorders of communication, such as those encountered daily in the world of trade and industry.

Preventing Troubles

In this connection, let me call attention to the fact that Professor Irving Lee of the School of Speech at Northwestern University has written a book on *How to Talk with People*,[6] which is of particular interest to anyone concerned with such disorders. Its subtitle describes it as "a program for preventing troubles that come when people talk together." The sorts of troubles with which Professor Lee is concerned in this book are among those of greatest interest and importance to personnel managers and business administrators and executives generally, and there would seem to be no better way to make my diagram take on a very practical kind of meaning than to sketch briefly what Professor Lee did and what he found in his studies of men in the world of business trying to communicate with one another.

---

6. Irving Lee, *How to Talk with People* (New York: Harper & Brothers, 1952.)

Over a period of nearly ten years Professor Lee listened to the deliberations of more than 200 boards of directors, committees, organization staffs, and other similar groups. He made notes of the troubles he observed, and in some cases he was able to get the groups to try out his suggestions for reducing such troubles as they were having; and as they tried out his suggestions, he observed what happened and took more notes.

Among the many problems he describes in *How to Talk with People* there are three of special interest, which can be summarized thus:

(1) First of all, misunderstanding results when one man assumes that another uses words just as he does. Professor Quine of Harvard once referred to this as "the uncritical assumption of mutual understanding." It is, beyond question, one of our most serious obstacles to effective thinking and communication. Professor Lee suggests a remedy, deceptively simple but profoundly revolutionary: better habits of listening. We must learn, he says, not only how to define our own terms but also how to ask others what they are talking about. He is advising us to pay as much attention to the righthand side of our diagram as to the lefthand side of it.

(2) Another problem is represented by the person who takes it for granted that anyone who does not feel the way he does about something is a fool. "What is important here," says Lee, "is not that men disagree, but that they become disagreeable about it." The fact is, of course, that the very disagreeable disagreer is more or less sick, from a psychological and semantic point of view. Such a person is indulging in "unconscious projection." As we observed in considering the amazing transformation of the physiological goings-on at Stage 3 into words or other symbols at Stage 4, the only way we can talk about the world outside is to filter it through our private inner states. The disagreeable disagreer is one who has never learned that he possesses such a filter, or has forgotten it, or is so desperate, demoralized, drunk, or distracted as not to care about it.

A trained consciousness of the projection process would seem to be essential in any very effective approach to this problem. The kind of training called for may be indicated by the suggestion to any administrator who is inclined to try it out that he qualify any important statements he makes, with which others may disagree, by such phrases as "to my way of thinking," "to one with my particular background," "as I see it," and the like.

(3) One more source of trouble is found in the executive who thinks a meeting should be "as workmanlike as a belt line." He has such a business-only attitude that he simply leaves out of account the fact that "people like to get things off their chests almost as much as they like to solve problems." Professor Lee's sensible recommendation is this: "If people in a group want to interrupt serious discussion with some diversion or personal expression—

let them. Then bring them back to the agenda. Committees work best when the talk swings between the personal and the purposeful."

Constructive Factors

Professor Lee saw something, however, in addition to the "troubles that come when people talk together." He has this heartening and important observation to report:

"In sixteen groups we saw illustrations of men and women talking together, spontaneously, cooperatively, constructively. There was team-play and team-work. We tried to isolate some of the factors we found there: (1) The leader did not try to tell the others what to do or how to think; he was thinking along with them. (2) No one presumed to know it all; one might be eager and vigorous in his manner of talking, but he was amenable and attentive when others spoke. (3) The people thought of the accomplishments of the group rather than of their individual exploits."

This can happen—and where it does not happen, something is amiss. The diagram presented in *Exhibit 1,* along with the description of the process of communication fashioned in terms of it, is designed to help us figure out what might be at fault when such harmony is not to be found. And it is intended to provide essential leads to better and more fruitful communication in business and industry, and under all other circumstances as well.

Conclusion

Mr. A talking to Mr. B is a deceptively simple affair, and we take it for granted to a fantastic and tragic degree. It would surely be true that our lives would be longer and richer if only we were to spend a greater share of them in the tranquil hush of thoughtful listening. We are a noisy lot; and of what gets said among us, far more goes unheard and unheeded than seems possible. We have yet to learn on a grand scale how to use the wonders of speaking and listening in our own best interests and for the good of all our fellows. It is the finest art still to be mastered by men.

The Nature of Communication

Stephen W. King

Three weeks into a course entitled "Small Group Communication" an earnest student raised her hand and asked, "Now that we know what a 'small group' is, Professor, what is 'communication'?" Many students snickered, thinking the question tremendously naive and trivial.

However, I was apprehensive. Was this student going to force me to deal with the difficult but essential question of definition? I tried to get out of the tense moment by flippantly saying, "What is *not* communication?"

Undaunted, the student pressed her question, "You didn't answer the question; you merely circumvented it."

Trapped! So I said, "Well, Stevens defined it as 'the discriminatory response of an organism to a stimulus,' Miller and Steinberg asserted that communication 'involves an intentional, transactional, symbolic process,' and Samovar and Mills concluded that communication 'includes all methods of conveying any kind of thought or feeling between persons.' "[1]

Gaining confidence the student looked at me and said, "Professor, that was simply a smorgasbord of definitions offering me a great deal of choice but not much clarification."

I prayed for the bell to ring indicating the end of the period. No bell, so I said, "O.K., Miller and Steinberg's definition is the right one. Now, do you understand?"

"No," said the student, "that's the point. You gave me a definition but I don't understand why that definition captures the essence of 'communication' while the others do not. I guess I want to understand 'communication' not define it."

Of course, she was right. Thus, I begrudgingly began a dialogue aimed at understanding communication, its fundamental nature and conceptual boundaries. I invite you to join us on this expedition in search of understanding.

We can begin our expedition with a brief story:

(1) Professor Samuel Withit left the library one morning and saw

---

1. S. S. Stevens, "A Definition of Communication," *Journal of the Acoustical Society of America,* 22 (1950), p. 689; G. Miller and M. Steinberg. *Between People: A New Analysis of Interpersonal Communication.* Chicago: Science Research Associates, 1975, p. 34; L. Samovar and J. Mills. *Oral Communication: Message and Response,* 3rd ed. Dubuque, Iowa: Wm. C. Brown Publishing Co., 1976, p. 4.

one of his students across the quad wave to him. He waved back. (2) A few moments later Professor Withit walked by another of his students who gave a friendly "hello" smile. (3) Professor Withit did not see the student and continued to walk to his office without acknowledging the smile. The student, miffed by the rebuff, cut class for the rest of the week. (4) Upon entering the departmental offices, Professor Withit overheard one of his ex-students telling another student, "Professor Withit's class is one of the toughest in this department." (5) Later, Professor Withit dictated a letter to his secretary and requested that the letter be mailed that day. Two days later the letter left the office.

How many of these five incidents would you classify as examples of communication? All five? Two? None of them? Very probably other people would disagree with whatever answer you decided upon. Such difference of opinion is more than just an interesting disagreement; we must ask the question, "Why?" Quite simply, the answer centers on the fact that to decide to call something by a name, in this case "communication," reflects your understanding and, at this point in your study of communication, you *all* probably have different ideas about what is or is not "communication." Let's look at each of these five incidents and try to discover the points at which some of your understandings might differ.

In incident number one (1) no words are exchanged. Because of this, did you exclude this as an example of communication? In incident two (2), a signal—a smile—was sent but not received. Is reception necessary for communication? Professor Withit's behavior in incident number three (3) unintentionally affected his student. Are such accidental effects communication? In incident four (4), Professor Withit was not the intended receiver of the signal sent by one of his ex-students. Did the student communicate anyway? Finally, in incident five (5), the professor's instruction to the secretary was apparently received but not effective. Is the study of communication limited to effective communication?

Possibly your concept of communication allows you to include all the incidents as examples of communication. However, if another person conceived of communication as only those exchanges of ideas through words, incidents one, two, and three would be dropped because words were not uttered. If another individual thought communication dealt only with messages intentionally sent, incidents three and four would not qualify. If success was a prerequisite for yet a third person, incidents two, four, and five would not be included. It is apparent that if we are going to go much further in this study of communication, we must come to a shared understanding of the term.

One way to understand a phenomenon is to identify its parts or components. Accordingly, let's try to decide what the fundamental ingredients of communication are. First, nonverbal communication, which does not rely on words, is a reality. If it were not, why do people get so upset over various hand gestures? Why did Professor Withit's student skip class for a week? Second, to concern ourselves only with successful idea exchange is like calling "teaching" only that which results in the student getting an "A." The result would be that neither education nor communication would ever be improved since no one would have investigated the causes of failure. We must look at both successful and unsuccessful communication. Finally, if we limit ourselves to only those messages intentionally sent, two problems become apparent. First, we have to make some very questionable decisions about what is going on inside a sender's head. Second, and more importantly, we must ignore many messages that do, in fact, have impact, such as Professor Withit's unintentional slight of his student. With these distinctions in mind, let me suggest a description of communication that reflects our understanding of communication to this point: *Communication is a process whereby symbols generated by people are received and responded to by other people.*

Understood in this way we would include all the incidents of Professor Withit's morning except number two (2). In that case the student sent a message, a smile, but it was not received and responded to. Communication was attempted but not achieved. All the other incidents, however, were examples of communication.

Characteristics of Communication

Another way to test the adequacy of our understanding of communication is to see if our concept can accommodate basic truths about communication. Accordingly, let's see if our description of communication fits with five commonly accepted characteristics of communication:

(1) Communication is a process.
(2) Communication is complex.
(3) Communication is symbolic.
(4) Communication is a receiver phenomenon.
(5) Communication is transitory.

Communication is a process. This statement implies that communication "does not have *a* beginning, *an* end, *a* fixed sequence of events. It is not static, at rest. It is moving. The ingredients within a process interact; each affects all of the others."[2] Viewed in this way, communication is both dynamic—that is, constantly changing—and interactive—at least two actively participating individuals are involved. We can separate the ingredients only if we stop the process to look at it. For example, in an argument between an employer and employee many things are happening simul-

---

2. D. Berlo. *The Process of Communication.* New York: Holt, Rinehart and Winston, 1960, p. 24.

taneously, each one affecting the others—e.g., the employee thinks his boss hates him, the rebuke confirms that impression, the employee's reaction is seen as a challenge to the boss's authority, other employees giggle at the exchange, increasing the employer's determination to reassert authority, etc. To sum up, the idea of process means that many ingredients—variables—are interacting at the same time to produce results.

Communication is complex. The complexity of communication is reflected in two important observations. First, being a process, it is not as direct and one-way as an injection into the arm administered by a physician. Rather, communication proceeds on verbal and nonverbal levels, in both directions.

Second, communication is complex because it involves so many variables, or ingredients. Consider, for example, how many variables are operative during a simple conversation between you and a friend. It is more than just a matter of exchanging ideas with another person; "whenever there is communication there are at least six 'people' involved: the person you think yourself to be; the man your partner thinks you are; the person you believe your partner thinks you are; plus the three equivalent 'persons' at the other end of the circuit."[3] To these six "people" we must add the topic, the communication setting, the goal of communication, and the many other variables that affect any communication event. In addition, everyone has an individual personality, a set of needs, a past history, important personal relationships, and a unique way of seeing the world.

Communication is symbolic. One obvious but important characteristic of communication is that it involves the use of symbols of some kind. Symbols are arbitrary, man-made signs that represent thought. Two important implications of symbol use concern us here. First, a given symbol means something different to everyone. Symbols such as "beauty," "intelligence," and "democracy" illustrate well the many meanings invoked by single symbols. Therefore, communication is not the simple transfer of thought from one person to another. Rather, it is a process in which one individual encodes—translates—his thoughts into a symbol and sends that message via some medium to a receiver. The receiver then translates the message into thought—decodes the symbols. Thought and meaning are not transferred: messages are. Once the student of communication sheds the idea that communication is the transfer of meaning and adopts the view that *communication is an exchange of symbols,* a more realistic conception of the communication process is achieved.

The second important consequence of the fact that communication is symbolic is that not all symbols are words. The peace symbol, "thumbs down," long hair, and sarcastic voice inflection are all symbols that com-

---

3. D. Barnlund, "Toward a Meaning-Centered Philosophy of Communication," *Journal of Communication,* 2 (1962), p. 40.

municate ideas or sets of ideas. Indeed, many researchers contend that more than half of the meaning we gain in face-to-face communication is achieved through these nonverbal cues. The recognition and study of the importance of these nonverbal symbols is a critical aspect of understanding human communication.

Communication is a receiver phenomenon. Remember the second student that Professor Withit met earlier in this essay? That student smiled (an attempt to communicate nonverbally) but the professor did not see the smile. According to the description of communication we developed, the student did not communicate because the professor did not receive and respond to the symbol. This example illustrates an important aspect of communication: "Communication always occurs *in* the receiver."[4] Notice how the concept of communication differs from a concept like "love." It is possible to love someone and not have the person aware of it. Even though the object of one's love is unaware of the existence of the feeling, the feeling nevertheless is real. Communication, on the other hand, requires that the receiver be just that—a receiver. Communication attempts that do not reach the receiver, like the attempts of our hapless smiling student, are merely attempts at communication, not communication.

There is another implication we must keep in mind. If communication occurs within the receiver, the intention of the sender is largely unimportant. For example, whether or not Professor Withit intended to slight his student, he did. Whether or not the student whose discussion Professor Withit overheard intended it, his message was nevertheless picked up. Communication occurred because an individual received and responded to a set of symbols.

Third, if communication is identified by receiver response, we ought to examine the types of responses that occur. Let's again examine the episodes with which this essay began. Clearly, one result of the communication was a change in attitudes: the first student probably likes his professor a little more and the second student a little less, or maybe a lot less. Additionally, the professor probably did not think much of his secretary when he found out that the letter was mailed late. Apparently, then, one general effect of communication is that our attitudes toward people and things change. Another type of response was illustrated by the student who skipped class for a week. Obviously, the student's behavior was changed by the communication. By reading this essay, your knowledge of communication will be affected. Clearly, change in knowledge is another general type of response to communication. At this point, we should understand that communication occurs in the receiver and that its potential effects on the receiver are numerous.

---

4. L. Thayer, *Communication and Communication Systems,* Homewood, Illinois: Richard D. Irwin, Inc., 1968, p. 113.

Finally, being a receiver phenomenon means that communication occurs when the receiver attaches meaning to others' behavior. As a consequence of the dominant role of the receiver, some researchers have concluded that it is impossible to not communicate. Simply, "one cannot not communicate."[5] All behavior, when perceived by another, has potential message value or communicative significance. That is, people assign meaning to other people's behavior or nonbehavior. For example, Professor Withit's failure to respond to one of his students angered the student. Therefore, if *all* behavior can have message value or meaning, it is impossible to not communicate, since you can't stop behaving. Anything you do or do not do *may* have meaning for one who perceives it. A few examples may illustrate this important characteristic of communication.

If you were to ask your roommate a question, is there anything he/she could do that would not mean something to you? What if he/she ignored your question? What if he/she answered sarcastically? What if he/she responded in a very cheery way? What if he/she left the room? No matter what he/she did, you would interpret the behavior as meaning something to you.

When you sit next to a person in the campus coffee shop and he says "hello," he is obviously communicating. Is not the same person communicating when he just looks at his food and ignores your presence? Of course he is! He is saying, "I'm here to eat and not to carry on idle chatter with a person I don't know." Is there anything that person could do to which you would not attach meaning? Probably not.

The fact that "one cannot *not* communicate" is important. It means that the study of communication must focus on all your behavior and not just on that part of the time when your mouth is open. Furthermore, it increases your responsibility to recognize that what you say and do influences other people.

Communication is transitory. This principle has two parts. First, communication is irreversible. It can only go onward: it cannot back up and try again. This characteristic of communication is best illustrated by the absurdity of the judge's admonition, "The jury will disregard the testimony just given." Impossible! Second, communication is unrepeatable. Even if the message is repeated word for word, the audience has been changed by the first attempt. Therefore, they are different receivers attaching a different meaning to the same message. This principle of communication is well illustrated by the common experience of either telling or hearing a joke the second time; it just is not the same.

So far it works! If we conceive of communication as a "process whereby symbols generated by people are received and responded to by other

---

5. P. Watzlawick, J. Beavin, and D. Jackson. *The Pragmatics of Human Communication.* New York: W. W. Norton, 1967, p. 48.

people" we can account for the observations that communication is a process, is complex, is symbolic, is a receiver phenomenon, and that communication is transitory. Let's test our understanding in yet another way.

Myths of Communication

Another test of the adequacy of our concept of communication is whether it helps us reject myths or misconceptions about communication. Using our description of communication see how it allows us to avoid five of the most common mistaken conclusions about communication.

1. "I understand communication. I've done it for years." Because of this false assumption, people have communicated poorly for centuries. You have breathed for years, driven cars for years, listened to radios for years, and thought for years, and yet you probably realize that knowing more about physiology, engineering, electronics, and psychology could improve your own performance. Many successful salespersons do not understand persuasion. Doing something does not necessarily imply that one understands what he or she is doing.

2. "Communication can be improved simply by improving communication skills." This myth is based on two fallacies. First, it assumes that there are "certain unequivocal laws which, if followed, lead to success, and, if not, to failure."[6] That simply is not the case. Communication is far too complex a process and our investigation (so far) too unsophisticated for such rules to exist. If such rules were available, they could be printed and distributed at freshman orientation, and all departments of English and Speech Communication could be disbanded.

Second, this myth focuses attention on the speaker, which, according to our description of communication, is stressing the wrong person. Remember, communication is a receiver phenomenon. The study of communication, therefore, should not focus on what the speaker *does to* a receiver (which treats the receiver as a passive, mindless blob), but should focus on what happens within the receiver as the result of the speaker's behavior.

Communication is not necessarily improved merely by improving communication skills. Indeed, communication is improved "first, by the communicator's understanding of the communication process, then by the communicator's attitudes and orientations; and only then by the techniques the communicator employs."[7]

3. "I didn't misunderstand him, he misunderstood me." Because of human nature, we are always convinced that we are right and the

---

6. Thayer, p. 8.
7. Thayer, p. 8.

other person is wrong. For example, I have heard students say things like, "It was John's fault, his speech was so confusing nobody could have understood it." Then, two minutes later, the same student remarked, "It wasn't my fault, what I said could not have been clearer. John must be stupid." Poor John! He was blamed when he was the sender *and* when he was the receiver. John's problem was that he was the *other* person, and that's who is always at fault.

To understand and to improve communication, you have to be willing to accept the idea that communication is a two-way process with at least two active participants and "fault" must be divided between them.

4. "Most problems, from interpersonal to international, are caused by communication breakdowns. These breakdowns are abnormal and easily correctable." Let's look at the first sentence of this most common of myths. In recent years a number of widely discussed, little understood, and generally ambiguous terms and phrases, such as "communication breakdown," "communication gap," and "credibility gap," have been introduced into our everyday vocabulary. These terms have become the dumping ground for many phenomena we can't explain in an easier or more direct way. The fact that college administrators and students disagree is not a communication breakdown. The fact that teenagers frequently argue with parents is not a communication gap. The fact that minorities demonstrate for a greater share of the economic "action" in this country is not a communication breakdown. Calling these problems gaps or breakdowns ignores the psychological, economic, political, and physical realities which caused the symptom of poor or infrequent communication.

The second part of this myth is equally erroneous. Ineffective communication is not abnormal. Communication is complex and poorly understood; is it any wonder that without much knowledge or training in communication we are not very good at it? Further, since communication is so complex, can we expect it to be easily corrected when it is found to be inefficient?

5. "All communication is attempting to achieve perfect understanding between participants." This myth is dangerous on two counts. First, it assumes that "perfect understanding" is possible. Second, it denies an important reality: sometimes the goal of communication is to be misunderstood.

To achieve "perfect understanding" through communication limited to a humanly-devised symbol system is impossible. Our symbols frequently do not come close to fitting the ideas they are supposed to represent; at best, they are approximations. There is always a very real possibility, indeed probability, that the idea you try to communicate will not be the idea your communication partner decodes from the symbols you have chosen to represent the idea. Recognizing that symbols are inexact, we should try to make our communication as efficient as possible. This, rather than "perfection," is a realistic and attainable goal.

Do you always want to be perfectly understood? Probably not. Have you never answered a test question vaguely to avoid demonstrating ignorance? Have you never sidestepped giving an opinion about a friend's new car or clothing? Often we intentionally garble our messages so as to avoid embarrassment or hide our true feelings. The following selection from an Oscar Wilde play illustrates this use of communication well.

THE DUCHESS: "Do, as a concession to my poor wits, Lord Darlington, just explain to me what you really mean."

LORD DARLINGTON: "I think I had better not. Nowadays to be intelligible is to be found out."[8]

What Is Not Communication

One final test of our understanding of communication is whether we can use such understanding to identify what is not communication. That is, we should be able to answer the question, "What isn't communication?"

We have said that communication takes place whenever someone attaches meaning to another's behavior. It is clear that unless one's behavior is perceived by someone, communication has not occurred. That is, what one does or says in isolation is not communication.[9] Furthermore, we must exclude those behaviors which, though perceived, have no meaning or significance for the perceiver. Perceived behavior to which the perceiver does not attach meaning is not communication. Every day we interact with others in ways that result in no significant interpretation or meaning being attached to the perceived behavior. For example, when you jostle your way in or out of a crowded lecture hall, your behavior and that of many others are mutually perceived, but only in the rare circumstances of inordinate rudeness does anyone attach meaning to that type of perceived behavior. Note that this argument retains the focus of our study on the receiver: Does the receiver attach meaning to that which is perceived? Obviously, what is meaningful for one person might be inconsequential for another. For example, you would probably ignore the fact that your friend does not

---

8. O. Wilde, *Lady Windermeir's Fan,* cited by Thayer, p. 306.

9. Of course, communication with ourselves can be considered communication—intrapersonal communication. However, this essay has focused on the social or interpersonal nature of communication.

wear a watch, but a psychiatrist may take that to mean something significant about your friend's psyche.

Thus, to answer the original question, behavior that is not perceived by another or to which no significant meaning is attached is not communication. Behavior that is both perceived and meaningful is communication. You may now argue, "O.K., but earlier you said that communication can't be turned off, and now you say some perceived behavior is not communication. Isn't that contradictory?" Not at all. Not all behavior communicates, but it has the *potential* for communication. The important distinction is that you cannot *avoid* communicating. It is impossible for you to turn communication off as you do a radio. When this point was presented earlier in the essay, I was looking at the sender and forcing him or her to recognize all the ways he or she is constantly giving off communicative behavior. When I say that all behavior need not be communication, I am focusing on the receiver and asking the question—does the receiver actually assign meaning to perceived behavior? Not all behavior actually communicates, but it does have communication potential.

Summary

Are you now ready for a definition? We described communication and then tested our understanding of the thing described in many ways. We found that our understanding of communication helped us identify what is and isn't communication, it assisted in rejecting fallacious myths about communication, and it can accommodate several basic truths about communication. Accordingly, we can now define communication in a way that *reflects* our understanding, rather than merely assert a definition that is separate from our understanding. Simply, we understand communication to be "a process whereby symbols generated by people are received and responded to by other people."

Elements of Group Communication

John E. Baird, Jr. and Sanford B. Weinberg

In chapter 1 [Baird-Weinberg text], we defined communication as "the process involving the transmission and reception of symbols eliciting meaning in the minds of the participants." We further suggested that those symbols, which can take the form both of words and of nonverbal behaviors, have no meaning of their own—that they serve simply to stimulate meaning in the mind of the receiver. But this suggestion might be a bit misleading, implying that we need not be concerned about words or behaviors because they have no special importance. Quite the reverse. Certain meanings are conjured up by certain words; specific ideas are stimulated by distinct gestures. To understand the meanings which form in the minds of group participants, then, we first must understand the nature of the symbols which elicit those meanings. In this chapter, we will examine the symbols which comprise the communication process.

To facilitate our examination of human messages, we will go beyond the verbal-nonverbal distinction and divide communication into three categories: verbal, paraverbal, and nonverbal. Verbal communication is what you say, paraverbal is how you say it, and nonverbal is what you do while you are saying it. In the following sections of this chapter, we will analyze the verbal, paraverbal, and nonverbal elements of human communication, noting their general characteristics and the ways in which they operate in the group setting.

Verbal Communication

The verbal communication channel serves as a good starting point not because it is necessarily the most important element, but because it is the most obvious. When observing a group, we are most likely to notice the spoken and written messages which the members exchange. Nonverbal and paraverbal messages must be carefully focused upon, while the declamations, memos, agendas, and protestations of group members tend to hit the observer squarely between the eyes.

Verbal communication is of two sorts: oral and written. In some formal groups, written communication is dominant. Members exchange and ponder carefully prepared reports, ask a few minor questions, and vote to

From John E. Baird Jr. and Sanford B. Weinberg, *Communication The Essence Of Group Synergy* (Dubuque, Iowa: Wm. C. Brown Publishing Co. 1977). Reprinted by permisssion of publisher.

accept, to reject, or to modify. Most groups, however, rely much more heavily on oral communication. While there may be a group secretary furiously scribbling notes throughout the meeting, the most important messages are those exchanged orally. Hence the observations we will make in this section will apply to both oral and written communication, but we will be concentrating primarily on the former. But a comment about written communication is in order. Such communication has both advantages and disadvantages. The advantages are that written messages may be carefully prepared, so that they are exact in tone, specific in detail, and presumably exact in wording. In addition, the message has permanence, so that if the receiver forgets what the message said, he can always look it up again. But written messages also have important disadvantages. The most obvious is a loss of immediacy: the sender and receiver do not confront one another. But this leads to a second, more serious disadvantage. A written message is not open to modification through feedback. You cannot correct misunderstandings easily—indeed, you probably will not detect misunderstandings in the first place—and you cannot readily revise the message should misunderstandings occur. A great deal of flexibility is therefore lost, and a high risk of misunderstanding and miscommunication is incurred.

Napoleon is said to have hit upon a solution of sorts. He appointed an idiot to his staff, and had the unfortunate soul read all messages before they were sent to Napoleon's generals. Napoleon reasoned that if a written message was so clear that an idiot could understand it, there was a good chance that his generals would be able to handle it as well. Still, Napoleon met his Waterloo. Our advice, then, is to use oral communication whenever possible, employing direct and immediate feedback to evaluate the receiver's understanding of your message and to clarify that message if further explanation is needed. Your communication practices may not make history, but you will be able to communicate more effectively and, in the process, save wear and tear on corporals, your memorandum-writing and -sending abilities, and your nerves.

Semantics

Rather basically, verbal communication involves words and phrases. Ideally, member *A* forms a mental concept, selects the proper word for it, speaks that word, and relaxes. Member *B* hears the word, translates it, and receives the mental image *A* intended. Unfortunately, things are rarely so simple.

Take a deep breath. With what did you fill your lungs? air? oxygen? gases? smog? Do you stand on earth? on ground? on dirt? on soil? or in a yard? Do you drive a car? an auto? some wheels? a vehicle?

Perhaps the words in each of these sets are identical to you. But you might note certain minute but meaningful differences. Often, connotative differences have little effect. But an eleven-year-old called a *child* instead of a *kid* or *young person* or a black person called a *Negro* might disagree. The study of words and word meanings is called *semantics,* and it is a complex field overlapping linguistics, philosophy, psychology, and speech.

Some semanticists have been portrayed as eclectics, more concerned with the proper word than with communicative intention. We shall try to avoid a perspective trap here; for the moment we'll accept the hypothesis that words are a method of expressing ideas rather than a tool for forming ideas themselves. And, unlike the semanticist of Ogden Nash's famous poem, we'll try not to get lost debating over whether the approaching lizard is an alligator or a crocodile while the beast is attacking.

Before examining the verbal linguistic code itself, let's take a broad perspective. A few observations ought to be noted. It is helpful that all group members share a common language. Rather basic, you say, but it may be an important problem in international negotiations where certain phrases may not readily translate from one language to another. Until the "universal translator" of Star Trek fame is perfected, we'll have to be sensitive to this problem. *Sympatico,* for example, has no English equivalent. The Russian word for *policeman* is not readily translatable as *cop.* And slang idioms—well, we'll consider that tangle a bit later. Suffice it to say that our initial observation about verbal communication is that, with all the confusion occurring from homonyms, dialects, and connotative differences, a common group language provides the group with at least a fighting chance of success. Perhaps it is for this reason that the Boy Scouts tried desperately to teach Esperanto, an international language, to all boys attending the Internation Jamboree held in Japan.

Another general observation about verbal communication in groups involves the frequency of interaction. Several researchers have reported a strong correlation between leadership and verbal contribution (see research cited in chapter 7). Apparently, more talkative group members tend to be perceived as group leaders regardless of the worth of their verbal contributions. In one experiment, for example, subjects sat around a table upon which were a series of colored lights. Each subject could see only the set of lights directly in front of him. Participants were instructed to talk whenever their green light was on and to stop talking when their red light was illuminated. The experimenters manipulated the frequency of interaction by changing the duration and pattern of light signals. Even though subjects often could think of nothing valuable to say and spent their green light time repeating nonsense, there was a strong and significant correlation between perceptions of leadership and duration and frequency of the light signals (Hayes and Meltzer 1972). It was possible to make one subject appear as the group leader simply by increasing the talking time of that person.

The phenomenon does have a limit, however. Individuals who dominate conversation to the exclusion of others are considered less benevolent than are relatively quieter group members. This lowering of benevolency ratings produces a reduction in the perceived leadership ratings as well (Smith, Brown, Strong, and Rencher 1975). Talking too much, then, like talking too infrequently, can have a negative effect upon perceptions of leadership contributions. Group members evidently tend to ascribe leadership qualities to individuals who interact frequently but not dominantly.

Rate of speech, vocal inflection, and tone will be discussed later as elements of paraverbal communication. Now, let's look in more detail at the verbal content of the group communication process.

We discover and assign meaning to words through a number of channels: nonverbally, using gestures as clues; paraverbally, relying upon volume, pitch, or inflection; and verbally, attempting to translate the words themselves. While the phrase may be the most meaningful unit for examination, we know that words themselves do have relatively specific meanings. Through the examination of word meanings we can discover information about group communication and group functioning.

S. I. Hayakawa, one of the most famous and persuasive semanticists, has suggested that several problems potentially arise from attempting to ascribe meaning to words (Hayakawa 1949). These problems may produce confusion, false impression, and general misinterpretation of message meaning. For our purposes in examining group communication, we'll concentrate on the three most frequently encountered pitfalls of verbal exchange: the map-territory dilemma, the problem of abstraction, and the purr-snarl controversy.

A map, says Hayakawa, is not a territory. Territory is a concrete thing: we can see it, stand on it, sell it, build a house on it, and pay taxes for it. The map of that territory is merely a summary diagram attempting to represent the major qualities of that land. Do you remember as a child looking for a physical line drawn on the ground when passing from one state into another? Do you expect school buildings to be square with little black flags? While a map denotes (represents) the characteristics of the territory, we sometimes expect the physical land to share some of the connotations (implications) of the map. Here lies the source of some confusion.

Words are simply maps of ideas or physical things. A thing is not its word. But we may expect a *custodial engineer* to be more dignified than a *janitor* and a *multimedia-printed-matter center* to be more than a *library*. We are, in effect, confusing maps and territories. We sometimes expect physical items to share the connotative characteristics of the word describing that item. Is a *memo* more terse than a *message*? Does a committee's *charge* require more dynamic action than a committee's *responsibility*?

Does a *board* have more normal tasks than a *group* or *committee?* If you read implications of this sort into the words employed, you may be confusing maps and territories. But what is the danger? Perhaps there is none *if* all of the groups members share the same connotations. But because a map is an abbreviated diagram of a territory, the same map may describe closely two similar but distinct pieces of property.

Similarly, the same word with varying connotations may imply very different meanings. Remember that individuals united in a group have some characteristics in common and differ on some other criteria. They have a general unity of purpose, but retain individuality within the group. What if the individual group members have different assumptions which they attach to words? Let's assume, for example, that we're in a group working on the problems of how to help poor children in our community. One member proposes funding a camp for these disadvantaged children. You, perhaps, having worked in a summer camp last year, fully approve of the idea. Another group member is appalled and calls you a Nazi. Why? Perhaps the connotation he attached to the noun *camp* involves the adjective *concentration.* He sees the plan as a method of eliminating the poor kids from the area. A fight is on, and it is likely that neither of you understands why—you don't really disagree about the concept; you simply have different territories associated with the same map.

If this seems contrived, try another example. Discuss the possibility of providing poor people with free birth-control devices. Are you attempting a subtle form of genocide? or providing a vital service that will eventually help people overcome their poverty? or subverting their religion? or commenting on imagined loose morals? or attempting to corrupt the youth? A single map, but widely differing connotative territory.

This problem is closely related to and confounded by yet another verbal difficulty: abstraction. We can, in reality, draw a variety of different maps of the same territory, each varying in exactness of detail and symbolism. A photograph is a map, as is a geological survey map made from the photograph. In the photograph mountains are represented by film images of mountains. On the map, mountains look like curving thin brown lines (contours). From the geological survey map, we could construct a road map which would portray mountains as gray inverted *v*'s ($\underset{\wedge}{\wedge} \underset{\wedge}{\wedge}$). Or, we could draw a sketch, writing *mountain* in the proper place. Our maps vary in their levels of abstraction, and our verbal interaction varies in much the same way. We can describe a student government election as a *polling,* a *school activity,* or a *youth project.* The ultimate territory is identical, but the maps vary greatly in their specificity. The level of abstraction chosen for a particular message has a significant effect upon the reception of that message. The more concrete a term is, the more likely it is that the individual group members will be able to associate with and understand that term.

For example, we may have some trouble grasping a plan that will "improve the internal decision-making balance capacity of a multinetwork collective organization," but we can more clearly appraise a proposal to "let everyone in the group have a chance to speak." Some organizations and individuals seem to purposely strive for ambiguity and high-level abstraction, perhaps to hide the fact that they are not doing anything important. Generally, the more concrete a message, the more convinced the sender is that the group ought to grasp the full meaning of that message. High-level abstractions diffuse group responsibility, limit concretized understanding, and block full realization of implications. Low levels of abstraction are, in effect, votes of confidence in the group members. You might want to examine your income tax form with that thought in mind.

Some politicians running for office often power their campaigns with abstraction. If asked "Do you favor forced busing?" either yes or no is likely to lose you votes. The response of "I favor an equal opportunity for all Americans" is a safe, spineless out, tempting to many would-be leaders.

The third contribution of Hayakawa we'll consider is the use of purr and snarl words. Often two descriptive terms can be given for the same item or phenomenon. For example, an overweight person can be called *plump* or *a toad*. A smart person might be termed an *egghead* or an *intellectual*. The dictionary tells us these terms are synonyms, but they actually have very different connotative meanings. Hayakawa calls words with a positive connotation "purr" words (as in a loving kitten's calls) and words with a negative connotation "snarl" words (as in a mean cat's growl). For example, what you might call *persuasive* your friend might label *manipulative*. What you think of as *sexy* your parents might consider *lewd*. You have the same territory, but are changing maps to imply different characteristics about that territory.

In a group situation, each member may employ snarl or purr items, each term may elicit a variety of different territories, and each territory might be viewed as one of a number of abstraction levels. In interpersonal communication face-to- face contact allows rapid clarification of a great deal of the resulting confusion. In group communication nonverbal and paraverbal clues aid in interpretation, but some confusion is still likely. In many kinds of groups, the individual members share a common orientation, philosophy, educational level, and background. You and your friends are likely to share a common orientation. Faculty-student committees, while often composed of individuals of varying backgrounds, nonetheless generally contain members used to and trained in dealing with persons of different backgrounds. You, for example, have been trained for at least sixteen years in understanding teachers.

In some groups, however, wide educational and status levels are coupled with the problems of individuals not experienced in communicating with members of differing backgrounds. Perhaps the jury is the prime example of this situation. Since juries are designed to represent a cross section of society, we can expect that some jury members will have difficulty communicating on the same level as their peers. Resulting confusions of map-territories, abstraction levels, and snarl-purr connotations are likely. Perhaps this explains in part the insistence upon complete agreement in most jury decisions.

The verbal code is certainly a major channel of communication in groups and as such is a major source of misunderstanding and misinterpretation. When two people communicate, variations as described by Hayakawa may produce a great deal of confusion. When those problems are multiplied by the five or more group members involved in a discussion, it may be surprising that anything is ever accomplished. Misunderstandings can be minimized, of course, by modifying behavior to avoid the pitfalls just identified. In fact, three relatively simple rules should help greatly:

1. Double check map-territory agreement. Techniques include reliance upon feedback from other group members to make sure that you are all talking about the same thing, careful definition of terms, and identification of important elements through the use of alternate maps (terms) for key concepts. For example, you might begin a discussion by asking each member what the best way to help disadvantaged youngsters might be, and use that description as a concrete territory for the map *camp*. You can alternately reinforce the meaning by calling the experience a *summer play opportunity* (different abstraction level) instead of a *camp*.

2. Move up and down the abstraction level to ensure that all members have an idea of the specific and general implications of the concept. Be as concrete as possible most of the time to avoid ambiguity, but occasionally use an alternate term that clarifies the implications of the idea. Plan an *election,* but remember that it is a *student feedback opportunity.*

3. Strive for neutral terminology. Snarls and purrs both distort meaning and subvert free discussion. If other group members use connotative terms in discussion, ask them to explain what they mean. If you are planning to write a newspaper, don't let the group refer to it as a *rag sheet* or as a *journalistic enterprise* if unrealistic connotations accompany those terms.

These suggestions should help in all communication activities, for they deal with problems that are not unique to group situations. But there is one important communication barrier that does occur only in (or most commonly in) small groups. Before concluding this section on verbal channels of group communication, we'll consider the phenomenon of ingroup speech.

Ingroup Speech

As groups thrive and function and grow, they tend to develop a unique vocabulary to accompany the new syntality. Originally, group members brought to the group a variety of linguistic and verbal patterns. Those terms and phrases with common meaning hopefully became the group staple, forming a specialized vocabulary code for communicating within the group. Eventually, however, some of these terms began to be uniquely abbreviated to save time, or began to take on uncommon specialized meanings, or perhaps began to be used to represent new concepts not easily expressible. Perhaps if the group exists long enough and functions intensively enough, a special sublanguage of terms evolves. This unique language is understandable only by the other group members. Often, the group members are not even aware they have a special code. Probably, they would have difficulty translating a great deal of it to an outsider.

The code typically speeds and eases communication within the group. It is likely to be rapid, simple, and be common to all the group members. So far, of course, no problems exist. The ingroup speech code is an aid, not a barrier, to communication. Before considering the possible difficulties that might arise, though, let's examine the existence and extent of the ingroup speech phenomenon.

Consider your campus as a defining characteristic of a group. How many specialized slang terms can you find? Some, no doubt, are unprintable. After all, ingroup speech is a rather informal code. But some terms are common to insiders on campuses all over the country. Is your undergraduate library known as the *Ugly?* Are easy courses at your school called *slides, guts, cribs,* or *cake?* Do you try to *ace* exams? Are tests called *hourlies?* We've collected samples of ingroup speech from campuses in several different parts of the country, and these terms seem to be the most common. But would your parents understand if you told them you had "spent the night at the ugly so that you could be sure to ace the hourly in your cake course"?

Slang speech changes rapidly over time and distance. Ask one of your older teachers to define *making out* or *fagging.* Do these meanings conform to your usage? In the Midwest, order a *pop* if you are thirsty—*soda* will get you seltzer water. When you buy something in North Carolina, the salesperson will put it in a *sack;* in Florida you're likely to be asked if you want it wrapped; in New York, a *bag* is used. These kinds of slang differences can be represented in ingroup speech, too. But unique group activities and focuses may have other effects.

Some professions, for example, rely heavily on ingroup terms. The medical profession, for instance, has long been accused of confusing lay persons by employing a highly specialized vocabulary. To your doctor, for example, a *nose job* is *rhinoplasty.* And we've often wondered why psychologists term the inability of an individual to express an idea lying just below the conscious level the *TOT phenomenon*—an acronym for "tip of the tongue."

Ingroup speech, then, has two very definite handicaps: it hinders communications between groups or subgroups, and it slows the integration process when a new member joins a group. Outsiders have difficulty understanding ingroup codes, and hence are clearly identified, perhaps confused, and certainly excluded.

Since the development, use, and problems of ingroup speech are so important to an understanding of the verbal code of group communication, let's examine a few key testable hypotheses concerning the unique vocabulary of slang in group situations.

1. Ingroup speech tends to increase group cohesion. It reinforces the commonalities of group members while identifying and excluding outsiders. Does your group have certain in jokes? As a child, did you ever belong to a group with a secret code word? do you today? The Greek letters of most fraternal organizations stand for some secret motto. Even the name of Phi Beta Kappa, the national honorary scholarship society, is a secret coded message. And, no doubt, somewhere there is someone who cares enough to remember what that message is.

We conducted an informal experiment in which nonfraternity members were invited to fraternity houses for dinner. The use of slang in the fraternity membership was more than double the normal levels with the presence of an outsider. The brothers of that house consciously or subconsciously excluded the visitor and bolstered their cohesion through the use of ingroup speech.

2. Ingroup speech may be used for ease in communication. Some pioneer industries and groups have been forced to invent new terms as they invent new techniques. Hence a stage, motion-picture, or television crewman who moves equipment is called a *grip,* and a computer printout is *debugged* to correct errors.

Ingroup speech may also save time. Hospitals have OB units instead of *obstetrical wards.* Graduate students may be working on an MA or PhD degree. These abbreviations may confuse outsiders, but do ease communication significantly.

3. Ingroup speech seems to proliferate in minority groups. Perhaps in order to maintain identity or prestige, minorities have traditionally developed elaborate ingroup vocabularies. The black culture, for example, has provided a rich and rapidly changing torrent of slang terms. Black English and Yiddish are paralanguages which have emerged from and are maintained in minority groups. Elements of these languages maintain group cohesion and identity.

At the same time, majority groups tend to co-opt slang, perhaps to integrate outsiders or to join desirable subgroups. Do you occasionally use some medical terminology you learned from television to impress your physician? Do you parrot the slang you learned from overhearing another group? Do you find yourself employing minority-group phrases when you talk to members of those groups? It has been suggested that the slang of the youth culture dies as soon at Johnny Carson uses it.

4. Ingroup speech often has a disguised meaning. Words mean the opposite of their usual meaning. To be *bad* is (or was) to be *good*. Some words are developed from other slang. A *deejay* plays records—the name, of course, comes from the slang of the last generation: disc jockey.

This disguised effect may be due in part to the desire to avoid being infiltrated. The more obscure the meaning, the easier it is to isolate outsiders. If the meaning is obvious, most of the exclusionary value is lost.

5. Many terms have forbidden connotations. Perhaps ingroup speech is sometimes a way of talking about the untalkable. Many terms have sexual connotations. But would a foreign-speaking listener realize that the person you called an *ass* does not necessarily share the characteristics of a beast of burden? Perhaps the writing on bathroom walls loses something in the translation.

Of course, if this hypothesis is correct, we ought to see fewer and fewer sexual slang terms as sex increasingly becomes a fit subject of undisguised conversation. No doubt members of some groups, however, will find something else to restrict, for the development of ingroup vocabularies seems to have a universal appeal.

Ingroup speech tends to magnify the commonalities of group members, hence strengthening group cohesion. The increased group efficiency, however, decreases the flexibility of intergroup communication. The result is a strong but communicationally isolated group.

The unusual characteristics of verbal communication shed a great deal of light upon group communication as a whole. We stated earlier that communication was a process of information transference. By now it ought to be obvious that *group* communication, though, serves a dual role. While communication is allowing the group to perform its task as efficiently as possible, that same verbal communication is performing an important maintenance function. By avoiding semantic confusions, we can avoid unnecessary dissention and argumentation within the group that might serve to weaken it. In a further effort to conserve important synergy for task purposes, group communication can increase cohesion through the use of sophisticated slangs. The more tightly knit the group is, the less likely it will develop severe maintenance difficulties. And of course the less energy used for maintenance, the more energy can be devoted to task.

Communication is a tool which allows energy channeled for task accomplishment to serve the dual purpose of maintenance and cohesion building. It is then, the key to efficient synergy utilization. Even while synergy is the essence of groups, communication is the essence of efficient synergy. An examination of nonverbal and paraverbal communication will further illustrate the important linking function communication performs. Through communication, energy need not be divided between the two group functions; it can unite for mutual benefit.

Paraverbal Communication

Group meetings are oral experiences in which a great deal of information is communicated *paraverbally*. As you sit in a group while another member drones on, you presumably are listening to what is being said. You are translating verbal messages, striving to understand the things which the current speaker is trying to say. At the same time, however, you are probably reacting to and translating a more subtle message: you are listening to *how* the speaker is communicating as well as *what* he or she is saying. The way in which a verbal message is delivered is termed *paraverbal communication*. Paraverbal messages are based upon such factors as the speaker's oral style, phraseology, intensity, articulation, and interpretive expression.

Before examining in detail the five most significant variables of paraverbal communication, let's consider for a moment the all-important role that paraverbal messages play in group situations. In a mass lecture, you are not likely to be able to see subtle nonverbal cues (such as gestures) and will probably have to concentrate on paraverbal messages. You will be striving to write down or remember or evaluate what it is the speaker actually says. Of course, some perceptive students concentrate upon the speaker's intensity, thinking that when the professor gets excited a test question is in the air. Most of the audience, though, is probably spending a great deal of their energy on the verbal channel.

Incidentally, television does have a modifying effect upon this generality. When you watch Walter Cronkite you are, in fact, a member of a mass audience. Psychologically, however, you may feel like a participant in an interpersonal conversation and hence devote more of your listening energy to nonverbal and paraverbal channels.

In an interpersonal setting, you can hear the speaker, see the speaker's nonverbal communications, and evaluate paraverbal cues all at the same time. Each channel is generally utilized, and each becomes important.

A group situation magnifies the importance of paraverbal communication in two ways. First, as we just explained, group members come from greatly varying backgrounds but share a common focus. While the focus does much to aid communication, the variety of background may significantly increase ambiguity and confusion. We saw how verbal difficulties may cause distortion and misunderstanding. The other two communication channels, therefore, become increasingly important for interpreting and clarifying verbal messages.

Second, the nonverbal channel may be impeded. While all group members are physically close enough to hear intonations and inflections, they may not be situated properly to observe subtle nonverbal cues. Physical limitations such as rectangular tables, size restrictions, and attention diversions (more than one person speaking, for example) may make it difficult to clearly see what is happening.

Restrictions on verbal communication caused by semantic variations and limitations of the nonverbal channel resulting from observational impediments therefore conspire to increase the significance of the paraverbal communication channel. With this increased importance in mind, let's examine the effects of paraverbal communication in groups.

Although there are many different variables included under the rubric "paraverbal," we will just concentrate on the five that have the greatest significance in group communication. Those factors are *oral style,* the delivery of words chosen in conversation; *articulation,* the pronunciation and clarity of those words; *intensity,* the emotional impact conveyed by the voice in delivery; *phraseology,* the stringing of words together; and *interpretive expression,* the emphasis or implication of those words and phrases. Before investigating these concepts, however, allow us to make a mild disclaimer. We are well aware that the categories just identified are not distinct. Many situations will overlap the divisions suggested, just as the divisions of verbal, nonverbal and paraverbal sometimes seem to flow together. We suggest, then, that you read the following section not with the intent of being able to cubbyhole interactions, but rather in the hope that these arbitrary and somewhat leaky categories will aid your understanding of the broad process of communication, which transcends all of our attempts to subdivide it.

Oral Style

You have your own unique oral style. Perhaps you are aggressive or assertive. Or you might have a passive, apathetic personality. When you communicate, your choice of words and style of delivery broadcast hints about the person you are. Can you think of someone you instantly disliked as soon as he or she opened a conversation? even before you mentally registered the topic of discussion? Much research is currently being conducted concerning the effect that oral style has on other variables such as trust, willingness to self-disclose, and willingness to assume risk (Norton and Miller 1973). There is apparently a strong link between the paraverbal cues of oral style and interpersonal ties established during the interaction.

If oral style is a valid predictor of relationships between communicators, this aspect of paraverbal communication has important implications for group situations. Consider the possibility that in a small group you form close ties with one person because of his use of inflection, word choice, and speaking pattern. His task-oriented communication can therefore have a significant effect upon maintenance functions within the group. And, of course, the less energy spent on maintenance, the more synergy is available to accomplish that task. Having synergy serve double-duty is the most efficient method of group operation.

Oral style, then, is a potentially invaluable tool for smoothing the wheels of group syntality. A pleasant, amiable style can have considerable impact in arriving at a group decision, while an obnoxious style can add new barriers to consensus.

Articulation

Of course, if people don't understand what it is you are saying, the style with which you say it is of little importance. We saw that speaking in a foreign language is potentially disasterous. Equally serious, and much more common, is speaking with poor articulation.

In normal conversation you receive immediate feedback if the target cannot understand what you are mumbling. In a group setting, however, you are likely to get positive assurance from the members close to you while those on the physical outskirts of the group have difficulty understanding. The point is so obvious that it makes little sense to repeat it: in a group situation, speak up and speak distinctly so that everyone can hear what it is you have to say.

Incidentally, poor articulation can also lead to misunderstanding. How many fights have erupted because of "But I thought you said . . ."? Some research has shown that poor articulation reduces individuals' credibility and persuasiveness (Underwood 1964) as well as waste maintenance synergy. For very real and demonstrable reason, then, it pays to make certain you are communicating whenever you are speaking.

Intensity

The intensity with which a message is delivered may have a significant effect on the importance attached to that message (Mortensen 1972). We tend to pay more attention and to be more impressed by a person who is obviously emotionally involved in his message. Again, the point is important in all communication: utilizing emotionally charged language and intense delivery increase audience interest. In a group setting, a serious payoff is involved. Because groups are ongoing organizations, group members have to make a series of compromises over time. You might have your way on one issue and have to defer to someone else's opinion on a subsequent question. At times, however, you feel so strongly about your position that compromise is impossible. If the group fails to recognize your position, a great deal of synergy can be wasted on simple maintenance functions. If your paraverbal message clearly informs others that you have a strong ethical or moral commitment to your position, or that you have significant ego-involvement in a particular decision, other group members can defer to your position or offer face-saving compromises. If, on the other hand, you purposely feign a high commitment on an insignficant issue, you lose the flexibility to compromise at that time, and force the group to expand synergy unnecessarily. The rule of thumb, then, is this: if your blood is beginning to boil, let others know it. But if the controversy really isn't important, don't paraverbally cry wolf. Remember, the more time the group wastes on disagreement and maintenance, the more difficult it is to arrive at a decisive action.

Phraseology

Sometimes, particularly in more formal group situations, the phrasing of a point or speech may be important. We are not talking here about avoiding obviously biased terminology. Obviously, if you are going to have to work with the group members in the future, name-calling today is likely to backfire tomorrow. But some kinds of phrasing can add significant drama to a statement, emphasizing intensity and suggesting a shift of oral style. For example, consider these three rhetorical devices:

1. Chiasmus: crossing-over or reversing normal word patterns. Isn't "Ask not what you can do . . ." more moving than "Don't ask . . ."?

2. Alliteration: repeating consonant or vowel sound for emphasis. We wonder whether this wording works wonders. If overdone, the effect may be humorous. Properly used, however, the message seems more moving, more meaningful, more motivating, more . . .

3. Parallelism: placing concept in phraseological contrast. Even as synergy is the essence of groups, syntality is the essence of synergy. "We shall pay any price, bear any burden, meet any hardship, support any friend, oppose any foe . . ." (John F. Kennedy, January 20, 1961).

While these stylistic devices can obviously be overdone in a group situation, do not underestimate (underestimate not) their value when you are trying to persuade other group members. Paraverbally they add great impact to your verbal message.

Interpretive Expression

Finally, the interpretive expression of a message can have significant additive meaning. Much of what we said previously applies here, too. One can easily add a note of disbelief, of sarcasm, or of horror to an otherwise innocuous message through paraverbal inflection. How many ways can you interpret the following line?

These statements seem to be reliable.

Is the speaker implying that the statements may seem reliable on the surface, but that they are really distortions? or that other facts seem more reliable? or that previously examined statements are highly questionable? or that while reliable the statements are incomplete, or inconsequential or not relevant? There may be some confusion in reading the message, but in hearing it the paraverbal interpretation is likely to remove all doubt.

In a group situation, paraverbal inflection can add greatly to understanding by serving as a readily observable commentary on the message itself. If the meeting is being transcribed, though, or if you are afraid of being quoted, better avoid sarcasm. Your "Me, rob a bank? Sure I would!" looks much more compromising on paper than it might when heard. Although some inflection may aid in understanding, undue use of sarcasm may boomerang and reduce effective group communication.

Clearly, paraverbal communication is a minor stepchild: it is not intrinsically as important as either verbal or nonverbal channels, while it possesses overlapping qualities of both. Yet paraverbal communication is powerful. As a tool used properly it can add an interpretive dimension important in face-to-face group settings that is almost impossible in written communication. Unless you are careful, however, sarcasm, inflection, articulation, intensity, and style can greatly complicate the already complex process of communication. As we'll see in the next section, nonverbal feedback may provide the clue to proper understanding of both verbal and paraverbal communication channels.

Nonverbal Communication

Investigation of nonverbal phenomena has recently become a booming fad. Every time you look over your shoulder, some researcher is trying to talk to your body (in its own language), to read your eyes (to see what they mirror about your soul), to measure your territorial claim (presumably to determine whether you are a claim jumper), or in some other way to assess the ways in which you inadvertently communicate with your environment. Scholars are watching your use of space, your choice of seat, your favorite color, your recurrent gestures. Everything you do and do not do is being observed, classified, catalogued, examined, and analyzed. Feel paranoid? Don't show it—nonverbal communicologists can spot that, too.

Really, we ought not be too harsh in our judgment of those who measure pupil dilations, muscle twitches, tongue lolls, and so on—they are conducting research in an area of communication which has immense importance. The behaviors which accompany the words we transmit have significant impact upon the meanings which ultimately are elicited in the minds of our receivers. Indeed, Raymond Birdwhistell (1955), an appropriately named authority on nonverbal communication, estimates that in face-to-face interactions nonverbal messages account for approximately two-thirds of the total meaning produced, while words account only for about one-third. Certainly, precise measurement of the sources of meaning is difficult; nevertheless, Birdwhistell's argument indicates the importance of nonverbal cues in group communication. In this section, then, we will try to achieve a more thorough understanding of nonverbal message cues, noting some types of nonverbal messages, the functions which these messages can play, and some of the effects which these messages produce in group settings.

Types of Nonverbal Cues

Although researchers have suggested many systems by which nonverbal messages might be categorized, the following list seems to us to comprise those elements most germane to group communication:

1. The environment: the physical setting in which communication occurs including room color and lighting, general attractiveness of the surroundings, temperature, etc.
2. Proxemics: placement of individuals relative to other individuals (includes such aspects of geographical location as physical distance, seating arrangements, bodily orientation, and other details of one's location)
3. Appearance: characteristics of an individual which are readily observable by others including general attractiveness, body shape or physique, bodily odors, hair, clothing, jewelry, and other apparent features
4. Kinesics: general bodily movements including postures, gestures, and movements of the head, limbs, hands, and feet
5. Facial expressions: movement of the facial features and/or movement of the eyes

Within these categories, we believe, fall the types of nonverbal cues which have significant impact upon group communication. Behaviors or elements in each category have a message potential such that any of them can elicit some meaning in the mind of the receiver. If as sources of communication we are careful to monitor our own nonverbal messages, we may be able to elicit meanings in our receivers which are congruent with the meanings we intend. If, however, we behave as most people do, sending nonverbal messages without paying much attention to their potential impact, we run the risk of disrupting our communication with other group members. In the following sections, we shall consider in more precise terms some potential effects of nonverbal cues; for now, simply note the types of cues which have message potential so that you can be aware of their impact when you deal with groups in real-world situations.

Functions of Nonverbal Cues

To understand the operation of nonverbal messages, we must consider the relationship between nonverbal cues and the words they accompany or symbolize. We thus turn to a brief consideration of the functions performed by nonverbal cues—functions defined in terms of the relationship between nonverbal behaviors and verbal messages.

1. Repeating. Nonverbal behaviors may simply restate the content of the verbal message. This function is most readily seen when one gives someone else directions while simultaneously pointing the way, or when someone tells you "Sit here, please" while pointing at a specific chair. But repeating also operates on a much less obvious level. Facial expressions, for example, usually repeat the emotional state described by one's words, or a letterman's jacket may repeat someone's claim that "I play football for Michigan."

2. Contradicting. Just as nonverbal cues may repeat messages, so too can they contradict them. For example, in one group discussion we observed, one member became particularly upset. As the discussion progressed, his voice became increasingly shrill and loud, his face grew redder, veins bulged from his face and neck, and his knuckles turned white as he grabbed the top of his desk harder and harder. Finally, someone said to him, "Geez, Don, you don't need to get so upset about this." Screaming, Don replied, "Dammit, I'm not upset!" Clearly, his nonverbal cues were suggesting something else.

3. Substituting. Occasionally nonverbal cues may operate in place of verbal messages. The peace or V-for-victory sign, the gesture indicating OK, and a variety of obscene gestures all take the place of words, as do the slumped posture, tired look, and soft snore which say to the other group members, "Wow, is this discussion boring!"

4. Elaborating. Nonverbal cues may also complement or elaborate upon verbal messages. Hands held five feet apart elaborate on the words "I caught a fish this long." Note that in this instance, the same gesture substitutes for the words "I lie like a dog." Moreover, expressions of emotion are usually accompanied by facial expressions, postures, and gestures which indicate the extent to which the emotion is felt, thus elaborating upon the spoken words.

5. Accenting. In this text, we have used italics, boldface type, and capitalization to add emphasis and meaning to the words we have written. Similarly, we use nonverbal cues to emphasize certain portions of our

spoken messages. The stereotypical politician who pounds the podium to emphasize his points is using nonverbal cues to accent his message, as is the group member who uses changes in volume to emphasize certain spoken words.

6. Regulating. When people communicate, they use some nonverbal cues to regulate the interaction. That is, we do certain things to indicate that we want to speak, that we are about to finish speaking, or that we would like someone else to speak. A forward lean, for example, may indicate that we have something to say; looking directly at someone as we near the end of a statement may suggest to him that we are finishing and that we expect him to respond; looking away from someone as he starts to speak to us usually shows that we would rather not hear what he has to say. By controlling the flow of interaction, then, cues such as these serve a regulatory function.

The meaning elicited by nonverbal cues seems thus to be a function largely of the role these cues play in relation to the spoken message. Nonverbal behaviors may produce or alter meaning by repeating verbal messages, contradicting them, substituting for them, elaborating on them, accenting them, or regulating them. Each of these functions is important, and each of them illustrates the crucial nature of nonverbal communication.

Effects of Nonverbal Cues

Group situations make nonverbal communication particularly difficult to analyze. Despite our insistence that groups operate on a face-to-face basis, there is a sense in which group communication is not face-to-face. Realistically, as a listener you cannot always directly face the person speaking, and as a speaker you cannot constantly be watching every listener. Yet, unlike public-speaking situations, you also cannot afford to generalize about your audience's reaction—you must treat all group members as individuals and adapt to their individual reactions. So groups pose a unique problem. As a speaker, you need to know how the other members are reacting, but you cannot watch them all. As a listener, your own reaction is an important message element for the speaker, but he cannot always watch you.

Obviously, these problems are not beyond solution. Groups have been functioning successfully long before communication researchers told us how difficult group communication is. People have been reading nonverbal communication for centuries before anyone decided that bodies have a language of their own. So it is possible to overcome the difficulties posed by nonverbal communication. But we believe that we should do more than overcome nonverbal problems—we should use nonverbal cues deliberately to increase group synergy. Therefore, our purpose in this section will be to examine some effects of nonverbal cues and, through that examination, to suggest to you the probable consequences of your own nonverbal transmissions. We will consider in turn the types of nonverbal messages which we described a few paragraphs ago.

Environment While several characteristics of a group's surroundings such as temperature, lighting, room color, and so on, probably affect the group's interactions, two dimensions of the environment seem of particular importance. First is the concept of territory. Generally, we tend to think of groups as collections of people sitting around a table. In truth, groups may occupy any one of a number of kinds of territories. A group of high school teachers, for example, may define as their territory a teachers' lounge. Four bridge players might consider their bridge table to be their own territory. A group of children might protect their mound of dirt from all comers. In each instance the principle is the same: the group claims as its own some physical location and defends that claim against invasion by outsiders. The claim may not be a legal one, and the group may not have explicitly agreed that the territory is theirs, but deep down inside each member feels that this particular space is theirs.

Consider again the teachers' lounge. If a nonteacher were to enter that smoke-filled room, he likely would be greeted by silence, snarls, or softly muttered oaths. Certainly, this response would make the intruder feel uncomfortable, and probably he would either try to justify his presence there, perhaps by delivering a message or striking up a conversation with a group member, or he would quickly exit. Obviously, he had every legal right to be in the room, but the group's feeling of territoriality caused the members to protect their claim through the use of social disapproval. Similarly, most groups try to protect their territories from invasion by outsiders.

Just as ingroup speech constitutes a verbal territory, the physical area owned by a group is likely to be a valuable tool in building group identity. Whyte (1949) reported that restaurant workers tended to define and defend the territory of the kitchen, and that this common area lent a unity and cohesion to the staff which contributed to group maintenance and probably increased group productivity. In accordance with this evidence, we have, in the past, advised leaders of Boy Scout units to assign each small patrol a specific corner of the meeting hall to build group teamwork. And we offer the same advice to you. If you are responsible for a group, you should consider the power of territory in building unity. Providing a group with a specific territory is a simple and valuable technique in which nonverbal factors are used to increase group spirit so that more synergy is generated and devoted to task concerns, rather than to social concerns.

A second important environmental element is the attractiveness of the surroundings. Maslow and Mintz (1956) and Mintz (1956) asked subjects to evaluate a series of photographs while working in three different settings: an ugly room (made to appear as a messy janitor's closet), an average room (professor's office), and a beautiful room (a living room with nice furniture, drapes, carpeting, and so on). Comparisons of the ratings obtained in these settings demonstrated that people felt much more positively toward the people in the photographs when those photographs were viewed in the beautiful room than when they were viewed in the ugly room. In addition, the subjects reported changes in their own emotional states. In the ugly room, they described their experience as irritating, tiring, dull, and generally unpleasant, while in the beautiful room they reported feeling comfortable, pleasant, and anxious to continue the activity. It seems reasonable to conclude, then, that the feelings aroused in us by our surroundings may be transferred to the people who also are present. If the room makes us feel good, we tend to respond well to the other people; if the room makes us uncomfortable, we find it more difficult to interact well with the others. Finding a room which is attractive to all group members thus seems another measure which will contribute to group cohesiveness.

Proxemics Physical location is particularly important in group settings. A great deal of evidence exists suggesting that seating arrangement has a significant impact upon patterns of group communication. Steinzor (1950) and Strodtbeck and Hook (1951) found that interaction tended to occur most often between individuals seated directly across the table from one another or between the individual seated at the end of the table and the rest of the group. These effects on interaction in turn had implications for leadership since emergent leaders typically are those individuals who communicate most often with the most group members, the end positions on a rectangular table typically produced the emergent leader.

A similar conclusion was reached by Howells and Becker (1962). They seated two group members on one side of a table, and three members on the other side. Arguing that more communication would take place between members across from one another than between members next to each other, they hypothesized that one of the members on the two-person side, by virtue of his easy access to the three people on the opposite side, would emerge as leader. Their experiments confirmed this hypothesis: usually, one of the two people on the two-person side would emerge as leader. The lesson therefore seems to be this: if you want to be group leader, establish direct contact with as many group members as you can. The end position of a rectangular table is ideal—it gives you direct access to almost everyone. Second best is to sit on the least-populated side of the table so that you face most of the group members. On the other hand, another lesson emerges from all this: if you want leadership to be a product of something other than seating arrangement, establish a setting which is advantageous to no one. Typically, a circle is best, although having an equal number of people seated on each side of a rectangular or square table is almost as good.

Appearance Although we repeatedly are told that we can't judge a book by its cover, a great deal of evidence exists demonstrating that we do precisely that—that we judge people, at least initially, on the basis of their appearance. And these judgments have significant impact upon our reactions to those people. Studies by Singer (1964), Mills and Aronson (1965), and Widgery and Webster (1969) all found that sources judged attractive by their receivers were more influenced or persuasive than were sources judged unattractive. One aspect of appearance, clothing, seems particularly important. In a particularly interesting study, Lefkowitz, Blake, and Mouton (1955) hired an accomplice, presumably a professional daredevil, to wander about a large city violating the Don't Walk sign at street corners while the experimenters observed the behaviors of other pedestrians in the vicinity to determine how many of them would follow the accomplice's example.

They found that when the accomplice was dressed in a suit and tie which suggested high status large numbers of pedestrians followed him across the street, while virtually no one followed him when he was dressed in an outfit indicating low status. Similarly, Bickman (1974) discovered that people who had found money lying in a public telephone booth (money cleverly planted by Bickman and his associates) were more willing to return the money to a well-dressed confederate who claimed he had lost it than to a poorly dressed confederate who made the same claim. In both these studies, then, people dressed in ways indicating high status exerted more influence than did people dressed in outfits conveying low status.

It is difficult to make suggestions about appropriate manners of dress in group situations. Certainly, the preceding studies ought not lead you to the conclusion that you always should wear a suit and tie—in some groups such dress would make you an immediate outcast. Perhaps the principle which we can draw from all this is that specific groups typically value certain forms of dress. In some groups, a formal outfit is called for so that status is conferred only to members wearing clothing of that sort. In other groups, the valued pattern of dress may be a sweat shirt with Harvard scrawled across the front, a jacket with Hell's Angels scrawled across the back, a pair of Adidas tennis shoes, a leather jacket, and so on. If you discover what form of dress is preferred by your group and then adopt that form, your status and influence will probably rise. Note that we are not suggesting you set out and dress to please other people; we simply want to make you aware of the impact which your choice of clothing has. If you want to increase your standing in a group, you may do so by wearing the things they value. If you choose not to conform to group clothing preferences, that, too, is your option.

Kinesics In view of the difficulties group situations pose for those of us interested in observing nonverbal behaviors, it is hardly surprising to discover that almost no research has been conducted in an effort to delineate the role of gestures, postures, and movements in group discussions. Still, some relevant research exists which provides us with an insight into the impact of kinesics. Rosenfeld (1966) found that people exhibit frequent gesticulations and positive head nods when they are seeking approval from other people, and he noted that frequent shifts of posture seemed to indicate discomfort, perhaps resulting from failure to obtain the desired approval. In a related study, Mehrabian and Williams (1969) found that people who are trying to persuade others show an increase in frequency of gesticulation and positive head nodding and a decrease in postural shifts. These two studies share a common implication: since approval from other members and the exertion of influence both are related to leadership, these kinesic variables should play a role in the leadership emergence process.

O'Connor (1971) tested this implication by having observers rate each group member's general nonverbal behaviors according to four dimensions: dynamism (a general measure of arm and hand movements), alertness (head and face movements), involvement (overall posture), and participation (mouth movement). He found that participation and dynamism, in that order, were most related to perceptions of leadership. Baird and Schubert (1974), on the other hand, actually counted instances of eight nonverbal behaviors: head agreement, head disagreement, facial agreement, facial disagreement, eye contact, postural shift, gesticulation of the shoulder, arm, or wrist, and gesticulation of the fingers and hands. They also distinguished between task and social groups to determine whether the same sorts of behaviors are related to leadership in each group type. Their findings indicated that in both types of groups, leaders gave more positive head nods (head agreement) than did nonleaders, and that leaders in task-oriented groups showed greater gesticulation of the shoulders, arms, and wrists than did leaders in social groups or nonleaders in either group type. While both of these studies are exploratory in nature, they provide an indication that our nonverbal gestures and postures may have an impact upon the perceptions of the other group members. Perhaps subsequent research will provide further information concerning the nature of this aspect of nonverbal communication.

Facial Expressions Without doubt, the face is the most expressive and complex source of nonverbal cues. This complexity has created particular problems for researchers who, because of the variety of meanings conveyed by almost undetectable changes in expression, have been unable to establish the specific consequences of particular facial cues. Some progress has been made by the students of Rosenfeld (1966) who found that people exhibit smiles more frequently when they are seeking approval, and Mehrabian and Williams (1969), who noted that people trying to persuade show an increase in facial activity, but a great deal of work is left to be done. Perhaps the most promising avenue of research in facial expression is the technique developed by Ekman, Friesen, and Tomkins (1971), who have determined that certain areas of the face usually express particular emotions. Their findings indicate that happiness is shown most by the lower face and eye areas, that sadness is shown primarily in the eyes, that surprise is indicated by the eyes and lower face, that anger is reflected in the lower face and the brows and forehead, that disgust is seen in the lower face, and that fear is shown most clearly in the eyes. Perhaps research such as this ultimately will provide us with a complete understanding of the role of facial expression in group communication.

More precise findings have been produced by studies of eye contact in human communication. Taken together, these studies indicate that we seek eye contact with others when we want to communicate with them, when we are physically distant from them, when we like them, when we are extremely hostile toward them (as when two boxers try to stare each other down before a fight), and when we desire feedback from them concerning messages we have just sent. Conversely, we avoid eye contact if we do not want to communicate with someone, if we are physically close to him, if we dislike him, if we are trying to lie to him, and if we expect him to say something which we are not particularly interested in hearing. Given the positive meanings conveyed by eye contact and the negative meanings conveyed by eye avoidance, we are not surprised to discover that eye contact seems to improve communication. Mehrabian (1969) observed that high-status individuals usually receive more eye contact from other group members than do individuals of low status, and Exline and Eldridge (1967) discovered that messages accompanied by eye contact tend to be more favorably interpreted by the receivers. Clearly, maintaining eye contact with other group members usually is desirable.

In this section, then, we have seen some of the effects produced by nonverbal cues. But we must sound a note of caution. While we have tried to be specific in our interpretations of nonverbal behaviors, these interpretations ought not be seen as inflexible rules. A postural shift during a group discussion could, as we suggested, indicate discomfort resulting from lack of approval, but it also could indicate nervousness, desire to enter into the discussion, severe muscle cramp, or tight pants. Similarly, each of the nonverbal behaviors we have discussed may spring from a variety of causes and may produce a variety of results. Our aim here was to suggest some, but by no means all, of the causes and consequences of certain nonverbal cues. Our hope is that despite the imprecision of nonverbal research this last section has made you more aware of your own and others' nonverbal cues so that you may become a more effective communicator in small group settings.

Summary

Just as chapter 1 [Baird-Weinberg text] considered the elements of which groups are composed, this chapter focused on the elements which make up the communication process in groups. We considered three basic communication categories: verbal cues, which involve problems of semantics, ingroup codes, and interpretation; paraverbal cues, which take into account oral style, articulation, intensity, phraseology, and interpretive expression; and nonverbal cues, which consider individual behaviors, territory, distance, and seating arrangement. By understanding these elements and their interactions with the group context, we should be better able to comprehend and utilize the principles which we will discuss in subsequent chapters.

References

Baird, J. E., Jr., and Schubert, A. "Nonverbal Behavior and Leadership Emergence in Task-Oriented and Informal Group Discussions," Paper presented at International Communication Association Convention, 1974, New Orleans.

Bickman, L. "Social Rules and Uniforms: Clothes Make the Person," *Psychology Today* 7 (1974): 48-51.

Birdwhistell, R. "Background to Kinesics," *ETC* 13 (1955): 10-18.

Ekman, P., and Friesen, W. "The Repertoire of Nonverbal Behavior: Categories, Origins, Usage, and Coding," *Semiotica* 1 (1969): 49-98.

Ekman, P.; Friesen, W.; and Tomkins, S. "Facial Affect Scoring Technique: A First Validity Study," *Semiotica* 3 (1971): 37-58.

Exline, R., and Eldridge, C. "Effects of Two Patterns of a Speaker's Visual Behavior upon the Perception of the Authenticity of his Verbal Message." Paper presented to Eastern Psychological Association, 1967, New York City.

Hayakawa, S. *Language in Thought and Action.* New York: Harcourt, Brace Jovanovich, 1949.

Hayes, E., and Meltzer, L. "Interpersonal Judgments Based on Talkativeness: Fact or Artifact?" *Sociometry* 35 (1972): 538-61.

Howells, L., and Becker, S. "Seating Arrangements and Leadership Emergence," *Journal of Abnormal and Social Psychology* 64 (1962): 148-50.

Lefkowitz, M.; Blake, R.; and Mouton, J. "Status Factors in Pedestrial Violation of Traffic Signals," *Journal of Abnormal and Social Psychology* 51 (1955): 704-46.

Lott, D., and Sommer, R. "Seating Arrangement and Status," *Journal of Personality and Social Psychology* 7 (1967): 90-95.

Maslow, A., and Mintz, N. "Effects of Esthetic Surroundings: I. Initial Effects of Three Esthetic Conditions Upon Perceiving 'Energy' and 'Well-Being' in Faces," *Journal of Psychology* 41 (1956): 247-54.

Mehrabian, A. "Significance of Posture and Position in the Communication of Attitude and Status Relationships," *Psychological Bulletin* 71 (1969): 365.

Mehrabian, A., and Williams, M. "Nonverbal Concomitants of Perceived and Intended Persuasiveness." *Journal of Personality and Social Psychology* 13 (1969): 37-58.

Mills, J., and Aronson, E. "Opinion Change as a Function of the Communicator's Attractiveness and Desire to Influence," *Journal of Personality and Social Psychology* 1 (1965): 73-77.

Mintz, N. "Effects of Esthetic Surroundings: II. Prolonged and Repeated Experience in 'Beautiful' and 'Ugly' Room," *Journal of Psychology* 41 (1956): 459-66.

Mortensen, C. *Communication: The Study of Human Interaction.* New York: McGraw-Hill Book Co., 1972.

Norton, R., and Miller, L. "Oral Style: An Effect of Dyadic Perception." Paper presented at Speech Communication Association Convention, 1973, New York City.

O'Connor, J. "The Relationship of Kinesic and Verbal Communication to Leadership Perception in Small Group Discussions." Ph.D. dissertation, Indiana University, 1971.

Rosenfeld, H. "Instrumental Affiliative Functions of Facial and Gestural Expressions." *Journal of Personality and Social Psychology* 4 (1966): 65-72.

Russo, N. "Connotations of Seating Arrangements," *Cornell Journal of Social Relations* 2 (1967): 37-44.

Singer, J. "The Use of Manipulative Strategies: Machiavellianism and Attractiveness," *Sociometry* 27 (1964): 128-54.

Smith, B.; Brown, B.; Strong, W.; and Rencher, A. "Effects of Speech Rate on Personality Perception," *Language and Speech* 18 (1975): 145-52.

Sommer, R. *Personal Space: The Behavioral Basis of Design.* Englewood Cliffs, N.J.: Prentice-Hall, 1969.

Steinzor, B. "The Spatial Factor in Face-to-Face Discussion Groups," *Journal of Abnormal and Social Psychology* 45 (1950): 552-55.

Strodtbeck, F., and Hook, L. "The Social Dimensions of a Twelve Man Jury Table," *Sociometry* 24 (1961): 397-415.

Underwood, B. "Articulation and Verbal Learning," *Journal of Verbal Learning Behavior* 3 (1964): 146-49.

Whyte, W. "The Social Structure of the Restaurant," *American Journal of Sociology* 54 (1949): 302-08.

Widgery, R., and Webster, B. "The Effects of Physical Attractiveness Upon Perceived Credibility," *Michigan Speech Journal* 4 (1969): 9-15.

Nonverbal Communication in the Small Group

Lawrence Rosenfeld

You cannot *not* communicate. You are always communicating something to other people, even when you are not speaking. The way you place your hands, the position of your body, your facial expression, your tone of voice, the way you touch, the clothes you wear, and where you position yourself communicate something to others. The shape of the room, the color of the walls, the type and size of the chairs, the temperature, time, and day communicate something to you and thereby affect your behavior in the small group.

Research in the area of nonverbal communication rarely focuses on the impact of nonverbal communication on small group interaction. Yet, the implications of research findings are relevant to the small group setting for several reasons. First, individuals working in groups have a great deal at stake: they value group membership, good interpersonal relationships, and effective task completion. Because of the value of successful interaction, group members seek cues to increase the probability of their effectiveness. Nonverbal cues, if interpreted correctly, provide one means.

Second, nonverbal communication is the means whereby group members project their feelings and attitudes. Therefore, nonverbal communication is closely related to a group's socio-emotional development. The greater a group's awareness to nonverbal cues, the greater the sensitivity to implicit meanings in gestures, vocal intonations, and various postures, the greater the probability of smooth and effective socio-emotional development. The effect is cumulative: effective socio-emotional development helps task development.

Finally, the small group, functioning as a microcosm for the larger society, makes it easier to focus upon the effects of verbal and nonverbal communication. Interaction in a small group appears concentrated, so the causes and effects may be more apparent than on the societal level.

Because of the nature of the nonverbal stimuli, attempts to systematically describe the area have yielded ambiguous results. Three approaches to the study of nonverbal communication have helped to define the object of study. The *transcription* approach, developed by Birdwhistell (1970) and Hall (1963), attempts to identify individual units of behavior and codify them. The complexity of the Birdwhistell system is testimony to the difficulty of this approach which, from the outset, seems contrary to one basic feature of the nonverbal code, that is, it is made up of continuous, not discrete, parts.

From Lawrence Rosenfeld, *Human Interaction In The Small Group Setting* (Columbus, Ohio: Charles E. Merrill Publishing Company, 1973). Reprinted by permission of the publisher.

The *external variable* approach devised by Ekman and Friesen (1968) appears to be more reasonable. The meaning of nonverbal behavior is a complex function of (a) the behavior exhibited and (b) a given context. A broad classification schema helps pinpoint the object of study, e.g., facial expressions or body movements, and then the behaviors are observed and measured. Meaning is abstracted from the data.

Third, the *contextual* approach designed by Scheflen (1964) attempts to describe the rules and structure of the nonverbal language code. Units of behavior have meaning because they occur in patterns under similar contexts. A behavioral unit contains specific parts, organized in a certain way, and fitted into a larger system of behavior. This approach recognizes the continuous nature of the stimuli under investigation.

Verbal and nonverbal codes differ in how they are learned. Whereas the verbal code is consciously acquired, the nonverbal code usually is learned in a more intuitive fashion. Words and sounds are arbitrary symbols, and each culture has to teach its young exactly what a particular symbol represents. This makes verbal language intellectual and, therefore, suitable for transmitting information in a reasonably sophisticated manner. Nonverbal behavior is less intellectual and more spontaneous than verbal behavior. Because of the basic differences between the two codes, each serves a different purpose. The nonverbal language code is best for expressing emotions and attitudes, noncognitive information. Therefore, nonverbal communication is more suitable than verbal communication for establishing interpersonal rapport.

Although the two language systems have been contrasted for purposes of clarification, it is obvious that they work together. When we express ourselves verbally, we are, simultaneously, expressing ourselves nonverbally. Our tone of voice, our facial gestures, and all the other nonverbal behaviors we perform, complement, supplement, and provide a context for our verbal behavior. At times the two may be incongruent, we may say one thing with our words and express the opposite with our gestures. For instance, hardly a day goes by that we do not say yes to someone while screwing up our eyebrows. The two languages are incongruent; one says yes, the other says no. This, of course, raises problems. Which code do you read when you receive conflicting information?

Nonverbal Communication

For purposes of analysis, nonverbal communication may be broken down into several areas. These areas are interdependent and interactive; that is, they often produce effects that cannot be predicted by examining each area (apparel, facial expression, posture, vocal cues, territoriality, personal space, environment, and body rhythms) separately. When we first join a group, we immediately form impressions of the other members. We most likely base our judgments on physical characteristics and apparel. We are attracted by what we consider well-formed and pretty, and repelled by what we consider malformed and ugly. Beyond this, our first impressions are formed by the clothes and jewelry worn by other members of the group. Then we observe facial gestures and posture, and listen to the other members speak —their vocal nonverbal cues (for example, pitch, variety, and volume) provide us with some of the best data available on which to base our judgments. After a while we notice that each person seats himself a certain way and in a certain place. Finally, we take notice of the environment and how it affects the interaction.

Apparel

Clothes and jewelry often serve as symbols of status in our society. As a consequence, we choose what we wear carefully, since our clothes "tell" something about ourselves.

A number of significant relationships exist between the dress an individual selects and various personality measures. Aiken (1963), studying undergraduate women students, correlated responses to questions concerning dress likes and dislikes to several personality measures. The questions were divided into five topics: decoration in dress, comfort in dress, interest in dress, conformity in dress, and economy in dress. Aiken found that a correlation exists between women who like decoration in dress and such traits as conformity, sociability, and nonintellectualism. Comfort in dress correlated with controlled extroversion. Interest in dress correlated with social conscientiousness, as well as uncomplicatedness. Conformity in dress correlated with conformity (in general) and submissiveness. Lastly, economy in dress correlated with intelligence and efficiency. The Aiken study was conducted in 1963. It may be that the changes in style and attitudes toward clothing would yield different results today. Regardless, clothing is taken as an indication of emotional states, certain personality characteristics, and other personal qualities. Because clothes are consciously selected, they offer a fairly accurate statement of the individual wearing them.

Apparel not only affects our judgments of others, but often influences our own behavior directly. Lefkowitz, Blake, and Mouton (1955) found that pedestrians were more likely to follow a well-dressed individual (shined shoes, white shirt, tie, and freshly pressed suit) violating a pedestrian "wait" signal than a poorly dressed one (worn shoes, soiled, patched pants, and blue denim shirt).

If you have been keeping a group process diary, look back at your first entries. Can you think back and determine the effect of apparel on your first impressions? Is there a relationship between apparel and the roles adopted by the various members? Do some members consistently dress more formally or casually than others? Do they differ in terms of their roles in the group?

Facial Expression

Osgood (1966), Shapiro (1968), and Shapiro, Foster, and Powell (1968) found that observers make relatively accurate judgments of the emotions expressed by various facial expressions. The judgments, though, are subject to stereotyping (Secord 1958). Secord, Bevan, and Katz (1956) found that Caucasian judges rated pictures of Negroes lower on traits such as alertness, honest face, air of responsibility, and intelligent look, and higher for lazy, superstitious, untidy, and immoral. What is interesting about this study is that there was no difference in the degree of personality stereotyping of Negro photographs varying widely in physiognomic "negroidness." Individuals tend to focus on a few unique characteristics, and then assign the whole range of stereotypes.

Secord (1958) found that cultural factors play a role in how an individual learns to respond to facial expressions. The culture dictates which features are to be attended to and which ignored. The general American culture teaches individuals to attend to slight variations in facial cues in order to attribute thoughts or sentiments to a speaker, whereas Navajos seldom make such attributions from facial cues, but instead depend upon explicit statements.

Pupil size has also been investigated as a source of information about the person observed. Hess (1965) found that pupil size related to the interest value of the stimuli, as well as the emotional state of the subject. Pupil dilation accompanied observation of a picture that was deemed interesting or stimulating, such as a pin-up or a picture of a mother and child. Another interesting finding was that men liked women with larger pupils. Consequently, an aspect of facial expression to which we respond, but are often unaware, is pupil size.

Facial expressions, including pupil size, are context bound, and often idiosyncratic. Culture and the surrounding stimuli help determine how we interpret these cues. Isolating any one cue from its total context will result in misleading conclusions; on the other hand, an awareness of the specific factors which make up the whole of any situation is likely to facilitate an accurate reading of individuals.

Posture

How we stand and sit, the way we organize our bodies, may reveal something about how we feel. Davis (1958) observed elementary school children and hypothesized psychological divergencies from postural variations. Two basic signs of tension were noted: static and kinetic (moving). Static signs of tension were characterized by sitting in a chair with legs wrapped tightly around the chair, clasping hands tightly, clenching fists, and holding the head rigidly to one side. Kinetic signs of tension were continually moving feet or hands, twisting the head from side to side, and running about the room. Although Davis observed elementary school children, the conclusions are applicable to groups composed of older individuals. Individuals who engage in a great deal of extraneous activity, such as foot movements and constant changing of postural position, *appear* anxious or tense, whether they are or not. The *perception* of their tension may disrupt group activity, deflecting conversation to tangential matters, such as personal problems and their possible resolution.

The presence or absence of chairs can affect interaction significantly. Without chairs, group members sit closer, touch more, and assume relaxed postures. Members who refuse to give up their chairs may be refusing to become intimate with the group.

Mehrabian and Friar (1969) focused on *projected* postural arrangements of individuals. Subjects were asked to assume the posture they would use if addressing a friend, a person of higher status, male or female, and a person they did not like. Researchers noted such things as eye contact, distance between the subject and the imagined person, head orientation, leg orientation, shoulder orientation, arm and leg openness, and the degree of limb relaxation. Results indicate that the more important variables for communicating positive attitude use a small backward lean of the torso, close distance, and great eye contact. Interacting with persons of higher status is accompanied by more eye contact and less sideways lean than interaction with persons of lower status.

Select a group meeting and focus on the postural messages of other members. Make inferences about their psychological states. Can you detect tension in the group? What adjustments do other members make to changes in postural cues?

Vocal Cues

The paralinguistic dimension of language, the vocal features which accompany our words and sentences, including pitch, clarity, breathiness, articulation, rhythm, resonance, and tempo, are more likely to convey information about the speaker than the literal message.

The paralinguistic dimension offers a variety of interpretable cues to listeners. Studies conducted since the early 1930s have produced fairly consistent results: listeners tend to agree on the characteristics they ascribe to speakers based on the paralinguistic code of their speech (Addington 1968).

In a summary article by Ernest Kramer (1963), the following conclusions were posited. (1) *Physical characteristics* that can be judged from the voice include speaker's age, height, overall appearance, Kretschmerian body type, and whether the speaker has a particular form of brain damage. (2) *Aptitudes and interests* that can be judged from the voice include the speaker's intelligence, dominant values, and vocation. (3) *Personality traits* that can be judged from the voice include whether the speaker is a dominant person, whether he is extroverted or introverted, and his degree of sociability. (4) Concerning the *personality as a whole,* listeners are able to match voices with personality sketches of several speakers, and can sort normal speakers from those with hypertension. (5) The final area concerns judgments dealing with an individual's *adjustment and psychopathology.*

More recent studies confirm Kramer's conclusions and expand the realm in which listeners make accurate judgments. Nerbonne (1967) studied the performance of listeners identifying the following characteristics: ethnic group, education, and dialect region, as well as those variables enumerated in Kramer's summary. Nerbonne concluded that listeners correctly differentiate Negro from Caucasian speakers, speakers with less than a high school education, a high school education, and college graduates, and speakers from the Eastern, Southern, and General American dialect regions.

Anisfeld, Bogo, and Lambert (1962) compared the stereotypic personality characteristics attributed to speakers speaking American English with and without a Jewish accent. They conclude, "The accented guises were comparatively devalued on height, good looks, and leadership for both gentile and Jewish subjects and when the accented guise was perceived as being either Jewish or non-Jewish. The gentile subjects did not consider the accented guise as more favorable on any trait while the Jewish subjects [did]" (p. 230).

Ruesch and Priestwood (Starkweather 1961) concluded that anxiety can be transmitted by sound alone and that some vocal aspects of anxiety were common enough to be detected immediately. Davitz and Davitz (1961) identified certain voice qualities with different emotional states. Active feelings were associated with loud voice, high pitch, blaring timbre, and fast rate. Passive feelings were associated with quiet voice, low pitch, resonant timbre, and slow rate.

Variations in the expression of emotion have been linked to force differences, differences in the rate of expiration, speech rates, breathing rates, and differences in the duration of phrases. Listeners recognize the intended emotion of speakers with better than chance accuracy. However, when speakers and listeners were of the same socio-economic background, judgments were more accurate. This infers that the expression of emotion is, in part, a cultural product.

Communication Variables

Status

Status is an important mediating variable. Ascriptions of high or low status affect credibility ratings, attitude change, and judgments of speaker background which relate to status, such as the level of education attained. Two studies indicate that accurate judgments of status are possible based on vocal cues alone.

Harms (1961) presented subjects with a 40 to 60 second sample of speech and asked subjects to judge each speaker's status and credibility. Both speakers and subjects were objectively classified as being of either high, middle, or low status, using the Hollingshead *Two Factor Index of Status Position* (which considers education and occupation). Harms concluded that subjects, regardless of their own status, could differentiate among speakers according to status, and that these distinctions are in accordance with the Hollingshead measure. Also, speaker status and credibility are positively correlated regardless of listener status. Exactly which dimension of the paralinguistic code is used as the basis for ascribing status is not known.

Ellis (1967) attempted to isolate the variables used by listeners as the basis for ascribing a certain level of status to a speaker. He concluded that status may be ascribed from cues given in single words (eliminating variables such as vocabulary, grammatical usage, and fluency), and that even under conditions of faking vocal qualities, listeners can still identify primary social status.

Credibility and Attitude Change

Perhaps two of the most important areas in speech communication are credibility and attitude change. As already discussed, the Harms study (1961) considered judgments of status and credibility based on vocal cues. Concerning credibility, Harms concluded that regardless of their own status, listeners found perceived high status speakers more credible than perceived low status speakers.

Recent studies by Miller and Hewgill (1964), Addington (1971), and Pearce and Conklin (1971) attempted to discover how various aspects of the paralinguistic code affect ratings of source credibility: the effects of nonfluencies; the effects of speaking rate, pitch variety, voice quality, and articulation; and the effects of "conversational" and "dynamic" delivery styles. Sereno and Hawkins (1967), Bowers (1965), Pearce (1971), and Pearce and Brommel (1971) considered the effects of nonfluencies and different delivery styles on credibility in relation to attitude change.

The following variables were found to be associated with decreases in speaker-credibility: increases in the number of nonfluencies (vocalized pauses, such as "uh," and repetitions); decreases in pitch; increases in nasality or denasality; increases in tenseness; and increases in throatiness. Those factors which had either no effect or an inconsistent effect on credibility were: increases or decreases in speaking rate; and increases in pitch. Delivery style had no effect on the perceived competence of the speaker, although it did affect other perceptions. A "conversational" delivery style was perceived as more trustworthy than a "dynamic" one.

The relationship between vocal cues, credibility, and attitude change is a complex one. Generally, variations in vocal cues produce variations in credibility ratings, but not attitude change, unless high or low credibility is established with an introduction (which is not always available in the same group setting) and a dynamic delivery is used. Although credibility has been classed as a major factor in attitude change, it is interesting that variations in vocal cues, which produce variations in credibility, do not produce variations in attitude change. It may be that *changes in attitudes are affected by a dimension or combination of dimensions of credibility which are unaffected by variations in vocal cues.* (See Hovland, Janis, and Kelly [1953]; Weiss and Fine [1955, 1956].)

Conclusion

Questions may be raised concerning the accuracy of listeners' judgments. Raymond Hunt and Tip Kan Lin (1967) conducted a study concerned with the accuracy of judgments of personal attributes from speech. Their findings provide evidence of accurate judgment and also some evidence of individual performance consistency across samples of speech expressive of dissimilar personalities; they also found that accuracy was greater for affective attributes than for behavioral-physical ones. They conclude,

> The most noteworthy findings to emerge from this research are those that support the idea that stable cues to personality are carried by general voice "qualities" *independently of the lexical content* of speech. The fact that listeners could judge personality accurately from speech samples, but that passage content had no effect on accuracy suggests either that speech content tends to be no more than redundant with voice quality or simply irrelevant to the judgmental task. (p. 453)

A more basic question which must be answered about listener judgment and agreement concerns the validity of the assigned personality characteristics. Ernest Kramer (1964) concluded that interjudge agreement concerning assigned personality characteristics to unseen speakers is not without validity. However, the role of seeking correlations with external criteria, e.g., objective personality measures, has not been fully understood. An objective personality measure, like *any* measure including one provided by a *single* judge, taps only part of the construct being measured. Judgments from aural cues may be prompted by another part or aspect of the same construct untapped by objective measures. The fact that judges agree with one another may be taken to represent only concurrent validity.

Territoriality

If you went so far as to "steal" someone's seat in the library, you probably noticed that when he returned, you were either the object of some verbal/nonverbal deprecation or that you became subject to an argument based on territorial rights. You may have argued that the seat does not belong to anyone, that it is available for all the students. The angry reply may have been that the books and coat should have indicated to you that the seat was, indeed, occupied. You may have countered that all the seats are the same, after all, and that the whole argument is silly. The nonverbal messages you encountered may have forced a retreat.

The tree fort became a *cause celebré*. The group of nine-year-olds returning to their tree fort probably wasted no time in talking. Icy stares and a show of teeth are the usual outcomes when the defense of territory is at stake. The odds are that the builders won. But the question which remains is an important one. What was at stake? Was it simply the chair in the library? Was it simply the fort? Or was it a great deal more?

What do you do when you walk into a classroom after the first few weeks of class and someone is in "your" seat? Immediately aware that something is "wrong," you probably stand in front of your seat and stare at its new occupant. You look slightly idiotic, and you certainly, by now, feel that way. Now what? You cannot stand there all period. One of two things occurs to you: either ask the person to move or find another seat. But how can you ask him to move when there is no *real* reason? Frustrated, you find another seat, either close to your original territory or far enough away so you can establish a new territory.

Territoriality is characterized by two features. First, there is the assumption of proprietary rights toward a geographical area and, second, there is the recognition that there is no legal basis for proprietary rights. The library seat is yours because you were there first. The classroom seat is yours because you have been occupying it for the greatest length of time. Proprietary rights with the tree fort are "stronger" because the four boys built the fort with their own tools, materials, and labor. The investment is greater than time. The fight, if one were to occur, is likely to be more physical. By the same token, a fight is less likely to occur at all; the claim to the territory is stronger.

The notion of territoriality has been examined in animals more extensively than in humans (Ardrey 1966, 1970; Hall 1969; Mowat 1963; Henderson 1952). Hall defines territoriality as "behavior by which an organism characteristically lays claim to an area and defends it against members of its own species." The net result of this behavior is that territoriality regulates the species density in a given area and provides a framework for coordinating the activities of the group.

Territoriality may be as much an aspect of human behavior as it is of other animals (see Alland [1972] for an opposing view). The entire concept of territoriality first became clear to one student when, she reported, "It wasn't until two weeks ago at dinner when one of the neighborhood dogs graciously left a sampling on our front lawn and my aggressive father arose from the table and ran out screaming, 'That's my bush!' as if he intended to use it next, that I knew . . . the concept of territoriality" (Ullrich 1971, p. 1). Studies of isolated pairs (Altman and Haythorn 1967) and old age homes (Lipman 1968) also indicated that territoriality is a human characteristic. Several researchers have focused on territorial behavior in humans. Whyte (1949), reporting on the social structure which exists in restaurants, found a clear relationship between status and territory. Each worker had his own territory and invasions caused disruptions.

The relationship between territoriality and dominance has been subject to little systematic investigation with humans. De Long (1970) hypothesized that in a seminar situation, a direct relationship would exist between seating position and rank within the student hierarchy. Members closer to each other in rank would also be closer spatially. After the fifth meeting, the teacher withdrew as the authority figure. At the end of the eleventh and twenty-third meetings, the group ranked its membership for demonstrated leadership ability, quantity and quality of participation, aggressiveness, relaxation, positive and negative attitudes, and friendliness. Over the first eleven meetings, there was no clear relationship between dominance and territoriality. The next group of eleven meetings supported De Long's hypothesis.

A territorial analysis of a classroom is quite easy and often very revealing. Where does the professor sit? Who sits around him? Who has access to chalk, the lights, the door, the window shades? Spatial position and role are closely related. The person nearest the window usually assumes the responsibility of opening and closing it, while the person nearest the chalkboard usually fetches chalk or erases. What other examples of position and role relationships can you think of?

Territoriality in humans is more complex than in other animals. We claim territory and define it for a variety of reasons, some conscious, some unconscious. By the same token, how we defend our territory varies. Animal species have fewer choices; they defend first by threatening sounds, then by physical aggression. Humans, on the other hand, have many alternatives. Sommer (1969) describes the numerous ways that individuals maintain territory. For example, books may be left on a seat, someone may be asked to "save my place," "occupied" signs may be left, and so on.

Personal Space

Whereas territory remains stationary, personal space is carried around with you. Personal space is the space that you place between yourself and others, the invisible boundaries which become apparent only when they are crossed.

Our personal space varies according to the situation and the persons with whom we are interacting. Comfortable and intimate situations call for a smaller personal space than situations which are uncomfortable or threatening. The closer we feel to a person psychologically, the closer we will stand physically. If the relationship becomes less friendly, the physical distance will increase (Willis 1966; Little 1965; Justice 1969).

The average distance in a nonthreatening situation with strangers is approximately two feet. This, of course, varies from culture to culture (Hall 1959) and from subculture to subculture. For example, Jones and Aiello (1972) found that blacks in the first grade stand closer to each other than do whites in the first grade. Adding this finding to those of a previous study (Jones 1971), the authors concluded that "lower-class blacks maintain a closer interaction distance than middle-class whites in the first grade" (Jones and Aiello 1972, p. 12).

Sommer (1962), studying pairs and groups, found that two people prefer to sit across from one another, at a slight angle, rather than side-by-side, but, if the distance across is too great, they will prefer to sit side-by-side. A comfortable distance for conversation for people sitting across from each other is five and a half feet between heads (three and a half feet between couches). Sommer (1959) also found that women sit closer to both men and women than do men. Finally, people will arrange themselves around a *corner* of a table to facilitate discussion.

Personal space in animals is related to flight distance and fight distance. Flight distance refers to the distance an animal will allow an intruder to approach before it flees. Fight distance refers to the distance an animal will allow an intruder before he attacks him. The relationship between personal space and self-protection is also apparent in humans.

Dosey and Meisels (1969) presented subjects with three situations in either stress or nonstress conditions. In the first, subjects were instructed to walk toward each other; in the second, subjects were instructed to trace a silhouette representing themselves in a room with a printed silhouette of the opposite sex; and, in the third situation, subjects entered a room in which the experimenter was seated and were told to be seated—they could choose either a near or far seat. In the stress condition, subjects were told that the purpose of the experiment was to determine their physical attractiveness, sex appeal, and feelings about initiating relationships with strangers. In the nonstress condition, subjects were told that the purpose of the experiment was to study the "orienting reflex," a natural reaction in all people. In all three situations, there was a significant difference between the stress and nonstress conditions. In general, personal space was greater in the stress than nonstress conditions.

Our personal space determines the degree of contact that we have with other people. In a study by Bardeen (1971), subjects interacted with a confederate on either a tactile, verbal, or visual level. For the tactile mode (blindfolded without conversation), the subjects described the confederate as trustful and sensitive. For the verbal mode (blindfolded without touching), the subjects described the confederate as distant and noncommunicative. For the visual mode (no talking or touching), the subjects described the confederate as artificial, arrogant, and cold. Although Bardeen was not interested in personal space, note the implications of his findings for the area.

The tactile condition provided the most complete circumstances for a violation of personal space. The confederate was described as trustful. In the verbal condition there was no invasion of personal space. Since the circumstance was an impersonal one (in that there was no physical contact or eye contact, which are intimate), the confederate was described as distant. Compare this to the first condition in which the source of contact was intimate and in which personal space was violated. The third condition, visual, also constituted an invasion of personal space, but not to the degree as in the first condition. Eye contact is an intimate form of communication, and so an invasion of personal space occurred, but not enough information was provided to sanction the invasion. Subjects could maintain enough distance to label the confederate as arrogant.

Environment

Environmental surroundings have a direct influence on group behavior. Maslow and Mintz (1956) studied the effects of different room decorations on subjects' ratings of pictures of faces on dimensions of "energy" and "well-being." Subjects were placed in a beautiful room—two large windows with drapes, beige walls, indirect overhead lighting, and attractive furnishings; an ugly room—two half-windows, battleship gray walls, overhead bulb with a dirty lampshade, and furnishings to give the impression of a dirty storeroom; or an average room—a professor's office with three windows with shades, battleship gray walls, indirect overhead lighting, and somewhat attractive furnishings. Subjects in the beautiful room gave significantly higher ratings to the faces in the pictures than the subjects in either of the other rooms. The ratings of subjects in the average room were closer to those of the subjects in the ugly room than those of the subjects in the beautiful room.

In a follow-up study, Mintz (1956) attempted to determine if the effects of being in a beautiful or ugly room were long-term. Whereas in the first study subjects were in the experimental rooms for approximately ten minutes, this second study required that each subject be in the room a total of eight hours, four one-hour sessions, and two two-hour sessions.

> Observational notes showed that in the [ugly] room the examiners had such reactions as monotony, fatigue, headache, sleep, discontent, irritability, hostility, and avoidance of the room; while in the [beautiful] room they had feelings of comfort, pleasure, enjoyment, importance, energy, and a desire to continue their activities. It is concluded that visual-esthetic surroundings . . . can affect significantly the persons exposed to them. These effects are not limited either to laboratory situations or to initial adjustments, but can be found under naturalistic circumstances of considerable duration. (p. 466)

The size of a particular room and the furniture arrangement also affect interaction. Hare and Bales (1963) found that the way chairs are placed in a room determines the type and amount of interaction. In a circle, individuals talk to those opposite them, rather than to those sitting on either side. At a rectangular table, the individuals who sit at the corners contribute least to the discussion, and the central and head positions appear to be dominant. Whether the position is the major factor in determining the amount of member participation, or whether members who normally contribute a certain amount select the position which seems to best suit them, is difficult to assess. Most likely, it is a combination of the two.

Sommer (1962) found that room size affects the distance that individuals sit from each other. The relationship is an inverse one: as the size of the room increases, the distance between individuals decreases. Sommer also determined that in a private home, as opposed to a larger public room, eight feet is a comfortable distance for conducting conversations.

The environment may also influence the amount of contact between groups and, therefore, influence intergroup relations. Deutsch and Collins (1951) studied conditions which favor friendly outcomes of intergroup relations. They hypothesized that proximity and friendliness are inversely related, that is, the closer the two groups, the greater the friendliness. Two housing projects were used for the study. In one, families were assigned to apartments without regard to race; in the other, families were segregated with regard to race. In the interracial housing project, there were many more instances of friendly contact between members of different races. Also, there were more favorable attitudes toward blacks and Chinese as well as toward living in an interracial housing project.

Body Rhythms

Do you sometimes refer to yourself as a "day" or "night" person? If so, then you are already acquainted with certain body rhythms. Our bodies have certain biological rhythms which affect our capacity to perceive, respond, and perform according to outside stimuli. These rhythms are referred to as *circadian,* i.e., rhythms synchronized with environmental cycles. For example, our sleep cycle is synchronized with the day and night cycle.

Lane (1971) reviews some of the effects of circadian rhythms on our communicative behavior, and the specific implications they have for interpersonal relations. "A recent experiment demonstrated that an individual can become synchronized with the activities of a social group and if removed desynchronized, as revealed in changes in the concentration of sodium, potassium, and calcium in the urine, and variations in body temperature" (p. 20). Although the specific cause-and-effect relationships have yet to be discovered, "the identification of social activity and daily routine as synchronizers means that formation of opinion, as it involves the individual's association with his social groups, depends to some extent on a biological synchronization between individuals, and between individuals and their environments" (Lane 1971, p. 20).

Luce (1971) provides us with a method for determining our own body rhythms, consisting of questions such as, "At what hour do you rise?" "When do you prefer to make love?" and "A what time during the day are you happiest?" By answering these and other questions, you may be able to chart your own body cycles and, therefore, determine the "best" and "worst" times for you to be interacting with your groups. For instance, your sleep schedule synchronizes other internal rhythms. Changes in your sleep patterns may adversely affect your ability to work well with others. In general, it is best to synchronize sleep patterns with activity patterns, timing it so sleep precedes a period of great activity.

Empathic Skills and the Development of Interpersonal Communication Effectiveness

Gerald R. Miller and Mark Steinberg

To communicate interpersonally, one must be able to leave the cultural and sociological levels of prediction and psychically travel to the psychological level. We have already examined some ways in which a communicator's patterns of control, as well as his cognitive style, influence his attempts to reach the interpersonal level. Certainly, the communicator's journey is more likely to be successful if he develops his ability to empathize. In this chapter we will discuss the importance of empathy in interpersonal communication. More specifically, we will develop a definition for empathy, suggest a model for viewing an important dimension of the empathic process, and survey some strategies for improving empathic skills. As the chapter proceeds, it will become apparent that acquiring these skills is crucial to becoming effective in interpersonal communication. In fact, empathic skills and interpersonal communication effectiveness may come to seem almost synonymous.

Toward a definition for empathy

Although the term *empathy* is relatively common, it means many things to many people. After surveying some of the literature in aesthetics and theatre, Gunkle pessimistically concluded that "the term, stretched to mean almost anything, has come to mean nothing" (1963, 15). Katz (1963) devotes a substantial part of his book to examining meanings for *empathy,* as well as distinguishing it from sympathy, projection, and insight. This rich background of meanings can be grouped into two broad categories: psychophysiological response and social perception skill.

Empathy as a psychophysiological response

All of us can probably remember watching someone suck a lemon and feeling the sour taste permeate our mouths. This response is not limited to citrus fruits. When asked her meaning for empathy, a student in one of Gerry's classes replied tersely, "Empathy is when you throw up, I throw up, too!" In a similar vein, we speak of the contagion of laughter, tears, or

From *Between People* by Gerald R. Miller and Mark Steinberg. © 1975, Science Research Associates, Inc. Reprinted by permission of the publisher.

yawns. Indeed, it is a rare person who has never experienced this sort of psychophysiological identity with another, both in real life and vicariously through the entertainment media.

In its psychophysiological sense, empathy probably occurs most frequently when the empathizer uses multiple sensory channels. While the lemon effect can be produced by mere mention of sucking a lemon, observation of the lemon-sucker heightens it. Still, the auditory channel alone is often sufficient—as it was for listeners to radio soap operas, a vivid childhood remembrance of Gerry's. On weekday visits to his grandparents' home he invariably found people listening to "Valiant Lady," "Lorenzo Jones," "Ma Perkins," "Backstage Wife," ad nauseam. Tears flowed between commercials; joy was eagerly shared, and angry words ("You'll get yours, you _____!") were voiced. The demise of radio in America as a major source of entertainment resulted in more than unemployment for many organists. Today television and films have supplanted this mode of vicarious identification, combining auditory and visual sensations.

So intense is the psychophysiological response and so strong the sense of identity with another that some writers have resorted to rather mystical ways of describing the emphatic process.

> When we experience empathy, we feel as if we were experiencing someone else's feelings as our own. We see, we feel, we respond, and we understand as if we were, in fact, the other person. *We stand in his shoes. We get under his skin . . . When we take the position of another person, our imagination projects us out of ourselves and into the other person.* (Katz, 1963, p. 3) [italics ours]

Katz's words are by no means atypical. Empathy is most often defined using phrases akin to "putting yourself in someone else's shoes." Since all of us are forever trapped inside our own skins, however, any judgments we make about the emotional or cognitive states of others must be inferential. The raw materials for our inferences are the actual behaviors of other individuals and our own experiences with similar kinds of behaviors. Thus, when we say we can identify, or empathize, with someone sucking a lemon, we are saying that we have observed his lemon-sucking behavior and that our own experiences with lemons call forth biochemical changes similar to those occurring in his mouth.

We shall avoid bestowing an aura of mysticism on empathy, preferring to treat it primarily as a behavioral process. Although our approach may lack the imaginative or emotional appeal of the mysterious, we believe it has considerable comunicative utility. To tell a prospective empathizer to put himself in another person's shoes, or to get inside someone else's skin, is not so helpful as giving him pointers on how to spot behavioral cues presented by others.

A psychophysiological response to someone can express support and understanding, but certainly empathy occurs more often than just when people share the same sensory-emotional reactions. The recipient of such an expression of empathy may or may not consider it to be a desirable response. If, for example, he becomes sick to his stomach, he may well get little relief from an empathic friend who does likewise. The friend is more likely to be perceived as empathically admirable if he tries to help alleviate the sick person's distress. We will have more to say about this later in this chapter when we set forth our transactional definition of empathy.

Empathy as a social perception skill

In the social perception arena, empathy refers to *the accuracy with which an individual predicts the verbal responses of another.* More specifically, empathic ability is concerned primarily with responses reporting the person's emotional states or the way he feels about himself. High accuracy is equated with high empathic skill; low accuracy is taken as evidence of empathic limitations.

Self-other ratings

To illustrate how empathic ability is assessed, we will briefly describe one of the most popular procedures, the self-other rating developed by Dymond (1949). This approach requires two persons (A and B) to provide the following ratings:
For person A:
   1. A rates himself (A).
   2. A rates B as he (A) sees him.
   3. A rates B as he thinks B would rate himself.
   4. A rates himself (A) as he thinks B would rate him.
For person B:
   1. B rates himself (B).
   2. B rates A as he (B) sees him.
   3. B rates A as he thinks A would rate himself.
   4. B rates himself (B) as he thinks A would rate him.
Typically, the raters use a five-point scale of intensity for rating such personality traits as self-confidence, superiority, unselfishness, friendliness, leadership, and sense of humor. The measure of A's empathic ability, for example, is determined by calculating how closely A's predictions of B's ratings correspond with B's actual ratings.

Suppose two friends, Mary and Ruth, wished to assess their mutual degree of empathy, using the sense of humor trait. On a five-point scale ranging from high to low, Mary would (1) rate her own sense of humor, (2) rate Ruth's sense of humor, (3) provide a rating that *predicts* how Ruth sees her own sense of humor, and (4) provide a rating that *predicts* Ruth's perception of Mary's sense of humor. Ruth would carry out the identical rating procedures. If both predicted the other's responses quite accurately, we would probably conclude that they have established an interpersonal relationship; if one was relatively successful but the other was not, we would say that the relationship reflects a mixed, interpersonal/noninterpersonal level; and if neither was very accurate, we would call the relationship noninterpersonal.

Degree of empathy and levels of relationship

We see empathy, when viewed as a social perception skill, as closely akin to the predictive process that characterizes interpersonal communication. To some extent, accurate prediction of another's self-perceptions requires the predictor to spot relevant individual differences. Still, we are not willing to view the processes of empathizing and communicating interpersonally as totally synonymous, particularly when research procedures such as the self-other approach are used as measures of empathy. Examination of some of the characteristics of this research method will reveal why we are reluctant to equate the two processes.

Typically, self-other ratings of empathic ability focus on personality traits. While the ability to make accurate discriminations about others' perceptions of their personalities may frequently aid the interpersonal communicator, his range of concern is naturally much broader. Consider once again our salesman seeking to move to the interpersonal level with a reluctant customer. He is not primarily concerned with predicting the customer's level of self-confidence accurately, but with selling his product. On many occasions, the salesman will achieve greater success by avoiding unnecessary speculation about unobservables, such as personality traits, and by focusing on the ways in which the customer is responding to his messages. In particular, he must ask himself how a customer's response differs from the responses of other customers with whom he has communicated successfully and, given these differences, how he might alter his communicative strategy to increase the likelihood of a sale. Successful discrimination is based on the salesman's skill in spotting subtle behavioral cues and then predicting appropriate message changes. In some instances, prediction may be improved by concern with personality traits, but in many others, the inclusion of personality inferences as part of the predictive equation only confuses and complicates the issue.

Predicting personality traits from cultural or sociological data

It is often possible to make accurate predictions about others' perceptions of their personality traits solely on the basis of cultural or sociological data, since people do not vary much in their self-ratings on certain personality characteristics. To demonstrate this consistency to yourself, ask several of your friends whether they have a good sense of humor. If more than one or two reply negatively, it will be surprising. By the same token, how many people are likely to see themselves as relatively unfriendly? Since our society assigns a positive value to traits such as having a good sense of humor or being friendly, most people like to believe they possess these personal characteristics.

Graphologists and fortune tellers have long been aware of such invariant areas of self-perception. If you wish to amaze your friends with your psychic powers, try this experiment. Ask several of them for handwriting samples, and tell them you will use the samples to provide them with descriptions of themselves. (If you think friends will feel you based your descriptions on other data, get the samples from relative strangers.) Then for every person, write the same description, including comments such as the following:

> Generally, you are friendly with other people and accept them for what they are. While you trust people most of the time, there are times when you feel others are taking advantage of you and when you believe you have not been given enough credit for things you have done. Occasionally you suffer from feelings of inadequacy. You have a good sense of humor and you are able to laugh at yourself when the occasion warrants.

Return the description to each of your friends and ask them whether it is accurate. Having performed the experiment several times in our classes, we are certain that most of your friends will marvel at the accuracy of your evaluation.

Empathy and stimulus discrimination

This tendency for persons to perceive themselves similarly on certain personality dimensions poses an interesting dilemma for the prospective interpersonal communicator. If such perceptions are accurate—e.g., if almost everyone does have a good sense of humor—these traits are worthless predictive vehicles because variation is a necessary condition for discrimination. If, as is more likely, considerable variability is associated with these traits, many people are victims of their own self-delusions; they do not see themselves as others see them. Since empathic accuracy is defined as the correspondence between the ratings of the empathizer and those of the person with whom he is empathizing, a "good" empathizer accepts self-delusion as a given. By contrast, stimulus discrimination, as we have defined it, deals primarily with the ability to differentiate one person's behavior from another's. Thus, an important distinction can be drawn between the two processes: *when viewed as a social perception skill, empathy involves the ability to predict accurately others' self-perceptions; when conceived of as a crucial determinant of interpersonal communication effectiveness, stimulus discrimination involves the ability to identify ways that the actual behaviors and attitudes of an individual differ from the behaviors and attitudes of others.*

Given this distinction, a social perception skill view of empathy may sometimes actually prevent a communicator from moving to the interpersonal level. How could this apparently contradictory result occur? Assume you are a salesman for a company engaged in manufacturing a new multiple lock system for apartment doors—a flourishing business in this era of high crime rates. During your training period, the sales manager describes some customer problems you are likely to encounter. In particular, he points out that since most people see themselves as friendly and accessible, they are likely to resist the prison-like, inaccessible atmosphere created by an intricate lock system. Consequently, he stresses that your sales pitch should specifically minimize the infringement upon movement and the hostile atmosphere imposed by the adoption of such a system; in fact, he arms you with a particular sales pitch designed to overcome customer resistance on this point.

You successfully use this sales routine with your first three customers. Not only do you accept the manager's dictum concerning people's perceptions of their own friendliness, you detect behavioral cues that these three customers are genuinely reluctant to further isolate themselves from their fellowmen. But now you are face-to-face with customer four. Like the preceding three customers, he probably perceives himself as friendly and outgoing. Still, he is not behaving the same way they behaved. His words, his tone of voice, his reluctance to open the door fully are all cues that he is hostile, suspicious, and prefers to be left alone. Spontaneously, you decide to emphasize, rather than downplay, the increased privacy and inaccessibility offered by the lock system, and you are rewarded with a quick sale.

It is possible, though not probable, that the standard sales pitch would have yielded the same outcome. What is important is that a commitment to basing communicative predictions on empathic grounds, rather than stimulus discrimination, would have resulted in a different message strategy, one less likely to clinch the sale. Had an empathic framework been adopted, you would have been forced to reason as follows: "I know this customer perceives himself as friendly and outgoing, even though his behavior belies this perception. Hence, my messages should minimize the extent to which the new lock system will create a more inaccessible, remote environment." By contrast, a prediction based on stimulus discrimination stems from this line of reasoning: "Even though this customer thinks of himself as friendly and outgoing, his behavior indicates suspicion and hostility. Consequently, I should emphasize the greater privacy and inaccessibility to be gained from the lock system, rather than playing those factors down."

A final deficiency

From a communication standpoint, there is yet another crucial deficiency in the typical definition of empathy as a social perception skill: it is *unidirectional, rather than transactional.* The social perception viewpoint holds that a good empathizer is one who can accurately predict others' responses, particularly in regard to the ways they perceive themselves. From a transactional communication perspective, this definition is inadequate, for when we say that someone is a good empathizer, we mean not only that he can predict how we feel, but also that he communicates with us in ways we find rewarding. We believe a transactional definition of empathy best suits the dynamics of human communication in general and interpersonal communication in particular.

A transactional definition for empathy

Assume you have an acquaintance who is remarkably adept at sensing your current emotional state, even though you may try to conceal it from him. When you are upset or unhappy, he detects your mood unerringly; when you are joyous and happy, this fact never escapes his attention. But despite his sensitivity to your every emotion, you avoid contact with him because he is unable or unwilling to communicate in ways you find satisfying. Rather than reducing your sadness, he heightens or ignores it; rather than rejoicing with you, he discovers a communicative means of transforming your happiness to gloom. In short, you view him as a "bad news" communicator.

Most of you probably know the kind of person we have just described. We doubt that you would characterize him as a good empathizer, even though he is extremely talented at reading your emotional states. Transactionally, empathy embraces two major steps:

1. *The prospective empathizer must be able to discriminate accurately the ways that the individual's motivational and attitudinal posture differs from others.*
2. *Accurate discriminations must be followed by behaviors that are viewed as desirable, or rewarding, by the persons who are the objects of prediction.*

While our hypothetical acquaintance has no trouble accomplishing the first step, he falls short on the second.

Step 1 closely parallels the previously discussed definitions of empathy as a social perception skill. Even here it differs in one important respect, placing emphasis on accurate behavioral prediction based on subtle verbal and nonverbal cues, rather than on predictive agreement with the self-perceived attitudes and motives of the other. In drawing this distinction, we are not arguing that there is one correct, preferred way to gauge motives and attitudes. Sometimes, the best evidence we have is the other person's verbal descriptions of his feelings. At times, however, as we have already indicated, these verbal responses may conflict with other behaviors, e.g., an individual may say that he is friendly and outgoing, and yet he may behave just the opposite. Given such conflicting evidence, predictive accuracy is usually enhanced by relying on behavioral cues other than the individual's verbal report about his usual attitudes toward others.

Step 2 places the definition within the transactional view of communication discussed in chapter 2 [Miller-Steinberg text]. Like beauty, empathy is in the eye (or perhaps more descriptively, the perceptions) of the beholder. No matter how accurately someone reads us, we do not bestow the title "good empathizer" upon him unless he also communicates with us in rewarding ways. This fact suggests that the most effective interpersonal communicators not only read cues well, but also select the appropriate communication behaviors implied by the cues.

This transactional definition should not be interpreted as an attempt to impose our values on the communication process. We do not think it necessary to equate "good empathizers" with "nice guys." Still, from a transactional perspective, communicators reserve the accolade "good empathizer" for those who respond to them in rewarding ways. For that matter, an unscrupulous communicator, skilled in exercising effective environmental control, may meet both of our conditions for empathic response and still use his empathic skills to manipulate the other person in devious ways.

The Development of Self-Concept in Small Groups

Bruce K. Eckman

Who Am I? The answer to this question is the basis of a person's self-concept. It is asked by all persons throughout their lives. Some of us have more answers than others, some of us like our answers more than others, and some of us are more certain of our answers than others. One reason for this is that people are different in how publicly they ask, Who am I? Some individuals are very willing to share their answers with others and even hope to learn more about themselves in the process. Others, unfortunately, prefer not to ask that question out loud.

Regardless of your individual baseline pattern (a combination of your personal security, motivation and value structure), there are times that there will be an increase in your questioning behavior. These times occur when your self-definition becomes unclear, such as when you are rejected by your girl friend/boy friend, you are finishing college and don't know what you want to do, or a host of other stressful situations. The point is that your lack of a clear definition of yourself creates anxiety and stress and leads you to reduce it by trying to clarify who you are.

Systems theory would suggest that when a person leaves an established system for an unknown one, uncertainty and anxiety result. As you grow up and leave adolescence for adulthood, for example, that happens. You are in the process of leaving home and the dependencies that accompany that protected and familiar environment. While this is usually highly desired, it is also accompanied by high anxiety. First, leaving the home, either literally or psychologically or both, creates a loss. There is a loss of security. The order of responsibility for your security is reversed from the parents being primarily responsible, to you being primarily responsible. There is also a loss of dependency. You are becoming more self-reliant. There is a loss of structure. Your time is increasingly your own, and you have to make decisions as to how to spend it. No longer do family responsibilities dictate how you organize your time, nor do your parents tell you what to do and when to do it. Finally, there is a loss in your role definition. You are no longer thinking of yourself as somebody's son or daughter but rather as Bill or Jane, an independent self.

Secondly, when you leave the home, you move into a vast, unknown, exciting experience. But since it is new, you have, by definition, had little experience with it. Therefore, if you have experiences which you don't like, you don't understand, or you don't want to have recur, you don't have the backlog of other similar or better experiences to give you a sense of perspective. Consequently, leaving the home generates a good deal of anxiety and uncertainty, which can be reduced through clarification of who you are.

I remember when I was going through an identity crisis in college. I rejected much of my past capitalistic background and decided I was a Marxist. I read a lot of Marx, Engels, Lenin and Trotsky. I idealized the class struggle, identified with the group where we discussed the issues, and felt very self-righteous. In my sophomore year, however, I read Hesse's *Siddhartha* and rejected all Western thought, including Marxism. I decided to become a Buddhist monk and reject material belongings and the class struggle altogether. My contemplative life was altered when I took a philosophy course in existentialism. Nietzsche, Kierkegaard, and Hegel became my new heroes. In each case I was trying to find the answer to "Who Am I?" Clearly, I wasn't too certain of my answers.

Some Definitions

What does all this have to do with self-concept? First a few definitions should be developed. Self-concept, self-esteem and self-confidence are frequently used interchangeably but they don't mean the same thing. Self-concept is a hypothetical construct that was made up so people could talk to each other about their subjective phenomenological realities. It is the set of beliefs a person has about who he is. It includes answers people give themselves, answers others give to them, and answers people thought others gave them. It is all that people believe about themselves.

Self-esteem is related but different. It is how a person feels about that set of beliefs he has about himself (his self-concept). If you tried to do well in college and got average grades, your self-concept would be, "I am an average college student academically." If everyone in your family had been an excellent student, you might not feel very good about yourself. On the other hand, if no one in your family had expected you even to go to college, you would probably feel proud of yourself. Self-esteem is the positive-negative evaluation a person makes about each belief in his self-concept. The very same behavior (average grades) in two different students (assuming both were trying to do well) leads to similar self-concepts but not necessarily to the same self-esteem.

Self-confidence is the degree of certainty a person has about his self-concept and self-esteem. In the example I gave earlier of my own college identity crisis, my self-confidence was low because I was not certain who I was. If you say, "I am an independent person, attractive to the opposite sex," that is a belief you have about yourself (your self-concept). How sure you are about that is a measure of your self-confidence. If you would *like* to be independent and attractive to the opposite sex but don't evaluate yourself that way, you would be low in self-esteem and low in self-confidence. If on the other hand, you have experiences which confirm your self-concept, you will, in most cases, increase your self-confidence.

Does this mean that when your self-confidence increases your self-esteem will also increase? Often, but not always. Self-confidence is how certain you are of your self-concept. As an example, let's say Andy wanted to be tall. And further, let's assume Andy was very short and knew with painful certainty that he was short. His self-confidence would be high (he would not doubt that he was short) but his esteem would be low.

It is my thesis that sharing who you think you are, and sharing who you think others are, in a small group setting can facilitate knowledge of your self-concept, raise your self-esteem and increase your self-confidence. This paper will develop that position and present some methods used to achieve those goals.

Development of Self-Concept

Information about who you are is gained through several primary sources. First, you gain information from your direct experience of the world. A baby learns to distinguish inside-outside, pleasure-pain, real-not real, good-bad rather early in life. Eventually it discriminates me and not-me. From this it constructs who it is and who others are. "I am good," "Mommy is pleasurable." Later on in life, the statements become more specific. Since Joe plays basketball well, he thinks of himself as strong and well-coordinated.

Information is also obtained from other people who are significant to you, such as your parents. A young child has a very unclear sense of who he is. His parents continuously provide him with workable answers to his questions about the world. As a result, his parents' opinions about who he is are often adopted without critical reflection and then maintained as long as possible. If the parents' perceptions were accurate, there is no problem. But if the parents were wrong or made their judgments on the basis of whom their son or daughter should be, each will have to revise his or her belief structure at some point to fit actuality.

Information is also gathered by a child when he hears his mother telling a third party about him. A child often experiences his mother saying things she doesn't mean. She will at times say "don't do that" and then let him do it. He learns to discriminate when she is serious and when she is not. But when the mother remarks to a friend, "my son is such a brat," the son sees little reason to question her statement. It must be true, why else would she tell her friend? This information, once started, will be heard repeatedly from other friends in the community.

The final source of information to be discussed is social comparison. Children do not live in a vacuum. A child lives with his siblings and plays with friends who are going through a similar process. Through his inter-action he forms concepts about himself such as his leadership ability, his dominance patterns, and his ease at forming friendships. He also forms opinions about whether he is better or worse at these things than his friends. A child growing up seeks information about himself from himself, from others, from others telling others, and from comparing himself to others. From these, he forms his self-concept.

If your sources of information are congruent, that is, each says the same thing about you, your certainty about whom you are will be high (self-confidence). Unfortunately these sources of information are frequent-ly not congruent. Sometimes you delude yourself. You want so badly to be liked that you think what you do is likable, when it is not. Other times, your parents want you to be something in particular, i.e., a doctor or a lawyer, and exaggerate your abilities in those areas and downplay others. And at other times, your more remote friends don't want you to be con-fident of yourself, don't know you well or see themselves in you and, therefore, they give you inaccurate information. A group setting gives people an opportunity to re-examine those original sources of information, discover whose perceptions are accurate, and increase the congruency be-tween adult self-concept and the other group members' perceptions.
From these, he forms his self-concept.

Some Contributions the Group Makes to Your Self-Concept

The most obvious way a group makes a contribution is through feed-back, both positive and negative. Positive feedback tends to generate more of the same behavior. If a member laughs spontaneously at your jokes, you will probably joke with him some more. Negative feedback often reduces the chance of a behavior recurring, or returns the group to equilibrium. If a group member starts being catty about an absent mem-ber and you say, "I don't think we should talk about Joe behind his back. If it really bothers you, why don't you tell Joe to his face next week?" the effect is to reduce that behavior (being catty) and return the group to a more stable equilibrium point.

Positive and negative feedback are used to confirm positive and nega-tive aspects of your self-concept. If you think you are likable and the group responds warmly to your presence, you confirm a part of your self-concept. Likewise, if you know you can be short-tempered, the group's negative feedback helps confirm this perception. Confirmation of your self-concept leads to an increase in self-confidence.

When people are first meeting, they often present their most desirable traits. At other times people put on false fronts, knowingly or not. When this happens in a group, someone will frequently say, "I don't see you like that" or "Get off it." The group member's reaction is not congruent with the person's self-concept or their self-presentation. This is useful to the person because it eliminates ambiguities that he himself has created, through ideas he has about who he should be or would like to be. Disconfirmation also fosters self-confidence because it eliminates uncertainties.

Another positive outcome of the group's feedback is when you become aware of something you never thought of before. For example, a student of mine said that he thought another group member was strong because he always faced up to mistakes he had made. This took the other member by surprise. He had always felt inadequate in such situations. Strength was a perception that never occurred to him. The effect of this feedback was to enhance his knowledge of his self-concept and raise his self-esteem. Confirmation and disconfirmation, on the other hand, don't enhance self-knowledge, but rather, increase self-confidence.

You may be saying by now, "That's fine when it works, but what about when a group member's reaction is wrong or, worse yet, an outright lie?" That is a good question, and it brings me to the second contribution that the group makes to your self-concept, that of risk-taking. Regardless of whether the group confirms or disconfirms your self-concept, or whether the group is correct or incorrect in its assessment, one of the greatest benefits of self-disclosure is taking a risk. Risk is the root of change and growth. Without risk there would be no excitement.

When you take a risk, several things happen. First, you reinforce your self-concept that you are courageous. This tends to increase self-esteem. Secondly, taking a risk is a statement that you accept yourself as you are. When you take a risk you are putting yourself on the line, not an image of yourself. You are saying implicitly, this is who I am, react to me. When you are willing to take these risks by disclosing who you are, the other person(s) tends to do the same. This is the principle of mutual self-disclosure developed by Jourard. If the other person follows your lead and discloses who he is, there is less reason to protect your self-concept. Neither he nor you are attacking, but instead, making yourselves more vulnerable to each other. And in the process you are both strengthening your self-concept, self-esteem, and self-confidence. Finally, risk-taking brings the person to the point of confrontation from which he either reinforces what he already knew or is forced to change and grow. In either case, confidence is increased. Therefore, I would argue it is better to take the risk and disclose who you are honestly and sincerely to the group, regardless of whether their confirmations or disconfirmations are accurate or not. Disclose first, for yourself: to reinforce your own sense of courage and acceptance; and secondly, because the group often can be accurate and genuinely helpful.

In those rare situations* where someone actually lies or is maliciously intent on hurting you, disconfirmation of your actual self can lead to confusion which would lower self-confidence. However, there is still another, unmentioned benefit to be derived from taking a risk under these circumstances. That benefit is to learn that the most basic authority you can rely on is your own experience. This is an important learning to be derived in all group settings, but it is particularly heightened when your actual self is disconfirmed. If Bill's experience of himself conflicts with Jim's judgment of Bill, the first step is for them to be open to being wrong. They should examine both positions fully by reversing roles. After each has examined what the other has to say, Bill should try to get more in contact with his own experience. To do this he should heighten his experience by exaggerating and focusing on himself. Then he should try to accept it as his own self. If he can accept it readily, he should rely on it, regardless of what Jim or others say.

If acceptance does not come easily, then Bill should recognize that Jim might have been right, or that he is not yet ready to accept the truth of his own experience. If this process were repeated in your group, you would learn to trust yourself. This leads to higher self-esteem and self-confidence. To review, taking a risk, disclosing sincerely, even when the other person lies in return, leads to your getting more fully in contact with your experience, accepting it as yours, trusting yourself and learning that your experience is better than what someone else or, even you, thinks you *should* experience.

Some Effects Group Members' Self-concepts Have on Group Interaction

If the group members began with positive self-concepts and high self-esteem, or their self-esteem were elevated through the group experience, a positive feedback spiral results. This means that positive feedback leads to more positive feedback which leads to even more positive feedback. It is somewhat akin to falling in love, i.e., the rush of ebullience that always accompanies the beginning of romantic love. A positive feedback loop is

---

*I say rare because while everyone can think of a time he or she has been hurt by someone lying or being mean; it is often due to one of two things: First, people seem to remember much more vividly the time(s) someone hurt them, rather than all the times someone didn't, and hold that up as reason not to take risks; or second, people fear being hurt so strongly it seems as if it happened, when it rarely has actually happened to them.

self-perpetuating and makes all its participants feel worthwhile, liked and cohesive. This cycle obviously fosters a gain in self-esteem for the group members. Unfortunately, as in romantic love, it can't last forever. It may last until the group's interaction is frustrated in some way, i.e., a task they couldn't accomplish. Or it may last until a particular member feels the group is getting too close or means too much, which scares him. In either case of frustration or fear, negative feedback is initiated and the group moves toward a more stable point.

When the attractive forces are positive, the group experience is remembered with pleasure and satisfaction. But what about when there is limited self-esteem among the group members? What does that do to the interaction? The most common reaction is a reduction in total interaction. There is less reinforcement for each other and so less behavior occurs. Secondly, when the interaction does occur, it is less flowing. The choppy nature of the interaction could be due to flighting, the approach-avoidance conflict of trying to be there and not wanting to be there, or the lack of reinforcement for being there. In any case the outcome is alienation; from the group, from the interaction, from the self. This result, unfortunately, only exacerbates the problem. Alienation lowers a person's self-esteem and self-confidence, which makes for less interaction, which makes for more alienation. This is a classic negative feedback spiral, which is destructive to the person's self-esteem and to the effectiveness of the group.

How does a person or a group get out of such a spiral? One typical reaction is to repeat what a person does when in a positive spiral—more of the same behavior. But since the behavior in this case is withdrawal and alienation, more of the same behavior becomes destructive and leads to waiting and wishing: waiting for things to get better, for the class to end, or until you leave home; and wishing for a better situation, a better group, a better lover. In each case more of the same behavior, which works in a positive spiral, leads to not taking responsibility for your part in the situation and dependency on someone else to do it for you. Neither outcome is effective in a negative spiral. How much of your time do you spend waiting for something better to happen, rather than taking steps to make it happen?

One step you might take in a group that is locked into a negative spiral is to metacommunicate. Metacommunication is communication about the group's communication pattern. To do this you must be able to step out of the system you are in and discuss the group from a larger perspective. For example, let us suppose that Mike and John are competing for the leadership of the group. Every time a new decision has to be made either Mike or John initiates a solution and the other always disagrees. If either one would step outside his desire to lead and recognize that whenever a decision has to be reached they argue, and then discuss this problem in the group, perhaps, they could resolve the basic issue of leadership and eliminate the arguments. This metacommunication could also be made by a third party not involved in the basic leadership battle.

A second step you might take to break a negative spiral is to make yourself vulnerable to the other members. Remember, I argued before that self-disclosure is a courageous act and ultimately enhances your self-esteem, which is a way of breaking the spiral. In addition, your self-disclosure leads to the other member's self-disclosure. Instead of attacking each other, you are making yourself vulnerable to each other. Even if someone didn't follow the disclosure pattern and did attack or put you down, the other members usually are quick to protect you, creating the beginnings of a positive spiral.

A third possible step to break out of the alienation of a negative spiral is for you to accept your alienation. If you were to talk about it, share it with the other members, your alienation from the interaction would disappear. This is a form of self-acceptance which raises self-esteem, necessary for a positive spiral. And, if by chance the other members could identify with your alienation from the present interaction (which in a negative spiral, they probably could do), a weak but positive spiral results, centering around what you don't like.

When a negative spiral is broken and a positive spiral has begun, the ensuing interaction process reinforces several aspects of the group members' self-concept. As the group develops cohesion through positive interactions, a sense of belonging also develops. When a person feels that he is a member of something, it implicitly suggests that he is wanted and desired by the other members. This is a confirmation of his value or worth as a human being and certainly adds to his self-esteem.

Negative spirals are not all bad. Having worked a negative spiral into a positive spiral teaches an important lesson not learned in a group which has had only positive spirals. That lesson is to be as you are, not as you should be. Since there are less rewards in a negative spiral, you will be less rewarded for emitting behaviors others want or think should be emitted. Likewise, since the group has already seen you in an alienated and negative state, you have less to lose for being who you actually are. There is less reason to maintain ideal, but false, self-presentations. In a positive spiral, people are often rewarded when they act as others think they should. Since the reward structure is different, a group who develop a negative into a positive spiral have a greater chance to discriminate between their actual and ideal selves, and of learning to be as they are, than a group who never worked through a negative spiral, or only experienced positive spirals. This knowledge is another form of self-acceptance which benefits self-esteem.

In conclusion, it is my belief, which is congruent with my own personal experience and my observation of my group members' experiences, that a person's self-concept, self-esteem and self-confidence benefit tremendously from group experience. The benefits derive primarily from other's positive and negative feedback, self-disclosure, and learning to trust your own experience. Once these have been risked, feedback loops create positive and negative spirals, which give the group members a clearer sense of their actual selves and enrich their self-esteem.

SUGGESTED READINGS

Chapter 6

Argyle, Michael. *The Psychology of Interpersonal Behavior.* Baltimore: Penguin Books, 1967.

Ashcraft, Norman and Scheflen, Albert E. *People Space: The Making and Breaking of Human Boundaries.* New York: Anchor Press, 1976.

Barnlund, Dean C., ed. *Interpersonal Communication: Survey and Studies.* Boston: Houghton Mifflin Company, 1968.

Gergen, K. *The Concept of Self.* New York: Holt, Rinehart and Winston, 1971.

Gilbert, Shirley J. and Horenstein, David. "The Communication of Self-Disclosure: Level Versus Valence," *Human Communication Research* 1 (Summer, 1975): 316-322.

Harrison, Randall. *Beyond Words.* Englewood Cliffs, N.J.: Prentice-Hall, Inc., 1974.

Knapp, Mark L. *Nonverbal Communication in Human Interaction.* New York: Holt, Rinehart and Winston, 1972.

Leathers, Dale G. *Nonverbal Communication Systems.* Boston: Allyn and Bacon, 1976.

Luft, Joseph. *Of Human Interaction.* Palo Alto, CA: National Press Books, 1969.

Mehrabian, Albert. *Silent Messages.* Belmont, CA: Wadsworth Publishing Company, Inc., 1972.

Miller, Gerald R., ed. *Explorations in Interpersonal Communication.* Beverly Hills, CA: Sage Publications, Inc. 1976.

Mortensen, C. David. *Communication: The Study of Human Interaction.* New York: McGraw-Hill Book Company, 1972.

Ofshe, Richard R., ed. *Interpersonal Behavior in Small Groups.* Englewood Cliffs, N.J.: Prentice-Hall, Inc., 1973.

Sommer, Robert. *Personal Space: The Behavioral Basis of Design.* Englewood Cliffs, N.J.: Prentice-Hall, Inc., 1969.

Triandis, Harry C. *Interpersonal Behavior.* Monterey, CA: Brooks/Cole Publishing, 1977.

Watzlawick, Paul; Bearin, Janet H.; and Jackson, Don D. *Pragmatics of Human Communication.* New York: W. W. Norton & Company, Inc., 1967.

Wenburg, John R. and Wilmot, William W. *The Personal Communication Process.* New York: John Wiley & Sons, Inc., 1973.

Practice

Clear Interpersonal Communication

John Stewart

Usually my interpersonal communication classes begin working on clarity and accuracy with two exercises. In the first one a three-by-five card is put on a table or lectern where it can't easily be seen. On the card is a relatively simple set of geometric shapes, for example

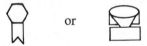

A volunteer stands where he can see the card and tries to interpersonally communicate in such a way that everyone is able to reproduce on a piece of paper exactly what's on the card. The only rules are that he cannot touch the card, he cannot draw on the blackboard, and no one can ask him any questions. Almost everybody is able to get this shape

in two or three minutes. This card, however, challenges the clearest communicator and has entertained classes for over half an hour:

Stewart, *Bridges Not Walls,* © 1973, Addison-Wesley, Reading, Massachusetts.

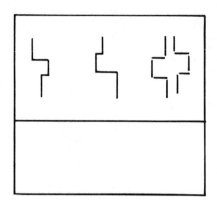

The second exercise is called the "block T." A small movie screen is used to separate two chairs. The person in one chair is given four puzzle pieces that look like this:

The person in the other chair is given a completed puzzle:

The one with the completed puzzle is supposed to tell the other how to assemble the T. The first time we try it no questions or answers of any kind are allowed. Then we let each person ask and answer "yes and no" questions. Finally they are permitted to converse freely, so long as what they do remains hidden from the other person. As in the first exercise, the results vary widely, but the "T" often looks something like

after the first couple of times. When the two persons are able to talk freely they usually can put it together in four or five minutes.

The Difficulty of Communicating Clearly

After the class has completed these exercises, we discuss what's been illustrated about accuracy and clarity in interpersonal communication. Three kinds of insights usually emerge from our conversations. First, we're all graphically reminded of the difficulty of communicating clearly and accurately. The evidence is right in front of us:

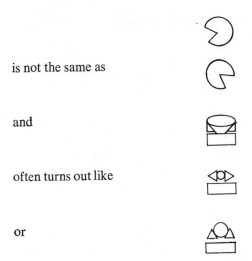

is not the same as

and

often turns out like

or

We remember the times we've been asked for directions and been hopelessly confused by them, or when we've tried to tell someone how to get to the stadium only to see the polite nodding of glazed eyes above a fixed smile that tells us we aren't making sense.

General semanticists explain that our difficulties are created by the "map-territory" problem. Just as a map is not the land it charts, words are not the things we use them to talk about. If they were, my description of

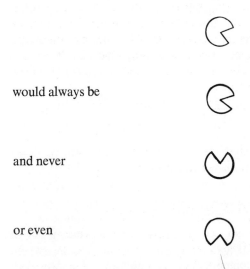

would always be

and never

or even

What words mean depends on the persons communicating and the communication situation. I may describe the figure as "a pie with a slice out at the bottom." You may locate the missing piece at "the southeast side," "between four and six o'clock," or "between 130 and 180 degrees." Or you may call the figure a poker chip partly hidden by the corner of a card. In short, our discussion of the exercises reminds us that although the relationship aspect is a vital and seldom-emphasized part of every human communication, content is also important. Teachers, lawyers, executives, accountants, foremen, telephone operators, presidents, and even people all need to know how to be clear.

A Definition of Clarity

After some discussion, we're also usually able to identify or define what communication accuracy or clarity consists of. The exercises enable us to define the terms operationally. That is, if your shape of puzzle looks like mine, then I've communicated accurately and clearly. One way to express that definition is to call communication accuracy "the degree of correspondence between the referents decoded, or inferred, from a set of communication behaviors by an addressee and the referents encoded, or represented, in those communication behaviors by the communicator."[1] As someone usually points out, however, that definition begins to break down as soon as you talk about something like justice, poverty, racism, enthusiasm, sportsmanship, studying, enjoyment, etc.—something too abstract to have clearly "encodable and decodable referents." It's difficult enough to locate a referent or thing-in-the-world that "justice" refers to, let alone to decide whether your "referent" corresponds poorly or well with mine.

When our discussion gets to that point, we usually move in the direction suggested by information theorists. They treat accuracy or clarity as the degree to which uncertainty is reduced by communication. In other words, before you communicate at all with someone, he could be 100% uncertain about you, and could conceivably believe that you're almost anything—a slumming Tibetan Lama, president of the Chicago Fresh Air League, or Hawaii's only Ukrainian orthodontist. As soon as the two of you begin to communicate—verbally or nonverbally—his range of possible beliefs is restricted; that is, his uncertainty is reduced. The more you communicate; the less uncertain—or the more certain—he will become about you. And vice versa. Similarly, if I say to you, "Slap your knee" you know that I want you to behave *in a certain way.* The content of your communication reduces your uncertainty by eliminating the possibility—in most situations anyway—that

1. Albert Mehrabian and Henry Reed, "Some Determinants of Communication Accuracy," *Psychological Bulletin,* LXX (1968), 365.

I want you to wiggle your ears or blow your nose. (Of course there are still several possible ways you can slap your knee, and two possible knees. As I mention below, uncertainty can *never* be totally reduced.) As Francis Cartier puts it, "a sentence, then, may be viewed as a series of words chosen to successively modify each other in such a way as to eliminate more and more unintended concepts from the listener's choice as the sentence progresses. At the end of the sentence, the listener's freedom of choice is then as restricted as may be necessary for the purpose of the communication."[2] *Accurate or clear communication is thus communication that adequately reduces uncertainty.* What's "adequate" depends on the situation. "Draw a circle" might be adequate to tell someone how to begin reproducing this figure

but *not* this one.

One feature of this definition of clarity is that it is consistent with a transactional view of human communication. Since communication is a transaction, whatever happens when we communicate happens because of us and our relationship; consequently, it's nonsensical to talk about the clarity of "my" "message" or yours. But we *can* talk about—and work toward—communicating in ways that reduce uncertainty for both of us. The discussion in our class also usually moves in that direction. We are able to identify several strategies that helped clarify the communication about the shapes or the "block T," and to generalize from these to more common and significant communication situations. Eventually we come up with a number of practical suggestions or principles for reducing the uncertainty and thus increasing the accuracy and clarity of our interpersonal communication.

These suggestions or principles usually relate to four aspects of the overall communication situation: (1) the subject or topic of the communication, (2) the persons communicating, (3) the context in which the communicating takes place, and (4) the language the persons use.

Topic of Communication

Subject- or topic-related suggestions for increasing accuracy are pretty straightforward and obvious. For example, the more complex a subject, the more difficult it is to communicate clearly about it. An eraser has relatively

2. Francis Cartier, "Three Misconceptions of Communication," *ETC.: A Review of General Semantics*, XX (July 1963), 137.

few parts; it's not very difficult to say something definitive about one. An automatic transmission or a sorority is much more complex and much harder to discuss clearly. Another pretty obvious generalization is: the more ambiguous a subject, the more difficult it is to communicate clearly about it. Some colors and facial expressions are easy to discuss accurately; for example, black or a smile. Others, like "brownish-greenish-orange" or "a puzzling grimace" are more difficult to discuss clearly because of their ambiguity. The color I call "brownish-greenish-orange" you might call "reddish-greenish-gold."

The Communicators

Generalizations about the persons communicating are a little less obvious. In the first place, communication accuracy varies with the attitudes of the persons toward whatever they're talking about. Whether you evaluate your topic positively or negatively, whether you're for or against it, the further from neutral your attitudes are about it, the less accurate the communication will tend to be. A similar principle applies to persons' attitudes toward each other. You might assume that you can communicate more accurately with someone you admire or love. But it's been demonstrated that accuracy is inversely correlated with the magnitude of *positive or negative* attitudes of the communicators to each other.[3]

It might seem to follow from all this that if you want to communicate clearly, you should avoid talking with anyone you like or dislike about any topic you're interested in one way or the other. But that's pretty ridiculous. Instead, what I'm suggesting is that you recognize the effect attitudes have on the accuracy and clarity of your communication, and that you work to diminish that effect by applying the principle of adaptation. The principle of adaptation says that you can increase the clarity of your communication by constantly trying to put yourself in the psychological frame of reference of the other person. As Dean Barnlund suggests, try to become a *meaning*-centered communicator. Remember that you're working to reduce uncertainty, and you can't do that as long as your communication behavior is affected by unexamined assumptions about the people you're talking with. Try to see the communication situation from their point of view. Try not to assume, for example, that people always respond in a way that you'd call "rational." What's reasonable to you is often ridiculous to somebody else. Try not to assume that every time you talk everybody automatically listens, or that other people don't care what happens, or that most problems have a simple cause

---

3. H. C. Kelman and A. H. Eagly, "Attitude toward the Communicator, Perception of Communication Content, and Attitude Change," *Journal of Personality and Social Psychology*, I (1965), 63–78.

and a simple cure, or that there's only one way to look at a problem and it's your way, or, most importantly, that words mean for everybody what they mean for you. Actually, the principle of adaptation can be helpful in almost *all* communication situations. Whether or not you're aware of interfering attitudes—your own or somebody else's—try to put yourself in the psychological frame of reference of the other.

This advice is especially applicable to intercultural or intersubcultural communication. Blacks, Chicanos, native Americans, Puerto Ricans, and Asians have been unfairly downgraded for years because people who write the tests that often determine scholarly and job placement have not applied the principle of adaptation. Only recently have linguists, for example, begun to explain that the dialects spoken by blacks in urban ghettos are not "substandard"; what's "standard" depends on who's measuring. Black dialects are at least as rich and reasonable as dialects spoken in white subcultures. But our methods of observing and classifying this kind of language behavior have mistakenly assumed that anything nonwhite was substandard. When you put yourself in the psychological frame of reference of the other in an intersubcultural communication situation, you recognize that *both* of you operate out of a rich cultural background and both need to find out "where the other guy is coming from."

Communication Context

Clarity is also affected by the communication context. The most obvious contextual factor is noise, which usually means anything in the communication situation that distracts a communicator. The distracting influence can range from what we normally call noise—unwanted, interfering sound—to a headache, high humidity, or a hidden agenda. The problem is, one man's noise is another man's information. For some persons, President Kennedy's repetitive right-handed sawing the air distracted from what he was saying; for others it was an integral part of their total image of J.F.K. The relative nature of noise is another reason to use the principle of adaptation. If you try to put yourself in the other's psychological frame of reference, you'll be more easily able to understand what's liable to distract him. In addition, you can reduce the noise level in your communication by making it as unobtrusive as possible. Again, a lot depends on the situation. But generally, clear communication doesn't call attention to itself with distracting elements like an inappropriately formal or informal style, repetitive interminable pauses, giggles, nonstop exclamation points, etc.

Channel availability is also an aspect of the communication context that affects accuracy and clarity. The more channels you can utilize when you communicate, the better are your chances of reducing uncertainty. This factor is often illustrated in the "communication of shapes" exercise when the volunteer tries to communicate clearly without gesturing. Although the rules do not prohibit drawing the shapes in the air, most people assume that such a channel is not available and end up taking much longer than they need to.

Channel availability also explains why it's often harder to communicate accurately in a letter than face-to-face. We only use one channel for written communication; several are available when we communicate in person. And it's been demonstrated that communication accuracy increases to the degree that all communication behaviors of one person are made available to the other.[4] For example, two experimenters found that when inconsistent attitude communications are observed simultaneously in the facial, vocal, and content channels, the blocking of the facial or vocal channels can significantly change the quality of attitude being communicated.[5] Another study found that the availability of visual cues from the lips of the communicator increases the intelligibility of his communication.[6]

If you avoid looking at the other person and habitually talk in a listless monotone, or if you ignore what's communicated by facial gestures and spatial relationships, you're eliminating some opportunities to reduce communication uncertainty. Similarly, if you don't promote multi-channel communication in your family, office, classroom, etc., you're reducing the possibilities for clear communication. Since you can't "transmit" ideas, but can only *evoke* them, you don't know what the other person is thinking unless he tells you. And vice versa; he can't know how you've heard him unless you tell him. Too often, however, we either refuse to give what the interaction theory calls "feedback" or we refuse to receive it. Those channels should be open too. In short, be aware of all the channels that are available to you, and to communicate clearly, utilize as many of them as you can.[7]

Up to this point I've mentioned eight suggestions that usually emerge from our discussion of the effects on accuracy and clarity of the persons communicating, the topic, and the context: (1) beware of the complex topic; (2) be also aware of the ambiguous or vague topic; (3) remember that your chances of being accurate and clear decrease as your positive *or* negative feelings about the other communicator(s) increase, and (4) as your attitudes toward the subject or topic shift from neutral; (5) in order to combat (3) and (4), try constantly to put yourself in the psychological frame of reference of

---

4. Mehrabian and Reed, 375.

5. Albert Mehrabian and S. R. Ferris, "Inference of Attitudes From Nonverbal Communication in Two Channels," *Journal of Consulting Psychology,* XXXI (1967), 248–252.

6. K. K. Neely, "Effect of Visual Factors on Intelligibility of Speech," *Journal of Acoustical Society of America,* XXVIII (1956), 1275–1277.

7. There are exceptions to this "rule." Especially when information in one channel contradicts that in another, multi-channel communicating can be confusing. The communication needs to be as consistent-across-channels as possible.

the other person(s), and (6) avoid basing your communication on unexamined assumptions about either yourself or others; (7) try to reduce distracting communication noise; (8) utilize as many available communication channels as you can.

In the next several pages I want to suggest six more principles that should increase the accuracy and clarity of the *language* you use to communicate.[8]

Language

The first is the Principle of Parsimony or Economy: use only necessary words. I could have worded the principle this way: "When you're talking to someone, you want to remember not to use any more words than you absolutely have to in order to get across the point that you are primarily interested in communicating at a given particular time." But that would probably be too obvious.

This principle, like the others that deal with language, is based on a *functional, content*-centered view of communication; consequently, when you're concerned about *relationship* communication, it may be invalid. But if you want the content aspect of your spoken language to be clear, make it succinct. Partial sentences if necessary. Bare bones. Only necessary words. O.K.?

The second is the Principle of Prior Definition: define before you develop; explain before you amplify. Remember that the simplest terms can be unclear. Where would you go, for example, if I said, "I'll meet you at the side of this building"? When you're dealing with terms more complicated than "side," the need for definition and explanation is obviously even greater. Jargon also creates problems. We're often guilty of increasing uncertainty instead of reducing it by using the jargon or "in-group terms" of our favorite field of organization. When I get together with some of the people I work with, we have a delightful time talking about analogically coded metacommunicative cues, symmetrical escalation, overrigid complementarity, illocutionary acts, the argument from circumstance, and other fun things. You probably do something similar in a group you belong to. It's often harmless and maybe even helpful in some situations. But jargon can frustrate and confuse someone who wants to understand you accurately. Remember to define or explain unfamiliar terms before you use them. Recognize, too, that you're not always able to rely on *prior* definition. Especially if the terms or concepts are unfamiliar or unusual, you may have to redefine or reexplain to make your language as accurate and clear as possible.

---

8. I'm very much indebted to Professor C. David Mortensen for the outline of these six "Keys to the Kingdom of Clarity."

The Principle of Single Topic Development is simple but important: one idea at a time, one step at a time, one direction at a time. Often communication is unclear because it is overloaded with information. When we're asked to comprehend too much, we either forget or become confused. Or both. How would you respond, for example, if you were told to begin putting the "block T" together this way: "Take the largest, five-sided piece and put it on the table so that the longest sides are diagonal to the top and bottom of the table and the long side of the right angle is parallel with the nearest to the left side of the table"? The directions would be easier to follow if they went one idea, step, and direction at a time: "Take the largest puzzle piece, the one with five sides. Locate the right angle on that piece. Put the piece on the table so that the long side of the right angle is vertical. Check to see that the short side of the right angle is on your left. Notice the two parallel sides of that piece. Those sides should be running diagonally across the table."

Creative writers in advertising demonstrate the effectiveness of the principle of single topic development every day. Whatever else advertising is, it's almost always clear: "Certs stops bad breath." "Tastiest mint of all." "Ajax is stronger than dirt." "I hate it. But I use it twice a day." "All you add is love." "Ultra Brite gives your mouth sex appeal."

The Principle of Repetition is important. Very important.[9] You can reread a written message, but speech only comes by once. So it's especially important to use repetition in oral communication. Obviously, however, you shouldn't repeat everything you say. So what should your strategy of repetition be? First, repeat key points. Know your topic well enough to recognize what's crucial and what isn't. Second, repeat or restate difficult ideas. Third, pay careful attention to the other persons communicating, so you can recognize when they need to have you go back over something. For the sake of both clarity and economy, repeat the smallest possible units. Finally, remember that just saying something again often won't significantly reduce uncertainty. If you are not familiar with "analogically coded metacommunicative cues," my repetition—"that's analogically coded metacommunicative cues" —won't be much help. In those cases some kind of explanation, restatement, extension, capsulization, or example is needed.

How do you get to the stadium from here? Go south on highway 405 to route 522. Take 522 across the Evergreen floating bridge. Take the second exit beyond the bridge to Montlake Avenue. Cross the Montlake bridge and bear right on twenty-fifth. Twenty-fifth goes in front of the stadium, which will be on your right. That's 405 to 522, across the bridge, and Montlake exit to twenty-fifth.

The Principle of Analogy takes advantage of our proclivity to relate or

---

9. Sorry. Couldn't resist.

associate ideas. You can often clarify your communication by associating what you're talking about with something the other person is familiar with. In other words, link the unknown to the known. This principle applies most obviously to the "communication of shapes" exercise I mentioned. The figure

is usually called a stop sign—even though it's six-sided—with a medal ribbon or prize ribbon hanging from it. I think the key to the "block T" puzzle can be the number seven that I see in the largest piece. If you start by making a seven with that right angle, the rest of the puzzle will go together fairly easily. Analogies can also help clarify descriptions of, discussions about, or instructions related to less concrete topics. How is fixing the derailleur on a ten-speed bike like threading a sewing machine? How is writing a paper like composing a letter? How is the Chicago Conspiracy trial like the trial of Daniel Berrigan and the Catonsville Nine? Remember whenever possible to reduce the uncertainty of your communication by linking whatever you're talking about with something the other communicators are already familiar with.

Number six is the Principle of Sequentiality or Structure. Many psychologists contend that our mental processes consist primarily of activities which relate, arrange, contrast, classify, rank, or in some other way deal with experiences so as to place them in some meaningful order. If they are right, if we habitually think in patterns or sequences or structures of some kind, then it follows that communication with some structure will be more cognitively compatible, that is, easier to think about and understand, than a disordered conglomeration of apparently unrelated ideas.

Since we're talking about communication from a functional point of view, I think psychological structure is much more important than logical structure. As a result, I am not going to suggest that each time you communicate you must have, as some Greek and Roman rhetoricians believed, an "exordium," "narration," "confirmation," "refutation," and "peroration." I'm not even sure you always need an "introduction," "body," and "conclusion." But you *do* need to have some structure. You need to link your ideas together in some way that makes sense. Generally, you need to move from first principles to second principles, from premises to conclusions, from antecedents to consequents. Those things that should come first, should. Those things that should come second, should. Always. Or as Walt Kelly has Pogo say, you should "start at the beginning, go 'till you get to the end, and then stop."

Pogo's aphorism is actually pretty sound advice. The trick is discovering the beginning, identifying an orderly way to get through the material, and knowing when and how to stop. To do all that, you have to be familiar with what you're talking about and the persons you're talking with. If you were to explain to a nonstudent the structure of a class you have taken, where would you begin? With its size? Schedule? Subject? Instructor? Mood? Students? *Why*? What considerations would affect your choice of where to begin? How would you decide where to go next? The important point is this: if you want to communicate clearly, think through the communication decisions you invariably make until you have *reasons* for doing what you do.

Your decisions about internal structure depend on a variety of factors—you, the other persons, your relationship with them, the topic, etc. You should try, however, to discover the simplest and clearest possible way to deal with your topic. Remember that there are many possible "sequences of ideas" to choose from. Chronological or time order, for example, works well for some topics. Directions frequently require some kind of spatial order, that is, front to back, point to point, bottom to top, inside to outside. etc. Comparison and contrast or problem-solution order can usually help clarify complex topics. Some topics suggest their own developmental sequence. The federal government, for example, can be characterized by talking about the executive, legislative, and judicial branches. Other topics can be treated in terms of the parties involved, fields of activity, parts of the whole, etc. If you'd like a detailed treatment of organizational sequences, consult the chapter on organization in almost any public speaking text.[10] I just want to emphasize the importance of structure. For your communication to be clear, the various parts of it need to hang together somehow. They need to be interrelated in a way that makes some sense. You need to have some reason for saying first what you say first, second what you say second, etc. . . . and last what you say last.

One final suggestion. Sometimes communication that's pretty clearly structured still comes across like a disordered jumble of thoughts. In other words, what one person thinks is organized sometimes sounds disorganized to others. The problem is often a lack of transitional signposts. Remember that other persons don't think about things as you do, and don't know how a set of ideas hangs together for you until you tell them. Telling them means letting them know how what you're saying now relates to the point you made a few seconds ago, and how both are connected to the main point you want to make. You let them know by employing transitions—words, phrases, sentences, pauses, changes in tone of voice, etc.—that indicate how the various things you say are related. Sometimes I feel that my transition storehouse isn't as well supplied as it might be. If you'll look back over this chapter, you'll see me using—and sometimes probably overusing—"similarly," "in short," "for

---

10. See, e.g., Thomas H. Olbricht, *Informative Speaking* (Glenview, Ill., 1968), Chapter 4; or Ray E. Nadeau, *A Basic Rhetoric of Speech Communication* (Reading, Mass.: Addison-Wesley Publishing Company, 1969), Chapter 6.

example," "however," and "in addition" to move from one idea to another and indicate how the ideas are interrelated.

In sum (there's one!), transitions are important for clarity. Your communicating can be much clearer if it's reasonably structured, and the best way to let others know how you've related your ideas is to provide them with transitional signposts to point the way.

Conclusion

That's the gist of what I know about communicating accurately and clearly. Communication uncertainty will never be reduced to zero—at least not until we can directly link minds. But we can move toward less uncertainty. And it's been my experience that these suggestions work toward that end.

If you're not being clearly understood, or if you're unable accurately to understand others, ask yourself how much of the problem is due to a vague or ambiguous topic. Be aware of distortions introduced by positive or negative attitudes toward the topic or the persons involved. Try to put yourself in the psychological frame of reference of the others communicating, and minimize—or at least be conscious of—the assumptions you're making about them, the situation, and yourself. Try to reduce noise in the system, and use as many available channels as you can. Finally, increase your clarity by being as succinct as you can; by applying the principle of prior definition; by talking about one idea at a time, one step at a time, in one direction at a time; by strategically repeating or restating key ideas (this summary is a form of repetition); by employing analogies; and by being as clearly organized as you can.

Empathic Listening

Charles M. Kelly

In a research project exploring listening behavior, industrial supervisors gave the following reasons for communication problems in large management-level meetings and conferences: "things discussed here are often side issues that don't interest everyone," "I think about my job upstairs," "they get off the subject," and "a lot of people like to hear themselves talk." A content analysis was made of these and other responses dealing with the perceived deficiencies of meetings and discussions. Results indicated that most of the dissatisfaction centered around the general feeling that many different issues were discussed at a typical meeting, and that usually some of these issues were not directly related to all of the participants.[1]

Complaints such as the above are not unusual, and frequently are justified. Every text of discussion and conference methodology deals with the problems of keeping the discussion on relevant and significant issues, and of motivating the participants. However, most of the emphasis in the past has dealt with the obligations of the discussants (both leaders and participants) as *speakers,* rather than as *listeners.* This unbalanced emphasis, especially as it actually affects persons in real discussions, could be an important *cause* of the problems that speaking is supposed to cure: e.g., the reason a discussion leader may have difficulty clarifying the comments of another, may be that he did not listen carefully to begin with; when one is overly concerned about what *he* is *going* to say, he really can't devote his full attention to what *is* being said by others. If a person in a group preoccupies himself by privately bemoaning the irrelevancies that inevitably occur in discussion, he may be less able to get the group back on the track; he misses opportunities for constructive action because he lacks an *accurate* analysis of the flow of ideas, even the irrelevant ones.

Of course, listening is a multi-faceted activity and it can be considered from different viewpoints, but at least two ways of categorizing listening seem especially fruitful for theoretical analysis: *deliberative listening* and *empathic listening.* More recent writers have treated listening as a unitary skill, i.e., as a rather definite and "deliberative" ability to hear information, to analyze it, to recall it at a later time, and to draw conclusions from it. Commercially-

This original essay appeared in print in the first and second editions. All rights reserved. Permission to reprint must be obtained from the publishers and the author.
1. Charles M. Kelly, "Actual Listening Behavior of Industrial Supervisors as Related to Listening Ability, General Mental Ability, Selected Personality Factors and Supervisory Effectiveness," Unpublished Ph.D. Dissertation, Purdue University, 1962, p. 129.
Charles Kelly is Director of Personal Development, Celanese Fibers Group, Fiber Industries, Charlotte, North Carolina.

published listening tests and most listening training programs are based on this, the deliberative listening, viewpoint. On the other hand, empathic listening occurs when the person participates in the spirit or feeling of his environment as a communication *receiver*. This does not suggest that the listener is uncritical or always in agreement with what is communicated, but rather, that his primary interest is to become fully and accurately aware of what is going on. (See Figure 1.)

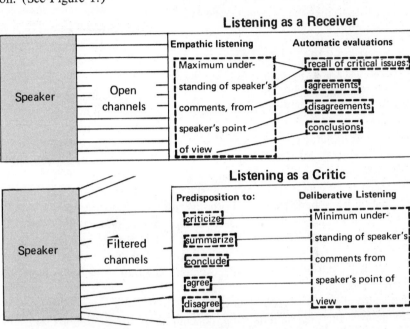

Figure 1. The differences between empathic listening and deliberative listening are primarily motivational. Both listeners seek the same objective: accurate understanding of the communication from another. The model suggests that the motivation to receive information is superior to the motivation to use critical skills. The empathic listener lets his understanding of the speaker determine his modes of evaluation, which are automatic; the deliberative listener's understanding of the speaker is filtered through his predetermined modes of selective listening, and actually spends less time as a communication receiver. The empathic listener is more apt to be a consistent listener, and is less prone to his own or other distractions. This theory is correct, only if the assumption is true that persons can and do think critically without deliberate effort— *while listening.* (Of course, if persons do not make the effort to listen *per se,* little or no understanding will occur.)

It should be observed that the terms "deliberative listening" and "empathic listening" are not mutually exclusive or exhaustive. Their main purpose is to differentiate between two basic ways of viewing the same listening activity. The desired result of both deliberative and empathic listening is identical: accurate understanding of oral communication. However, this understanding is achieved by different routes. The deliberative listener *first* has the desire to critically analyze what a speaker has said, and secondarily tries to understand the speaker (this can be the result of personal inclination or of training which emphasizes procedure at the expense of listening). The empathic listener has the desire to understand the speaker first, and, as a result, tries to take the appropriate action.

The former kind of listening is characteristic of the discussant who is predisposed to be disagreeable, or to summarize, or to clarify—even when there is little that is significant to disagree with, when there is no need to summarize, or when further clarification is a waste of the group's time. The latter kind of listening is characteristic of the person who is able to adapt quickly to the real needs of a situation because he has a presence of mind and a greater confidence in the accuracy of his awareness—he does not handicap himself by deciding in advance that he does not have to listen to a particular person who is poorly dressed, or that he must be sure to expose all faulty reasoning if he is to demonstrate his competence.

This is not to say that various skills in critical thinking are less important than emphatic listening. Without critical analysis, listening in a problem-solving discussion would be useless. The point is, however, that a person uses quite naturally whatever critical skills he has already acquired, as long as he is interested and actively listening; to the extent that he is not listening, critical skills will be of little value. Actually, a case can be made that "deliberative listening" is a self-contradiction and a misnomer—and that "empathic listening" is a redundancy. To the extent that one is deliberating (mentally criticizing, summarizing, concluding, preparing reports, etc.) he is *not listening,* but formulating his own ideas. And listening, by its very nature, *has* to be empathic; a person understands what he has heard, only to the extent that he can share in the meaning, spirit, or feeling of what the communicator has said.

There is some evidence that this line of reasoning is correct. In one experiment,[2] a researcher presented a 30-minute talk dealing with "The Supervisor and Communication" to 28 supervisors at a regularly scheduled business meeting. The supervisors were in no way led to believe that they were in an experiment or that their listening performance would be tested. Following the presentation, they were given a 30-item multiple-choice "surprise" listening test. During the following two weeks, the supervisors were given the Brown-Carlsen Listening Comprehension Test, the STEP Listening Test, the Otis Quick-Scoring Mental Ability Test, and the Cattell 16 Personality Factor

---

2. This study is reported in detail: Charles M. Kelly, "Mental Ability and Personality Factors in Listening," *Quarterly Journal of Speech,* XLIX, (April, 1963), 152–156.

Questionnaire. (Because of the nature of the Crown-Carlsen and STEP listening tests, subjects have to know in advance that their listening ability is being tested.)

The results (Table 1) indicated that the supervisors' "listening ability" (as measured by the Brown-Carlsen and the STEP) was indistinguishable from general mental ability (as measured by the Otis) when they knew in advance that their listening was being tested. In fact, the listening tests correlated *lower* with each other, than each did with the test of mental ability. In other words, when the supervisors had the extra motivation of a test, or were constantly listening, they made full use of their general mental ability, and the listening tests became orally-presented tests of general mental ability, rather than of "listening." On the other hand, when the supervisors did not know their listening was being tested, their listening performance was significantly less related to general mental ability.

Table 1

Correlations (Pearson r) Among the "Surprise" Listening Test,
the Brown-Carlsen Listening Test, the STEP Listening
Test, and the Otis Test of General Mental Ability[a]

	Brown-Carlsen	*STEP*	*Otis*
Surprise Listening test	.79	.78	.70[bc]
Brown-Carlsen		.82	.85[b]
STEP			.85[c]

[a] All correlations are significant at the 0.1 level.

[b] The difference between the two correlations so designated is significant at the 0.5 level, t = 2.205.

[c] The difference between the two correlations so designated is significant at the .05 level, t = 2.162.

Further insight can be gained by analyzing the results in terms of personality variables (Table 2). Again, the Brown-Carlsen and STEP listening tests are indistinguishable from the Otis, when compared on the basis of personality variables; the same personality factors appear about equally important (as expressed in chi square values) in the test of general mental ability as in the tests of listening ability. However, the "surprise" listening test showed significantly more substantial personality differences between good and poor listeners than did the other three tests.

The most significant differences between good and poor listeners, when they had no unusual motivation to listen because of test awareness, were that good listeners were more adventurous (receptive to new ideas), (emotionally), stable, mature, and sophisticated. Although the other six differences in Table 2 (under "surprise listening test") were not statistically significant, it is interesting to note that all were in the same direction, with the good listeners being more emotionally mature: outgoing, bright, dominant, enthusiastic, trustful and controlled (will control). The opposite ends of the personality scales, describing the poor listeners in the surprise listening test, were: aloof, dull, emotional, submissive, glum, timid, suspecting, simple, lax, and tense.

Table 2
Statistical Significance of Differences (Chi Square with Yates' Correction) Between "High" and "Low" Criterion Groups (as Determined by Scores on Each of Four Tests) on the Cattell 16 PF Scales

Cattell Scale Low Score vs. High Scores	Surprise Listening Test[bcd]	Brown- Carlsen[b]	STEP[c]	Otis[d]
Aloof vs. Outgoing	.14	.00**	.14	.00
Dull vs. Bright (intelligence factor)	.57	5.16	2.29	2.29
Emotional vs. Mature	3.57***	1.28	3.57***	1.28
Submissive vs. Dominant	.14	.00	.00	.15
Glum vs. Enthusiastic	.14	.00	.00	.00
Casual vs. Conscientious	.00	.00	.00	.00
Timid vs. Adventurous	9.19*	.57	2.29	.57
Tough vs. Sensitive	.00	.00	.00	.57[a]
Trustful vs. Suspecting	.57[a]	.00	.00	.00
Conventional vs. Eccentric	.00	.00	.00	.00
Simple vs. Sophisticated	3.65***	1.31	1.31	1.31
Confident vs. Insecure	.00	.57[a]	.00	.00
Conservative vs. Experimenting	.00	.59[a]	.00	.00
Dependent vs. Self-sufficient	.00	.00	.00	.00
Lax vs. Controlled	2.29	.00	.00	.00
Stable vs. Tense	7.00*[a]	.14[a]	1.31[a]	2.29[a]

*X^2 of 6.64 = 1% level.
**X^2 of 3.84 = 5% level.
***X^2 of 2.71 = 10% level.
[a] High scorers on the test scored low on the Cattell personality scale.
Using the sign test for statistical significance, the following differences were observed between tests, on the basis of personality scales (intelligence scale, "Dull vs. Bright," was not included):
[b] difference between tests so designated was significant at p = .03
[c] p = .008
[d] p = .055

This and other studies[3] strongly indicate that when persons know that their listening comprehension is being tested, differences between individuals are primarily matters of general mental ability; when they do not know their listening performance is being tested, differences are due to personality dif-

---

3. For a detailed analysis of this issue, see: Charles M. Kelly, "Listening: Complex of Activities—and a Unitary Skill?" *Speech Monographs*, XXXIV (November, 1967), 455–466.

ferences (including motivation to listen), as well as general mental ability. Of these two kinds of research situations, the latter is more representative of realistic listening events.

It is likely that most communication problems arise either because of participant inattention (poor motivation), or because of a lack of general mental ability—not because of anything that can be called "listening ability." Do teachers in a faculty meeting miss the details of registration because of a lack of listening ability, or because of a lack of motivation? Does an engineer fail to understand an explanation of a new process because he lacks listening ability, or because he simply has not yet been able to visualize unfamiliar relationships? In the rare cases when a discussion is vitally important to everyone and motivation is high (as in a listening test), there is little chance of an important point (or its significance) being missed, unless the listener simply lacked the mental ability to understand or appreciate it to begin with. But in most of the everyday discussions that deal with the nagging problems of industrial production, proposed new school construction, traffic safety, curriculum changes, etc., motivation to participate (and, hence, listen) is moderate at best and is not evenly distributed among the discussants—and with some persons, inattention seems to be habitual.

In terms of *listening* theory, it is far more important to stress empathic, rather than deliberative, listening in discussion. This observation in no way depreciates the need for education and practical experience in critical analysis, debate, general semantics—or in any of the various mental skills brought into play *while* listening. But it is a mistake to consider these skills *as* listening, since this viewpoint suggests that the listener's analysis is part of the receiving process.

The degree to which one is able to listen, and to perform other mental acts at the same time is an open question; research into the exact nature of listening, as it relates to other general mental abilities, is unclear at best. However, because of the obvious difficulties that occur in discussion when listener motivation is poor or nonexistent, and in view of the probability that problems in discussion are due to factors other than listening *ability* when participant motivation is high, the following suggestions seem warranted:

Listening Suggestions

Remember the characteristics of the poor listener. It is easy to sit back in your chair and complain to yourself that the discussion is boring or unimportant. However, the description of the kind of person who habitually does this is not very flattering, and should serve as an incentive to better listening; research suggests that the poor listener is less intelligent, and less emotionally mature than the good listener. Obviously, there are times when a person may be just as well off *not* listening, but the poor listener tends to make this a crutch for the easy way out of difficult listening events.

Make a firm initial commitment to listen. Listening is hard work and it takes energy. If you have had difficulty listening in the past, and now decide merely to *try* to listen and to participate in the spirit of the discussion as long as you can, you will soon fall into old habits. Above all, don't make an initial decision *not* to listen; if discussions in the past have proved deficient, according to your standards, accurate listening will better enable you to correct them in the future.

Get physically and mentally ready to listen. Sit up, and get rid of distractions; put away paper you were reading, books, pencils, papers, etc., unless you plan to use them. Try to dismiss personal worries, fears, or pleasant reverie until a later time. Will these kinds of thoughts be more productive of personal gain than your participation in this discussion?

Concentrate on the other person as a communicator. View the others in a discussion as sources of ideas and information, not as personalities. If you are reacting to another as being dishonest, unethical, stupid, tedious—or as a college professor, or Republican, or student rioter, or disgruntled parent—it will be difficult for you to accurately perceive what he is trying to say. There is little to fear in such an open approach. Shoddy thinking or speaking needs no label to be recognized, and fewer good ideas will be discarded because they were never really listened to. Of course, it goes without saying that persons communicate with gestures as well as with their voices, and the listener is concerned with perceiving the total communication environment as accurately as possible.

Give the other person a full hearing. Avoid interrupting another person unless you are sure you understand him fully, and that it is necessary. If you feel that you aren't sure you understand him, a well phrased question is usually more appropriate than an attempt by you to clarify his position. Impatience with others can lead to false understanding or agreement, and eventually leads to greater difficulties.

Use analytical skills as supplements to, not instead of, listening. To the degree that successful participation in discussion requires your understanding of others, rather than your speaking contributions, it is important not to be distracted by your own note taking, mental review of main points, critical analysis, or preparation for argumentative "comeback." An especially dubious recommendation frequently found in articles on listening is that, since listeners can listen faster than speakers can talk, the extra time should be used to review main points, "read between the lines," etc. Whether this conscious effort is exerted between words, sentences, or major ideas is never made clear. However, interviews with subjects following "surprise" listening tests have indicated that one of the major causes of listener distraction was a speaker's previous point: "I suddenly realized that I didn't know what he was talking about, because I was still thinking about what he had said before."

Omitted from this list are the many sound suggestions that have been made by other writers about: analyzing the speaker's intent, figuring out what he is going to say or what he has not said, note-taking, mental reorganization of a speaker's comments, etc. These, and others, are perfectly valid tools to be used in an oral communication setting, but their success is due to factors other than listening. For example, a discussion leader may wisely decide to mentally review the progress of a discussion while "listening" to a certain person unnecessarily repeating himself—but the wisdom of his action is due to his prior analysis, not to "listening ability." While listening to a specific individual, he may briefly jot down the person's main ideas for future reference; if he has developed an efficient note-taking skill, he may not miss anything significant—but he is effective because he is able to take notes with very little or no conscious effort, not because note-taking is a *listening* activity. Other less talented persons may never be able to take notes without distracting them from what is truly listening.

Conclusion

Many factors make up a discussion, and listening is only one of them; however, it is an extremely important factor, and it has been diluted in the past by a shift of its meaning from one of reception to one of critical analysis.

Empathic listening cannot of itself make a good speaker out of a poor one, a clear thinker out of a dull thinker, or a good discussion out of a bad discussion. But to the extent that problems result from a lack of participant reception and understanding of the discussion interaction, empathic listening appears to be the best answer.

Characteristics of Effective Feedback

Elliot Aronson

The Importance of Immediacy

As I mentioned previously, members of T-groups are encouraged to express their feelings directly and openly. When the participants abide by this, each is able to receive immediate feedback on how people interpret what he says and does. In this way, a participant is able to gain insight into the impact that his actions and statements have on other people. Once he gains this insight, he is free to do whatever he wants with it: that is, people are not advised to perform only those actions that no one finds objectionable; rather, they are allowed to see the consequences of their behavior and to decide whether the price they are paying is worth it. They are also given the opportunity of finding out that there may be more options open to them than they may have realized. To illustrate, suppose I perform an action that angers my wife. If she doesn't express this anger, I may never become aware of the fact that the action I've performed makes her angry. On the other hand, suppose she gives me immediate feedback; suppose she tells me how these actions on my part make her feel angry. Then, I have at least two options: I can continue to behave in that way, or I can stop behaving in that way—the choice is mine. The behavior may be so important that I don't want to give it up. Conversely, my wife's feelings may be so important that I choose to give up the behavior. In the absence of any knowledge of how my behavior makes her feel, I don't have a choice. Moreover, knowing exactly how she feels about a particular set of actions may allow me to explore a *different* set of actions that may satisfy my needs as well as her needs.

The value of feedback is not limited to the recipient. Frequently, in providing feedback, a person discovers something about himself and his own needs. If a person feels, for example, that it's "wrong" to experience anger, he may block out his awareness of this feeling. When the expression of such feelings is legitimized, he has a chance to bring them out in the open, look at them, and to become aware that his expression of anger has not caused the world to come to an end. Moreover, the direct expression of a feeling keeps the encounter on the up-and-up and, thus, helps to prevent the escalation of negative feelings. For example, if my wife has learned to express her anger directly, it keeps our discussion on the issue at hand. If she suppresses the anger, but it leaks out in other ways—at different times and in different situations—I do not know where her hostility is coming from. I may get self-righteous about being abused for no apparent reason. This makes me angry, and the escalation is on.

Feelings versus Evaluations

People often need some coaching in how to provide feedback. We often do it in a way that angers or upsets the recipient, thereby causing more problems than we solve. Indeed, one of the aspects of T-groups that sometimes frightens and confuses people who have never been in a properly conducted group in that their prior experiences with providing and receiving feedback have not always been pleasant. This is one of the reasons why it is so difficult to communicate what happens in a T-group to people who have never experienced one. Specifically, when we describe this aspect of a T-group, we are describing behavior of a sort that all of us have had experience with—much of it unpleasant. And yet, we're trying to say that such behavior can be productive in a T-group. To say this, however, may make the group seem to be a magical, mystical thing, which it's not. The way this can happen is better illustrated than described in the abstract. I will do this by providing an example of "improper" feedback, and of how people can be taught to modify their method of providing feedback (without modifying its quality) in order to maximize communication and understanding. This example is an event that occurred in an actual group session.

In the course of the group meeting, one of the members (Sam) looked squarely at another member (Harry) and said, "Harry, I've been listening to you and watching you for a day and a half, and I think you're a phoney." Now, that's quite an accusation. How can Harry respond? Another way of asking the question is: What are Harry's options? He has several: he can (1) agree with Sam; (2) deny the accusation and say that he's not a phoney; (3) say, "Gee, Sam, I'm sorry that you feel that way"; (4) get angry and call Sam some names; or (5) feel sorry for himself and go into a sulk. Taken by themselves, none of these responses is particularly productive. In the "real world," it is unlikely that Sam would have come out with this statement; if he had come out with it, there almost certainly would have been trouble. But doesn't Sam have the right to express this judgment? After all, he's only being open.

This seems to be a dilemma: T-groups encourage openness, but openness can hurt people. The solution to this dilemma is rather simple: It is possible to be open and, at the same time, to express oneself in a manner that causes a minimum of pain. The key rests in the term *"feeling"*: Sam was not expressing a feeling, he was expressing a judgment. As I mentioned previously, openness in a T-group means the open expression of feelings. By "feeling," I mean, specifically, anger or joy, sadness or happiness, annoyance, fear, discomfort, warmth, and the like.

How was this encounter handled in the T-group? In this situation, the group leader intervened by asking Sam if he had any *feelings* about Harry. In our society, people are not accustomed to expressing feelings. It is not surprising, then, that Sam thought for a moment and then said, "Well, I *feel* that Harry is a phoney." Of course, this is not a feeling, as defined above. This is an opinion or a judgment expressed in the terminology of feelings. A judgment is nothing more or less than a feeling that is inadequately understood or inadequately expressed. Accordingly, the leader probed further by asking Sam *what* his feelings were. Sam still insisted that he felt that Harry was a phoney. "And what does that do to you?" asked the leader. "It annoys the hell out of me," answered Sam. Here, another member of the group intervened and asked for data: "What kinds of things has Harry done that annoyed you, Sam?" Sam, after several minutes of probing by various members of the group, admitted that he got annoyed whenever Harry showed affection to some of the women in the group. On further probing, it turned out that Sam perceived Harry as being very successful with women. What eventually emerged was that Sam owned up to a feeling of jealousy and envy—that Sam wished that he had Harry's smoothness and success with women. Note that Sam had initially masked this feeling of envy; rather, he had discharged his feelings by expressing disdain, by saying Harry was a phoney. This kind of expression is ego-protecting: because we live in a competitive society, if Sam had admitted to feeling envious, it would have put him "one down" and put Harry "one up." This would have made Sam vulnerable—that is, it would have made him feel weak in relation to Harry. By expressing disdain, however, Sam succeeded in putting *himself* "one up." Although his behavior was successful as an ego-protecting device, it didn't contribute to Sam's understanding of his own feelings and of the kinds of events that caused those feelings; and it certainly didn't contribute to Sam's understanding of Harry or to Harry's understanding of Sam (or, for that matter, to Harry's understanding of himself). In short, Sam was communicating ineffectively. As an ego-defensive measure, his behavior was adaptive; as a form of communication, it was extremely maladaptive. Thus, although it made Sam vulnerable to admit that he envied Harry, it opened the door to communication; eventually, it helped them to understand each other. Moreover, a few other men also admitted that they felt some jealousy about Harry's behavior with women. This was useful information for Harry, in that it enabled him to understand the effects his behavior had on other people.

As we know, Harry has several options: he can continue to behave as he always has, and let other people continue to be jealous, and, perhaps, to express their jealousy in terms of hostility; or he can modify his behavior in any one of a number of ways in order to cause other people (and, ultimately, himself) less difficulty. *The decision is his.* Should he decide that his "enviable" behavior is too important to give up, he has still gained enormously from his encounter with Sam in the T-group. Specifically, if a similar response occurs in the real world, Harry, who now knows the effect his behavior may have on other men, will not be surprised by their responses, will be more understanding, will be less likely to overreact, and so forth.

But who needs a group? Couldn't Sam and Harry have done just as well by themselves? No. They almost certainly would have ended simply by calling each other names, hurting each other's feelings, and making each other angry. But suppose they had the benefit of a trained counselor in human relations— wouldn't that be as good as a group? Probably not. One of the great advantages and excitements about the T-group is that we don't deal with expert opinion (in the traditional sense). Rather, each person is considered an expert on his own feelings. By sharing their feelings, the other members of the group can be enormously helpful to Sam and Harry. Specifically, the other group members contributed to the data Harry was gathering by expressing their own feelings about Harry's behavior.

Indeed, if the other members of the group do not spontaneously express their feelings, the group leader might specifically ask them to do so. Why is this important? Let's take two opposite cases. First, let us assume that Sam was the only person in the room who felt envious. In that case, it would have been relatively safe to conclude that the situation was largely Sam's problem, and he could then work on it. Sam would have gained the understanding that he is inordinately jealous or envious of people who do particular things, as evidenced by the fact that no one else experienced such feelings toward Harry. On the other hand, if it came out (as it did in reality) that several people also felt envious of Harry, it would be clear that the problem was one that Harry himself might want to face up to.

This is another reason why it is important for the group that each member be honest and open in expressing his feelings. If all of the members of the group actually experienced envy of Harry, but (out of kindness, or fear, or shyness) none of them admitted to it, then it would have left Sam with the feeling that he was an extraordinarily envious person. If, on the other hand, very few of the other members felt this envy, but they wanted to support Sam and did so by claiming this feeling of enviousness, then this would have left Harry with the feeling that he was causing a lot of negative feelings in other people by his behavior when, in fact, he wasn't. It would also leave Sam with the feeling that his behavior was not extraordinary. Thus, a desire to protect Sam would certainly not be doing him any good—it would be protecting him from an understanding of himself.

Of course, the preceding example was a relatively easy one to deal with. It ended up with Sam feeling admiration and envy for Harry. But what if Sam hates Harry—should he express his hatred? What if Sam believes that Harry is an evil person—should he express that belief? Here again, we can see the difference between a feeling and an evaluation. It would be useful if Sam would express the feelings underlying his judgments and evaluations. Did Harry do something that hurt Sam and made him angry? Is this why Sam hates Harry and thinks he's an evil person? Sam will not get very far by discussing Harry's evilness. *Sam:* "I hate you, Harry; you are evil." *Harry:* "No, I'm not." *Sam:* "Well, that is the way I see it; I'm just giving you feedback like we're supposed to do in here." *Harry:* "That's your problem—besides, you're not so great yourself." By calling Harry names, Sam sets up the situation in a way that invites Harry to defend himself and counterattack, rather than to listen. But if Sam were to lead with his own feelings ("I am hurt and angry"), it would invite Harry into a discussion about what he (Harry) did to hurt and anger Sam. That is not to say that it is pleasant to hear someone say that he is angry at us or hurt by us—it's not. But it helps us to pay attention and to try to deal with the problem at hand.

Why is it tempting for Sam to call Harry evil, rather than to talk about his own hurt? The reasons for this behavior should be clear by now. Being hurt puts us "one down"—it makes us vulnerable. In this society, we tend to glide through life protecting ourselves; in effect, each of us wears a suit of behavioral armor, so that other people can't hurt us. This results in a lot of inauthentic behavior—that is, we mask our true feelings from other people. This is often accomplished through the process of short-circuiting. Sometimes, we are so successful at it that we mask our feelings from ourselves as well.

In summary, then, feedback expressed in terms of feelings is a lot easier for the recipient to listen to and deal with than feedback in the form of judgments and evaluations. This is true for two major reasons: First, a person's opinions and judgments about another person are purely a matter of conjecture. Thus, Sam's opinions about Harry's being a phoney and about Harry's being an evil person may reflect reality, or they may, just as likely, not: they are merely Sam's theories about Harry. Only Harry knows for sure whether he's being a phoney; Sam is only guessing. But Sam's statement that he is feeling envious or angry is not a guess or a theory—it is an absolute fact. Sam is not guessing about his feelings—he knows them; indeed, he is the only person in the world who knows them for sure. Harry may or may not care about Sam's intellectual theories or pontifical judgments, but, if he is desirous of interacting with Sam, he is probably very interested in knowing about Sam's feelings and what role he (Harry) plays in triggering those feelings.

The second major reason why feedback expressed in terms of feelings is preferable to feedback expressed in terms of judgments is that, when Sam states an opinion or a judgment about Harry, he is saying something about

Harry only, but when he states a *feeling* about Harry, he is also talking about himself. Thus, the statement of feeling is a gift: metaphorically, it is Sam opening the door to his home and letting Harry in. When Sam states a judgment about Harry, however, he is storming Harry's barricades and laying something on him. Harry has good reason to resist this, because Sam has no right to be in his home without an invitation. Harry can let him in by telling him what his feelings are; likewise, Sam can let Harry in by telling him what *his* feelings are.

Feelings and Intentions

Frequently, in a T-group (or in the "real world"), one person will say or do something that hurts another. If the recipient (*R*) *does* get to the point of expressing his hurt, the person (*P*) may insist that hurting wasn't his intention. It is important that he expresses this; but, in a T-group, it is important to move beyond this. If *P* says, "Oh, I'm sorry, I didn't mean to hurt you—I really like you," and *R* answers by saying "Oh, that's fine, I feel better about it now," that may smooth things over and make things tolerable. Much of the time, all we're after is interpersonal relations that are tolerable. But sometimes we want more than that—we want to learn something about ourselves and the other person. We accomplish this by moving beyond our tendency to paper over events such as this—by moving toward an exploration of the process. "Why is it that I hurt people when I don't intend to?" or, "Why am I so easily hurt?"

If *P* does not *intend* to hurt *R*, there is often a tendency for him to deny the legitimacy of *R*'s hurt, saying, in effect, "What right do you have to be hurt, now that you know that I didn't intend to hurt you?" Again, this kind of attitude does not increase *P*'s learning. If I spilled a cup of hot tea on my friend's lap, the fact that I did not intend to does not completely remove the hurt. I may want to reach out to my friend and express concern that he's hurt —and then examine my own clumsiness, to try to learn from it, so that the probability of my doing it in the future will be reduced. At the same time, it may be that the tea wasn't all that hot. The group may be useful in helping my friend and me explore the ins and outs of this complex relationship—not to decide who is right and who is wrong, but to help us understand ourselves, each other, and the nature of our relationship. In a T-group, people do not attempt to decide who is right and who is wrong; rather, an attempt is made to determine what can be learned. If a person is misunderstood, it is not enough for him to sulk and say, "Alas, nobody understands me." It can be far more productive if he tries to find out why it is that people don't understand him, and what he can do to increase the probability that he will be understood in the future. In order to accomplish this, each individual must assume some part of the responsibility for what happens to him.

Conflict and Its Resolution

Bobby R. Patton and Kim Giffin

What does the word *conflict* mean to you? To many people it means quarreling, arguing, and fighting. We would suggest, however, that there is a positive dimension to conflict. Just as we know that conflict is inevitable because of the differences in people, we know that without conflict there would be no innovations, creativity, or challenging of existing norms and practices. The key to whether or not conflict should be viewed positively is in the method of its resolution.

In this chapter we shall discuss the levels of conflict within the individual, within the group, and among groups, the differences in competitive and cooperative orientations, and the methods of handling conflict.

The Levels of Conflict

Conflict typically involves some obstacle to achieving a desired goal; it often arises when someone has a chance to win at the expense of someone else. Competition in a game or a particular job exemplifies this type of conflict. Yet it doesn't take two to quarrel; sometimes we are in conflict with ourselves.

Conflict Within the Individual

If our desires are denied, we become frustrated. If there are alternative routes to satisfying our desires, we feel internal conflict:[1] "Conflict [is] . . . a pulling in two directions at the same time. The obstacles one meets are not brick walls but drags that pull back as one goes forward . . . frying-pan-and-fire situations, or donkey-between-the-bales-of-hay situations."

Conflict forces the individual to choose, to make a decision among available alternatives. An individual may respond to conflict with disruptive or with constructive effects.

Among the disruptive approaches are the following.

1. *Aggression.* A direct attack may be made on one or another alternative. Wright studied the behavior of children three to six years of

From pp. 90-97, 100-102 in *Problems Solving: Group Interaction* by Bobby R. Patton and Kim Giffin. Copyright © 1973 by Bobby R. Patton and Kim Giffin. Reprinted by permission of Harper & Row, Publishers, Inc.

1. H. J. Leavitt, *Managerial Psychology*, Chicago, University of Chicago, 1964, p. 53. Cited and abstracted in W. V. Haney, *Communication and Organizational Behavior Text and Cases*, Homewood, Ill., Irwin, 1967, p. 124.

age in conflict situations. In a free-play period the children were allowed to play freely with toys for fifteen minutes. Frustration was then induced by placing the best toys behind a wire screen. The experimenter became the target of direct aggression by 37 percent of the children during the frustrative session. The aggression ranged from calling him names to hitting him with blocks and tearing his records.[2]

2. *Withdrawal.* Some persons have little tolerance for conflict situations and withdraw into themselves rather than be forced to make a decision. In a group situation such a person will change the subject, joke, mediate, or become silent, when areas of conflict become exposed.

3. *Ego-defensive reactions.* The purpose of this approach is not to solve the problem but to protect the ego and maintain a possibly inaccurate feeling of self-esteem. Haney cites as examples of such reactions:[3]

> . . . *fantasy* (wish-fulfilling dreams, day-dreaming, etc.); *projecting* (imputing one's thoughts and desires to others); *rationalization* (finding "justifiable" reasons for our behavior or convincing ourselves that the goal is really undesirable—assuming the "sour grapes" attitude); *repressing* (attempting to ignore, deny, or forget troublesome things); *regressing* (reverting to childish ways); *identifying* (becoming ego-involved with others); *blaming others* (excusing ourselves by finding others responsible for our failures—"scape-goating"); *overcompensating* (trying to overcome one's deficiencies, to "make up" for one's feelings—but in an excessive manner); *sublimating* (getting indirect but socially acceptable satisfaction).

These "defense mechanisms" protect the individual from anxiety, though at the price of a certain degree of reality denial, or distortion.

A possible constructive effect of internal conflict for the individual may be that he is impelled to make a greater effort to reach the goal in the best way. If the conflict is still unresolved, he may redefine the problem or change the goal, as suggested by Krech and his associates:[4]

> One obvious way of removing conflict, its consequent frustration, and increased tension is to make choices among the alternatives . . . sometimes the choice is an absolute one; in other cases the person decides to attain this goal first, and later that one. In either case the increased tension helps to force a choice—and choice in conflict situations is adaptive behavior. The tension has brought about a redefining of the situation, so that the conflict is eliminated.

Conflict may thus make a person reexamine himself, his goal, and the means of attaining that goal.

---

2. M. E. Wright, "The influence of frustration upon the social relations of young children," *Character and Personality,* 12 (1943-1944), 111-122.

3. Haney, *op. cit.,* pp. 124-125.

4. D. Krech, R. S. Crutchfield, and N. Livson, *Elements of Psychology,* New York, Knopf, 1969, p. 757.

Another way of considering internal conflict is in terms of cognitive dissonance. In Chapter 2 [Patton-Giffin text] we referred to Festinger's theory, which postulates that, when a person engages in behavior inconsistent with his attitudes or beliefs, he will feel the discomfort of cognitive dissonance, which serves to motivate him to resolve it. This dissonance, or inconsistency, forces a person to make an attitudinal adjustment.

One source of internal conflict is an individual's affiliations with divergent reference groups in which different needs are fulfilled. A teenager, for example, may feel conflict between peer pressures and family expectations on such issues as dating behavior, drinking, and the use of drugs. Speaking of another level, Kiesler and Kiesler cite research on the conflicting role demands of school superintendents:[5]

> They found that the school superintendent has three roles to play: the role of school superintendent from the point of view of the school board; the role of school superintendent as regarded by the parents; and his role *vis-a-vis* the teachers within the school system. The school board wants the school run smoothly and as inexpensively as possible. The parents would like to see their children in smaller classes, but not at the expense of a tax increase. The teachers want higher salaries. At particular times of the year these three roles become especially divergent, and the conflict thus produced for the school superintendent becomes torturous indeed.

These internal conflicts are often the result of group influences and may, conversely, affect the progress of the group.

Conflict Within the Group

There are numerous sources of internal group conflict. Any perceived changes, ranging from leadership roles to group structure to activities to new membership, may provoke conflict. The conflicts are inevitable; the nature of the group will determine if they are handled openly or reduced to the level of the hidden agenda (discussed in Chapter 3 [Patton-Giffin text]). Even the changing nature of a group's membership may introduce conflict. In a teenage gang the member's interests and maturity levels may change at different rates of time.

Kemp calls for a "creative handling of conflict" and proposes a "fresh, incisive look at conflict" by consideration of the following points:[6]

---

5. C. A. Kiesler and S. B. Kiesler, *Conformity,* Reading, Mass., Addison-Wesley, 1970, pp. 37-38. From research reported in N. Gross, A. W. McEachern, and W. S. Mason, "Role conflict and its resolution," in *Readings in Social Psychology* (E. E. Maccoby, T. M. Newcomb, and E. L. Hartley, Eds.), New York, Holt, Rinehart & Winston, 1958, pp. 447-458.

6. C. G. Kemp,, "The creative handling of conflict," *Perspectives on the Group Process,* Boston, Houghton Mifflin, 1970, p. 262.

1. Productive conflict arises because group members are so bound together that their actions affect one another; that is, they have accepted the fact that they have become interdependent.
2. Conflict occurs because people care. Often group members who have great creative differences share a very deep relationship. Because they care about one another and the group as a whole, they are willing to make, if necessary, a costly emotional response to help improve a situation.
3. Each member has different needs and values. These differences become evident and produce conflict unless the members repress their individual differences and assign the direction of the group to an authority figure. Sometimes, rather than accept the fact of their creative differences, members allow themselves to be taken over by such a leader.

Conflict situations in groups may be classed as two types, *distributive* and *integrative*.[7] A distributive situation is one in which a person can win only at someone else's expense, such as in a poker game. An integrative situation is one in which the members of the group integrate their resources toward a common task, as in working together on a jigsaw puzzle. Research teams work in an integrative manner, whereas a buying and selling transaction involves distributive bargaining.

The National Training Laboratories have identified two opposite modes of behavior, Approach A and Approach B. Approach A is associated with behavior in distributive social situations; Approach B, with behavior in integrative.[8]

Approach A	*Approach B*
1. Behavior is purposeful in that one's own goals are pursued.	1. Behavior is purposeful in that goals held in common are pursued.
2. Secrecy.	2. Openness.
3. Accurate personal understanding of own needs, but these are publicly disguised or misrepresented: Don't let them know what you really want most, so that they won't know how much you are really willing to give up to get it.	3. Accurate personal understanding of own needs and accurate representation of them.
4. Unpredictable, mixed strategies, utilizing the element of surprise.	4. Predictable; while flexible behavior is appropriate, it is not designed to take the other party by surprise.
5. Threats and bluffs.	5. Threats or bluffs are not used.

---

7. This analysis was made in the *1968 Reading Book* of the National Training Laboratories Institute of Applied Behavioral Sciences.
8. Ibid.

6. Search behavior is devoted to finding ways of appearing to become committed to a position; logical, nonrational, and irrational arguments alike may serve this purpose.

7. Success is often enhanced (where teams, committees, or organizations are involved on each side) by forming a bad stereotype of the other, by ignoring the other's logic, by increasing the level of hostility. These tend to strengthen ingroup loyalty and convince others that you mean business.

8. A pathological extreme occurs when one assumes that everything that prevents the other from reaching *his* goal also must facilitate one's own movement toward *his* goal; thus, one would state his own goals as being the negation of others' achievement.

9. Etc.

6. Search behavior is devoted to finding solutions to problems and utilizing logical and innovative processes.

7. Success demands that stereotypes be dropped, that ideas be given consideration on their merit regardless of sources, and that hostility not be induced deliberately. In fact, positive feelings about others are both a cause and an effect of other aspects of Approach B.

8. A pathological extreme occurs when one will assume that whatever is good for others and the group is necessarily good for oneself. Cannot distinguish own identity from group or other person's identity. Will not take responsibility for own self.

9. Etc.

Engaging in the distributive approach causes problems for the task-oriented group. Among the problems are:[9]

1. Development of we-they and superiority-inferiority complexes within the group. The group may splinter if the distributive behavior is sustained.

2. In groups with internal competitive pressure individuals tend to overestimate their contributions and unrealistically downgrade the work of others.

3. Under competitive pressures group members think they understand one another when in fact they do not. These distortions in perception cause areas of agreement to go unrecognized.

Labor-management negotiations characteristically utilize this distributive approach in a between-groups pattern of interaction. Labor wins at management's expense. An integrative approach would attempt to discover ways that both parties might gain. We shall discuss this alternative in greater detail when we suggest alternative modes of handling conflict.

Conflict of the integrative type can have positive benefits for the group. Only when members feel comfortable in the group can conflict safely emerge. Basic problems cannot usually be resolved without some

---

9. These consequences and others are reported in R. R. Blake and J. S. Mouton, "Reactions to intergroup competition under win-lose conditions," *Management Science,* July, 1961.

conflict due to the different values, feelings, and perceptions of the members. That the conflict center on issues rather than on personalities and exaggerations requires an acceptance of individual differences and some degree of mutual trust.

Group conflict may either bring out the best in a group or literally tear the group apart. The over-all social structure of the group may determine which occurs. As sociologist Lewis Coser states: [10]

> In loosely structured groups and open societies, conflict, which aims at a resolution of tension between antagonists, is likely to have stabilizing and integrative functions for the relationship. By permitting immediate and direct expression of rival claims, such social systems are able to readjust their structures by eliminating the sources of dissatisfaction. The multiple conflicts which they experience may serve to eliminate the causes for dissociation and to re-establish unity. These systems avail themselves, through the toleration and institutionalization of conflict, of an important stabilizing mechanism.
>
> In addition, conflict within a group frequently helps to revitalize existent norms; or it contributes to the emergence of new norms. In this sense, social conflict is a mechanism for adjustment of norms adequate to new conditions.

Although conflict is inevitable in groups, it may be either functional or disruptive.

Conflict Among Groups

Whether or not we are aware of it, our future goals and fortunes are greatly affected by the states of harmony or conflict between groups. Problems of intergroup relations include conflict between political groups, religious groups, economic groups, labor and management, and young and old, and across international boundaries.

The classic study of conflicts between groups was made by Sherif and Sherif.[11] They studied groups of young boys eleven and twelve years old at camp sites under experimentally manipulated conditions. The boys were all selected from stable, white, Protestant families from the middle socioeconomic level; they were well adjusted and had no past records of behavioral problems. No cultural, physical or economic differences were present in the sample. In a 1954 "robbers' cave" experiment two groups were formed separately and kept unaware of the presence of the other until competitive tournament games in various sports between the two groups were arranged. A series of mutually frustrating events arose naturally in the course of the tournament events. Stealing and burning of the oppo-

10. L. Coser, *The Functions of Social Conflict,* New York, Free Press, 1964, p. 154.
11. M. Sherif and C. W. Sherif, *Social Psychology,* New York, Harper & Row, 1969, pp. 239, 221-266.

2006 Ed.
5:00

nent's flag, scuffling cabin raids, and name calling resulted. The experimenters tested and validated the following hypotheses:[12]

1. *When members of two groups come into contact with one another in a series of activities that embody goals which each group urgently desires but which can be attained by one group only at the expense of the other competitive activity toward the goal changes with time into hostility between the groups and among their members.* Prizes were offered in the sports contests, and cumulative scores were kept for the various events, which included baseball, football, a tug of war, a treasure hunt and tent pitching. Good sportsmanship deteriorated as the events progressed, and the cheer "2-4-6-8, who do we appreciate?" changed to "2-4-6-8, who do we apprecihate?" Accusations of "dirty players" and "cheaters" abounded and led to the overt physical attacks.

2. *In the course of such competitive interaction toward a goal available only to one group, unfavorable attitudes and images (stereotypes) of the out-group come into use and are standardized, placing the out-group at a definite social distance from the in-group.* Members of each group were asked to rate their fellow members and the opponents in the other group during the height of friction. Adjectives applied to the in-group were: "brave, tough, and friendly," while the out-group were "sneaky, smart alecks, stinkers." The ratings were assigned on the basis of "all of them are . . ." to "none of them are . . ."

3. *Conflict between two groups tends to produce an increase in solidarity within the groups.* Pride and group solidarity increased as the conflict and hostility grew. After the tournament the sociometric choices became exclusively restricted to one's group, and members of other groups were rejected. At a beach outing, each group stuck together despite many distractions.

4. *The heightened solidarity and pride in the group will be reflected in an overestimation of the achievements of fellow members and in a lower estimation of the achievements of members of the out-group.* A game of bean toss was introduced, in which the goal was to collect as many of the beans scattered on the ground as possible within a limited time. A judgment was called for by exposing, with an opaque projector, the supposed collection of each individual. Actually thirty-five beans were exposed each time. The members of each group overestimated the number of beans collected by his fellow group members and made significant lower estimates of the performance of the out-group members.

5. *Relations between groups that are of consequence to the groups in question, including conflict, tend to produce changes in the organization and practices within the groups.* In one group the leadership changed hands when the leader who had emerged prior to the conflict was reluctant to take aggressive actions. In the other group a boy perceived as a low-status bully during group formation emerged as a hero during the inter-group encounters.

---

12. Ibid.

In the study it became unmistakably clear that overt differences are unnecessary for the rise of intergroup hostility, social distances, stereotyped images, and negative attitudes in a group of "normal" youngsters. Although physical appearance, language, and culture may serve to intensify differences, conflict itself becomes a major contributing variable. . . .

. . . .

Methods of Handling Conflict

We have repeatedly suggested that conflict, whether at the individual, the group, or the intergroup level, has a potential for both functional and disruptive consequences.

We shall now note some of the specific means of channeling conflicts into productive results.

At the individual level internal conflicts may be viewed as dissonance problems. One way of minimizing the discomfort that a person experiences when he finds himself doing something inconsistent with his attitudes is to modify those attitudes. A group of college students was tested to determine their attitudes on the three controversial issues of universal military training, dorm hours for women students, and deemphasis of collegiate athletics. Students with definite opinions were asked to debate the topic on the side opposite to their true beliefs. Half the subjects were reinforced by being told that they had won the debate, according to the votes of members of the class; the other half were told they had lost the debate. The winners underwent a significant attitude change, in the direction of the argument they had publicly supported, while the losers went in the opposite direction, intensifying their original beliefs.

Another way of minimizing discomfort is by reconciling discrepant judgments. In a group situation this approach forces an individual to look for good reasons that rationally account for the disagreement in such fashion as to allow him to accommodate both his judgment and that of the group. Thus he may decide that the question asked actually could be interpreted in quite different ways, leading to different and equally correct answers. This form of cognitive reconciliation obviously makes it easier for a person to stick to his own judgment.

Within a group conflict can best be handled through open communication based upon mutual trust. The conflict should be kept to the issue instead of becoming a personalized, polarized argument. Feelings have a place and should be communicated, but they should not become confused with the central issue. As Zaleznik and Moment state:[13]

---

13. A. Zaleznik and D. Moment, *The Dynamics of Interpersonal Behavior,* New York, Wiley, 1964, p. 178.

The optimum norm would allow free expression of feelings but would require that the expressions be treated as data and processed as is the other data related to the group task. Thus the individual may express himself, but he is forced to think twice. If he does not concern himself with how his feeling relates to what is going on in the group, he can be sure that others will do so. This does not imply prosecution or justification; it means that the group and its individual members accept responsibility for understanding and processing all the relevant data at their disposal. It also implies a model for responsible individual behavior.

Conflict may move to the hidden-agenda level and persist long after an issue has apparently been settled.

Hopefully, if group members utilize a cooperative integrative approach, a genuine integration of ideas will be found to meet the full demands of all parties in disagreement, or else a compromise may be identified, in which each receives part of what he wants. The significant variable of communication, needed for the prerequisite stage of mutual trust, will be discussed in the next chapter.

At the *intergroup* level Sherif and Sherif utilized what they called *superordinate goals* to bring the boys in the "robber's cave" experiment out of the state of conflict. The operating principle was that "if conflict develops from mutually incompatible goals, common goals should promote cooperation."[14] Camp activities were planned in such a way that desirable goals could not be achieved by the efforts of only one in-group; both groups were forced to cooperate toward the common goal. One such goal involved repairing a sabotaged water-supply system. Others included cooperatively raising money to obtain a movie that both groups wanted to see and moving a stalled food truck. All the tasks were accomplished by the cooperative efforts of the two groups.

After the boys had participated in these cooperative activities, sociometric tests were again administered. The results revealed that attitudes toward members of the out-group had clearly changed. While the friendship choices remained primarily within each in-group, the choices of out-group members as friends had increased, and there was less total rejection of out-group members. As Sherif says[15]:

> Our findings demonstrate the effectiveness of a series of super-ordinate goals in the reduction of intergroup conflict hostility, and their by-products. They also have implications for other measures proposed for reducing intergroup tensions.
> It is true that lines of communication between groups must be opened before prevailing hostility can be reduced. But, if contact

---

14. Sherif and Sherif, *op. cit.* p. 266.

15. M. Sherif, "Superordinate goals in the reduction of intergroup conflicts," *Am. J. of Sociol.,* 63 (1958), 356.

between hostile groups takes place without superordinate goals, the communication channels serve as media for further accusations and recriminations. When contact situations involve superordinate goals, communication is utilized in the direction of reducing conflict in order to attain the common goals.

The identification and utilization of superordinate goals seem to have genuine effectiveness in reducing intergroup conflict.

Summary

Although conflict is inevitable, it may be positive in some instances negative in others, and irrelevant in still others.

Individuals can resolve their internal conflicts by resorting to aggression, withdrawal, and ego-defense mechanisms or by changing their attitudes so as to bring about internal consistency or by accepting differences as they exist.

Within a group a distributive approach to conflict problems leads to distrust and competition, whereas an integrative approach promotes openness and cooperaton.

Between groups sustained conflict over mutually desired goals attainable to only one group provokes hostile and aggressive acts, social distance, negative stereotypes, and also internal group solidarity and changed relationships. Establishing superordinate goals provides a framework of cooperation among the rival groups and effectively reduces the negative conflict.

Cooperativeness leads to coordination of effort, productivity, good human relations, and other positive benefits. Competitiveness leads to distrust and insecurity. The implications for all groups are readily apparent.

Defensive Communication

Jack R. Gibb

One way to understand communication is to view it as a people process rather than as a language process. If one is to make fundamental improvement in communication, he must make changes in interpersonal relationships. One possible type of alteration—and the one with which this paper is concerned—is that of reducing the degree of defensiveness.

Definition and Significance

Defensive behavior is defined as that behavior which occurs when an individual perceives threat or anticipates threat in the group. The person who behaves defensively, even though he also gives some attention to the common task, devotes an appreciable portion of his energy to defending himself. Besides talking about the topic, he thinks about how he appears to others, how he may be seen more favorably, how he may win, dominate, impress, or escape punishment, and/or how he may avoid or mitigate a perceived or an anticipated attack.

Such inner feelings and outward acts tend to create similarly defensive postures in others; and, if unchecked, the ensuing circular response becomes increasingly destructive. Defensive behavior, in short, engenders defensive listening, and this in turn produces postural, facial, and verbal cues which raise the defense level of the original communicator.

Defense arousal prevents the listener from concentrating upon the message. Not only do defensive communicators send off multiple value, motive, and affect cues, but also defensive recipients distort what they receive. As a person becomes more and more defensive, he becomes less and less able to perceive accurately the motives, the values, and the emotions of the sender. The writer's analyses of tape recorded discussions revealed that increases in defensive behavior were correlated positively with losses in efficiency in communication.[1] Specifically, distortions became greater when defensive states existed in the groups.

Reprinted with permission from *Journal Of Communication*, Vol. XI, No. 3 (September, 1961), pp. 141-148.

1. J. R. Gibb, "Defense Level and Influence Potential in Small Groups," in L. Petrullo and B. M. Bass, eds., *Leadership and Interpersonal Behavior* (New York: Holt, Rinehart and Winston, Inc., 1961), pp. 66–81.

The converse, moreover, also is true. The more "supportive" or defense reductive the climate the less the receiver reads into the communication distorted loadings which arise from projections of his own anxieties, motives, and concerns. As defenses are reduced, the receivers become better able to concentrate upon the structure, the content, and the cognitive meanings of the message.

Categories of Defensive and Supportive Communication

In working over an eight-year period with recordings of discussions occurring in varied settings, the writer developed the six pairs of defensive and supportive categories presented in Table 1. Behavior which a listener perceives as possessing any of the characteristics listed in the left-hand column arouses defensiveness, whereas that which he interprets as having any of the qualities designated as supportive reduces defensive feelings. The degree to which these reactions occur depends upon the personal level of defensiveness and upon the general climate in the group at the time.[2]

Table 1
Categories of Behavior Characteristics of Supportive
and Defensive Climates in Small Groups

Defensive Climates	Supportive Climates
1. Evaluation	1. Description
2. Control	2. Problem orientation
3. Strategy	3. Spontaneity
4. Neutrality	4. Empathy
5. Superiority	5. Equality
6. Certainty	6. Provisionalism

Evaluation and Description

Speech or other behavior which appears evaluative increases defensiveness. If by expression, manner of speech, tone of voice, or verbal content the sender seems to be evaluating or judging the listener, then the receiver goes

2. J. R. Gibb, "Sociopsychological Processes of Group Instruction," in N. B. Henry, ed., *The Dynamics of Instructional Groups* (Fifty-ninth Yearbook of the National Society for the Study of Education, Part II, 1960), pp. 115–135.

on guard. Of course, other factors may inhibit the reaction. If the listener thought that the speaker regarded him as an equal and was being open and spontaneous, for example, the evaluativeness in a message would be neutralized and perhaps not even perceived. This same principle applies equally to the other five categories of potentially defense-producing climates. The six sets are interactive.

Because our attitudes toward other persons are frequently, and often necessarily, evaluative, expressions which the defensive person will regard as nonjudgmental are hard to frame. Even the simplest question usually conveys the answer that the sender wishes or implies the response that would fit into his value system. A mother, for example, immediately following an earth tremor that shook the house, sought for her small son with the question: "Bobby, where are you?" The timid and plaintive "Mommy, I didn't do it" indicated how Bobby's chronic mild defensiveness predisposed him to react with a projection of his own guilt and in the context of his chronic assumption that questions are full of accusation.

Anyone who has attempted to train professionals to use information-seeking speech with neutral affect appreciates how difficult it is to teach a person to say even the simple "who did that?" without being seen as accusing. Speech is so frequently judgmental that there is a reality base for the defensive interpretations which are so common.

When insecure, group members are particularly likely to place blame, to see others as fitting into categories of good or bad, to make moral judgments of their colleagues, and to question the value, motive, and affect loadings of the speech which they hear. Since value loadings imply a judgment of others, a belief that the standards of the speaker differ from his own causes the listener to become defensive.

Descriptive speech, in contrast to that which is evaluative, tends to arouse a minimum of uneasiness. Speech acts which the listener perceives as genuine requests for information or as material with neutral loadings is descriptive. Specifically, presentations of feelings, events, perceptions, or processes which do not ask or imply that the receiver change behavior or attitude are minimally defense producing. The difficulty in avoiding overtone is illustrated by the problems of news reporters in writing stories about unions, communists, Negroes, and religious activities without tipping off the "party" line of the newspaper. One can often tell from the opening words in a news article which side the newspaper's editorial policy favors.

Control and Problem Orientation

Speech which is used to control the listener evokes resistance. In most of our social intercourse someone is trying to do something to someone else

—to change an attitude, to influence behavior, or to restrict the field of activity. The degree to which attempts to control produce defensiveness depends upon the openness of the effort, for a suspicion that hidden motives exist heightens resistance. For this reason attempts of nondirective therapists and progressive educators to refrain from imposing a set of values, a point of view, or a problem solution upon the receivers meet with many barriers. Since the norm is control, noncontrollers must earn the perceptions that their efforts have no hidden motives. A bombardment of persuasive "messages" in the fields of politics, education, special causes, advertising, religion, medicine, industrial relations, and guidance has bred cynical and paranoidal responses in listeners.

Implicit in all attempts to alter another person is the assumption by the change agent that the person to be altered is inadequate. That the speaker secretly views the listener as ignorant, unable to make his own decisions, uninformed, immature, unwise, or possessed of wrong or inadequate attitudes is a subconscious perception which gives the latter a valid base for defensive reactions.

Methods of control are many and varied. Legalistic insistence on detail, restrictive regulations and policies, conformity norms, and all laws are among the methods. Gestures, facial expressions, other forms of nonverbal communication, and even such simple acts as holding a door open in a particular manner are means of imposing one's will upon another and hence are potential sources of resistance.

Problem orientation, on the other hand, is the antithesis of persuasion. When the sender communicates a desire to collaborate in defining a mutual problem and in seeking its solution, he tends to create the same problem orientation in the listener; and, of greater importance, he implies that he has no predetermined solution, attitude, or method to impose. Such behavior is permissive in that it allows the receiver to set his own goals, make his own decisions, and evaluate his own progress—or to share with the sender in doing so. The exact methods of attaining permissiveness are not known, but they must involve a constellation of cues, and they certainly go beyond mere verbal assurances that the communicator has no hidden desires to exercise control.

Strategy and Spontaneity

When the sender is perceived as engaged in a stratagem involving ambiguous and multiple motivations, the receiver becomes defensive. No one wishes to be a guinea pig, a role player, or an impressed actor, and no one likes to be the victim of some hidden motivation. That which is concealed, also, may appear larger than it really is with the degree of defensiveness of the listener determining the perceived size of the suppressed element. The intense reaction of the reading audience to the material in the *Hidden Persuaders* indicates the prevalence of defensive reactions to multiple motivations behind strategy. Group members who are seen as "taking a role," as feigning emotion, as toying with their colleagues, as withholding information, or as having special sources of data are especially resented. One participant once complained that another was "using a listening technique" on him!

A large part of the adverse reaction to much of the so-called human relations training is a feeling against what are perceived as gimmicks and tricks to fool or to "involve" people, to make a person think he is making his own decision, or to make the listener feel that the sender is genuinely interested in him as a person. Particularly violent reactions occur when it appears that someone is trying to make a stratagem appear spontaneous. One person has reported a boss who incurred resentment by habitually using the gimmick of "spontaneously" looking at his watch and saying, "My gosh, look at the time—I must run to an appointment." The belief was that the boss would create less irritation by honestly asking to be excused.

Similarly, the deliberate assumption of guilelessness and natural simplicity is especially resented. Monitoring the tapes of feedback and evaluation sessions in training groups indicates the surprising extent to which members perceive the strategies of their colleagues. This perceptual clarity may be quite shocking to the strategist, who usually feels that he has cleverly hidden the motivational aura around the "gimmick."

This aversion to deceit may account for one's resistance to politicians who are suspected of behind-the-scenes planning to get his vote, to psychologists whose listening apparently is motivated by more than the manifest or content-level interest in his behavior, or to the sophisticated, smooth, or clever person whose "oneupmanship" is marked with guile. In training groups the role-flexible person frequently is resented because his changes in behavior are perceived as strategic maneuvers.

In contrast, behavior which appears to be spontaneous and free of deception is defense reductive. If the communicator is seen as having a clean id, as having uncomplicated motivations, as being straightforward and honest, and as behaving spontaneously in response to the situation, he is likely to arouse minimal defense.

Neutrality and Empathy

When neutrality in speech appears to the listener to indicate a lack of concern for his welfare, he becomes defensive. Group members usually desire to be perceived as valued persons, as individuals of special worth, and as objects of concern and affection. The clinical, detached, person-is-an-object-of-study attitude on the part of many psychologist-trainers is resented by group members. Speech with low affect that communicates little warmth or caring is in such contrast with the affect-laden speech in social situations that it sometimes communicates rejection.

Communication that conveys empathy for the feelings and respect for the worth of the listener, however, is particularly supportive and defense reductive. Reassurance results when a message indicates that the speaker identifies himself with the listener's problems, shares his feelings, and accepts his emotional reactions at face value. Abortive efforts to deny the legitimacy of the receiver's emotions by assuring the receiver that he need not feel bad, that he should not feel rejected, or that he is overly anxious, though often intended as support giving, may impress the listener as lack of acceptance. The combination of understanding and empathizing with the other person's emotions with no accompanying effort to change him apparently is supportive at a high level.

The importance of gestural behavioral cues in communicating empathy should be mentioned. Apparently spontaneous facial and bodily evidences of concern are often interpreted as especially valid evidence of deep-level acceptance.

Superiority and Equality

When a person communicates to another that he feels superior in position, power, wealth, intellectual ability, physical characteristics, or other ways, he arouses defensiveness. Here, as with the other sources of disturbance, whatever arouses feelings of inadequacy causes the listener to center upon the affect loading of the statement rather than upon the cognitive elements. The receiver then reacts by not hearing the message, by forgetting it, by competing with the sender, or by becoming jealous of him.

The person who is perceived as feeling superior communicates that he is not willing to enter into a shared problem-solving relationship, that he probably does not desire feedback, that he does not require help, and/or that he will be likely to try to reduce the power, the status, or the worth of the receiver.

Many ways exist for creating the atmosphere that the sender feels himself equal to the listener. Defenses are reduced when one perceives the sender as being willing to enter into participative planning with mutual trust and respect. Differences in talent, ability, worth, appearance, status, and power often exist, but the low defense communicator seems to attach little importance to these distinctions.

Certainty and Provisionalism

The effects of dogmatism in producing defensiveness are well known. Those who seem to know the answers, to require no additional data, and to regard themselves as teachers rather than as co-workers tend to put others on guard. Moreover, in the writer's experiment, listeners often perceived manifest expressions of certainty as connoting inward feelings of inferiority. They saw the dogmatic individual as needing to be right, as wanting to win an argument rather than solve a problem, and as seeing his ideas as truths to be defended. This kind of behavior often was associated with acts which others regarded as attempts to exercise control. People who were right seemed to have low tolerance for members who were "wrong"—i.e., who did not agree with the sender.

One reduces the defensiveness of the listener when he communicates that he is willing to experiment with his own behavior, attitudes, and ideas. The person who appears to be taking provisional attitudes, to be investigating issues rather than taking sides on them, to be problem solving rather than debating, and to be willing to experiment and explore tends to communicate that the listener may have some control over the shared quest or the investigation of the ideas. If a person is genuinely searching for information and data, he does not resent help or company along the way.

Conclusion

The implications of the above material for the parent, the teacher, the manager, the administrator, or the therapist are fairly obvious. Arousing defensiveness interferes with communication and thus makes it difficult—and sometimes impossible—for anyone to convey ideas clearly and to move effectively toward the solution of therapeutic, educational, or managerial problems.

Alienation from Interaction

Erving Goffman

I. Introduction

When the individual in our Anglo-American society engages in a conversational encounter with others he may become spontaneously involved in it. He can become unthinkingly and impulsively immersed in the talk and carried away by it, oblivious to other things, including himself. Whether his involvement is intense and not easily disrupted, or meager and easily distracted, the topic of talk can form the main focus of his cognitive attention and the current talker can form the main focus of his visual attention. The binding and hypnotic effect of such involvement is illustrated by the fact that while thus involved the individual can simultaneously engage in other goal-directed activities (chewing gum, smoking, finding a comfortable sitting position, performing repetitive tasks, etc. yet manage such side-involvements in an abstracted, fugue-like fashion so as not to be distracted from his main focus of attention by them.

The individual, like an infant or an animal, can of course become spontaneously involved in unsociable solitary tasks. When this occurs the task takes on at once a weight and a lightness, affording the performer a firm sense of reality. As a main focus of attention talk is unique, however, for talk creates for the participant a world and a reality that has other participants in it. Joint spontaneous involvement is a *unio mystico,* a socialized trance. We must also see that a conversation has a life of its own and makes demands on its own behalf. It is a little social system with its own boundary maintaining tendencies; it is a little patch of commitment and loyalty with its own heroes[1] and its own villains.

Taking joint spontaneous involvement as a point of reference, I want to discuss how this involvement can fail to occur and the consequence of this failure. I want to consider the ways in which the individual can become alienated from a conversational encounter, the uneasiness that arises with this, and the consequence of this alienation and uneasiness upon the interaction. Since alienation can occur in regard to any imaginable talk,

From "Alienation from Interaction" by Erving Goffman in *Human Relations,* Volume 10, Number 1, pp. 47-60, 1957. Plenum Publishing Corporation, N.Y.

1. One of its heroes is the wit who can introduce references to wider, important matters in a way that is ineffably suited to the current moment of talk. Since the witticism will never again be as telling, a sacrifice has been offered up to the conversation, and respect paid to its unique reality by an act that shows how thoroughly the actor is alive to the interaction.

we may be able to learn from it something about the generic properties of spoken interaction.

II. Involvement Obligations

When individuals are in one another's immediate presence, a multitude of words, gestures, acts, and minor events become available, whether desired or not, through which one who is present can intentionally or unintentionally symbolize his character and his attitudes. In our society a system of etiquette obtains that enjoins the individual to handle these expressive events fittingly, projecting through them a proper image of himself, an appropriate respect for the others present, and a suitable regard for the setting. When the individual intentionally or unintentionally breaks a rule of etiquette, others present may mobilize themselves to restore the ceremonial order, somewhat as they do when other types of social order are transgressed.

Through the ceremonial order that is maintained by a system of etiquette, the capacity of the individual to be carried away by a talk become socialized, taking on a burden of ritual value and social function. Choice of main focus of attention, choice of side-involvements and of intensity of involvement, become hedged in with social constraints, so that some allocations of attention become socially proper and other allocations improper.

There are many occasions when the individual participant in a conversation finds that he and the others are locked together by involvement obligations with respect to it. He comes to feel it is defined as appropriate (and hence either desirable in itself or prudent) to give his main focus of attention to the talk, and to become spontaneously involved in it, while at the same time he feels that each of the other participants has the same obligation. Due to the ceremonial order in which his actions are embedded, he may find that any alternate allocation of involvement on his part will be taken as a discourtesy and cast an uncalled-for reflection upon the others, the setting, or himself. And he will find that his offense has been committed in the very presence of those who are offended by it. Those who break the rules of interaction commit their crimes in jail.

The task of becoming spontaneously involved in something, when it is a duty to oneself or others to do so, is a ticklish thing, as we all know from experience with dull chores or threatening ones. The individual's actions must happen to satisfy his involvement obligations, but in a certain sense he cannot act *in order* to satisfy these obligations, for such an effort would require him to shift his attention from the topic of conversation to the problem of being spontaneously involved in it. Here, in a component of non-rational impulsiveness—not only tolerated but actually demanded—we find an important way in which the interactional order differs from other kinds of social order.

The individual's obligation to maintain spontaneous involvement in the conversation and the difficulty of doing so place him in a delicate position. He is rescued by his co-participants, who control their own actions so that he will not be forced from appropriate involvement. But the moment he is rescued he will have to rescue someone else, and so his job as interactant is only complicated the more. Here, then, is one of the fundamental aspects of social control in conversation: the individual must not only maintain proper involvement himself but also act so as to ensure that others will maintain theirs. This is what the individual owes the others in their capacity as interactants, regardless of what is owed them in whatever other capacities they participate, and it is this obligation that tells us that, whatever social role the individual plays during a conversational encounter, he will in addition have to fill the role of interactant.

The individual will have approved and unapproved reasons for fulfilling his obligation *qua* interactant, but in all cases to do so he must be able rapidly and delicately to take the role of the others and sense the qualifications their situation ought to bring to his conduct if they are not to be brought up short by it. He must be sympathetically aware of the kinds of things in which the others present can become spontaneously and properly involved, and then attempt to modulate his expression of attitudes, feelings, and opinions according to the company.

Thus, as Adam Smith argued in his *Theory of the Moral Sentiments,* the individual must phrase his own concerns and feelings and interests in such a way as to make these maximally usable by the others as a source of appropriate involvement; and this major obligation of the individual *qua* interactant is balanced by his right to expect that others present will make some effort to stir up their sympathies and place them at his command. These two tendencies, that of the speaker to scale down his expressions and that of the listeners to scale up their interests, each in the light of the other's capacities and demands, form the bridge that people build to one another, allowing them to meet for a moment of talk in a communion of reciprocally sustained involvement. It is this spark, not the more obvious kinds of love, that lights up the world.

III. The Forms of Alienation

If we take conjoint spontaneous involvement in a topic of conversation as a point of reference, we shall find that alienation from it is common indeed. Joint involvement appears to be a fragile thing, with standard points of weakness and decay, a precarious unsteady state that is likely at any time to lead the individual into some form of alienation. Since we are dealing with obligatory involvement, forms of alienation will constitute misbehavior of a kind that can be called "misinvolvement." Some of the standard forms of alienative misinvolvement may be considered now.

1. External Preoccupation. The individual may neglect the prescribed focus of attention and give his main concern to something that is unconnected with what is being talked about at the time and even unconnected with the other persons present, at least in their capacity as fellow-participants. The object of the individual's preoccupation may be one that he ought to have ceased considering upon entering the interaction, or one that is to be appropriately considered only later in the encounter or after the encounter has terminated. The preoccupation may also take the form of furtive by-play between the individual and one or two other participants. The individual may even be preoccupied with a vague standard of work-activity, which he cannot mantain because of his obligation to participate in the interaction.

The offensiveness of the individual's preoccupation varies according to the kind of excuse the others feel he has for it. At one extreme there is proccupation that is felt to be quite voluntary, the offender giving the impression that he could easily give his attention to the conversation but is wilfully refusing to do so. At the other extreme there is "involuntary" preoccupation, a consequence of the offender's understandably deep involvement in vital matters outside the interaction.

Individuals who could excusably withdraw involvement from a conversation often remain loyal and decline to do so. Through this they show a nice respect for fellow-participants and affirm the moral rules that transform socially responsible people into people who are interactively responsible as well. It is of course through such rules, and through such reaffirming gestures, that society is made safe for the little worlds sustained in face-to-face encounters. No culture, in fact, seems to be without exemplary tales for illustrating the dignity and weight that might be given to these passing realities; everywhere we find enshrined a Drake who gallantly finishes some kind of game before going out to battle some kind of Armada, and everywhere an outlaw who is engagingly civil to those he robs and to those who later hang him for it.[2]

2. Self-consciousness. At the cost of his involvement in the prescribed focus of attention, the individual may focus his attention more than he ought upon himself—himself as someone who is faring well or badly, as someone calling forth a desirable or undesirable response from others. It is possible, of course, for the individual to dwell upon himself as a topic of

---

2. Yet different strata in the same society can be unequally concerned that members learn to project themselves into encounters; the tendency to keep conversations alive and lively may be a way in which some strata, not necessarily adjacent, are characteristically different from others.

conversation—to be self-centered in this way—and yet not to be self-conscious. Self-consciousness for the individual does not, it seems, result from his deep interest in the topic of conversation, which may happen to be himself, but rather from his giving attention to himself as an interactant at a time when he ought to be free to involve himself in the content of the conversation.

A general statement about sources of self-consciousness ought to be added. During interaction the individual is often accorded by others and by impersonal events in the situation an image and appraisal of self that is at least temporarily acceptable to him. He is then free to turn his attention to matters less close to home. When this definition of self is threatened the individual typically withdraws attention from the interaction in a hurried effort to correct for the incident that has occurred. If the incident threatens to raise his standing in the interaction, his flight into self-consciousness may be a way of rejoicing; if the incident threatens to lower his standing and damage or descredit his self-image in some way, then flight into self-consciousness may be a way of protecting the self and licking its wounds. As a source of self-consciousness, threat of loss seems more common and important than threat of gain.

Whatever the cause of self-consciousness, we are all familiar with the vacillation of action and the flusterings through which self-consciousness is expressed; we are all familiar with the phenomenon of embarrassment.

Self-consciousness can be thought of as a kind of pre-occupation with matters internal to the interactive social system, and as such has received more common-sense consideration than other kinds of internal preoccupation. In fact we do not have common-sense words to refer to these other kinds of improper involvement. Two forms of these I shall refer to as "interaction-consciousness" and "other-consciousness" to emphasize a similarity to self-consciousness.

3. Interaction-consciousness. A participant in talk may become consciously concerned to an improper degree with the way in which the interaction, *qua* interaction, is proceeding, instead of becoming spontaneously involved in the official topic of conversation. Since interaction-consciousness is not as famous as self-consciousness, some sources of it may be cited by way of illustration.

A common source of interaction-consciousness is related to the special responsibility that an individual may have for the interaction "going well," i.e. calling forth the proper kind of involvement from those present. Thus, at a small social gathering the hostess may be expected to join in with her guests and become spontaneously involved in the conversation they are maintaining, and yet at the same time if the occasion does not go well she, more than others, will be held responsible for the failure. In consequence, she sometimes becomes so much concerned with the social machinery of the occasion and with how the evening is going as a whole that she finds it impossible to give herself up to her own party.

Another common source of interaction-consciousness may be mentioned. Once individuals enter a conversation they are obliged to continue it until they have the kind of basis for withdrawing that will neutralize the potentially offensive implications of taking leave of others. While engaged in the interaction it will be necessary for them to have subjects at hand to talk about that fit the occasion and yet provide content enough to keep the talk going; in other words, safe supplies are needed.[3] What we call "small talk" serves this purpose. When individuals use up their small talk, they find themselves officially lodged in a state of talk but with nothing to talk about; interaction-consciousness experienced as a "painful silence" is the typical consequence.

4. Other-consciousness. During interaction, the individual may become distracted by another participant as an object of attention—exactly as in the case of self-consciousness he can become distracted by concern over himself.[4]

If the individual finds that whenever he is in the conversational presence of specific others they cause him to be overly conscious of them at the expense of the prescribed involvement in the topic of conversation, then they may acquire the reputation in his eyes of being faulty interactants, especially if he feels he is not alone in the trouble he has with them. He is then likely to impute certain characteristics to those who are thus perceived, doing so in order to explain and account for the distraction they cause him. It will be useful to our understanding of interaction to list a few of the attributes imputed in this way.

By the terms "affectation" and "insincerity" the individual tends to identify those who seem to feign through gestures what they expect him to accept as an uncontrived expressive overflow of their behavior. Affectation, as Cooley suggests, ". . . exists when the passion to influence others seems to overbalance the established character and give it an obvious twist or pose." . . . "Thus there are persons who in the simplest conversation do not seem to forget themselves, and enter frankly and disinterestedly into the subject, but are felt to be always preoccupied with the thought of the impression they are making, imagining praise or depreciation, and usually posing a little to avoid the one or gain the other."[5] Affected individuals seem chiefly concerned with controlling the evaluation an observer will

---

3. The problem of safe supplies is further considered in my "Communication Conduct in an Island Community," Unpublished Ph.D. Dissertation, Department of Sociology, University of Chicago, 1953, ch. XV.

4. Other-consciousness is briefly but explicitly considered in James Baldwin, *Social and Ethical Interpretations in Mental Development* (London, 1902), pp. 213-14.

5. Charles H. Cooley, *Human Nature and the Social Order* (Charles Scribner's Sons. New York, 1922), pp. 196, 215.

make of them, and seem partly taken in by their own pose; insincere individuals seem chiefly concerned with controlling the impression the observer will form of their attitude toward certain things or persons, especially toward him, and seem not to be taken in by their own pose. It may be added that while those who are felt to be self-conscious give the impression of being overly concerned with what will happen or has happened to them, those who are felt to be insincere or affected give the impression that they are overly concerned with what they can achieve in what is to follow and are willing to put on an act in order to achieve it. When the individual senses that others are insincere or affected he tends to feel they have taken unfair advantage of their communication position to promote their own interests; he feels that they have broken the ground rules of interaction. His hostility to their unfair play leads him to focus his attention upon them and their misdemeanor at the price of his own involvement in the conversation.

In considering the attributes imputed to those who cause another to be conscious of them, we must give importance to the factor of immodesty. On analytical grounds overmodesty should equally count as a source of other-consciousness, but, empirically, immodesty seems much the more important of the two. What the individual takes to be immodesty in others may present itself in many forms: immodest individuals may seem to praise themselves verbally; they may talk about themselves and their activity in a way that assumes greater interest in and familiarity with their personal life than the individual actually possesses; they may speak more frequently and at greater length than the individual feels is fitting; they may take a more prominent "ecological" position than he thinks they warrant, etc.

One interesting source of other-consciousness is to be found in the phenomenon of "over-involvement." During any conversation, standards are established as to how much the individual is to allow himself to be carried away by the talk, how thoroughly he is to permit himself to be caught up in it. He will be obliged to prevent himself from becoming so swollen with feelings and a readiness to act that he threatens the bounds regarding affect that have been established for him in the interaction. He will be obliged to express a margin of disinvolvement, although of course this margin will differ in extent according to the socially recognized importance of the occasion and his official role in it. When the individual does become overinvolved in the topic of conversation, and gives others the impression that he does not have a necessary measure of self-control over his feelings and actions, when, in short, the interactive world becomes too real for him, then the others are likely to be drawn from involvement in the talk to an involvement in the talker. What is one man's overeagerness will become another's alienation. In any case we are to see that over-involvement has the effect of momentarily incapacitating the individual as an interactant; others have to adjust to his state while he becomes incapable of adjusting to theirs. Interestingly enough, when the impulse of the over-involved individual has ebbed a little, he may come to sense his impropriety and become self-conscious, illustrating again the fact that the alienative effect the individual has on others is usually one he cannot escape having upon himself. Regardless of this, we must see that a readiness to become over-involved is a form of tyranny practised by children, *prima donnas,* and lords of all kinds, who momentarily put their own feelings above the moral rules that ought to have made society safe for interaction.

A final source of other-consciousness may be mentioned. If the individual is to become involved in a topic of conversation, then, as a listener, he will have to give his aural and usually his visual attention to the source of communication, that is, to the speaker, and especially to the speaker's voice and face. (This physical requirement is underlined by social rules that often define inattention to the speaker as an affront to him.) If the speaker's communication apparatus itself conveys additional information all during the time that transmission is occurring, then the listener is likely to be distracted by competing sources of stimuli, becoming over-aware of the speaker at the expense of what is being said. The sources of this distraction are well known: the speaker may be very ugly or very beautiful; he may have a speech defect such as a lisp or a stutter; he may have inadequate familiarity with the language, dialect, or jargon that the listeners expect to hear; he may have a slight facial peculiarity, such as a hare lip, twitch, crossed or wall eyes; he may have temporary communication difficulties such as a stiff neck, a hoarse voice, etc. Apparently the closer the defect is to the communication equipment upon which the listener must focus his attention, the smaller the defect need be to throw the listener off balance. (It should be added that in so far as a speaker is required to direct his attention to his listener and yet not be overly conscious of him, defects in the appearance of the listener can cause the speaker to be uneasy.) These minor defects in the apparatus of communication tend to shut off the afflicted individual from the stream of daily contacts, transforming him into a faulty interactant, either in his own eyes or in the eyes of others.

In concluding this discussion of sources of alienating distraction, I should like to state an obvious caution. When the individual senses that others are unsuitably involved, it will always be relative to the standards of his group that he will sense the others have behaved improperly. Similarly, an individual who would cause certain others to be unduly conscious of him because of his apparent insincerity, affectation, or immodesty would pass unnoticed in a subculture where conversational discipline was less strict. Hence, when members of different groups interact with one another, it is quite likely that at least one of the participants will be distracted from spontaneous involvement in the topic of conversation because of what appears to him to be unsuitable behavior on the part of the others.[6] It is to these differences in expressive customs that we ought to look first in trying to account for the improper behavior of those with whom we happen to be participating and not try, initially at least, to find some source of blame within the personalities of the offenders.

SUGGESTED READINGS

Chapter 7

Adler, Ron and Towne, Neil. *Looking Out/Looking In: Interpersonal Communication.* San Francisco: Rinehart Press/Holt, Rinehart and Winston, 1975.

Bois, J. Samuel. *The Art of Awareness.* Second edition. Dubuque: William C. Brown Company, Publishers, 1972.

Duker, Sam. *Listening: Readings.* New York: Scarecrow Press Inc., 1966.

Goldhaber, Gerald M. *Organizational Communication.* Dubuque. William C. Brown Company, Publishers, 1974.

Haney, William. *Communication and Organizational Behavior.* Third edition. Homewood, Ill.: Richard D. Irwin, Inc., 1973.

Lindauer, J. S. *Communicating in Business.* New York: Macmillan Publishing Company, 1974.

Myers, Gail E. and Myers, Michele Tolela. *The Dynamics of Human Communication.* New York: McGraw-Hill Book Company, 1973.

Phelps, Lynn and Dewine, Sue. *Interpersonal Communication Journal.* New York: West Publishing Company, 1976.

Robbins, J. G. and Jones, B. S. *Effective Communication for Today's Manager.* New York: Chain Stone Age Books, 1974.

Tubbs, S. L. and Baird, J. W. *The Open Person: Self-Disclosure and Personal Growth.* Columbus, Ohio: Charles E. Merrill, 1976.

Vandemark, Jo Ann F. and Leth, Pamela C. *Interpersonal Communication.* Menlo Park, CA: Cummings Publishing Company, 1977.

Webb, Ralph. *Interpersonal Speech Communication: Principles and Practices.* Englewood Cliffs, N. J.: Prentice-Hall, Inc., 1975.

---

6. For example, in social intercourse among traditional Shetlanders, the pronoun "I" tends to be little used; its greater use by individuals from the mainland of Great Britain, and especially its relatively frequent use by Americans, leads the Shetlander to feel that these non-Shetlandic people are immodest and gross. Shetlandic tact, it might be added, frequently prevents non-islanders from learning that their manner causes Shetlands to be uneasy.

Section 4

GROUP LEADERSHIP:
CONCEPTS AND
PERFORMANCE

One of the most intriguing human behaviors is the leadership-followership phenomenon. Who are our leaders and what makes them leaders are fascinating questions to which man has been seeking answers since the beginning of civilization. We know there were tribal leaders before recorded history, and we know history is mostly a description of those who sought power and influence and those who were influenced. Yet, we are still uncertain why and under what circumstances some of us become leaders and others remain followers. Despite the extensive literature on leaders and leadership produced by philosophers, political scientists, and psychologists, we have no universal theory of leadership and no formula for producing leaders.

Plato believed that only a selected few with superior wisdom should be leaders. St. Paul said only those appointed by God could truly lead. Machiavelli felt that those princes who had the cunning and the ability to organize knowledge and power to meet political and military challenge should be followed. Thomas Carlyle held that certain men were born with superior courage and insight which caused them to rise to leadership positions. Hegel and Marx doubted that any individuals had superior strength and influence, but rather, some men understood history and the power of events and were able to lead by making people aware of the direction and force of socioeconomic changes. John Stuart Mill saw leaders as naturally endowed great men who used their powers of persuasion to enlighten groups and their political skill to bring followers to greater achievement. William James held that leaders arose out of moments or events that brought their genius to the fore, a genius not based on personal power but on the ability to help the group resolve the problems of the moment. Elton Mayo exemplifies the contemporary "impersonal leadership" school, holding that power and wisdom reside within groups and it is the leader's function to provide effective conditions for group interaction rather than impose his stamp on the group. This obviously oversimplified description of various theories of leadership serves only to show why it has been so difficult to arrive at a theory of leadership or agree upon the qualifications for a leader.

Not only have we been unable to agree on a theory of leadership, but there are those who argue that we have reached a leadership impasse. They believe that our present desire for individual liberty and democratic rights is at odds with our traditional reliance on strong leaders. Some people would purposely avoid leadership positions because they think it means manipulating other people and limiting freedom of choice. These persons tend to associate leadership with autocracy and the kind of power-seeking which has frequently led to corruption of group goals and unnecessary intergroup conflict. Some would go so far as to say that modern education and mass communication make leadership unnecessary. As yet, however, there has been no noticeable change in leaders or leadership and apparently no successful groups without leadership. Even when some members of a group consciously avoid leader roles, others arise to fill the void. The question then becomes not one of whether there should or should not be leaders but what constitutes the most effective and desirable leadership for a given group.

Some of the confusion about leadership can be traced to our failure in the past to distinguish between "leadership" and "the leader." If nothing else, twentieth-century research into the leader-follower phenomenon has established that leadership is a function of group process rather than a series of isolated traits residing in an individual. It is clear now that there is no such thing as "a leader" apart from some particular group. We have come to realize that individuals are in groups to satisfy needs that cannot otherwise be satisfied, and they accept direction for the same reason. Therefore, leaders arise because in groups there are practical problems of ordering and maintaining. The main characteristic of a leader is that he represents a means of having the group's needs fulfilled better than other members. The leader leads because it is a means of satisfying his and the group's needs. In this frame of reference, it is impossible to describe a leader qua leader or to describe the ideal leader. We can describe leadership functions or leadership roles, and we can find which persons perform these functions. In this way it is possible to distinguish between "leadership"—the function, and "the leader"—the person who is performing that function at a given time.

A focus on leadership functions as part of group process is the basis for the selections that appear in this final section. Each piece has been chosen because it sheds some light on the leadership needs created by group behavior and the means of satisfying these needs. The prevailing concepts of group leadership are presented in Chapter 8, "Concepts," and leadership types and roles are discussed in Chapter 9, "Performance."

Chapter 8 begins with a selection from T. O. Jacobs' book on Leadership entitled "Historical Perspective." In this piece Jacobs examines leadership theories and supporting research since the turn of the century. He notes the tremendous emphasis that was placed on leader personality traits and how little this focus has been supported by experimental research. He concludes that forty years of research has failed to demonstrate that leaders possess traits which make them leaders in all situations, rather it has been shown that leadership is always relative to the situation.

The second selection is from the book, *Leadership and Organization,* by Robert Tannenbaum, Irving Weschler, and Fred Massarik. These authors are concerned with building a basic, systematic theory of leadership (which they believe is still a long way in the future), and they start by presenting a frame of reference through which we can view variables underlying leadership effectiveness. Their frame of reference approach includes a brief history of leadership concepts, a communication-oriented definition of leadership, and a discussion of the components of leadership.

William E. Halal's article from a current journal presents a theory of leadership intended to integrate existing knowledge in the field of leadership. Prominent concepts, theories, and research evidence are synthesized to form a theoretical framework comprising five models of leadership. Each model specifies the conditions of task and motivation for which a particular style of leadership is congruent, thereby resulting in leadership effectiveness.

The final selection in Chapter 8 considers the contemporary problem of young persons who reject leadership positions and who are turned off by organizations and organized groups. Looking at the problem from a management focus David Berlew suggests modes of leadership based upon the emotional needs of persons in work groups who want meaning and excitement in their group functioning.

Chapter 9, our final chapter of readings, Leadership Performance, begins with an article from a Canadian personnel management journal. In this piece, James F. Kinder focuses on leadership styles, that is, on the behavior of leaders as observed by followers. He claims that there are four "styles" when viewed from this perspective: "dominant-hostile," "dominant-warm," "submissive-hostile," and "submissive-warm" and he presents a model for understanding each style.

Johnson and Johnson in the essay that follows are concerned with effective growth-group leadership. They explain that the goals of growth groups center around self-actualization and interpersonal effectiveness, therefore leaders (or group facilitators) must have special skills which are applicable to this type of group situation. They then describe what they consider to be the eight sets of skills necessary for effective growth-group leadership.

The fourth selection in this chapter, "The Leader's Diagnostic Skill and Group Effectiveness" by Walter M. Lifton presents a very practical schema to assist group leaders in spotting problem areas in group functioning. He categorizes nine problem areas, lists the specific problems associated with each category and describes the overt behaviors indicative of such problems. With this list of observable behavior indicators at hand, the leader can readily diagnose the type of problem the group is experiencing and move to provide the help needed to overcome the problem.

What is the leader's function is the question that William Schutz addresses himself to in an excerpt from his essay, "The Ego, FIRO Theory and the Leader as Completer." He stresses the application of FIRO Theory to group behavior and derives a leadership role based upon this application. FIRO Theory "states that there are three fundamental interpersonal needs—inclusion, control, and affection—and in order for an individual (or group) to function optimally, he [the leader] must establish and maintain a satisfactory relation in all three areas, with other people or with symbols of people." This to Schutz means that leadership is the act of guiding a group to optimal development in these three areas of interpersonal need. This approach establishes the leader as *completer*. He observes which functions are not being performed optimally and enables the group to accomplish optimal functioning. Whatever is needed that the group is not doing, he must do. When the group is functioning optimally, there is no function for the leader.

We end our book of readings on small group communication with this section on leadership, not because we think that leaders are the essential factor in effective group process, but because we think that all group members must assume responsibility for the assessment and evaluation of group needs and goals. This includes a continual interest in and evaluation of the group's leadership.

Concepts

Leadership: Historical Perspective

T.O. Jacobs

Leaders and leadership have been a focus of intense interest since, thousands of years ago, men first began to wonder about the ways in which leaders differ from other people. Outstanding leaders *are* challenging objects for study. Scientists and nonscientists alike have long sought to learn the nature of the exceptional talents and skills that have led to the significant accomplishments of exceptional leaders who have emerged over the centuries.

Indeed, such accomplishment has provided a basis for defining leadership, as the process of exceptional innovation with regard either to goal directions, methods of goal achievement, or the degree of achievement itself (e.g., Galton, 1925). One of the crucial issues in early leadership theory was probably generated by just this kind of observation. Thomas Carlyle, in 1910, postulated the so-called "great man theory," the essence of which was that the progress the world has experienced is a product of the individual achievements of great men who lived during the period in which advances occurred.

However, every theory seems to be capable of generating an antithetical position. While psychology might be defined as the study of the

From T. O. Jacobs, *Leadership And Exchange In Formal Organizations.* Alexandria, Va. 1971. Human Resources Research.

individual within society, sociology might be defined as the study of society itself. A sociological theory, in opposition to the great man theory, was that of "cultural determinism," which advocated the position that great men were not so much unique individuals in themselves, but rather were products of forces existing during the period in which they lived; had one "great man" not appeared, another "great man" *would* have. In this view, it is not that individuals appear who have the capability to effect great and sweeping changes, but rather that societal forces have reached such a magnitude that change must occur. Given such forces, an individual who can verbalize them and mobilize support for reasonable change will be accorded leader status. Clearly, the requirements for leadership would be different, depending upon which view is accepted—that of Carlyle or that of cultural determinism.

Of course, neither of these two conflicting positions could be demonstrated as scientifically "correct." Basically, they were conclusions drawn from observations, and both became obsolete as knowledge accumulated about the social dynamics of leadership processes. Nevertheless, the research on leadership has shown a continuing tendency for attention to be focused either on the individual in a leadership position, or on the structure of the social group in which the leader finds himself. Only quite recently have these two apparently conflicting emphases begun to seem compatible. The purpose of this introductory chapter is to outline some of the trends in leadership research and theory that have led to a blending of these opposite poles of thought.

During the last 40 years there have been several lines of development which, in some respects, seem to have proceeded almost independently of one another. Especially during the decade prior to World War II, there was great interest in the personality traits of leaders. Individuals who had achieved leadership status in one context or another were administered psychological tests of various sorts to measure personality characteristics that might be uniquely associated with their status. At nearly the same time, however, there were beginning movements in industrial psychology by Mayo (1933) and his associates that were concerned with the productivity of industrial work groups, and the impact of the organization on the work group's motivation to achieve high levels of productivity.

These approaches constitute foci of attention on (a) the personality of the leader and (b) the group itself—respective approaches that were conceptually almost in opposition to one another in that each very nearly excluded the other's subject as an element of importance. Even so, there was also a beginning awareness of interactive aspects of the leader-follower relationship, including such notions as the nearly universal emergence of structure in the small group, and power (or authority) relationships in such group structures. Smith and Krueger (1933) note that "In one sense at least it may be said that leadership is effective in face-to-face situations in proportion to the degree of control which the leader has over the follower group. That degree of control is due in part to the security and permanence of the leader in his position."

In this statement, there is implicit recognition of the need to consider group goals, the leader's bases of power, and, perhaps, the extent to which the leader's position may be supported by a larger organizational structure. As will be seen, these are all highly important elements of the total leadership equation.

One further complication in the study of leadership has been the problem of deciding who is a leader and who is not (and, perhaps, how *much* a leader each leader is). On the surface it appears absurd that this should be a problem—surely, it cannot be so difficult to decide whether a person is or is not a leader. But the fact remains that different standards *have* been applied, with the result that different studies sometimes reach apparently contradictory results that may not even be relevant to one another.

For example, Cowley (1928) made a distinction between "headmen" and leaders. Leaders were thought to have programs in their groups, and to be moving toward objectives in a definite manner. "Headmen," in contrast, were simply administrators, with no program and no objective, marking time while holding office. (Obviously, in some cases this distinction would be a difficult one to make.) Cowley was considering position-holders in general, and then applying a *criterion of effectiveness* to them. The problem is that it can sometimes be extremely difficult to judge effectiveness, so there might be considerable question as to whether a given position-holder was in fact a leader, or just a "headman."

Focus on Leader Personality Traits

During the two decades before World War II, it was natural that extensive effort was devoted to discovering the specific personal characteristics that distinguished leaders from non-leaders. This development was perhaps a consequence of the earlier attention given to the study of great men as leaders and perhaps, too, a result of the rapid growth of personality theory. This latter emphasis was evident in the proliferation of "personality" tests, which were supposedly effective in measuring various dimensions (or traits) of personality.

From the studies they reviewed, Smith and Krueger (1933) listed a number of traits that had been found to characterize leaders. These traits include the following:

Personality Traits	*Social Traits*
Knowledge	Tact
Abundance of Physical and	Sympathy
Nervous Energy	Faith in Others and Self
Enthusiasm	Patience
Originality	Prestige
Initiative	Ascendance-Submission
Imagination	*Physical Characteristics*
Purpose	Some advantage as to height,
Persistence	weight, and physical
Speed of Decision	attractiveness

Smith and Krueger noted, however, that some of these traits had ". . . been determined by statistical devices, others by mere observation of leaders in action, and still others by experimental procedure." They consequently included as one of 12 suggested areas for further work the following:

> One of the most suggestive attacks in the field of leadership would consist in selecting those who are considered leaders in any situation and in administering to them a battery of psychological tests in an effort to determine whether or not they actually are leaders and, if so, what characteristics they possess. Tests are available which are designed to measure such traits as the following: stability, sociability, ascendance-submission, extroversion-introversion, mental ability, academic standing, speed of decision, strength of will, self-confidence, and finality of judgment. A composite picture from the results of such an array of tests should give a rather definite idea as to whether an individual possesses the traits which may be considered characteristic of a leader in the situation studied.

As if in response to this injunction, studies of "leadership traits" became almost commonplace. Their objectives ranged from selection of business executves to identification of military leaders for hazardous combat duty. The logical assumption underlying this kind of approach was that there were leader characteristics which could be identified, and would be successful in separating leaders from non-leaders.

The Situation and Leadership

Unfortunately, the massive amount of effort invested in leadership-trait research during this period and indeed continuing until the present, has yielded very little in the way of generally useful results. Bird (1940) compared the results of 20 studies, finding that 79 traits had been investigated in the body of studies as a whole, with surprisingly little overlap from study to study.

Subsequent to World War II, Stogdill (1948) surveyed a total of 124 studies conducted to determine the traits of leaders. . . .

While the findings regarding traits shown in the listing appear convincing, comparison of these traits with those summarized earlier shows little similarity. A possible explanation for this lack of comparability is simply that the language being used may not be precise enough to cause the same basic trait always to be named by the same word. However, this explanation creates its own problems since, if trait names are this imprecise, it is difficult to see how the underlying concepts could have any substantial value for either selecting or training leaders.

In a summary discussion, Stogdill suggested that the personal factors that had been found associated with leadership could probably be categorized under five general headings: (a) capacity, (b) achievement, (c) responsibility, (d) participation, (e) status. These findings, to him, were not surprising. Within his frame of reference, a leader was a group member who served as an important motive force in producing group movement toward the attainment of group objectives. Thus, these factors were descriptive of group members who had special competence in producing movement toward the attainment of goals.

However, Stogdill listed yet another factor which needed to be considered, *the situation.* While there *had* been agreement among many studies as to specific traits that had been either positively or negatively associated with leadership, examination of the list [of traits] shows some surprising contradictions. The only reasonable explanation is that in these few cases, the demands of the situation itself were sufficiently different from the ordinary that "different from ordinary" requirements existed for the would-be leader.

Thus, the results of his survey, on the surface, seemed to support the theory that leaders do have at least some unique measurable traits. However, examination of *the extent to which these traits differed from situation to situation,* depending on particular situational demands, forced Stogdill to conclude that it may be more fruitful to consider leadership as *a relationship that exists between persons in a social situation,* rather than as a singular quality of the individual who serves as the leader. "A person does not become a leader by virtue of the possession of some combination of traits, but the pattern of personal characteristics of the leader must bear some relevant relationship to the characteristics, activities, and goals of the followers. Thus, leadership must be conceived in terms of the interaction of variables which are constant flux and change." (Stogdill, 1948, p. 64)

This is a very important conclusion. To consider its full impact, it is first necessary to consider what the implications would have been, had it been found that there were unique, measurable qualities, or traits, that leaders did have which others did not have. This would have implied that leaders either were *born* uniquely different, or had received a unique background of experience that made them successful in doing something that others could not do. Further, for a trait theory of leadership to hold true, it would have been necessary to find that leaders in one situation were leaders in other situations as well. (This is in contrast to Stogdill's conclusion, that the nature of the situation in which the leader finds himself determines what characteristics are required for success.) . . .

These findings may appear unreasonable; personal association with leaders who have "magnetic personalities" tends to produce disbelief that such persons might encounter a situation in which they would not be capable of leading anyone, anywhere, at any time. However, the findings summarized in the preceding paragraphs have been found to hold true in more recent research, which also demonstrates further the impact of the group task on leader selection.

For example, a study was made of the performance of groups of Air task requiring simultaneous participation by all group members. After each task requiring simultaneous participation by all group leaders. After each trial, the researchers reconstituted the groups, which consisted of three persons each. Substantial consistency of individual leadership status over different groupings of people was found, and the tendency for individual leadership status to persist from one group to another was highly significant. In this particular situation, a person who was a leader in one group tended, very strongly, to be a leader in a second group. However, *only one type of task was used in this experiment,* which means that—in contrast to the study by Carter and Nixon—the situation changed relatively little from trial to trial.

Barnlund (1962), on the other hand, used six different types of tasks while rotating the membership of groups from one session to another. When the task changed from one trial to another, the status (leadership) scores earned by specific individuals also varied substantially from one situation to another. There was a *tendency* for a person who was leader in one group to be high in the status hierarchy in other groups as well, but this was not nearly as strong as the tendency found in the study by Rosenberg, Erlick, and Berkowitz. Thus, changing the nature of the group's *task* reduced the *generality* of leadership. Apparently, the ability of the leader at the group's task is an important variable.

Additional studies have been conducted in more recent years to determine whether more modern methods and measuring instruments can produce findings that could not have been obtained in earlier years. In one of a substantial series of studies attempting to obtain predictive relationships with Officer Effectiveness Reports, Tupes (1957) correlated various *non-personality* measures with OERs obtained after commissioning. . . . The relationships are, in the main, very low and are of virtually no practical use in predicting effectiveness based on the OER criterion.

Similar findings continue to accumulate regarding *personality* measures. For example, Lee and Burnham (1963) conducted a study of students in a two-year program leading to the MBA degree. The study was designed to assess whether items in an extensive battery of 44 variables—43 of which were selected scales from such psychological tests as the Strong Vocational Interest Blank, the Minnesota Multiphasic Personality Inventory (MMPI), the Thematic Apperception Test (TAT), and so forth —were related to the subjects being rated as desirable or undesirable to have as bosses. These evaluations were made by their classmates, and thus were a form of peer ratings.

Lee and Burnham concluded that, of all 44 variables examined, the best and only stable predictor of the number of times a student was rated by his peers as desirable to have as a boss was that student's grade point average during the two-year period. This finding was repeated with a second sample of subjects.

An additional study provides a dramatic illustration of why the traits approach to leadership lacks utility. In this study, Sanford (1950) noted that there are seemingly few general leadership traits, if any at all. As did others at approximately the same time, Sanford concluded that the findings available at that time indicated a need to specifically include in any leadership theory not only characteristics of the leader, but also characteristics of the situation, *and follower.* While the characteristics of the situation were thought to determine the necessary relationship between the leader and follower, the follower was thought to be of unique importance because it is he who observes both the leader and the situation, and whose reaction is in terms of what he perceives.

Sanford had been particularly interested in the authoritarianism of the leader, where authoritarianism is defined in a manner somewhat synonymous with being arbitrary and unyielding. He had predicted that *followers would* react negatively toward an authoritarian *leader.* A measure of authoritarianism was included in a study of leaders in a formal organization (Vroom and Mann, 1960). The subjects were supervisors in a large delivery company. Two distinct groups of subordinates were also studied. The first group consisted of drivers who, on reporting to work, were assigned trucks and routes, and given any other instructions for the day. From 30 to 50 drivers reported to any one supervisor; the nature of their work restricted interaction among drivers, and between drivers and supervisors, to a few minutes at the beginning and at the end of each day. The drivers were on an incentive plan that was tied in with how many parcels they could deliver. The second group of subordinates consisted of positioners who were responsible for taking parcels from a conveyor belt and positioning them on shelves. Six- to 12-man crews worked together and were paid on a group incentive plan. There was a great deal of interaction among the positioners and their supervisor, who worked alongside them throughout the shift.

When attitudes of drivers and positioners toward their supervisors were correlated with the supervisors' authoritarianism scores, an interesting finding emerged. Positioners, as expected, tended to dislike supervisors with higher authoritarianism scores, but drivers *preferred* more authoritarian supervisors. In both cases, the size of the correlation was such that there could be no doubt of its statistical significance; further, the difference between the drivers' reactions to their supervisors, and the positioners' reactions to *the same supervisors* was also highly significant.

To account for these findings, it is necessary to re-examine the situation from which each of the two groups of subordinates viewed the supervisor during the day, and had only a brief time with him at the beginning (and end) of each day. In contrast, positioners had continual interaction with that supervisor in a situation that permitted, and perhaps required, continuing contact throughout the day.

Clearly, *for the drivers,* the supervisor behaved effectively when he was able to provide clearcut guidance, structure, and instructions for the day's work during the very few minutes available before that day's work started. This was especially relevant because the drivers were on an incentive plan; with more time, they could deliver more parcels and earn more money. Thus, with the drivers, the authoritarian manner, if such did exist, was effective because it produced what they needed—informative, rapid orders that enabled them to proceed efficiently to their jobs.

For positioners, on the other hand, continuing contact throughout the day could hardly be coldly efficient and directly to the point without eventually being perceived as just that. Further, since positioners were paid on a *group* incentive plan, they probably needed a supervisor who could help resolve intragroup tensions and facilitate group interaction that would aid goal attainment. They wanted, but did not perceive an opportunity for, involvement in group decision making, a supervisor with sensitivity to their needs and feelings, and help with group problems. It is not surprising that the positioners reacted negatively to the more authoritarian supervisor.

It is clear from this study that the same personality characteristic contributed positively to the effectiveness of the supervisor under one set of conditions (nature of task demands on the group, structure of working group, extent of intragroup cooperation required, and degree of contact with the supervisor, to mention only a few probable factors) and negatively under a different set. The fact that it was possible to compare reactions to the *same* supervisors under different conditions demonstrates conclusively the impact of situational factors on leader effectiveness, and illustrates why a focus on the *personality* of the leader alone is inadequate.

If further verification of this conclusion is needed, a review by Mann (1959) of more recent studies related seven personality dimensions (identified by factor analysis) to six measures of individual performance (e.g., leadership). While significant relationships were found, in no case was the median correlation between an aspect of personality and performance higher than .25, and most were closer to .15. The failure to find strong relationships confirms the fact that while personality is a significant variable in determining individual behavior and status in small groups, there must be other considerably more potent influences.

In summary, the research of well over 40 years has failed to demonstrate unique leadership qualities that are invariant from situation to situation. A leader with certain traits may be effective in one situation and ineffective in another. Further, leaders may be effective in the same situation with different combinations of traits.

This general set of conclusions provides the point of departure for the present volume for, as Gibb (1954) noted, ". . . leadership is always relative to the situation." It is difficult to conceive of a stable group that does not have objectives or goals that are mutually shared by the group's members. The situation impacts on leadership because the nature of these goals and the group member activities necessary to achieve them will determine which member has the *best combination* of skills and abilities to aid in their achievement.

In later sections, [Jacobs text], numerous studies will be cited that demonstrate this point. The conclusion will be reached that the success of any individual in a group leadership role will depend on the perception by the group's members that he has contributed uniquely toward goal attainment, and that *it is to the advantage of the group* for the individual to retain his leadership role. In simplest terms, the effective leader has functional utility for his group; he makes a significant contribution to it and, *in exchange,* is repaid as the group accords him the status and esteem of accepted leadership.

Leadership: A Frame of Reference*

Robert Tannenbaum, Irving R. Wechsler and Fred Massarik

Introduction

The word *leadership* has been widely used. Political orators, business executives, social workers, and scholars employ it in speech and writing. Yet, there is widespread disagreement as to its meaning. Among social scientists, the theoretical formulations of the leadership concept have continued to shift, focusing first upon one aspect and then upon another. Much still needs to be done to develop a basic, systematic theory. The time seems ripe for attempting a careful statement of a frame of reference which may serve to make available research more meaningful, and which may guide future research and practice.[1] Specifically, such a frame of reference can perform the useful function of pointing to the variables which need to be measured. It can help us to state hypotheses concerning the key variables underlying leadership effectiveness. It can also provide meaningful objectives for the development of more adequate leaders.

A Brief Historical View

The history of the "leadership" concept highlights the shifting focus in theoretical orientation. Early leadership research focused on the *leader* himself, to the virtual exclusion of other variables. It was assumed that leadership effectiveness could be explained by isolating psychological and physical characteristics, or traits, which were presumed to differentiate the leader from other members of his group. Studies guided by this assumption generally proved none too fruitful. Almost without exception universal traits proved elusive, and there was little agreement as to the most useful traits. Gouldner reviews some of the empirical and conservatively interpreted evidence relating to "universal traits," such as intelligence and psychosexual appeal. However, he concludes: "At this time there is no reliable evidence concerning the

* This chapter is a slightly modified version of an article under the same title by Robert Tannenbaum and Fred Massarik, *Management Science*, vol. 4, no. 1, pp. 1–19, October, 1957.
1. The evolution of the frame of reference proposed in this chapter cannot be attributed to any one individual; rather, most persons who have been members of the Human Relations Research Group, Institute of Industrial Relations and School of Business Administration, UCLA, during the past few years have played a significant role in its development. These persons, in addition to the present authors, are Paula Brown, Raymond Ezekiel, Arnold Gebel, Murray Kahane, Verne Kallejian, Gertrude Peterson, Clovis and Pat Shepherd, Eugene Talbot, and Irving R. Weschler.

existence of universal leadership traits."[2] It does not now seem surprising that this approach proved rather sterile. Leaders do not function in isolation. They must deal with followers within a cultural, social, and physical context.

With the fall from grace of the trait approach, the emphasis swung away from the leader as an entity complete unto himself. Instead, the *situationist* approach came to the fore. The situationists do not necessarily abandon the search for significant leader characteristics, but they attempt to look for them in situations containing common elements. Stogdill, after examining a large number of leadership studies aimed at isolating the traits of effective leaders, comes to the following conclusion: "The qualities, characteristics and skills required in a leader are determined to a large extent by the demands of the situation in which he is to function as a leader."[3]

More recently the *follower* has been systematically considered as a major variable in leadership research. This approach focuses on personal needs, assuming that the most effective leader is the one who most nearly satisfies the needs of his followers.[4]

There have been many attempts to assess recent developments in leadership theory. The trait approach, the situationist approach, and the follower-oriented approach have variously been discussed and evaluated by a number of authors including Stogdill, Jenkins, Gouldner, and Sanford.[5] On the basis of their work, it has become increasingly clear that, in the words of Sanford,[6]

> It now looks as if any comprehensive theory of leadership will have to find a way of dealing, in terms of one consistent set of rubrics, with the three delineable facets of the leadership phenomenon:
>
> 1. the leader and his psychological attributes
> 2. the follower with his problems, attitudes and needs, and
> 3. the group situation in which followers and leaders relate with one another.
>
> To concentrate on any one of these facets of the problem represents oversimplification of an intricate phenomenon.

Consequently, the frame of reference which we present is an attempt to take into account these three facets.

---

2. Alvin W. Gouldner (ed.): *Studies in Leadership* (New York: Harper & Brothers, 1950), pp. 31–35, especially p. 34.

3. See Ralph M. Stogdill, "Personal Factors Associated with Leadership: A Survey of the Literature," *Journal of Psychology,* vol. 25, p. 63, January, 1948.

4. For example, see Fillmore H. Sanford, *Authoritarianism and Leadership* (Philadelphia: Institute for Research in Human Relations, 1950), chap. 1.

5. See Stogdill, *Leadership;* Gouldner, *Leadership* (Introduction); William D. Jenkins, "A Review of Leadership Studies with Particular Reference to Military Problems," *Psychological Bulletin,* vol. 44, pp. 54–79, January, 1947; Fillmore H. Sanford, "Research in Military Leadership," in his *Current Trends: Psychology in the World Emergency* (Pittsburgh: University of Pittsburgh Press, 1952), pp. 45–59.

6. Sanford, "Research in Military Leadership," p. 60.

A Basic Definition of Leadership

We define leadership as *interpersonal influence, exercised in situation and directed, through the communication process, toward the attainment of a specified goal or goals.*[7] Leadership always involves attempts on the part of a *leader* (influencer) to affect (influence) the behavior of a *follower* (influencee) or followers in *situation.*

This definition has the virtue of generality. It does not limit the leadership concept to formally appointed functionaries, or to individuals whose influence potential rests upon the voluntary consent of others. Rather, it is applicable to *all* interpersonal relationships in which influence attempts are involved. Relationships as apparently diverse as the superior-subordinate, the staff-line, the consultant-client, the salesman-customer, the teacher-student, the counselor-counselee, the husband-wife, or the parent-child are all seen as involving leadership. Thus, our proposed frame of reference, based on the definition and given continuing substance through a flow of relevant research findings from many disciplines, can be useful in understanding a wide range of social phenomena.

One way of characterizing our definition of leadership is to say that it treats leadership as a *process* or *function* rather than as an exclusive attribute of a *prescribed role*. The subordinate often influences the superior; the customer, the salesman; and the group member, the chairman. In any given relationship, the roles of the influencer and the influencee often shift from one person to the other. Conceptually, the influence process or function is present even though the specific individuals taking the roles of influencer and influencee may vary. Thus, the leader role is one which is rarely taken continuously by one individual, even under specific conditions with the same persons. Instead, it is one that is taken at one time or another by each individual.

One criticism of our definition is that it unrealistically focuses on what appears to be a two-person relationship to the exclusion of group phenomena. For a number of reasons, we find this criticism unconvincing. First, the influencee at any given time may be more than one individual; an entire group may be considered to be the "follower." Second, since the leader role is not

---

7. Essentially, our definition subsumes definitions 1B, 1C, and 1E in the Ohio State "Paradigm for the Study of Leadership," all of which have to do with influence. The Ohio State definitions follow.

"1B. (The leader is the individual who exercises positive influence acts upon others.)

"1C. (The leader is the) individual who exercises more, or more important, positive influence acts than any other member in the group.

"1E. (The leader is the) individual who exercises most influence in goal-setting and goal-achievement."

See Richard T. Morris and Melvin Seeman, "The Problem of Leadership: An Interdisciplinary Approach," *American Journal of Sociology*, vol. 56, no. 2, p. 151, September, 1950. Reasons for our use of *situation* rather than *a situation* are presented on page 26.

restricted to a formally prescribed person, the notion of shared leadership is consistent with our view. Finally, the presence of other persons—with their values, beliefs, and customary modes of behavior—in the context of any given (and often momentary) interpersonal relationship represents a complex of variables which we take into account as a part of the situation. Our focus is on a relationship which is often transitory and always affected by situational contexts.

The Components of Leadership

Having made these general observations about the definition, we will now discuss in greater detail some considerations that arise in connection with its major components.

Interpersonal Influence

The essence of leadership is interpersonal influence, involving the influencer in an attempt to affect the behavior of the influencee through communication. We use the word *attempt* advisedly, in order to draw a distinction between influence efforts and influence effects.

To many, an act of leadership has occurred only if specified goals have been achieved. Under this interpretation, whether or not an individual may be called a leader in a given influence instance depends upon whether or not he is successful. If he is not, no leadership has occurred. Were we to accept this notion of leadership, we would be faced with the necessity of finding a satisfactory term for labeling unsuccessful influence efforts. It is our preference to let leadership refer to influence attempts and to treat the assessment of leadership effectiveness as a separate matter. Thus a person who attempts to influence others but is unsuccessful is still a leader in our view, although a highly ineffective one.

It is useful to draw a distinction between power and leadership. Power is potential for influence. However, even though an individual may possess considerable power in relationship to another, he may for a number of reasons (his personal values, apparent lack of necessity to do so, misjudgment) not use all of the power available to him. A leadership act reflects that portion of the power available to an individual which he chooses to employ at the time.[8]

It should be noted, in contrast to the above view, that the concept *power* frequently connotes a potential for coercion, based, for example, upon physical force, informal social pressure, law, and authority. In actuality, a given

---

8. For a relevant discussion of power, see D. Cartwright, *Toward a Social Psychology of Groups: The Concept of Power,* presidential address delivered before the Society for the Psychological Study of Social Issues, Cleveland, Ohio, Sept. 5, 1953, p. 19. Mimeographed.

leader typically has available not only these external sources providing him with power, but also power derived from such inner resources as understanding and flexibility.

Exercised in Situation

The concept *situation* is to be found in much of the recent writing on leadership. An analysis of this literature indicates that the term has been variously used to denote an activity or a particular set of activities engaged in by a group; group characteristics, including interpersonal relationships; group goals or needs; and the cultural context.[9]

It seems appropriate to us to define *situation* as including only those aspects of the objective context which, at any given moment, have an attitudinal or behavioral impact (whether consciously or unconsciously) on the individuals in the influence relationship, and to recognize that the situation of the leader and that of the follower may differ from each other in many respects. Both the phenomenological field and unconscious modes of response to external stimuli are relevant here. Stimuli having independent empirical reality, but having no impact on one or the other of the individuals, cannot be viewed as components of their respective situations. It is thus important to know, though not always easy operationally to ascertain, which stimuli external to the leader and to the follower affect each as they interact in the influence relationship.

The objective context of any influence relationship might include any or all of the following:

1. Physical phenomena (noise, light, table and chair arrangement, etc.)
2. Other individuals, including the members of the specific group of which the leader and follower are a part
3. The organization
4. The broader culture, including social norms, role prescriptions, stereotypes, etc.
5. Goals, including personal goals, group goals, and organizational goals

In reality, goals are an essential part of the concepts of group, organization, and culture. However, because of their special importance to the study of leadership, we here treat them separately.

---

9. For varying views of "situation," see Daniel Bell, " 'Screening' Leaders in a Democracy," *Commentary*, vol. 5, no. 4, pp. 368–375, April, 1948; Gouldner, *Leadership;* J. K. Hemphill, *Situational Factors in Leadership,* The Ohio State University Studies, Bureau of Educational Research Monograph no. 32 (Columbus: The Ohio State University, 1949); Jenkins, *Leadership;* Paul Pigors, *Leadership or Domination* (Boston: Houghton Mifflin Company, 1935); Sanford, *Authoritarianism and Leadership;* Melvin Seeman, "Role Conflict and Ambivalence in Leadership," *American Sociological Review*, vol. 18, pp. 373–380, August, 1953; Stogdill, *Leadership.*

An individual may influence the behavior of others by manipulating elements of their environment (situation). Thus, placing physical facilities in close proximity so that people can work near each other rather than in isolation may promote higher levels of productivity and/or job satisfaction. Since our definition limits leadership to interpersonal influence exercised through the communication process, we would not associate manipulation of situational components with leadership except in a special case—that in which such manipulation is intended by the leader as a communication symbol per se, carrying with it such implications as "this is a good place to work," "they always have our interests at heart," and the like.

The Communication Process

Our definition of leadership concerns only that interpersonal influence which is exercised through the communication process. We thus exclude, for example, the direct physical manipulation of another person, since such coercion, in its pure form, does not utilize symbolic means. On the other hand, we include threats and other coercive devices which can be imparted only by means of communication.

There are many problems involved in differentiating conceptually between the communication[10] and the leadership processes. We view communication as the sole process through which a leader, as leader, can function. The objective of a communicator, as communicator, is to transmit a message from himself to a communicatee which the latter will interpret as the former desires. The communicator's goal is to convey meanings, or ideas, without distortion.

The leader is interested in more than simply conveying ideas for their own sake. With rare exceptions, the leader's final objective is not solely to bring about attitude change. Rather, the leader makes use of communication as the medium through which he tries to affect the follower's attitudes so that the follower will be ready to move or will actually move in the direction of the specified goal. Of course, there is often a time lag between a change in the follower's attitude and the actual or potential goal movement.

An individual may communicate effectively without being an effective leader. He may desire, for example, that another individual leave the room, and he tells him so. The other individual may say, "I understand you want me to leave the room," and yet remain seated. The leader has been understood, the meaning he has transmitted presumably has been received without dis-

10. For two excellent discussions of the communication process, see Franklin Fearing, "Toward a Psychological Theory of Human Communication," *Journal of Personality*, vol. 22, pp. 71–88, September, 1953; Wendell Johnson, "The Fateful Process of Mr. A. Talking to Mr. B.," *Harvard Business Review*, vol. 31, pp. 49–56, January-February, 1953.

tortion, and effective communication has taken place. However, the leader has not succeeded in changing the follower's attitudes in such a way that this follower has been motivated to behave in accordance with the specified goal (overt behavior involving leaving the room). Thus, the leadership attempt has been ineffective.

As our later discussion will suggest, a leader, in order to be effective, needs to select those communication behaviors from his repertory which are likely to "strike the right chord" in the follower's personality make-up, resulting in changed attitudes and behavior in line with the desired goal.

Directed toward the Attainment of a Specified Goal or Goals

All leadership acts are goal-oriented. The leader uses his influence to achieve some desired (although often unconscious) goal or goals. These goals toward which individuals exert their influence fall into four categories, whose differences have considerable relevance for leadership theory. The following classification should not suggest that any given influence effort is necessarily aimed exclusively at one single goal. Often a complex of goals is involved, as when a leader brings about the attainment of organizational goals and at the same time satisfies some of his own needs.

Organizational Goals. In formal organizations, managers (as leaders) are those who are held responsible by their superiors for influencing others (subordinates) toward the attainment of organizational goals. These goals are the rationally contrived purposes of the organizational entity. Since these goals often have little or no direct motivational import to the followers, the manager's task of leadership often requires him to use other inducements which do have relevance to the need systems of the followers.

Group Goals. In small, informal, face-to-face groups the relevant goals are those which evolve through the interaction of the members of the group. They reflect (although not necessarily unanimously) "what the group wants to do." In such a situation, the leader is anyone who uses his influence to facilitate the group's attainment of its own goals. The achievement of a position of effective influence in such groups depends upon an individual's sensitivity to the group's objectives and upon his skill in bringing about their realization.

Personal Goals of the Follower. In such activities as teaching, training, counseling, therapy, and consulting, the leader often uses his influence to assist the follower in attaining his own (the follower's) personal goals.[11]

---

11. See, for example, Carl R. Rogers, *Client-centered Therapy* (Boston: Houghton Mifflin Company, 1951); and Thomas Gordon, *Group-centered Leadership* (Boston: Houghton Mifflin Company, 1955). No selflessness on the part of the leader is implied. His need satisfaction comes through remuneration for his services and/or gratification from serving others.

For example, through the establishment of an atmosphere of warmth, security, and acceptance, and through the use of facilitative methods, the leader aids another person to reach ends he has not been able to reach by himself.

Personal Goals of the Leader. Leaders also use their influence primarily to meet their own needs. At times such personal motives are at the level of consciousness and can be made explicit, but often they lie at the unconscious level where they are hidden from the leader. A teacher may think that he lectures to a class because "this is the best way to teach," without realizing that in so doing he feels more secure because the students never have a chance to "show him up." Likewise, a supervisor may harshly discipline a subordinate because "it is important to keep people in line," although a deep-felt need to express hostility receives some satisfaction through his behavior.

The issue of conscious and unconscious intent poses some knotty problems for both leadership theory and research. Should we be concerned only with objectives that can be made explicit by the leader, or should we admit unconscious motives? If we attempt the latter, by what operational methods do we define the hidden purposes? Unconscious purposes frequently do motivate the leader even though, with the exception of projective techniques, we have few methods available for operationalizing such hidden motives.

Leadership Effectiveness

Our definition of leadership focuses on influence efforts rather than upon influence effects. However, once leadership has been exercised, it becomes appropriate to raise questions about the effectiveness of such leadership.

The effectiveness of any influence attempt must always be assessed with reference to the leader's intended goal or goals. This again points up the crucial nature of the conscious-unconscious intent issue discussed above. No leadership act is inherently effective or ineffective; it might be either, depending upon the goals with reference to which it is assessed. Further, regardless of the leader's intended purpose, a given act of a leader might be seen as effective when viewed by his superior in terms of organizational goals, and at the same time be seen as ineffective when viewed by his subordinates in terms of informal-group goals.

Many operational problems are involved in assessing leadership effectiveness. The very multiplicity of coexisting goals encountered in most real-life situations makes clear-cut measurement difficult. Further, the usual goal clusters contain elements that have differential weight in the attainment of still "higher" goals in a hierarchy. An industrial organization, for example, may have many goals: high employee morale, labor peace, high productivity, contribution to community welfare, etc. These several goals may all contribute to a more inclusive goal, as culturally or organizationally espoused:

increased profits. High productivity and labor peace may be viewed as "more important" subgoals for the attainment of profits than employee morale or community welfare. Or, indeed, the opposite may be the case.

Specific leadership acts may also assist the attainment of certain goals while retarding the attainment of others. Finally, all leadership acts are in fact intertwined with numerous nonleadership acts (involving perhaps such factors as accounting procedures, production control, and technological progress), all of which may contribute to organizational success. Therefore, one often encounters real difficulty in the assessment of leadership effectiveness per se.

Our concept of leadership effectiveness is nonmoral in that it implies nothing about the goodness or badness of the goals of influence, nor for that matter, about the influence methods used to achieve these goals. The ethical evaluation involves factors different from those involved in effectiveness evaluation. For example, a gangster's effort—involving lies and coercion—to lead a teen-ager into a life of crime may prove to be a highly effective, although repugnant, leadership act.

Perhaps the most challenging question relating to leadership effectiveness is the one which focuses upon the variables most closely associated with such effectiveness. What can be said about the leadership process which may help us better to understand that which makes for leadership effectiveness?

Consistent with our definition of leadership, we feel that effectiveness in leadership is a function of the dynamic interrelationship of the personality characteristics of the leader, the personality characteristics of the follower, and the characteristics of the situation within the field of each individual.

We have already pointed out that the *situation* has a differential impact on both the leader and the follower as they interact. The *personality of the follower* (as it manifests itself in a given situation) becomes a key variable with which the leader must deal. The needs, attitudes, values, and feelings of the follower determine the kinds of stimuli produced by the leader to which the follower will respond. The *personality of the leader* (also manifesting itself in a situation) influences his range of perception of follower and situation, his judgment of what is relevant among these perceptions, and thence his sensitivity to the personality of the follower and to the situation. The leader's personality also has impact on his behavioral repertory (action flexibility) and on his skill in selecting appropriate communication behaviors.

Toward a General Theory of Leadership

William E. Halal

Introduction

Research in the field of leadership has been notably unsuccessful in producing theory which adequately explains leadership effectiveness. The early approach of identifying personal *traits* which distinguish effective leaders produced few sgnificant results (See Stogdill, 1948, for a review of this work) and attention has since then been directed toward determining modes of leader *behavior* which are most effective. In spite of the many studies which have now been conducted of leader behavior, a valid, comprehensive body of theory has failed to emerge. The wide variety of disparate theories which has been proposed is comprised of concepts which appear to be generally incomparable and causal relationships which often seem to conflict with one another.

Existing Theories of Leadership

Early theories of leadership behavior focused on discovering a single leadership style which is universally most effective. The most prominent of these include the classical, human relations, and participation theories. Considerable evidence has accumulated which indicates that all such theories are seriously limited in the applicability.

Although the *classical* form of leadership, as exemplified by the bureaucracy and scientific management models, may be effective if tasks are routine and subordinates are security oriented (March and Simon, 1958, Ch. 2; Whyte, 1969, pp. 3-9), many prominent studies have shown that classical leadership is frequently ineffective since these implicit assumptions are not often valid (Roethlisberger and Dickson, 1939; Kornhauser, 1962; Blauner, 1964). Similarly, the effectiveness of *human relations* seems to be limited to subordinates who are primarily motivated by social factors (Miles, 1965) since this style of leadership does not motivate other subordinates, such as professionals (Herzberg, 1959). It also seems that *participative* leadership may only be effective for subordinates with higher-order interests and for complex tasks; much recent evidence indicates that it is inappropriate for blue collar workers (Friedlander, 1965; Schwartz *et. al.,* 1966; Centers and Bugental, 1966), authoritarian personalities (Vroom,

From *Human Relations,* Volume 27, Number 4, pp. 405-410 and 412-414, 1974. Plenum Publishing Corporation, N.Y.
1. Now at The American University, Washington, D.C. 20016

1960), structured tasks (Fiedler, 1967), and undeveloped countries (Singh and Wherry, 1963; Whyte, 1969, Ch. 32).

As a result of this accumulation of evidence, it is now fairly well recognized that any single form of leadership may be effective for only a limited range of subordinate and task characteristics. As Strauss (1970) has effectively stated '. . . it has become increasingly clear that no one form of (leadership) is universally appropriate for all personalities, cultures, and technologies (p. 156).'

Several recent theories attempt to overcome the previous limitations by specifying frameworks comprised of various leadership styles which are each appropriate under various conditions of the leadership situation. These conditions are usually defined by some variable concerning subordinate personality or motivations, and some variable concerning tasks or technology (See Hollander, 1971, for a recent review of the situational approach).

Two main theories of this type are based upon partially substantiating evidence. Litwin and Stringer (1968) provided evidence indicating that three types of 'organizational Climate' (a variable in which leadership is most central) seem most effective for three types of tasks and motivational needs. Fiedler's contingency theory (1967) is supported by data indicating that low LPC (directive leadership) versus high LCP (permissive leadership) are most effective under three corresponding sets of conditions.

There are other frameworks which are unsubstantiated: Davis (1967, p. 480) proposes four types of leadership which are appropriate under four corresponding types of motivation; Bennis (1969) specifics two types of organization (which reflects leadership) for two types of tasks; and Etzioni (1961) distinguishes three types of authority which are most appropriate for three corresponding types of 'organizational purpose' (comparable to technology) and forms of 'member involvement' (roughly comparable to motivation).

Although these theoretical frameworks appear to be more valid than theories of a single leadership style, they remain lacking in two important respects: (1) None of these frameworks is broad enough to define the full range of leadership styles which are possible or the range of pertinent conditions under which various styles are appropriate, and (2) None of them has been shown to effectively synthesize the existing literature. The following framework which is proposed attempts to overcome these limitations.

An Integrated Theoretical Framework

The framework . . . proposed . . . defines five ideal models, each model being composed of a specific type of *leadership style, task technology,* and *subordinate motivation* which result in leadership effectiveness.

The question of effective leadership is thereby framed in a conceptual structure encompassing three independent variables which are defined as follows: leadership style is the type of working relationship between subordinates and superior; task technology is the type of work which subordinates perform; and subordinate motivation is the type of interests and values which characterize subordinate perceptions and behavior. As used here, leadership effectiveness refers to the optimum functioning of the social system which is formed by subordinates performing tasks under the direction of a superior. Subordinate job *satisfaction* and *performance* are defined as the criteria of effectiveness and, therefore, are the dependent variables of this theoretical framework. The five models are postulated to be optimum combinations of leadership style, technology, and subordinate motivation which result in maximum subordinate job satisfaction and performance.

The above framework is derived from a synthesis of salient literature concerning leadership behavior. . . .

The following descriptions of the five models of this framework briefly indicate the rationale for their validity. Since these are *ideal* models, in the Weberian sense, the concepts and the relationships they describe are, of course, idealizations rather than faithful descriptions of the more complex empirical world.

Model 1. Autocracy

'Autocracy' is considered to be the most rudimentary form of leadership characterized by the use of powerful, authoritarian methods for obtaining compliance, such as force and tradition. As a result, complete control may be exercised over all aspects of subordinate behavior. This form of leadership is expected to be appropriate only for 'primitive' forms of technology, such as warfare, hunting, and farming, which involve procuring the basic means of life at a subsistence level. Because of the exigencies of these precarious modes of existence, autocratic leadership is expected to be necessary to ensure swift and sure compliance. Persons living at such primitive levels of subsistence are postulated to have a motivational orientation toward the 'physical' needs of survival, such as obtaining food, shelter, and sex, which primarily concern the material aspects of life. Subordinates with such orientations are expected to respond best to primitive technologies and autocratic leadership because both reflect the material aspects of the world.

Model 2. Bureaucracy

'Bureaucracy' is defined as a rational, utilitarian relationship between subordinates and superior; assignments are highly specialized, the method of operation is entirely established by the superior in a rational manner, and financial rewards are offered in some proportion to performance. This form of leadership is believed to be most effective for 'routine' technologies involving repetitive operations since task specialization is then advantageous, and rigid supervisory control is required to ensure optimal performance. It is expected that subordinates who are primarily motivated by "security" needs will find the financial benefits, stability, and orderliness of this form of leadership and technology most desirable.

Model 3. Human Relations

'Human relations' emphasizes a social relationship between subordinates and superior in which social rewards and sanctions are employed to obtain compliance; the superior uses authority in socially acceptable forms, provides subordinates with emotional support, and encourages social interaction and affiliation. 'Service' forms of technology which involve providing personal service to assist others, such as the role of teachers, nurses, and receptionists, are expected to be most appropriate because human relations encourages social concern and enhances social skills. Subordinates characterized by the 'social' needs to give and receive affection and approval should respond best to human relations leadership and service technology since they will be particularly sensitive to these conditions.

Model 4. Participation

'Participation' is defined here as an egalitarian relationship in which subordinates are encouraged to share the problem-solving responsibilities of the superor. This leadership style is postulated to be most effective for 'influence' forms of technology: subordinate tasks which involve influencing or controlling the behavior of others. Typical examples would include the roles of supervisors, politicians, and salesmen. Participation is most appropriate for these tasks because the superior's sharing of responsibility with subordinates provides them access to greater knowledge, status, and authority, thus facilitating and legitimating their influence. These forms of leadership and technology are expected to be most effective for persons with 'ego' orientations, characterized by the need to enhance one's self-evaluation by obtaining prestige, recognition, and achievement. These conditions permit egoistic subordinates to elevate themselves above the ranks of others.

It should be noted that this model of leadership is applicable to leaders themselves, when acting in the role of subordinate with *their* superior. Thus, the framework also encompasses the trait approach to leadership since this model specifies ego motivations as a characteristic trait which distinguishes persons who are most effective at leadership tasks.

Model 5. Autonomy

'Autonomy' is defined as a relationsip in which no control is exercised over subordinates; the superior merely provides information and administrative support to *assist subordinates* in performing their jobs. Subordinates are free to select the tasks they will perform and the manner in which they will accomplish them. This form of leadership is postulated as most effective for 'creative' tasks involving the production of complex forms or ideas requiring great judgment or originality. Autonomy is expected to be essential for such tasks since freedom from constraints is necessary to allow individuals to develop their unique conceptions into creative works. The most compatible term of motivational orientation appears to involve 'intellectual' needs which concern abstract, conceptual ideals such as self-fulfillment, theoretical understanding, and aesthetic appreciation. This psychological orientation is expected to be most compatible with autonomous leadership and creative technologies since such persons seem to place a high value on freedom and creative activities.

A General Theory

Dimensions of Leadership, Technology, and Motivation

The above theoretical framework specifies discrete cases of the three independent variables of leadership, technology, and motivation by describing five specific states which each variable may assume. It is possible to develop a more general theory by specfying the continuous dimensions which are represented by these discrete cases. An inspection of the five models suggests the nature of these dimensions. The five forms of leadership, for example, primarily differ in the degree of control or influence exercised by the leader. A dimension of leadership could, therefore, be defined in terms of two opposing states at the ends of its range: 'directiveness' at one end and 'permissiveness' at the other. Using this approach, the previous theoretical framework may be collapsed into three continuous dimensions which are defined in Figure 1.

Thus, the variable of leadership is defined as continuously varying along a dimension of 'directiveness versus permissiveness.' The various forms of leadership of the five models represent various degrees of direction which a suprior may exercise over subordinates, or—conversely—various degrees of permission which he may allow. Model 1, autocracy, represents the case of maximum direction. Model 5, autonomy, corresponds with the opposite end of this dimension which defines maximum permission. Model 3, human relations, represent the middle of the dimension, and so on for Models 2 and 4. Similarly, the five forms of technology represent varying degrees of simplicity versus complexity', and the forms of motivation represent varying degrees of 'materialism versus idealism.'

Figure 1.

Definition of Dimensions

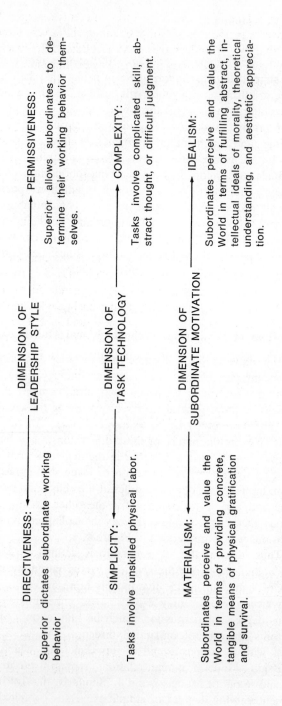

The reduction of this framework into three simple dimensions neces-sarily results in the loss of some meaning; however, these dimensions ap-pear to accurately reflect the most essential differences among the five models. Although the dimensions of leadership and technology appear to satisfactorily represent important differences in these two variables, the dimension of subordinate motivation does not seem to be so adequate. The five classes of motivational needs (which are essentially equivalent to the Maslow hierarchy) seem to defy being neatly incorporated into a single dimension; a variety of other dimensions also appear to be reasonable: 'physicalness vs. intellectualness'; 'concreteness vs. abstractness'; etc. How-ever, the dimension of materialism vs. idealism seems preferable and is, therefore, tentatively employed.

The Relativity of Leadership

Using the above dimensions of the three independent variables, the leadership effectiveness of the five models may be expressed in more gen-eral terms. The models were previously postulated to result in maximum leadership effectiveness because, within each model, the degree of permis-siveness of the leadership style, the degree of complexity of the task tech-nology, and the degree of idealism of subordinate motivations all represent equivalent points along the three dimensions. This equivalence among the three independent variables may be more conveniently defined as 'congru-ence' of the system. Thus, all five models were postulated to maximize effectiveness because they are congruent.

Conversely, to the extent that these three variables represent differing points along the three continuous dimensions, the system is 'incongruent' and effectiveness would be decreased. These relationships may be stated in precise form as follows:

Proposition 1. Leadership effectiveness is positively related to congruence among the permissiveness of leadership style, complexity of task technology, and idealism of subordinate motivation.

Proposition 1 is intended to summarize in precise form the implica-tions of the literature synthesized in the models of the theoretical frame-work: leadership effectiveness appears to be a function of leadership style *relative* to other pertinent conditions; congruence among leadership style, task technology, and subordinate motivation is postulated to cause leader-ship effectiveness because these variables are then *compatible* with one an-other. For example, the combination of more simple technology, material-istic motivations and directive leadership is congruent, and therefore com-patible, because these conditions all consistently reflect similar aspects of a *rudimentary* type of leadership situation characterized by a primitive technological environment, the predominance of physical concerns, and the use of power. Conversely, more complex technology, idealistic motivations, and permissive leadership consistently reflect aspects of more *advanced* leadership situations characterized by sophisticated technologies, intellectual concerns, and personal freedom.

Thus, identifying congruence as the cause of leadership effectiveness appears to resolve conflicts over the unique validity of various styles of leadership; the issue of leadership effectiveness is thereby reduced to more tangible questions concerning which leadership conditions of task technology and subordinate motivations prevail. These are empirical questions which are amenable to research study if the general theory is valid. . . .

The Tendency Toward Congruence

The previous proposition defines conditions under which leadership effectiveness would be decreased, resulting in low performance and low job satisfaction. However, it is reasonable to expect the subordinates and superiors are desirous of maximizing their respective goals of satisfaction and performance. Accordingly, it is likely that they would attempt to modify the social system they form to make it more congruent.

Subordinates may attempt to increase their job satisfaction by modifying the technology of their jobs and the leadership of their superior to match their motivational needs. They could, for example, change jobs, assume different tasks, change superiors, etc. to achieve increased congruence.

Similarly, the superior is likely to attempt to increase the performance of his subordinates by modifying his leadership style, and the motivations of his subordinates so they are congruent with the technology of the tasks for which he is responsible. He may change his style of leadership, replace subordinates, try to change them through training, etc.

Therefore, it seems reasonable to anticipate that a system of leadership would tend to adjust itself to a state of high congruence in order to improve its effectiveness.

Proposition 2. The permissiveness of leadership style, complexity of task technology, and idealism of subordinate motivation tend to be congruent.

The above proposition describes the state of equilibrium which social systems composed of a superior and subordinates tend to maintain. It is a condition in which leadership, technology, and motivation are congruent and, as a result, performance and satisfaction are high. Although not all systems can be expected to be so ideally stabilized—for a variety of dysfunctional reasons—most of them would have to approach this condition to a considerable degree in order to function effectively. Those systems which do not will be less likely to justify their existence (March and Simon, 1958, Chs. 3 and 4) and may perish.

Thus, when considering a large population of such systems, it is hypothesized that the three variables of leadership, technology, and motivation will be interrelated, and that aggregate satisfaction and performance will be above chance levels. These are testable hypotheses.

The Tendency Toward Evolution

The preceding discussion has been limited to the short-term dynamics of leadership systems; that is, it has only concerned the effects of congruence on leadership effectiveness at any specific time, and the tendency of such systems to adjust to a state of high congruence. There is also reason to believe that such systems evolve to higher levels of the three dimensions of leadership, technology, and motivation (or higher models of the theoretical framework) over the long-term.

At the conceptual level of the individual, for example, the Maslow (1954) theory of motivation (which is reflected in the motivation dimension of the theory presented in this paper) postulates the successive evolution of personality through five prepotent levels of characteristic needs. If there does exist such a tendency toward the evolution of motivations, proposition 2 suggests that the other two variables of leadership and technology would also evolve to higher levels in order to retain a state of congruence within the system. This prediction seems to be supported by the common observation that individuals progress to more complex jobs and are accorded greater freedom during the course of their lives.

At the societal level this phenomenon is observed in more striking clarity. Since the time of the industrial revolution, it is almost self-evident that prevailing cultural norms of leadership and authority have become increasingly permissive, and forms of technology have become more complex. There is evidence to suggest that forms of social character have also evolved to more sophisticated motivational orientations (Riesman, 1961). In this context, the five models of the theoretical framework may be interpreted to represent successive stages of industrial development. Thus, it is reasonable to postulate that there is a tendency for leadership systems to evolve over the long-term to higher forms along the three dimensions.

Proposition 3. Over the long-term, leadership style tends to become increasingly permissive, task technology increasingly complex, and subordinate motivation increasingly idealistic.

The above proposition also offers a tentative explanation of the origin and nature of some forms of social change and conflict. Over time, change is initiated when one of the three independent variables—say, the form of technology—advances to a higher level than the rest of the system. The resulting incongruence causes decreased satisfaction and performance which is experienced as conflict within the system. However, the tendency toward congruence of proposition 2 describes how the system's goal of increasing effectiveness acts as a restoring force which attempts to return the system to a state of equilibrium characterized by high congruence. The conflict within the system will be resolved, therefore, when the 'lagging' factors are advanced to regain a state of congruence.

This explanation of social change and conflict seems to be supported by recent phenomena experienced in most advanced industrial societies. Along with the recent great increases in complex forms of technology, such as television, the computer, and spaceflight, concomitant changes have been observed in the motivational characteristics of younger persons who have matured during this period. The social conflict experienced during the Sixties may be meaningfully interpreted as being a result of the 'lag' in cultural norms of leadership which have remained too directive for these advanced forms of technology and motivation. The demands of various social constituencies for greater participation in the management of educational, industrial, and governmental organizations can, therefore, be expected to persist until norms of authority have evolved to more permissive forms which are congruent with advanced societies.

Conclusion

There are several limitations to this theory which should be recognized. The particular concepts embodied within the three independent variables of leadership, technology, and motivation may not encompass other important determinants of leadership effectiveness. Other variables, such as the charismatic qualities of the leader, organizational structure, identification of subordinates with the goals of the organization, characteristic abilities and aptitudes of subordinates, cultural differences, etc., are probably also important determinants of leadership effectiveness. Also, the theory does not specify how *maximum* levels of effectiveness vary *along* the three dimensions (or among the five models). All of the above limitations obviously restrict the generality of this theory.

However, this theory appears to offer a useful means of synthesizing most of the existing concepts, theories, and research evidence concerning leadership into a more precise and complete conceptualization of the determinants of leadership effectiveness. Although there are certainly some serious limitations to this theory, it does appear to help us draw together our seemingly unrelated, contradictory, and bewildering morass of leadership literature into the most coherent form which may now be possible. In doing so, it may move us somewhat toward a more general theory which explains leadership effectiveness.

In a broader sense, this theory may also be valuable since it defines general relationships between three variables which are central to many aspects of social activity. If these relationships are valid, useful explanations could be provided for the interaction among leadership style, task technology, and subordinate motivation at the individual, organizational, and societal levels.

Leadership and Organizational Excitement

David E. Berlew

In the past several years, an increasing number of individuals—often new graduates and professionals—have rejected secure positions in apparently well-managed organizations in favor of working alone or joining up with a few friends in a new organization. Usually they are not protesting, but searching for "something more." The nature of this "something more" is the subject of this article.

Many executives have blamed this disenchantment with established organizations on changes in Western society which have made an increasing number of people unsuited for organizational life. They often express the view that changes in child-rearing practices and the breakdown of discipline in the family and in our schools has produced a generation which cannot or will not exercise the self-discipline and acceptance of legitimate authority required for bureaucratic organizations.

Because it has been so acceptable to fault society, the leadership of most organizations has felt little need to look inward for the source of the problem and to analyze their own and their organization's failure to attract and hold some of the best-trained people our society produces.

Those organizations which have tried to change to keep pace with society have often been frustrated. In analyzing our failure to stem the tide of increasing alienation in the workplace, Richard Walton describes "a parade of organization development, personnel, and labor relations programs that promised to revitalize organizations,"[1] such as job enrichment, participative decision-making, management by objectives, sensitivity training or encounter groups, and productivity bargaining. He argues that while each application is often based on a correct diagnosis, it is only a partial remedy, and therefore the organizational system soon returns to an earlier equilibrium. His prescription is a systemic approach leading to comprehensive organization design or redesign.

Whether we are concerned wth organizations that have viewed the problem as outside of their control or those that have been frustrated in their attempts to change, one factor which has not been adequately explored and understood is that of effective organization leadership. Only an organization with strong leadership will look within itself for causes of

© 1974 by the Regents of the University of California. Reprinted from *California Management Review,* Volume XVII, number 2, pp. 21-30 by permission of the Regents.

1. Richard E. Walton, "How to Counter Alienation in the Plant," *Harvard Business Review,* Nov.-Dec., 1972.

problems that can be blamed easily on outside forces. Exceptional leadership is required to plan and initiate signficant change in organizations, whether it is one of Walton's partial remedies or comprehensive organizaton redesign. Short-term benefits from change projects often result from leadership behavior which excites members of an organization about the *potential* for change rather than actual change introduced.

Current Leadership Models

Almost without exception, theories of managerial leadership currently in vogue postulate two major dimensions of leadership behavior.[2] One dimension concerns the manager's or leader's efforts to accomplish organizational tasks. Various writers have given this dimension different names, including task or instrumental leadership behavior, job-centered leadership, initiating structure, and concern for production. The second dimension is concerned with leader's relations with his subordinates; it has been labelled social-emotional leadership behavior, consideration, concern for people, and employee-centered leadership. Measures of the effects of leadership also usually fall into two categories: indices of productivity and of worker satisfaction. A leader or manager who is good at organizing to get work done and who relates well to his subordinates should have a highly productive group and satisfied workers.

There is nothing wrong with two-factor models of managerial leadership as far as they go, but they are incomplete. They grew out of a period in history when the goal was to combine the task efficiency associated with scientific management with the respect for human dignity emphasized by the human relations movement. They did not anticipate a time when people would not be fulfilled even when they were treated with respect, were productive, and derived achievement satisfaction from their jobs. As a result, two-factor theories of managerial leadership tell us more about management than about leadership. They deal with relationships between man and his work, and between men and other men, but they do not tell us why some organizations are excited or "turned-on" and others are not. They do not help us understand that quality of leadership which can ". . . lift people out of their petty pre-occupations . . . and unify them in pursuit of objectives worthy of their best efforts."[3]

---

2. Robert J. House, "A Path Goal Theory of Leader Effectiveness," *Administrative Science Quarterly*, 16, No. 3 (1971), pp. 321-338; and Abraham K. Korman, "Consideration, Initiating Structure, and Organizational Criteria—A Review," *Personnel Psychology*, 1966, Vol. 19, pp. 349-361.

3. John W. Gardner, "The Antileadership Vaccine," *Annual Report of the Carnegie Corporation of New York*, 1965.

	Stage 1	Stage 2	Stage 3
Emotional Tone:	Anger or Resentment	Neutrality	Satisfaction	Excitement
Leadership Mode:	CUSTODIAL	MANAGERIAL	CHARISMATIC
Focal Needs or Values:	Food Shelter Security Fair treatment Human dignity	Membership Achievement Recognition	Meaningful work Self-reliance Community Excellence Service Social Responsibility
Focal Changes or Improvements:	Working conditions Compensation Fringe benefits Equal opportunity Decent supervision Grievance procedures	Job enrichment Job enlargement Job rotation Participative management Management by objectives Effective supervision	Common vision Value-related opportunities and activities Supervision which strengthens subordinates

Figure 1. Organizational Emotions and Modes of Leadership

Leadership and Emotion in Organizations

In an effort to help fill that void, the outline of a model relating types of leadership to the emotional tone in organizations is presented in Figure 1. Stages 1 and 2 of the model are derived from familiar theories of work motivation and the two-factor models of leadership discussed earlier. Angry or resentful workers (Stage 1) are primarily concerned with satisfying basic needs for food, shelter, security, safety, and respect. Organizations in Stage 1 try to improve their situations by eliminating "dissatisfiers" through improved working conditions, compensation, and fringe benefits, and by providing fair or "decent" supervision. The type of leadership associated with a change from an angry or resentful emotional tone to one of neutrality, or from Stage 1 to Stage 2, has been labelled *custodial*. The workers are neutral, lacking either strong positive or negative feelings about their work or the organization. In the absence of "dissatisfiers," they tend to become increasingly concerned with group membership or "belonging" and opportunities to do inherently satisfying work and to receive recognition. In order to increase employee satisfaction organizations at Stage 2 introduce improvements such as job enrichment, job enlargement, job rotation, participative management, and effective (as opposed to decent) supervision. Changes are oriented toward providing work that is less routine and more interesting or challenging, building cohesive work teams, and giving employees more say in decisions that directly affect them. The type of leadership associated with this movement from neutral to satisfied workers, or from Stage 2 to Stage 3, has been labelled *managerial*.

Most of the advances in organization theory and management practice in the past few decades have related to Stage 2; defining and controlling the elements of supervision and the organizational environment that result in high productivity with high satisfaction. While these advances have been substantial and have led, in most cases, to healthier, more effective organizations, they have not prevented the increasing alienation of professional employees.

The addition of Stage 3 to the model to extend the emotional tone continuum to include *organizational excitement* is an attempt to deal with a phenomenon of the '70s—the increasing number of professionals and new graduates who are rejecting secure positions in established organizations. The model suggests that for this small but growing element of the population, the satisfaction of needs for membership, achievement, and recognition is no longer enough. The meaning they seek has less to do with the specific tasks they perform as individuals than the impact of their individual and collective efforts—channelled through the organization—on their environment. The feelings of potency which accompany "shaping" rather than being shaped or giving up (and dropping out) are a source of excitement. So, too, are the feelings that stem from commitment to an organization that has a value-related mission and thus takes on some of the characteristics of a cause or a movement. At the extreme, this can lead to total involvement or total *identification*—the breaking down of boundaries between the self and the organization so that the "individual becomes the organization" and the "organization becomes the individual."

Stage 3 Leadership

Although Stage 3 leadership must involve elements of both custodial and managerial leadership, the dominant mode is charismatic leadership. The word "charisma" has been used in many ways with many meanings. Here we will define it in terms of three different types or classes of leadership behavior which provide meaning to work and generate organizational excitement. These are:

● the development of a "common vision" for the organization related to values shared by the organization's members;

● the discovery or creation of value-related opportunities and activities within the framework of the mission and goals of the organization; and

● making organization members feel stronger and more in control of their own destinies, both individually and collectively.

The first requirement for Stage 3 or charismatic leadership is a common or shared vision of what the future *could* be. To provide meaning and generate excitement, such a common vision must reflect goals or a future state of affairs that is valued by the organization's members and is thus important to them to bring about.

That men do not live by bread alone has been recognized for centuries by religious and political leaders. All inspirational speeches or writings have the common element of some vision or dream of a better existence which will inspire or excite those who share the author's values. This basic wisdom too often has been ignored by managers.

A vision, no matter how well articulated, will not excite or provide meaning for individuals whose values are different from those implied by the vision. Thus, the corporate executive who dreams only of higher return on investment and earnings per share may find his vision of the future rejected and even resented by members of his organization. Indeed, he may even find his vision of a profitable corporate future questioned by stockholders concerned with the social responsibility of corporations. Progressive military leaders may articulate a vision or mission congruent with the needs and values of the young people they are trying to attract to an all volunteer service, only to discover that the same vision conflicts with the values of their senior officers.

An important lesson from group theory and research is that informal groups tend to select as leader the individual who is most representative of the group's needs and values. Thus his hopes and aspirations, and the goals toward which he will lead the group, are automatically shared by the group's members.

One problem for heads of complex organizations is that if they are to function as leaders (as opposed to custodians or managers) they must represent and articulate the hopes and goals of many different groups—the young and the old, the unskilled and the professional, the employee and the stockholder, the minority and the majority, union, and management. Only the exceptional leader can instinctively identify and articulate the common vision relevant to such diverse groups. But to fail to provide some kind of vision of the future, particularly for employees who demand meaning and excitement in their work, is to make the fatal assumption that man can *live* by bread alone.

There are dangers as well as advantages to a common vision. If top management does not sincerely believe in the desirability of the vision they articulate, they are involved in an attempt to manipulate which will probably backfire. Another danger might be called the "Camelot phenomenon": the articulation of a shared vision that is both meaningful and exciting, but so unrealistic that people must inevitably be disillusioned. Whether the responsibility in such cases lies with the seducer or the seduced is difficult to say, but the end result is a step backward into cynicism.

Finally, the effectiveness of the common vision depends upon the leader's ability to "walk the talk": to behave in ways both small and large that are consistent with the values and goals he is articulating. In this regard, my experience in the Peace Corps taught me that the quickest way to destroy or erode the power of a common vision is for the leader to allow himself to be sidetracked into bargaining over details instead of concentrating all of his attention on identifying, tracking, and talking to the value issue involved. For example, at a meeting where Volunteers are reacting negatively to a proposed reduction in their living allowance, the Peace Corps Director or leader cannot afford to get involved in a discussion of whether or not female Volunteers will be able to afford pantyhose with their reduced allowance. The role of the leader is to keep alive the common vision which attracted Volunteers to the Peace Corps in the first place: in this case, the idea of a group of Americans whose help will be more readily accepted if they live at about the same standard as their local co-workers. . . .

Our organizations and institutions have, for the most part, been quite uncreative about countering or controlling the increasing fragmentation of work and family life, and the many problems that result. I know from my relationships with my wife and children now that I work at home a few days a week compared to when I spent fifty to eighty hours at the office or out of town and came home tired and irritable, often with homework. I doubt if I am much different from most other professionals in this regard. Why not actively recruit husbands and wives as work teams when possible, with child-care facilities nearby? Or, where possible, encourage employees to work at home on individual projects when they may have fewer interruptions than at the office?

Many organizations have a manifest commitment to excellence in their products and services, and to carrying out their corporate responsibilities toward the community. Occasionally they are in a position to spearhead social change. Too frequently, however, the value-relevant message seems directed toward customers or stockholders and only secondarily toward organization members. When it is directed toward members, it usually comes from a staff department such as corporate relations or the house organ rather than directly from the senior-line officers. This is public relations, not leadership, and whereas charisma might substitute for public relations, public relations, no matter how good, cannot substitute for charisma.

Making Others Feel Stronger

The effective Stage 3 leader must lead in such a way as to make members of his organization feel stronger. To achieve the organization's goals as well as to meet the needs of his more confident and able employees, his leadership must encourage or enable employees to be Origins rather than Pawns.

Richard deCharms has described Origins and Pawns in the following terms:

> An Origin is a person who feels that he is director of his life. He feels that what he is doing is the result of his own free choice; he is doing it because he wants to do it, and the consequences of his activity will be valuable to him. He thinks carefully about what he wants in this world, now and in the future, and chooses the most important goals ruling out those that are for him too easy or too risky . . . he is genuinely self-confident because he has determined how to reach his goals through his own efforts . . . he is aware of his abilities and limitation. In short, an Origin is master of his own fate.
> A Pawn is a person who feels that someone, or something else, is in control of his fate. He feels that what he is doing has been imposed on him by others: He is doing it because he is forced to, and the consequences of his activity will not be a source of pride to him. Since he feels that external factors determine his fate, the Pawn does not consider carefully his goals in life, nor does he concern himself about what he himself can do to further his cause. Rather he hopes for Lady Luck to smile on him.[4]

---

4. Richard deCharms, *Personal Causation* (New York: Academic Press, 1968); and Richard deCharms, "Origins, Pawns, and Educational Practice," in G. S. Lessor (ed.) *Psychology and the Educational Process* (Glenview, Ill.: Scott, Foresman and Co., 1969).

Clearly, there may only be a few people in the real world of human beings who are *always* guiding their own fate, checking their own skill, and choosing their own goals, but some people act and feel like Origins more of the time than do other people. Similarly, there are only a few people who *always* feel pushed around like Pawns.

Some individuals—parents, teachers, managers—have the ability to relate on a one-on-one basis in ways that make another person feel and behave more like an Origin and less like a Pawn. Certain types of leaders can apparently affect entire groups of people the same way.

In an experiment conducted at Harvard University,[5] a group of business school students were shown a film of John F. Kennedy delivering his inaugural address. After viewing the film, samples of the students' thoughts or fantasies were collected by asking them to write short imaginative stories to a series of somewhat ambiguous pictures. The thoughts of students exposed to the Kennedy film reflected more concern with having an impact on others and being able to influence their future and their environment than the thought samples of students exposed to a neutral control film. J.F.K. made them feel like Origins.

Replicating this experiment in a number of leadership training sessions, I have found the same thing: exposure to a certain type of leader—such as John F. Kennedy—leaves people feeling stronger, more confident of being able to determine their own destinies and have an impact on the world. It was this type of reaction to J.F.K. that attracted many young people to the Peace Corps to "change the world" during the early and mid-sixties.

It is difficult to assess precisely what it was about Kennedy's leadership that had this strengthening effect. We do know that he articulated a vision of what could be which struck a resonant chord, particularly in young people and citizens of developing nations. He also projected extremely high expectations of what young people could do to remake their country, if not the world.

Although most organization leaders cannot count on such dramatic moments as a presidential inauguration, or perhaps on their oratorical powers, they nevertheless do have a powerful effect on whether those around them feel and behave like Origins or Pawns. A number of factors determine the effct they have on others in this critical area.

Beliefs about Human Nature.—One important factor is the manager's beliefs or assumptions about human nature. If he believes that the average human being has an inherent dislike of work and will avoid it if he can, that most people must be coerced or controlled to get them to put forth effort toward the achievement of organizational objectives, and that

---

5. David G. Winter, *Power Motivation in Thought and Action* (Ph.D. dissertation, Harvard University, Department of Social Relations, January 1967).

he wishes to avoid responsibility, has relatively little ambition and wants security above all, then the manager will organize and manage people as if they were Pawns. If, on the other hand, the manager believes that the expenditure of physical and mental effort in work is as natural as play or rest, that individuals will exercise self-direction and self-control in the service of objectives to which they are committed, and that commitment to objectives is a function of the rewards associated with their achievement, including psychological rewards, then he will organize and manage people in quite a different way, with the result that they will tend to behave more like Origins than like Pawns.[6]

High Expectations.—Another important factor is the expectations a manager has about the performance of his subordinates. To some extent, all of us are what others expect us to be, particularly if the others in question are people we respect or love. A dramatic demonstration of this phenomenon is the strong positive relationship between a teacher's expectations of how well a student will do and the student's actual performance, a relationship which persists even when the teacher's positive expectations are based on invalid information.[7] A second study, done in a corporate setting, demonstrated that new managers who were challenged by their initial assignments were better performers after five years than new managers who were initially assigned to relatively unchallenging tasks, despite the fact that the potential of the two groups was about the same.[8]

Reward Versus Punishment.—Some managers tend to focus their attention on mistakes—to intervene when there are problems, and to remain uninvolved when things are going well. Other managers look for opportunities to reward good performance. An overbalance in the direction of punishing mistakes as opposed to rewarding excellence lowers self-confidence and is relatively ineffective in improving performance. Rewarding examples of effective action, however, both increases self-confidence and improves performance.

Encouraging Collaboration.—Americans have a tendency to compete when the situation does not demand it, and even sometimes when competition is self-defeating (as when individuals or units within the same organization compete). Diagnosing a situation as win-lose, and competing, insures that there are losers; and losing is a weakening process. If a situation is *in fact* win-lose in the sense that the more reward one party gets the less

---

6. Douglas McGregor, *The Human Side of Enterprise* (New York: McGraw-Hill Book Company, 1960).

7. Robert Rosenthal and Lenore Jacobson, *Pygmalion in the Classroom* (New York: Holt, Rinehart and Winston, Inc., 1968).

8. David E. Berlew and Douglas T. Hall, "The Socialization of Managers: Effects of Expectations on Performances," *Administrative Science Quarterly*, 11, No. 2 (1966), pp. 207-223.

the other gets, competition and the use of competitive strategies is appropriate. This is usually the situation that exists between athletic teams or different companies operating in the same market. Diagnosing a situation as win-win and collaborating is a strengthening process because it allows both parties to win. A situation is *in fact* win-win when both parties may win or one can win only if the other succeeds, as is usually the case *within* a company or a team.

The leader who is effective in making people feel stronger recognizes collaborative opportunities where they exist and does not allow them to be misdiagnosed as competitive. When he identifies instances of unnecessary competition within his organization, he uses his influence to change the reward system to induce collaborative rather than competitive behavior. If confronted with a competitive situation which he cannot or does not want to alter, however, he does not hesitate to use competitive strategies.

Helping Only When Asked.—It is extremely difficult to help someone without making them feel weaker, since the act of helping makes evident the fact that you are more knowledgeable, powerful, wise, or rich than the person you are trying to help. Those familiar with this dynamic are not surprised that some of the nations that the U.S. has most "helped" through our foreign aid resent us the greatest, particularly if we have rubbed their noses in their dependence by placing plaques on all the buildings we have helped them build, the vehicles we have provided, and the public works projects we have sponsored.

Yet the fact remains that there are real differences between individuals and groups in an organization, and help-giving is a real requirement. The effective Stage 3 leader gives his subordinates as much control over the type and amount of help they want as he can without taking untenable risks. He makes his help readily available to those who might come looking for it, and he gives it in such a way as to minimize their dependence upon him. Perhaps most important, he is sensitive to situations where he himself can use help and he asks for it, knowing that giving help will strengthen the other person and make him better able to receive help.

Creating Success Experiences.—A leader can make others feel stronger, more like Origins, by attempting to design situations where people can succeed, and where they can feel responsible and receive full credit for their success. People, whether as individuals or organizations, come to believe in their ability to control their destiny only as they accumulate successful experiences in making future events occur—in setting and reaching goals. The leader's role is to help individuals and units within his organization accumulate such experiences.

When an organization, through its leadership, can create an environment which has a strengthening effect on its members, it leads to the belief that, collectively, through the organization, they can determine or change the course of events. This, in turn, generates organizational excitement. It also becomes an *organization* which has all the characteristics of an Origin.

SUGGESTED READINGS
Chapter 8

Asch, S. E. *Groups, Leadership, and Men.* Pittsburgh: Carnegie Press, 1951.

Deutsch, Morton, Pepitone, Albert and Zander, Alvin. "Leadership: The Small Group." *Journal of Social Issues,* 4 (Spring, 1948): 31-40.

Eagly, A. H. "Leadership Style and Role Differentiation as Determinants of Group Effectiveness." *Journal of Personality* 38 (1970), 509-524.

Ellis, Donald G. and Fisher, Aubrey. "Phases of Conflict in Small Group Development: A Markov Analysis." *Human Communication Research* 1 (Spring 1975): 195-221.

Fiedler, Fred E. *A Theory of Leadership Effectiveness.* New York: McGraw-Hill Book Company, 1967.

Gardner, N. P. *Group Leadership.* Washington, D.C.: National Training and Development Service Press, 1974.

Geier, J. "A Trait Approach to the Study of Leadership." *Journal of Communication,* 17 (1967): 316-23.

Gouldner, A. W. *Studies in Leadership.* New York: Harper & Row, Publishers, 1965.

Gouran, Dennis. "Perspective on the Study of Leadership: Its Present and Its Future." *Quarterly Journal of Speech* 60 (October 1974), 376-381.

Geutzkow, Harold, ed. *Groups, Leadership and Men.* New Jersey: Carnegie Press, 1951.

Heller, F. A. "Leadership, Decision Making, and Contingency Theory." *Industrial Relations* 12 (May 1973), 138-199.

Hill, Walter. "A Situational Approach to Leadership Effectiveness." *Journal of Applied Psychology* 53 (1969), 513-517.

Hollander, E. P. *Leaders, Groups and Influences.* New York: Oxford University Press, Inc., 1964.

Hollander, E. P. "Style, Structure, and Setting in Organizational Leadership." *Administrative Science Quarterly* 16, 1 (1971), 1-9.

Jacobson, W. *Power and Interpersonal Relations.* Belmont, CA: Wadsworth Publishing Co., 1972.

Lashbrook, Velma J. "Leadership Emergence and Source Valence: Concepts in Support of Interaction Theory and Measurement." *Human Communication Research,* 1 (Summer 1975): 308-315.

Liff, Z. A., ed. *The Leader in the Group.* New York: Jason Aronson, 1975.

Sherif, Muzafer, ed. *Intergroup Relations and Leadership.* New York: John Wiley & Sons, Inc., 1962, v-273.

Stogdill, Ralph M. *Handbook of Leadership: A Survey of Theory and Research.* New York: The Free Press, 1974.

Stogdill, R. and Coons, A., eds. *Leader Behavior: Its Description and Measurement.* Columbus, Ohio: Bureau of Business Research, Ohio State University, 1957.

Stogdill, R. M. "Leadership, Membership, and Organization." *Psychology Bulletin,* 47 (1950.)

Zaleznik, Abraham. *Human Dilemmas of Leadership.* New York: Harper & Row, Publishers, 1966.

Performance

Styles of Leadership

James F. Kinder

Many of us take leadership for granted and yet it is essential to business, government and the voluntary organizations that shape the way we live, work and play.

Each one of us is some way involved in leading others whether we happen to be the Prime Minister, president of our own company, chairman of a voluntary committee, or head of a family. The problems of leadership are important whether we have many subordinates, one subordinate or whether we are trying to influence members of our peer group.

Leadership is more than an appointed position—it's more than the personal qualities of the leader—it's more than just having authority over someone. Leadership is the process of influencing others so that they, along with you, reach a mutually acceptable goal in a way that is satisfying to all.

Implied in the discussion of leadership are the motives of the leader. Presumably a leader is interested in influencing others, in striving for effective results and in providing achievement satisfaction for himself and others.

The concept of leadership is usually analyzed in terms of the leader, those whom he is leading, and the situation in which leadership takes place. Our discussion focuses on the behavior of the leader and the reaction of the followers to his behavior.

Reprinted by permission of James F. Kinder and the *Canadian Personnel Journal*, May 1971, pp. 35-41.

Our focus then is on behavior: the behavior of the leader as it is *seen* by the persons he is leading. The key word here is *seen*. All of us tend to react to others in terms of the behavior which we observe. We do not usually make allowances for behavior which is unacceptable to us unless we have known an individual over many years, and most of our work associations are of relatively short duration. We interact with others in terms of observable behavior. As a subordinate I am concerned with *what* you do to me, not in what you *intended* to do.

In the study of leadership it is important then that we analyze various types of behavior initiated by the leader or to put it another way—the analysis of leadership styles.

A helpful way of identifying leadership styles is through the use of a behavioral model. For example, one of the earliest models portrays the implications of the use of democratic as opposed to autocratic leadership. Other models combine a leader's concern for production and his concern for people and describe four or five leadership styles.

There are many behavioral analysis models but all have one thing in common—they are concerned with how a leader gets the job done and how he handles people in getting that job done.

Lawrence Appley, retired President of the American Management Association once said that the world is composed of four kinds of people:

☐ those who make things happen
☐ those to whom things happen
☐ those who watch things happen
☐ those who do not even know that things are happening

This is one way of indicating that various "styles" of behavior exist.

The model to be used in our discussion combines four basic behavioral traits—Dominance, Submission, Warmth and Hostility. It may be shown visually this way:

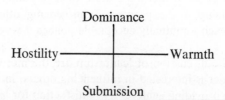

The evidence of dominance is shown by a person who leads, advises, directs, initiates, takes over situations, organizes, believes in structure, volunteers, and generally takes responsibility.

A person who is submissive is willing to accept others' leadership and guidance. In fact, he enjoys following others and tends to be a low risk-taker. In stituations that require leadership he tends to nominate others for the task.

Individuals who show warmth have a genuine concern for others. They tend to be confident, friendly, approachable, cheerful, have a sense of humor and, on occasion, can be self-sacrificing.

Hostile individuals tend to be cold, indifferent, competitive and intolerant of other people's ideas. A hostile person is self centered, does not listen to others and has very little sense of humor.

Using the four basic behavioral traits we can identify four leadership styles in our model.

An individual who combines the traits of dominance and hostility we call Dominant-Hostile and identify with the symbol L1.

The other three styles may be identified as follows:

Submissive-Hostile — L2
Submissive-Warm — L3
Dominant-Warm   — L4

The symbols L1, L2, L3 and L4 are useful to us in discussing the implications of the model. They are useful in the sense that we can establish almost instant understanding of the type of behavior we are seeking to understand.

Our model can now be shown as follows:

Dominant- Hostile		Dominant- Warm	
	L1	L3	
	L2	L4	
Submissive- Hostile		Submissive- Warm	

The style model we are using implies that all behavior may be analyzed in four separate categories: Dominant-Hostile, Submissive-Hostile, Submissive-Warm, and Dominant-Warm and that each of us fits neatly into one of the categories. Unfortunately human behavior is much more complex than this.

For example—a person who is usually Dominant-Warm will at times show evidence of submissiveness and/or hostility. Sometimes the submissive worm turns and shows flashes of leadership. On occasion the hostile person will show warmth toward certain people.

The point is that behavior should be analyzed in terms of what is happening in the current situation, not that a certain style once identified will always be used.

The purpose of behavior analysis through a style model is not to categorize but to be able to recognize here-and-now behavior in understandable terms.

With this purpose in mind, it might be helpful to illustrate briefly how the four styles may be recognized.

L1. Dominant-Hostile

The Dominant-Hostile leader is usually perceived as one who puts the immediate task above all other considerations. He is ineffective in that he makes it obvious that he has no concern for others' feelings and has little confidence in the efforts of other people. While this attitude promotes fear it also produces dislike and thus people are motivated to work only when the Dominant-Hostile is present. The Dominant-Hostile cannot understand why so many people are unco-operative; he does not fully realize that co-operation to him means doing it his way.

Further understanding may be achieved by considering the leader's action in handling certain managerial situations.

For example:

Control of Work Assignments

"Do it this way and do not change it unless you check with me."

Mistakes Made by Others

"Who is responsible for this?"

Decision Making

"My mind is already made up; do not confuse me with facts."

Attitude to Meetings

"Committees are a waste of time, the fastest way to get things done is to do it yourself."

Attitude to Suggestions Made by Others

"We tried that before and it does not work."

L2. Submissive-Hostile

The Submissive-Hostile leader is seen as one who often shows his lack of interest in both task and relationships. He is less effective not only because of his lack of interest but also because of his effect on others' morale. He may be seen not only as shirking his own duties but also as hindering the performance of others through intervention or by withholding information.

Likely to be resistant to change or accepts change and then sabotages it—withholds information, aims at minimum output, impedes others, lowers morale.

Control of Work Assignments
"I don't care how you do it, as long as it's done."

Mistakes Made by Others
"Forget it—we all make mistakes."

Decision-Making
"It's entirely up to you."

Attitude to Meetings
"Another meeting!—let's get it over with as soon as possible."

Attitude to Suggestions Made by Others
"Good idea. I'll pass it on to Bill."

L3. Submissive-Warm

The Submissive-Warm leader is basically a kindly soul who puts happy relationships above all other considerations. He is ineffective because his desire to see himself and be seen as a "good guy" prevents him from risking even mild disagreement in order to improve production.

He believes that happy people produce more and that production is less important than good fellowship. He strives to create a warm, pleasant, social atmosphere where an easygoing work tempo may be maintained.

He spends much of his time trying to find ways to make things easier for his people.

Control of Work Assignments
"How are things going, Charlie?"

Mistakes Made by Others
"Ah! forget it, we all make mistakes; better luck next time."

Decision Making
"I had nothing to do with the decision but it seems fair so I think we should go along with it."

Attitude to Meetings
"Yeh, the meeting may not accomplish much but it gives all of us an opportunity to get to know each other better."

Attitude to Suggestions Made by Others
"Wonderful idea, Joe, never thought of doing it that way. I'll discuss it with the others."

L4. Dominant-Warm

The Dominant-Warm leader is perceived as one who seeks his main task as maximizing the effort of others toward both short and long term goals. He sets high standards for production and performance but recognizes that because of individual differences he will have to treat everyone a little differently. He is effective, in that his commitment to both task and people is evident to all and acts as a powerful motivating force.

He welcomes disagreement and comment as they relate to the task. He sees such behavior as necessary, normal and appropriate.

He believes that differences can be worked through, that conflict can be resolved, and that commitment will result.

Control of Work Assignments

"Go ahead, Bill, I'll keep in touch to see if I can be helpful if you run into difficulty."

Mistakes Made by Others

"Let's see if we can determine *what* went wrong so it isn't likely to happen again."

Decision Making

"Let's discuss it before we proceed: I'd like your opinion."

Attitude to Meetings

"Tomorrow?—*great,* it will give us all an opportunity to express our views and decide on action."

Attitude to Suggestions Made by Others

"Sounds like a good idea; let's talk it over and see if it can be implemented."

A leader might ask himself—

What are some of the practical applications of behavior at work?

What does a study of behavior mean to me?

Is my leadership behavior consistent?

Is there a "best style of leadership?

What are my assumptions about people and how they work?

Can I really change my behavior?

The answers to some or all of these questions may be found in studying the model.

Research seems to indicate that we are basically consistent in our behavior and therefore we show a predominant style over a period of time. Our actions are a result of our value system about people and how work gets done. For example, if we believe that people are lazy, indifferent and irresponsible and therefore they will have to be pushed, coerced or ordered to do a job we will use a Dominant-Hostile style (L1).

There also seems to be some evidence that in most situations a style which involves others in planning and goal setting, that is, Dominant-Warm (L4), is the best style to use for effective results.

An understanding of behavior in style terms enables the leader to better understand the actions of others. For example, if a leader operates in a Dominant-Hostile fashion he should not be surprised if he gets either a Dominant-Hostile reaction or, worse still, a Submissive-Hostile attitude.

No behavior change in either the leader or the subordinate can take place until there is some understanding of what behavior choice is available; until there is some understanding of the results of a behavior choice; until there is some belief that by changing behavior a more effective result will be achieved.

In our society we tend to over-complicate issues and leadership is no exception. There have been guidelines in the past on good leadership practice. One of the best was stated by Lao-Tzu, a Chinese philosopher in the 6th Century, B.C. It is entitled "The Way of Life According to Lao-Tzu" and goes like this:

"A leader is best
When people barely know that he
exists,
Not so good when people obey
and acclaim him,
Worst when they despise him.
Fail to honor people,
They fail to honor you;
But of a good leader, who talks
little,
When his work is done, his aim
fulfilled,
They will all say, "We did this
ourselves."

A leadership style well worth adopting.

Leading Growth Groups

David W. Johnson and F.P. Johnson

Introduction

Literally tens of thousands of people each year now participate in small groups for the purpose of increasing their interpersonal effectiveness, self-actualization, group skills, personal awareness, and ability to function within organizations. In the last twelve years there has been an explosion of such groups, and more than a hundred "growth centers" in the United States now offer a wide variety of opportunities to join a small group for a weekend, week, or longer. Special group experiences have been designed to help improve couples' relationships, to bridge the gap between parents and children, to strengthen the communion and unity that have character-ized religious organizations in the past, to help people handle conflict more constructively, and to increase their ability to meditate, "center," and com-municate through touch. Training in human relations is becoming manda-tory for potential teachers, and intercultural experiences between blacks and whites, Indians and whites, middle· class and poor, are frequently offered to improve teaching and ethnic relations. There are sensitivity training groups, encounter groups, confrontation groups, personal growth groups, strength groups, and such a variety of other groups that no one can keep up with current labels. All such groups are generally referred to as *growth groups* in this book. With such a demand for small-group experiences, and such an expansion in the type of group experiences avail-able, it is difficult to conceive of a book on groups that does not cover growth groups.

To be an effective growth-group leader, a person needs three models: (1) of interpersonal and group effectiveness, self-actualization, human-ness, and so on (of where he is going), (2) of how these goals are to be achieved (of how he will get there), and (3) of leadership conduct (of how he will behave along the way). Models of interpersonal and group effectiveness have been presented in this book and in Johnson (1972), and models of self-actualization and humanness have been described in Johnson (1973); these goals, however, will be briefly reviewed in the next section. The method of reaching these goals is almost universally the inquiry-experiential method of learning discussed in Chapter 1. [Johnson and Johnson text] Inasmuch as this book is based on such a model, the subject

David W. Johnson, Frank P. Johnson, *Joining Together: Group Theory And Group Skills.* © 1975, pp. 287-293. Reprinted by permission of Prentice-Hall, Inc., Engel-wood Cliffs, New Jersey.

is not reviewed here. The reason why such a variety of group experiences can all be lumped together under the label of "growth group" is because and research to the behavior of the group members. To make such diag- chapter will focus upon presenting briefly a model for how a growth-group leader—hereafter termed a *facilitator*—behaves in order to promote learn- ing by group members. . . .

Leading A Growth Group

A facilitator needs several sets of complex skills in order to lead a growth group. The first set involves his being able to develop a growth- oriented climate in the group—that is, a climate of psychological safety that promotes openness, trust, and experimentation with alternative behaviors. A climate of psychological safety is built by communicating an authentic warmth and support for, an empathy with, and an accurate understanding and acceptance of the group members as individuals. A member is psycho- logically safe when he feels supported, accepted, understood, and liked. Being *supportive* is, basically, communicating to other individuals a recog- nition of their strengths and capabilities and the belief that they have the capacity to handle productively the situation they face. Being *accepting* is, basically, communicating a high regard for other people and a disposition to react to their behavior in a nonevaluative way. The specific skills in- volved being warm, supportive, empathetic, and accepting are presented in Johnson (1972). Much research on psychotherapy, experimental social psychology, and growth groups substantiates the necessity for such behavior. Leiberman, Yalom, and Miles (1973), for example, found that the most effective growth-group leaders cared a great deal (demonstrated such be- haviors as protection, friendship, love, affection, support, praise, encourage- ment) for group members.

A second set of skills required of an effective group leader involves his being a resource expert, an educator using inquiry-experiential methods, and a diagnoser of personal-interpersonal-group dynamics. Any growth- group facilitator should be skilled in the use of inquiry and experiential methods for learning, a subject discussed in Chapter 1 and in Appendix A. [Johnson and Johnson text] Almost all types of growth groups emphasize inquiring into the experiences of the group members. This inquiry is usu- ally based upon diagnosing the personal, interpersonal, and group dynamics being experienced, by applying a conceptual framework based upon theory and research to the behavior of the group members. To make such diag- noses, the facilitator must provide expertise in one of the behavioral sci- ences such as psychology or sociology. The presentation of conceptual frameworks enables members not only to gain insight into their behavior and their internal reactions to what occurs within the group, but to understand more fully the interpersonal and group dynamics they are involved in. Thus, a facilitator must have a solid knowledge of one of the behavioral sciences, an expertise in inquiry-experiential learning methods, and the ability to use his knowledge and expertise to help the members understand what they are experiencing. Leiberman, Yalom, and Miles found that the most effective leaders had a great ability to present conceptualizations that gave meaning to the experiences the members were undergoing. This one ability was the most important variable for promoting member learning found in their study. Such conceptualizations are especially useful to members after the group experience has ended, and they are able to use them to understand more fully their day-to-day interpersonal and group situations. The conceptualizations presented in this book and in Johnson (1972) are examples of the type of conceptual frameworks a facilitator must be able to communicate to members.

A third set of facilitator skills pertains to his making sure that members are provided with constructive feedback and confrontations. Helpful feedback means the sharing, upon request, of a description of how a person sees another person's behavior and its consequences, and a description of how the person is reacting to the other person's behavior. A confrontation is a deliberate attempt to help another person examine the consequences of some aspect of his behavior; it is an invitation to engage in self-examination. A confrontation originates from a desire to involve oneself more deeply with the person one is confronting, and it is intended to help the person behave in more fruitful or less destructive ways. The specific skills of feedback and confrontation are presented in Johnson (1972). The important point to keep in mind when feedback and confrontations are being facilitated is the difference among the behavior being observed, the conceptual framework the observer is using, and the inferences and interpretations made about the person engaging in the behavior. A facilitator should never let group members confuse these three elements involved in giving feedback and in confronting other members. The actual behavior being observed will be the same to all group members (given that the observations are valid), but the conceptual frameworks used to understand the behavior and to make interpretations and inferences about it can be widely disparate. Selling other group members on one interpretation of what is taking place is a much different activity from arriving at a consensus of what behavior is taking place.

A fourth set of skills required of a facilitator concerns his being able to model the behaviors he hopes members will learn from their group experience. Social-learning theory (Bandura, 1969) emphasizes the importance of modeling desired behaviors and then reinforcing group members (e.g., giving recognition and approval for imitating the facilitator); this procedure is probably the most effective way to teach new skills. The behaviors a facilitator may model are discussed in this book and in Johnson (1972). This would include such behaviors, for example, as sending and receiving communications, self-disclosure, giving and receiving feedback, experimenting with alternative behaviors, expressing acceptance and support for others. A willingness to model desired skills means that the facilitator will take an active part in interacting with other group members. Some research indicates that activeness on the part of the facilitator is to be preferred to passiveness (which, when it pertains to members, is associated with anxiety, dissatisfaction, silence, poor attendance, discontinuance, and lack of learning), except when the activeness turns into domination (Bierman, 1969). Peters (1966), in addition, found that members who imitate the facilitator learn more from growth groups than those who do not. Thus the facilitator may want to be the "ideal member" in the group in order to promote members' skill development. Finally, it should be noted that simply being an "authentic person" does not systematically present effective skills to be imitated by group members; a facilitator must be able to be interpersonally effective so she can model desired skills.

A fifth set of skills involves a facilitator's being able to engineer a problem-solving process with respect to the concern of members. This subject has been discussed in Chapter 10 of this book as well as in other chapters. In such a problem-solving process it may be important to bring in information about the person's past behavior and feelings as well as his behavior and feelings in the group (Leiberman, Yalom, and Miles, 1973).

A sixth set of skills a facilitator needs is to be able to promote corrective or reparative emotional experiences in the group. Highly personalized and relevant learning often arouses emotions, of anxiety while the learning is taking place and of happiness and satisfaction when it is achieved. To give and receive feedback, to confront and be confronted, to experiment with new behaviors, to bring out personal concerns to be problem solved, all promote considerable emotional reaction. High levels of warmth, anger, frustration, and anxiety are all found in most growth-group experiences. A facilitator may stimulate emotional reaction by confronting group members, by supporting attempts at experimenting with alternative behaviors, by promoting feedback and problem solving, by disclosing highly personal material about herself, and by expressing warmth and support for the members of the group. The most effective leaders in the Leiberman, Yalom, and Miles study engaged in a moderate amount of emotionally stimulating behavior. Though emotional experiences do not mean that learning will take place, genuine learning is often accompanied by emotionality. The facilitator needs to be certain that the members not only experience deep emotion, but also are helped to look at the experience objectively, in such a way as to give it meaning for the future. She should place emphasis upon reflection as well as experience, and guide members in applying their present experiences. In managing the emotionality of the group, the facilitator must also moderately stimulate learning that arouses emotions and provide conceptualizations that will promote learning from emotional experiences.

The seventh set of skills facilitators should be able to demonstrate concerns the social engineering of an effective group. All the skills discussed in this book are relevant to this point. Only in an effective growth group can the learning of members take place. The cohesion of the group; group norms that favor moderate emotional intensity, confrontation, and supportive peer control; the distribution of participation and leadership; the quality of communication; the management of conflict; and all the other aspects of group effectiveness are extremely important for productive growth groups. A facilitator must be able to promote effective group behavior among the members.

It is sometimes useful for a facilitator to have a clear contract with members concerning their responsibilities as group members. The contract might provide, for example, that members agree (1) to be completely open about themselves to the group with respect to both past and current behavior, (2) to take responsibility for themselves once they enter the group and not to blame others or circumstances for their predicaments, and (3) to get involved with the other group members and cooperate in increasing their learning. When an explicit contract is made, the facilitator becomes the "keeper of the contract" and should see to it that it is enforced.

Finally, a facilitator may have a variety of executive functions to carry out. Organizing the group, arranging for facilities in which it is to meet, providing it with needed materials, conducting an evaluation of its success, and so on may be the responsibility of the facilitator, all of which require a range of administrative and evaluation skills.

The Leader's Diagnostic Skill

Walter M. Lifton

To be helpful to a group, the counselor needs to be able to spot problems arising in groups and to have information he can offer the group, if asked, on ways to deal with these situations.

Presented below is a schema developed by Klein (36) to assist group counselors to spot problem areas in group functioning. He recognizes that symptom pictures can neither be precise nor reflect the many possible variables operating, but he has found the general schema helpful in assisting group leaders seeking to locate the sources of group malfunction.

I.   *Where the Problem Lies within the Individuals:*

  A.   Where the individuals in the group are so needful that they are unable to function in a group, are injurious to others, are in conflict within themselves:

   1.   Individuals cannot communicate or do not respond appropriately.

   2.   Individuals act out and their bizarre, seductive ego-alien behavior is frightening to others.

   3.   Individuals control the group by virture of nuisance value, fear, or contagion.

   4.   Behavior is withdrawn, apathetic, isolated, or fearful.

   5.   Members exacerbate problems of others.

   6.   Group support pathology or reinforces symptoms.

  Indications: Acting out, bizarre behavior, extreme provocation, distorted communication, withdrawn behavior, fear, etc.

  B.   Where individuals have no interest in the purpose or goal:

   1.   There is lack of cohesion.

   2.   There is lack of commitment.

   3.   There is lack of any group goal, contract, or agreed-upon goal, or where goals of the members are contra-indicated for each other, or for the group goal and purpose.

  Indications: Exploitation, apathy, conflict, scapegoating, do not listen to each other, ideas attacked before they are expressed, intolerance, no movement toward developing or working toward goals, etc.

C.   Where the grouping is inappropriate:
1.   The role behaviors set up an isolate at either end of the range of accepted behaviors.
2.   The individual symptoms cannot be tolerated by the group.
3.   The group composition is out of balance with group purposes.
4.   The group composition is out of balance, that is, the composition is weighted on the side of negative rather than positive factors and toward pathology instead of health; when taken as a whole its fulcrum is not at a modal point but skewed so that the negatives outweigh the positives.
5.   The grouping is not suited to the psycho-social level of tasks, needs, and resources.
6.   The members have primary allegiance to reference groups external to this group.

Indications: Reinforcement for existing behavior, anxiety about revealing self or sharing, absence of mutual aid, mistrust, punishing each other, absence of bond, etc.

D.   Where individuals have personal value conflicts.
E.   Where individuals have excessive superego controls.

II.   *Where the Group Is in Conflict with the Environment:*
A.   The environment superimposes demands.
B.   The demand of the environment is excessive.
C.   The structure of the environmental system is inadequate or inappropriate to carry its function, as for example, it is frustrating, rigid, and punitive for the group.
D.   The values of the group are in conflict with those of its environment.
E.   The group does not understand the demand.
F.   The group is unable to fill the demand.
G.   The group leadership is anti-social
H.   The group is rejected by the environment.
I.   The group is in conflict with authority such as worker, agency, subculture, community, culture of society.
J.   The environment is noxious, endangering, seductive, anomic, or contradictory.
K.   The environment does not provide access to resources that are needed by the group and its members.
L.   The kind, nature, and intensity of the relationship of the group to its environment is inappropriately dependent,

non-stimulating, overprotective, seductive, overly stimulating, overly demanding, defiant, exploitive:

1. The agency's values, procedures, and culture are contrary to the group's and the agency superimposes.
2. The neighborhood is hostile to the group and its members.
3. The forces of social control are hostile to the group and its members.
4. The members are impoverished economically and culturally.
5. The social values in the impinging society are inconsistent and rewards are given for deviant behavior.
6. The group leader is from reform school or local gang.
7. Worker is too different from members to be able to accept them, or they him.
8. The group lacks skills necessary to match the environment.
9. The group does not want to match environment and environment does not want to change.

Indications: Group solidarity and hostility to anything that is not of the group, anti-social acting out, low self-image, braggadocio, subvention, arguing inconsequential points, autocratic leadership, bullying, scapegoating, projection, rationalizing, ridicule, sadism, brutality, insecurity, etc.

III. *Where the Internal Structure of the Group Is not Appropriate or Is Inoperative:*

A. The structure is inadequate to meet the needs of the members.
B. The structure is insufficient to carry out tasks.
C. The structure is too formal, too ritualistic, or too much for the purpose, size, and functioning of the group.
D. The formal structure does not function.
E. The structure is in contradiction to the values of the group.
F. The structure is in contradiction to the group goals or there are no goals.
G. The structure blocks interpersonal interaction or group transaction.
H. The structure works against group movement:

1. Leadership is too strong, too weak, inept, inappropriate, absent, centralized, there is conflict for leadership, leadership is inappropriate for stage of group development, leadership denies access to resources and thwarts need-meeting, leadership operates through power, power is not distributed.

Indications: Attendance falls off, dropouts, participation index low, scapegoating, fighting, communication patterns centralized, poor movement toward goals, overstructured rituals and procedures, goal displacement, poor esprit de corps and low hedonic tone, high level of frustration, aggressive behavior, apathy and projection, informal channels wide open and formal channels neglected, taking sides with no compromises, etc.

2. Positions occupied or available do not meet needs of group or group members. Positions do not articulate or fit each other or the group. The formal positions do not match the informal functioning. Positions and status do not match. Status is not given for performing group requirements. Position and status are unfilled or in contention. Positions and status block person-to-person interaction.

Indications: Attendance fluctuates, poor interest in elections, positions unfilled or poorly carried, clique formation, conflict, inability to make group decisions or to keep those made, poor organization, and avoidance of communication channels, etc.

3. Communication is limited to few, or is skewed, is distorted, is lacking, is not heard or decoded, is double-bind, is not responded to, is not appropriate to desired goal, is delusional and not related to reality.

Indications: Poor participation, i.e., many do not talk, cross talk, talking all at once, responses inappropriate to what was said, movement diffuse and in all directions, schizoid behavior, unreal communication, group decisions made too quickly, etc.

4. Role patterns do not meet needs of individuals or of the group. There are role gaps; roles are inappropriate to purposes, task, or stage; are threatening or anxiety-producing to occupant; not complementary or reciprocal; ambiguous; con-

flicting; overlapping; non-functional; stereotyped; role paterns block person-to-person interaction.

Indications: Flight, fight, pairing, dependency, acting out, withdrawing, role playing, in appropriate role performance, difficulty in making group decisions, escape to irrelevancies and high-level abstractions, silences, hostility, anxiety, inappropriate reciprocal role relationships, etc.

5. The group procedures are faulty. They are too rigid, inappropriate, ritualistic, not followed, inconsistent, unformed or unknown, unsuited to group purpose or task, inappropriate to group values. Group procedures block person-to-person interaction or consensus. Procedures allow majority to dominate minority.

Indications: Excessive procedures and frustration, insufficient procedures and frustration, wrangling about procedures, undemocratic controls, floundering, impatience, dropping out, poor participation, goal displacement onto procedures and rituals, scapegoating, endless debate with no decision, decisions reached with too little or irrelevant discussion, railroading, etc.

6. Sociometric (affectional) ties are scarce and weak, skewed patterns, subgroup cleavage, few linkages, isolates, rejection.

Indications: Low cohesion, fighting, racial or ethnic intolerance, poor morale, diffusion of group goal, do not listen to each other, ridicule, diversity of interests, difficulty with program, each pushes own plan, idea possessiveness, do not help one another, no hedonic tone, do not share, group breaks under pressure or crisis, denial of access to resources, isolates, no closeness, interpersonal fear, etc.

7. Structure is designed to perpetuate domination, rigid decisions, keep clique in power, monopolize, thwart change, rationalize behaviors.

Indications: "Big Joes" and slaves, nondemocratic decisions, ingroup top clique, communication star pattern, domination, favoritism, power struggles, procedures ignored, punishment and fines, main concern is to gain status, subtle attacks on leadership, obeisance, contagion, physical force, etc.

8. The structure maximizes loyalty to outside reference groups.

9. The structure is a defense against interpersonal confrontation and a response to anxiety.

IV. *Where the Group Was Reasonably Well Grouped but the Group Composition Is out of Balance:*
  A. Because of group stage.
  B. Because the purpose has changed.
  C. Because individual behavior changes.
  D. Because a member is absent, dropped or added.
  Indications: Unusual acting out and withdrawal, reversal of decisions already made, realignments, attacks on leadership, discuss breaking up, unusual scapegoating, etc.

V. *Where the Group Is Reasonably Well Grouped and the Structure Is Adequate for Normal Functioning but there Is a Temporary Loss of Good Group Functioning:*
  A. There is a new, largely externally caused problem which is causing stress.
  B. There is a group crisis.
  Indications: Projection, tight ingroup, exclusion, fighting, delinquency, momentary loss of interest, self-discipline fails, reject limits, regression, etc.

VI. *Where the Group Is Reasonably Well Grouped, the Structure Is Adequate for Normal Functioning, but there Is Regression:*
  A. There is a change in the power structure.
  B. There is a change in the leadership.
  Indications: Conflict and infighting, seek to seduce worker to intervene, suspicion, childish behavior, random behavior, confusion, etc.

VII. *Where the Group Is Reasonably Well Grouped for the Purposes, the Structure Is Adequate, but the Worker Does not Promote Good Group Functioning:*
  A. Worker is not sufficiently skilled.
  B. Worker is not tolerant.
  C. Worker dominates the group.
  D. Worker lacks conviction.
  E. Worker does not listen and cannot understand.
  F. Worker is not responsive and does not enable.
  Indications: Fight authority, neurotic transference, retreat, conformity, gross defiance and discipline problems, hurt each other, submission, no movement, etc.

VIII. *Where the Group Is Reasonably Well Grouped, the Structure Is Adequate but the Program Fails:*
  A. Does not meet the interest or needs.
  B. Exacerbates problems of individuals or the group.

Indications: Apathy, heightened unrest and disinterest, aggressive behavior, destruction, regression, pathology, scapegoating, chaos, etc.

IX. *Where the Group Is Internally in Conflict over Values, Norms, and Standards, Is Ambivalent, or in Transition:*

Indications: Conflict, infighting, low cohesion, warring subgroups, poor decision-making, derision, low esprit de corps, vacillation, no group goal or commitment, etc.

Some of the behaviors which are listed above may be viewed, if one is judgmental, as deviant. A more useful way of looking at it is to see that behavior is a response and in most instances as such may be rational and appropriate. The behaviors also give a clue to the developmental stage of the group and therefore help the worker to adjust his stance to the immediate needs of the group in its struggle to become a viable group.

The Leader as Completer

William C. Schultz

The suggested framework for integrating group roles consists of listing all those things needed for a group to cope successfully with outer reality. interpersonal needs, and conflict-free factors. It is at this point that the FIRO theory of interpersonal behavior seems to offer a method of enumerating the necessary behaviors for coping with at least two of the three spheres. This theory states that there are three fundamental interpersonal needs—inclusion, control, and affection—and in order for an individual (or group) to function optimally he [the leader] must establish and maintain a satisfactory relation in all three areas, with other people or with symbols of people. The application of these notions to each area of influence of ego and leader development will now be pursued. The totality of requirements in these three areas may be considered necessary group functions for optimal group performance within the ego psychology—FIRO theoretical framework.

Outer Reality

The kinds of things that may go wrong in outer reality, the things that make it necessary for the leader to take some kind of action, are those in which the interpersonal needs of the group are not compatible with the requirements of external reality, or where somehow outer reality does not enhance (or even inhibits) the expression of the conflict-free area of the group. This suggests a way of categorizing outer reality for groups. FIRO describes various types of compatibility holding between people and suggests that this type of analysis can be expanded to include situations. Types of incompatibilities that can exist between the group and external reality may be described, parallel to person-person incompatibilities. Since, according to FIRO theory, individuals have three basic interpersonal needs— inclusion, control, and affection—there may be an incompatibility between a group and its environment in any of these three areas.

In the area of inclusion, a group can be incompatible with outer reality in that it wants either more or less contact and interaction with outer reality than it has. Too little contact is exemplified by military groups that live at

From the Ego, FIRO Theory and the Leader as Completer by William C. Schultz in *Leadership And Interpersonal Behavior,* edited by Luigi Petrullo and Bernard M. Bass. Copyright © 1961 by Holt, Rinehart and Winston. Reprinted by permission of Holt, Rinehart and Winston.

isolated outposts. If such a group, as a whole, wants more interaction with people than the setting provides, this dissatisfaction may be the source of incompatibility between the group and its environment. On the other hand, a family group for example, including a famous person, may be constantly besieged by invitations, visitors, and by other experiences that do not permit them to maintain sufficient privacy. In this case, outer reality becomes incompatible with the group by not allowing them sufficient withdrawal from interacton with their environment.

In the area of control, outer-reality incompatibility means that the group either has too little or too much control over its environment. Too little control is exemplified by a group living at the foot of an irregularly erupting volcano. Here, there is a fundamental incompatibility between the group and outer reality because the group has too little control. On the other hand, a group that is forced to control its outer reality too much is likely to feel it has more responsibility than it can handle. For example, in wartime, aboard key ships, young, inexperienced tactical radar teams have the enormous responsibility of controlling the actions of planes in combat with the enemy. In this case control is sometimes too great, and these groups would often be quite happy to be relieved of much of their control.

In the area of affection, a group may be incompatible with outer reality because it has too few or too many affectional ties with the environment. It often happens that a particular kind of group such as the Central Intelligence Agency is required to act in a very dignified and secret manner. This group is not allowed to become intimate with any other group because of the nature of its work. This aspect of too few ties may be unsatisfactory for most group members. On the other hand, intimacy and closeness for other groups may be excessive and may be forced upon them by the external situation. This is true of certain families living in suburbia, where the great closeness of their living forces them to become close and intimate with many people in their surroundings in ways they do not desire.

The above, then, are examples of a way in which, if one accepts the FIRO framework, all possible incompatibilities between a group and outer reality might be categorized. An area of influence on ego development as elaborated by FIRO theory indicates the following.

Leadership Functions re Outer Reality

(1) Establish and maintain sufficient contact and interaction with outside groups and individuals to avoid isolation of the group, but not so much contact that the group loses its privacy.

(2) Establish and maintain sufficient control over outer reality that the group can function satisfactorily without outside interference, and yet

not so much control that the group is forced to undertake more responsibility than it desires.

(3) Establish and maintain sufficient closeness and intimacy with outside reality that the group can feel the pleasures of friendship and affection, and yet not so much intimacy with outside reality that the actions of the group become distorted and detrimental to group objectives.

Interpersonal Needs

The leader functions for establishing and maintaining satisfactory relations among members follow the same lines as those given for outer reality, except that the compatibility must be among members within the group rather than between the group and outer reality. An extensive discussion of the problems of compatibility of this type is given in FIRO (Schutz, 1958c). For the present purposes, the primary leadership functions for each area are discussed.

Satisfaction of interpersonal needs is obtained through the establishment and maintenance of an optimal relation among group members in their need areas. Hence, in order to function effectively, the group must find comfortable balance in the amount and type of contact and interaction, control and influence, and personal closeness and affection.

Leadership Functions re Interpersonal Needs

Enough inclusion. It is neecssary to maintain the group's existence. It therefore is desirable that everyone feels part of the group and to some degree knows he belongs. A desire for inclusion is motivation for efficiency in activities such as notifying members of meetings. Activites that foster these feelings include introductions and biographical stories to identify members.

Not too much inclusion. It is necessary to allow group members to maintain some degree of distance from other group members and some individuality. To accomplish this end groups are divided frequently into subgroups, labor is divided, and perhaps in a more subtle way differences are established between subgroups (male-female, Negro-White, Catholic-Jew, etc.).

Enough control. It is necessary for members to influence other members to some extent in order to make decisions. Without this influence or control of others no decision-making system could be effective. Techniques used to accomplish this end are election of officers, establishment of power hierarchies, employment of brute force, and so on.

Not too much control. In most groups it is necessary to establish behavior patterns leading to a restriction of the amount of control some members have over others. If this is not done, the value of the independent operation of some persons is lost, and some members acquire too much responsibility. The institutional procedures of majority rule and consensus are often used to limit control.

Enough affection. The necessity for this need is more controversial. For the present purposes it is assumed that affection is necessary for the effective functioning of a group. Hence, it is required that people relate to each other with sufficient warmth and closeness for group processes to proceed. If there is not enough freedom to express feelings among members, then the productivity suffers because of the tie-up of energy in the suppression of hostile impulses. Widely used behaviors attempting to gratify this need include side-whispers, subgrouping, after-meeting coffee, parties, bringing food to meetings and coffee breaks.

Not too much affection. Excessive intimacy and closeness may have the effect of detracting from the main purposes of the group, and also of personalizing task issues to an undesirable extent. Hence, it is necessary to limit the degree of closeness in groups. Techniques used for accomplishing this end are nepotism rules, fraternization rules, agenda and other procedural techniques, discipline and punishment for too much affectional play.

These functions constitute those of leadership in the area of interpersonal needs. The leadership function must see to their satisfaction by means acceptable to the group for the group to perform optimally.

Conflict-free Behavior

Leadership Functions re Conflict-free Group Sphere

1. The establishment and clarification of the hierarchy of group goals and values.
2. The recognition and integration of the various cognitive styles (modes of approaching problem solving) existing within the group.
3. The maximal utilization of the abilities and capacities of the group members.

The essential difference between this area of leadership and the others is that the supposed physiological or somehow "purely" cognitive, thinking, characteristics of the group members must be mobilized. This requires assessing what they are and enabling them to be expressed fully. The area of cognitive style may also be included in this area. Measures of variables of this sort are now being developed and appear very promising. They may aid in explicating the conflict-free area and eventually lead to usable dimensions.

Rational and Irrational

The ego psychologists say that although the conflict-free ego sphere develops autonomously, it may still come under the influence of instinctual urges. This is a phenomenon widely noted in group behavior as well. Past studies (Schutz, 1955) indicate that for groups the task situation is commonly used to gratify interpersonal needs that have not been satisfied in the group. For example, a task is used to achieve prominence or withdrawal, power or dependency, emotional closeness or distance, until satisfactory resolution of these needs is made. If a member's strongest need is high inclusion, he works to the degree necessary to be an integral part of the group; if control, he attempts to gain the respect of the group by performing competently; if affection, he tries to be liked by all, perhaps by working, or joking, or by whatever technique he has found most effective. Similarly, people respond appropriately to the task situation if their interpersonal needs are gratified in the present group. *Appropriate* means "in such a way as to gratify themselves maximally in terms of their values and goals and within the limits of their cognitive capacities."

The Leader as Completer

In summary, by using the model of ego development presented by the psychoanalytic ego psychologists and elaborated by FIRO theory, a description may be made of the leadership functions in a small group. This description indicates the sameness of the problem for both the individual ego and the group leaders. In both cases, in order for the leader—or ego-functions— to develop optimally, the problems of the group, or individual, must be resolved: to outer reality with respect to contact, control and closeness; to interpersonal needs (or instinctual urges) with respect to contact, control and closeness; and to the autonomous conflict-free abilities and properties of the group or individual. In addition, the leader-or ego-functions must lead to a resolution of the interaction of these areas, partly through clarification and operation of value and goal hierarchies.

This approach leads to a somewhat more complicated picture of the leader function than those usually given—a picture which may be called the *leader as completer.* If all the above-mentioned functions must be performed for optimal group operation, the best a leader can do is to observe which functions are not being performed by a segment of the group and enable this part to accomplish them. In this way he minimizes the areas of group inadequacy.

Specifically, whatever is required to enable the group to be compatible with outer reality and whatever is not being done by the group itself, the leader has to do or get done. If this means making contact with outer reality, or enabling others to do it, or becoming a spokesman to outer reality for the group, or absorbing the hostility of the external world heaped upon the group—an effective leader must perform these tasks. Occasionally it becomes necessary for the leader to become the scapegoat for interpersonal problems within the group because the incompatibility, leading to hostility, in the group is so great that no work can be accomplished. If the leader drains off some of this hostility by being the scapegoat, the group is able to continue to function. This conception also implies that when the group is fulfilling all its functions adequately, the most appropriate behavior for the leader is inaction.

This may be a somewhat different notion of a leader, since typically he is not looked upon as someone who puts himself in this position. From this analysis of the parallel with the psychoanalytic concept of the individual, the general properties of a leader become simply those functions required to maintain a certain kind of equilibrium between outer reality and interpersonal needs and the conflict-free functions of the group. These sometimes are very unpleasant, even "unleaderlike" activities.

One implication of this conception is that for some people, fulfilling these particular leadership functions would not be gratifying to their own interpersonal needs. For some, being the scapegoat voluntarily is not a pleasant way to interact in a group. Hence, the prime requisites for a leader are: (1) to know what functions a group needs; (2) to have the sensitivity and flexibility to sense what functions the group is not fulfilling; (3) to have the ability to get the things needed by his group accomplished; and (4) to have the willingness to do what is necessary to satisfy these needs, even though it may be personally displeasing. This whole conception of leadership is reminiscent of an old saying that "the good king is one whose subjects prosper."

SUGGESTED READINGS

Chapter 9

Beal, George, *et. al. Leadership and Dynamic Group Action.* Ames, Iowa: Iowa State University Press, 1972.

Bednarek, Frank, "Identifying Peer Leadership in Small Work Groups." *Small Group Behavior Vol. 7, No. 3* (August 1976), 307-315.

Bradford, L. P. "Trainer-Intervention: Case Episodes," in *T-Group Theory and Laboratory Method: Innovation in Re-Education,* edited by L. P. Bradford.

Ewbank, Henry L., Jr. *Meeting Management.* Dubuque: William C. Brown Company, Publishers, 1968.

Golembiewski, R. T. "Three Styles of Leadership and Their Uses." *Personnel,* 38 (1961): 35-45.

Jacobs, T. O. *Leadership and Exchange in Formal Organizations.* Alexandria, Virginia: Human Resources Research, 1971.

Knutson, T. and Holdridge, W. "Orientation Behavior, Leadership and Consensus: A Possible Functional Relationship," *Speech Monographs* 42 (1975): 107-114.

Kwal, T. and Fleshler, H. "The Influence of Self-Esteem on Emergent Leadership Patterns," *Speech Teacher* 22 (1973): 100-06.

Maier, N. "Male Versus Female Discussion Leaders," *Personnel Psychology* 23 (1970): 455-61.

Sargent, J. and Miller, G. "Some Differences in Certain Communication Behaviors of Autocratic and Democratic Leaders," *Journal of Communication* 21 (1971): 233-52.

Schutz, William C. *FIRO: A Three Dimensional Theory of Interpersonal Behavior.* New York: Holt, Rinehart and Winston, Inc., 1958.

Steinmetz, Lawrence L. and David F. Hunt. "Understanding the Natural Born Leader That's Within You." *Administrative Management* 34 (October 1974), 30-36.

Zelko, Harold. *The Business Conference: Leadership and Participation.* New York: McGraw-Hill Book Company, 1969.

Index